McElhaney's
Trial
Notebook
by James W. McElhaney

SECOND EDITION

Section of Litigation
American Bar Association

To Penny

CONTENTS

FOREWORD

It is a paradox that the most popular column in a journal for trial lawyers comes from a law professor. But then, James W. McElhaney is a paradox. He is a graceful bear, a cocktail pianist, a pilot, a member of the choir, a teller of tales, a theorist whose hair would shoot out like Einstein's (if he had hair), and a writer of simplicity and grace. He is the only editor-in-chief of LITIGATION ever to address the annual meeting of editors in coat and tie. Yet none of his columns smell of the academy. You will profit from reading and rereading every one.

The author himself has edited this book. He has culled it from all of his columns published in twelve years of LITIGATION and reprinted forty-seven of them here. The articles have been grouped into the sequence of trial, beginning with the trial notebook itself. In that way, the book can be an aid to trial preparation and in the trial.

The first edition of *Trial Notebook*, published in 1981, contained about half the material printed here. The new edition has been corrected and the type entirely reset for uniform style and clarity. For the first time, the Section of Litigation has published a hardcover edition of this book as well as the softcover for those who wish to carry McElhaney into the courtroom.

Trial Notebook's first edition was the first book published by the Section. The editor of the first edition, Douglas D. Connah, Jr., of Baltimore, observed that the need for publication arose to forestall the constant demands to copy McElhaney's columns for distribution. The demand for reprints of the later columns has never slackened, which has led to this expanded edition.

The Section of Litigation is again pleased to present this book to the bar.

William Pannill
Houston, Texas
January 1, 1987

ACKNOWLEDGMENTS

Writing *Trial Notebook* involves not only ordinary legal research, but another kind as well—watching, listening to, and talking with all sorts of trial lawyers whose ideas and techniques have found their ways onto these pages. While I have tried to cite the techniques of individual lawyers whenever I can, my debt is not repaid. So first let me thank all those lawyers who have been teaching me trial advocacy since I started in law school, especially my brother, John H. McElhaney, whose late night advice by long distance telephone has been invaluable.

Many ideas in this book have come from trial demonstrations at programs sponsored by the ABA Section of Litigation or the National Institute for Trial Advocacy. I am delighted to be part of a system that borrows ideas from the profession and then returns them in print. Of course, if those ideas have suffered in the translation from action to the page, the fault is mine.

All of the essays in this book first appeared in LITIGATION. I am proud of that. LITIGATION will always have a special place in my affections. Even though I have served as an associate editor for ten years and editor-in-chief for two years, it has taught me far more than I have taught it.

I am proud of LITIGATION for more than selfish reasons, and much of what I love about the magazine has nothing to do with *Trial Notebook* or my editorial work. Charles H. Wilson from Washington, D.C. and Douglas D. Connah, Jr., from Baltimore, Maryland, are a pair of journalists-turned-lawyers who founded an extraordinary publication. Who would have thought that lawyers could produce a tasteful, attractive magazine, complete with high-quality paper, no advertisements, pleasant type style, timely topics, and fine art work?

LITIGATION is lively, lawyerly, and literate. That is quite a feat. The reason for its success is largely the design genius of Charlie Wilson, our first editor-in-chief, and the editorial tone set by Doug Connah. Connah, our second editor-in-chief, was a law student in my trial advocacy course at the University of Maryland in my fledgling days as a law teacher. He was a reporter with the Baltimore *Sun* before going to law school. He brought me into LITIGATION while it was being formed. He helped polish my work and encouraged me to keep writing *Trial Notebook*, and I am grateful.

The next editors all made their distinctive contributions. F. Wallace Pope, Jr., of Clearwater, Florida, made valuable suggestions for topics. John Koeltl of New York deftly shaped and directed. William Pannill from Houston, Texas, set new standards of excellence for LITIGATION. He turned out some of the finest issues the magazine has ever published, and inspired those who worked with him with his creative enthusiasm.

You can understand why writing for a magazine like that is a special challenge.

There are others to whom I am grateful. My special thanks go to Mrs. Hazel Hostetler of Cleveland, Ohio. Her thoughtful generosity in the memory of her late husband, Joseph C. Hostetler, has made all of my work at Case Western Reserve University possible. I am also grateful for the warm support and gracious encouragement of Deans Lindsey Cowen, Ernest Gellhorn, and Peter Gerhart of the law school.

I deeply appreciate the help given me by my secretary, Mrs. Arlene Hrisko, who has typed and listened and cared.

My family has contributed to these essays in ways they know and in ways they cannot know. I am grateful to my wife, Penny, and our boys, David and Ben.

Finally, let me thank the leaders of the American Bar Association Section of Litigation. Lawyers, judges, and the public all tend to think of the ABA as a stolid representative of the powers of inertia. That opinion is sadly out of date. It is most incorrect when it comes to the Section of Litigation. The list is impressive. George I. Meisel, William Emerson Wright, Robert Hanley, the late Paul R. Connolly, William J. Manning, Weyman I. Lundquist, Philip H. Corboy, Asa Roundtree, Ronald L. Olson, Joan M. Hall, Adrian M. Foley, Jr., John J. Curtin, Jr., N. Lee Cooper—Chairmen of the Section of Litigation—have nurtured the Section into an effective force that is improving our profession.

I am pleased that these essays have been associated with their efforts.

James W. McElhaney
Cleveland, Ohio
December, 1986

ix

PART I

Trial
Preparation

CHAPTER 1

The Trial Notebook

The young lawyer was cross-examining his opponent's chief witness, and was about to impeach him with a prior inconsistent statement that went to the heart of the case.

The witness, Mr. Charles Malloy, testified on direct examination that both the plaintiff and defendant met him in his office and entered into a verbal modification of the contract that was the subject of the suit. In his extensive deposition, Mr. Malloy had testified that he had never been with the plaintiff and defendant in his office at one time.

The set-up for the confrontation with the witness's contrary statement in his deposition was a textbook example of the right way to do it. But then came the confrontation itself:

Q: This is not the first time you have given testimony in this case, is it, Mr. Malloy?

A: I'm afraid I don't understand. What do you mean?

Q: Well, you gave your deposition in this case, didn't you?

A: Yes.

Q: You raised your hand and swore to tell the truth?

A: Yes.

Q: And you did tell the truth, didn't you?

A: Certainly.

Q: (Picking up the second volume of the 850-page deposition) Everything you said was transcribed by the court reporter?

A: Yes.

Q: And one of the questions I asked you then was (thumbing

through the deposition) . . . was . . . just a moment . . .
(riffling through the entire volume) . . . was (picking up the
first volume of the deposition) . . . ah . . . whether you
and, ah, Mr. Wellemeyer and Harold Stevenson . . . uh
. . . Your honor, may I have a moment, please?

The Court: You may.

[Thereupon there was a five minute recess]

Q: (Trying for a tone of confidence) All right, Mr. Malloy,
we will return to the meeting in your office in a little
while, but first, I want to ask you about your relationship
with Harold Stevenson . . . .

What happened?

Disaster.

Why?

The lawyer had engaged in exhaustive discovery. He had deposed every witness, asked every interrogatory, studied every statement, and made copious notes about everything. His files bulged with legal pads with his extensive analysis. He had a coherent theory of the case and was well versed in trial techniques.

The trouble was he used the legal pad, manila folder, brown accordion file system of trial preparation. John Alan Appleman was speaking about this method when he said, "Nothing so undermines the confidence of a court or jury in a lawyer as his constant groping and fumbling." J. Appleman, ed., *Successful Jury Trials* 100 (1952).

Unlike many more formal legal terms, the trial notebook is just what the name implies. It is a system of trial preparation that actually uses a notebook to organize everything in the trial.

There are many rewards to using the trial notebook system. First, and probably most important is that it helps you find things during the trial, from particular passages in a deposition to the right response to your opponent's objections. As A. Leo Levin and Harold Cramer said in *Trial Advocacy—Problems and Materials* 7 (1968), "The lawyer who has at his fingertips helpful authorities responsive to what may seem to others an unexpected objection on the part of his opponent is a professional advocate. Neither luck nor a photographic memory accounts for most instances of such effective advocacy."

Second, if you are a junior in a firm the trial notebook can help you in two ways: it can let a senior review your work in advance of trial, and it will impress your senior that you know what you are doing.

Third, if you prepare a good trial notebook, it is much easier for a colleague to take over if anything should keep you from trying the case.

So what goes in a trial notebook, and why? Before going into the list, please understand that one advantage of the noteboook system is its flexibility. What goes into the trial notebook and how detailed you make it depends on you and on the case. If it is to be a successful system, it must be made to work for you and not the other way around.

The Notebook Itself

Among those really dedicated to the system, the three-ring binder designed to hold 8½ by 11 inch paper is standard. If you decide to put in legal size papers, they can be turned sideways and punched at the top or folded and put in pockets. Anyway, larger size binders are not readily available. It is useful to get tabbed separators just like you used to buy in junior high school—only this time you will actually use them.

No matter what kind of binder you choose, pick one that can be easily opened in trial. There are new binders on the market with plastic rings that have a silent slide fastener, although there are some lawyers who enjoy the authoritative snap produced by the old metal rings of the more traditional binders. The snap, they claim, eventually produces a fearful anticipation on the part of the opponent as surely as Pavlov's bell made his dogs expect that dinner would be served.

Of more practical moment are the pockets that are now available in stationery stores. Punched for standard three-ring binders, these pockets are designed to hold papers as large as 8½ by 11 inches, and are just the thing for keeping documents, pictures, and other exhibits (as well as copies for the judge, your opponent, and the jury) that you do not want to punch. So much for the cover. Now to the contents.

Table of Contents and Index

The table of contents comes at the beginning, but its final version is written last. A preliminary table of contents, however, should be one of the first items to go into the book, just to show what needs to be done as preparation progresses.

Usually the table of contents need not list page numbers, just the sections of the trial notebook in order. Since things will go into and come out of the trial notebook continually, anything close to accurate pagination is impossible.

Ordinarily, an index is not used, although it can be helpful in protracted litigation. Instead of an ordinary index at the end of the trial notebook, a second table of contents, arranged alphabetically, will be more useful.

Analysis of the Case

A coherent theory of the case is an essential ingredient to effective litigation. That unifying concept which you will use to persuade the judge and jury is just part of the analysis of the case. Here is the place for all sorts of notes, whether formal or informal, that go to make up your battle plan—from ideas about preliminary motions and jury selection to thoughts about final argument and requests for instructions. For a detailed discussion, see Chapter 5, *The Theory of the Case*.

Analysis of the Opponent's Case

If you have done your job well, you have also done some daydreaming about your opponent's case. The analysis of your opponent's case need not be a separate entry, but is important enough to warrant separate mention.

Proof Checklist

A formal proof checklist is important for both plaintiffs and defendants. A good proof checklist has three levels: First, the formal facts the law requires you to prove—the elements of your cause of action or defense. Second, the evidence that supports each element. Third, the source of the evidence. It may sound complex, but it is not—especially if you think of the three levels as simply *elements, evidence,* and *source*. A short example from a plaintiff's trial notebook will suffice:

Defendant's Negligence
  Excessive speed
    Limit 25—Officer Lintz
    Eyewitness bystander—Karen Maguire
  No proper lookout
    Did not apply brakes—
    Admission in defendant's
    deposition
    Did not apply brakes—
    No skid marks, Officer Lintz

Writing the proof checklist is valuable for a number of reasons. First, it forces you to go over every facet of your case. If there are any gaps, they will show up on the proof checklist. Second, it helps you grasp the totality of the evidence that may refine your theory of the case. Third, going over your proof checklist immediately before trial will refresh your recollection about the case—especially if you have a number of active files in your office—and make you a better advocate. Fourth, the proof checklist will help you put all evidence in perspective as the trial unfolds. It is like a running scorecard, since you check off evidence as the trial goes on. Looking at the proof checklist will help you decide whether you need to take some remedial action, such as calling a rebuttal witness. Finally, when your case is finished, you can review what you have done and rest your case in confidence, knowing that if your opponent makes a motion for a directed verdict, your proof checklist will aid you in making the proper argument.

Jury Selection

Whether you have any real role in jury selection depends, of course, on the court you are in. What you do during voir dire is a subject all to itself. But whether you get to ask the veniremen questions or it is all done by the judge, you cannot tell the players without a scorecard. For this you need a chart, a group of squares assembled like a map of the way the panel of prospective jurors is arranged, in which to write their names and make some notes.

If you are conducting jury voir dire, then the outline or list of questions you are going to ask the jurors belongs in this section. On the other hand, if the judge is going to conduct the questioning, then here is where you put the list of supplementary questions you are going to request the judge to ask.

If you use the psychological point count system of juror evaluation—the method that relies on various factors in a juror's background being given a number of points which are totaled up for purposes of juror comparison—then the point count forms that you and your clinical psychologist advisor work out together to fit this particular case also belong in this section.

Opening Statement

Writing out your opening statement is usually not a good idea, because you may be tempted to read it at the start of trial. Reading any argument is almost always a mistake. Even though reading a prepared text may be smoother and more polished than an extemporaneous presentation, written language is different from spoken language. Moreover, no matter how hard you try, it is nearly impossible to duplicate exactly the progression of emotions you felt as you wrote your opening. The result is that if you read your opening statement, your feelings will not match the words and what you say will not sound quite sincere.

This does not mean you work without notes, however, and this is the place in the trial notebook to put those notes.

Stipulations and Pretrial Order

Here is a good place for these things. Often stipulations are read to the jury immediately after opening, although that is not the strongest way to start a trial. Usually it is better to start with a strong fact witness and weave in the stipulations where they make sense.

If you need to refer to the pretrial order (if there is one), it is good to know where it is, near the beginning of the book. If there is some reason for putting the pleadings into the trial notebook, they can go in here. On the other hand, if there is no need to refer to them during the course of the trial, the notebook need not be cluttered with them just because they look impressive.

Witnesses

There are two main subdivisions to this section. The first is the list of your witnesses in the order in which you intend to call them. If this list is more than one page long, it may make sense to have a second list arranged in alphabetical order.

Do not just put the witnesses' names on this list. It should also have their addresses and telephone numbers—both home and work—as well as a notation indicating whether they have been subpoenaed. Then if one of your witnesses does not show up at the appointed time, it is much easier to locate him.

In addition to this information, it is often helpful to give a short characterization of the witness's relation to the case. There is a good reason for this. Witness order has an important bearing on persuasion, and should be carefully worked out to fit the theory of the case. A notation such as "investigating officer"—strong witness can be very helpful.

The second part of the witnesses subdivision is the more important of the two. Here is the group of outlines on the direct examination of all your witnesses and the cross-examination of all the opponent's witnesses. Indeed, in the appropriate-sized case, you may want to break these into two separate sections, one for direct, the other for cross-examination. When the witness takes the stand, you merely turn to the appropriate page in the trial notebook, and you are ready to begin your examination.

Here is where the trial notebook system truly starts to outstrip the legal pad, manila folder, accordion file system. At the beginning of each witness's subsection is a page with the witness's name, address, telephone numbers, employment and statement about his relationship to the case—just the way it was on the witness list. Following that should be a short paragraph (just one or two sentences) explaining why this witness is being called to testify; just what it is you expect to prove with this person. Reading this introductory material and that paragraph of purpose just before the witness is called will tend to keep you right on track during the examination of the witness.

Following this should be an outline of your examination. Whether this is direct or cross-examination, write your outline on the *left hand side of the page* as Kenny Hegland suggests in *Trial and Practice Skills in a Nutshell* 142 (1978). You might even consider drawing a line down the middle of the page to force you to do this.

Why?

By leaving a wide right-hand margin, you have room for supplemental notes, and more importantly, a place to write particularly colorful language or important concessions from the witness you will later want to work into final argument. These are important notations you simply will not make unless you have a place to do it.

For most lawyers, writing out questions is not as successful as writing an outline. Written questions do not have as much flexibility as an outline when the witness does not answer as anticipated. Furthermore, unless one reads superbly—like the old radio drama actors—reading the questions verbatim gives the examination of a witness a sense of being ''canned,'' which is disastrous to the credibility of the witness (and the lawyer as well).

There are some questions, however, that should be written out and read verbatim. In rare instances it may be done with an ordinary witness. The more usual occasion for precisely worded questions is with expert witnesses, especially if they are asked hypothetical questions, a practice that has become optional under the Federal Rules of Evidence, Rules 703 and 705.

After the outline of the witness's examination is something nearly as important. It is a proof checklist for the particular witness. This is a short list of all the important bits of evidence you expect to elicit from the witness. When you have finished the examination of the witness, simply go down the checklist. Any gaps are obvious. If there are none, you can confidently say, ''No further questions.''

The time saved in witness examination will more than make up for the time spent preparing the trial notebook. Too many lawyers aimlessly flail around toward the end of both direct and cross-examination, hoping that they will somehow cover everything that way. The trial notebook system ends that, winning the gratitude of judges and juries alike.

And now to the point that got the young lawyer hopelessly snarled at the beginning: depositions and cross-examination.

It is not enough just to take a deposition and read it through before trial. One of the most important features of the trial notebook is the deposition index. With the deposition index comes one of the minor disputes about effective trial preparation: Is it something best done by the attorney trying the case, or can it be safely delegated to juniors or paralegals?

No matter how the question is answered, one thing is certain: the deposition index is not merely a formal matter. It can only be done by someone who understands the case thoroughly. For this reason, some lawyers who delegate many things to others actually dictate their own deposition indexes.

How complex the indexes need to be depends entirely on the case. Often a single page or two will do, listing topics and page numbers in the deposition. In complicated cases it may be more appropriate to prepare written summaries and cross-indexes, a system described in Paul Bergman's *Trial Advocacy in a Nutshell* 375-76 (1979).

Documents and Exhibits

Like witnesses, documents and exhibits are divided into two parts; first the list and then the things themselves.

If a document, picture, or other exhibit can be entirely authenticated and explained by one witness, you may wish to put it in a pocket as a part of the witness's file.

On the other hand, if there are a number of documents in the case, it is probably better to have them in a separate section or even a separate book. Under some circumstances it may be a good idea to prepare a copy of the entire document book (especially if the documents are pre-marked and admitted) for the court, each juror, and opposing counsel.

Before each document include a sheet with the requirements for the necessary foundation and the names of the witnesses who can do the job. If you anticipate trouble from your adversary about the foundation, you can even include a case citation on your foundation notes.

Evidence and Procedure Memoranda

Every case has the potential for some disputed areas of evidence or procedure. With a little thought, many can be identified in advance—such as the effect of a presumption when there has been contrary evidence or whether a doctor consulted just for treatment can testify to the person's medical history.

The answers to questions like these often vary from state to state. While they can have an important effect on the conduct of the trial, if the judge makes a mistake in ruling on one of them, it is usually not reversible error. It is important to understand that point, because it means that generally your one chance for a proper ruling on the issue is the first time it occurs.

Many lawyers do the necessary research on such questions, but then—through the quagmire caused by the legal pad, manila folder and brown accordion file system—either cannot find their research at the proper time, or fail to present their argument effectively.

Probably the best way to argue such an issue is both orally and in writing. The writing should be a miniature brief; no more than a few typewritten sentences in the middle of an otherwise clean paper. The effect of this sort of memoranda is startling, and it is worthwhile understanding why it works so well.

Watch what a judge does when a lawyer places a pile of books in front of him, and you will be cured of any temptation to do the same. The unspoken message of an opened book placed before the judge is, "I have not really finished my research. There may be contrary cases, and this may not really be on point, but I think it supports me."

The unspoken message of the long brief is a little different, but not much more persuasive: "I have really done my homework. This is a long and difficult point which is distinctly arguable either way. You may not have time to read this, but I would appreciate it if you would reward my diligence, even if I am wrong." Long briefs are not usually read during the heat of trial.

The unspoken message of the miniature brief is different still: "Here it is, the answer is clear. I have done my homework, and am certain of the right answer. Read this and you will instantly understand the right way to rule. Ignore it at your peril." Very short memoranda do get read during trial. To keep on top of things, you should have three copies of each, one for you, one for the judge, and one for your opponent.

Final Argument

Preparation for final argument really starts when the case comes in the door. Here is where all your notes will go. Their chance for actual retrieval is greatly enhanced because there is a place to put them.

Motions and Requests for Instructions

In some jurisdictions requests for instructions are rather informal, and all that is needed is a few notes unless the case presents some novel points. Other states, however, follow a more elaborate procedure. In Texas practice, for example, each requested instruction must be on a separate piece of paper, together with a brief form for the judge to indicate whether the instruction is granted or denied. Whatever the practice, the tabbed pocket is perfect for keeping requests for instructions and briefs in support of supplementary motions.

Having come this far, you are now in position to see the most valuable aspect of the trial notebook system of trial preparation. Using this method makes thorough preparation easy. Just paging through the book is an instant status report on the case; it shows exactly what needs to be done.

Finally, it is a system worth using because it works and helps win cases.

CHAPTER 2

Informal Investigation

It is one of the things law schools do not do well. While modern legal education has many virtues, teaching factual investigation is not one of them.

One reason is that the chief ingredient of most law school books is appellate cases, with their facts carefully arranged by the courts to support their decisions. A second is the very facility that good teachers have in spinning out hypothetical patterns in class. A third cause is the typical moot court problem in which the ''record'' is five or six pages long. But the biggest offender is the law school examination question that raises an unending stream of legal issues in just one or two paragraphs.

From all of it, the implication is clear—facts come in neat, ready-made packages so lawyers can manipulate rules to fit them.

It is a fascinating inversion of life outside the halls, where doctrine usually seems more stable than facts.

Academics are not the only ones to blame for our misshapen notions about facts. The law itself makes a contribution. Take the rules of discovery, for example. For the most part, the law is indifferent to how lawyers and witnesses get information.

But the law does regulate how lawyers get information from each other and how we record formal testimony before trial. That is the law of discovery, and because it is what the law controls, we tend to assume it is what is most important. The result is the notion that discovery is the best way to learn facts.

Wrong.

Discovery may be a good way to learn what a witness will say, and may be a good way to hold a witness or a party to a particular version of facts, but it is a very inefficent way to get information.

The suggestion is not to ignore discovery, but rather to stop ignoring informal methods of investigation. The subject, then, is not depositions, demands to admit, written interrogatories, the attorney-client privilege, or the work product doctrine. Instead, this discussion is about learning facts in other ways—by doing what Robert G. Vial of Dallas, Texas calls "trolling," or nosing about for essential information. Doing it well is one of the marks of a good trial lawyer.

Decent trolling requires a few basic ingredients: the right personal qualities, some simple techniques, a little equipment, and the proper sources.

Personal Qualities

Our starting point is the list of personal qualities, and there are three: curiosity, suspicion, and understanding. Each will require a little explanation.

Curiosity is a quality that most formal systems of education do not develop sufficiently after the first few grades ("put down the turtle, Johnny, it's time for science").

Consider the following example. Most lawyers, when trying a case involving a collision between a motor vehicle and a train, would be content with ordinary discovery and investigation when trying to determine how the wreck occurred. Surely we would read all the statements, reports, interrogatories, and depositions. We might do a few other things as well. We might learn some of the terminology and talk informally to an engineer or examine some pictures or diagrams.

Almost no one would climb into the cab of a locomotive to see how the engineer actually works the throttle and brakes.

Except Craig Spangenberg of Cleveland, Ohio. Climbing into the cab of a locomotive is what gave Craig the information that proved to be the undoing of the defendant in the case of "Whistling Sam."

Spangenberg represented the plaintiff in the case—a farmer who had been hauling a load of pig manure in his truck which was struck at a dangerous grade crossing.

The crossing was unprotected by any signal, just a sign advising motorists that the tracks were there, and the farmer claimed that the train did not sound either a whistle or bell as it approached the intersection.

14

The defendants laughed at the plaintiff's claim, because this particular train had been operated by "Whistling Sam," who had earned his nickname by always blowing the whistle.

From his experience in the cab, Spangenberg knew the kind of locomotive in the crash had separate quadrants for the brake and the throttle. One was operated by the right hand, while the other was controlled by the left hand. Both the brake and the throttle levers were about waist high. The whistle, however, was operated by pulling on an overhead rope that had a wooden handle attached to the end.

On the cross-examination of Whistling Sam, Spangenberg at first seemed not to control the witness enough, because several times Sam was able to slip in his reputation for blowing the whistle.

Then Spangenberg and Sam seemingly got lost in the finer points of handling a train as it goes around curves—especially when slowing down at the same time. In that maneuver, the engineer must actually work both the brake and the throttle at once. The brake is necessary to make the train slow down, while the throttle is necessary to keep the train stretched out lest the cars bunch up and risk derailment when braking on a curve.

Craig and Sam were working their imaginary throttles and brakes in this delicate operation when Craig had Sam explain that right as the train approached this grade crossing, it was rounding a tight curve and slowing from a high speed zone to a lower one. Sam suggested it was one of the most difficult operations on that run.

That was when Spangenberg put the key question:

    Q: Well, while you were working the brake with one hand and the throttle with the other, *which hand were you using to blow that whistle?*

The answer was classic:

    A: You got me there.

The second quality you need for trolling is suspicion. Not the common variety that turns a pleasant person into a raving paranoiac, but rather the little warning light kind of suspicion that sets off a small signal when something is not right. It is a sense (when properly developed) that will go off even when things do not appear wrong, but rather seem "too right."

An example comes from another train case—one that was tried in New England a few years ago.

It was also a grade crossing case. But instead of a farmer at work, the case involved an old car loaded with teenage boys late at night. The circumstances looked as if the boys had been trying to race the train, and the case for the plaintiffs seemed bleak.

Just to be sure he got everything, the lawyer for the plaintiffs asked for all the physical data about the train's stopping—the number of cars, the total weight of the train, its speed, the grade, the coefficient of friction between the wheels and the track, and the total length of skid after the engineer locked the brakes.

The train had been in a 35-mile-per-hour zone, and during the deposition, the engineer insisted that it was actually going under the limit immediately before the collision.

The request for all this information made it obvious that the plaintiff's lawyer was going to consult an expert to see if the information fit—that is, whether the weight of the train, the length of its skid, and the other factors fit with the speed the engineer claimed the train had been travelling.

And fit they did—with a mathematical precision that set off a warning signal in the lawyer's mind.

He shared his concern with an old friend of the family—a retired railroad conductor—who told him that it was the custom for train crews to try to make up lost time on the stretch where the accident occurred, and that speeds 20 to 30 miles per hour above the limit were common.

How, wondered the lawyer, could he tell which (if any) of the figures had been changed to cover up a violation of the speed limit by the train? Most of the other information seemed beyond dispute, and if the speed fit, would that not settle the matter?

The conductor asked the lawyer how he knew the weight of the train.

"They told me," replied the lawyer, "in answers to written interrogatories."

"What does that mean?" asked the conductor.

"They swore to the answer and put it in writing," said the lawyer.

The conductor was not impressed. "Did they give you the manifests listing the contents and weights of each car?"

When later discovery requests for the manifests resulted in the railroad saying they did not have any idea what might have happened to them, the lawyer knew he was on to something.

Now the problem was to get copies of those manifests.

That turned out to be easy. The retired conductor just dropped into the branch office of the railroad to see an old friend, and in a spare moment, checked the file and made Xerox copies of the manifests that the railroad had been unable to locate.

The results at trial were gratifying.

As expected, the railroad defended on the theory that the teenagers were trying to race the train. The railroad even put on an expert witness—a physicist who was armed with all the right formulas—to explain how the length of the skid, the weight of the train, the grade of the track, and coefficient of friction between the wheels and the track all proved that the crew's testimony about the moderate speed of the train was accurate.

Cross-examination was simple. First the expert agreed that if the facts were wrong—for example, the weight of the train—then the conclusion he reached must be wrong. Second, the expert admitted he got all his information from the railroad. When the plaintiff's lawyer had the railroad's expert recalculate the speed of the train—this time using the actual weight as shown by the "missing" manifests—the case was settled before the next witness was called.

The third quality needed for successful trolling is a special kind of understanding. From it comes an ability that outstanding lawyers share with the best investigative reporters—a creative sense for finding circumstantial evidence.

What does this have to do with understanding? Simply this: the gift for finding circumstantial evidence comes from a basic understanding about the world. It is a fundamental realization that facts do not just exist. Events do not arise in a vacuum. They have a context, and if you want to prove facts, you must look for their context.

Douglas Connah of Baltimore, Maryland (a reporter before he was a lawyer) showed that quality in a case he tried a number of years ago.

A young man had been given some shares of stock in a closely held corporation. The gift came from his father-in-law shortly after he was married, and represented 10 percent of a company that owned a radio station that carried programs for "mature audiences." No stock certificates ever changed hands, and nothing in writing was ever given to the son-in-law. It was a friendly, family affair, and the son-in-law was delighted to receive modest annual payments.

Then two things happened. The radio station changed its format to more popular music (and its ratings went up) and the daughter left the young man (and his ratings went down).

As a result, the father-in-law announced that the shares of stock went back to him. They had been, he said, a conditional gift, and had actually been given to the daughter or maybe to the couple's small children—but not to the young man.

Sensing something was wrong, the young man sought legal assistance. In time he saw three different lawyers, each of whom did approximately the same thing. They called the father-in-law or his lawyer, and decided the young man did not have a case. They told him there was no effective way to prove the stock had ever been his because there was nothing in writing.

Then the young man consulted Connah. In one afternoon of trolling, Connah had a briefcase full of information that settled the issue in the young man's favor.

Because he knew that facts do not just exist in a vacuum, he looked for their context. The corporate minutes were in the father-in-law's hands, and subject to easy manipulation, so he did not start there. But he knew that corporations had to pay taxes and list their owners. He also knew that radio stations had to file annual reports with the FCC and reasoned that they had to list their owners as well. He was right. There, on a stack of forms all filled out by the father-in-law, the young man was listed as a 10 percent owner for the last five years.

In the case that followed in federal court, the only issue was the amount of damages.

There they are—curiosity, suspicion and understanding—three personal qualities necessary for successful trolling. But there is more to it than that. You also need the proper techniques, some equipment, and the right sources.

Techniques

Following are some suggestions for different techniques that are worth thinking about.

1. *Do it yourself.* To be sure, you charge more per hour than an investigator, a paralegal, an associate, or a law clerk. It is also true that you must be able to delegate duties. It is impossible to do everything yourself.

On the other hand, there are some very good arguments for doing it yourself, particularly when it is early in your litigation career.

First, investigators and employees who are working for you know what you want and are anxious to please you. Their desire for approval sometimes shades their reports, and when it comes

18

to actually proving what they have reported, you may be disappointed.

Second, investigators and others simply do not think like lawyers. They are unlikely to know what is admissible and what is not. The result is that they will come back with information that may not be helpful, while they sometimes miss things you would spot.

A good approach for the beginning litigator is to do everything once, and learn how to do it well. Then you will have a better sense of when to delegate and when to climb into the cab of the locomotive yourself.

2. *Start trolling as soon as possible.* The sooner you start, the more likely your information will be complete. Memories are slippery, and events tend to melt away as time goes on. A second reason for talking to witnesses promptly is that people tend to identify with the party that values *them*—so it is useful to be the first to conduct interviews and take statements.

3. *Go in person.* Obviously you must use the telephone to talk to people. On the other hand, there are times when there is no substitute for meeting someone in person. Interviewing witnesses is a good example. Even if the witness tells you over the telephone that he will not talk to you, you may well win him over in person. Sometimes the witness who persists in telling you he will not talk to you will tell you everything he knows as part of his "refusal to talk" when you show up in person on his doorstep.

4. *Go to the scene.* Being there is invaluable. It will aid your understanding of what happened, assist in your investigation, make your direct examinations easier to follow, and sharpen your control over the witnesses on cross-examination.

Please do not feel that this advice is limited to personal injury cases. Go to the shopping mall that is the subject of the mortgage dispute, or inspect the defective cartons in which the goods were shipped. Nearly every type of litigation has a scene that will help.

5. *Get it recorded.* Whether it is the statement of a witness, the measurement or appearance of some physical relationship, or your impression how something happened, you should record it promptly.

Make a habit of getting statements from nonwitnesses (the ones who claim they know nothing about the incident) and adverse witnesses as well as those who help you. Do this in any way that makes sense—written statements, or tape or video recordings.

19

6. Protect your statement or recording. Experienced investigators often make at least one mistake per page when they write out statements for others to sign. They do this so the person making the statement can correct the mistakes—and if he does not spot them, they are pointed out to him. The corrections are evidence that every page has been checked and approved.

Other protective steps include having the witness initial each page and write that he has read the entire statement and that it is true. More sophisticated measures, such as never finishing a sentence at the end of the page and not skipping a line between paragraphs, will protect against the argument that some words or even a page was inserted or omitted. These and other suggestions are discussed more fully in A. Morrill, *Trial Diplomacy, Selected Text* pp. 171-178 (Court Practice Institute, 1973).

Equipment

Remember that while it is an advantage for you to have firsthand knowledge, it is a disadvantage for you to be a witness to a signature. You might have to withdraw from the case so you could testify to the execution of a statement. It is a good idea, then, to have someone else serve as a witness.

The next topic is simple, but for some, a romantic one. Just as a tackle catalog can excite some fishermen, so can the thought of hardware spark the imagination of some lawyers. And without a doubt, investigation can justify getting a nice portable cassette tape recorder and a good camera (probably an instant model, so you can see if the pictures turn out), especially if you are involved in personal injury work, either for the plaintiff or the defense. Carry them with you together with some pens and pads of paper.

You are likely to find Alan Morrill's list of equipment useful:
- one-hundred-foot tape measure;
- carpenter's six-foot rule;
- flashlight;
- magnifying glass;
- compass;
- clipboard; and
- a notebook.

See A. Morrill, *Trial Diplomacy, Selected Text* pp. 168-169 (Court Practice Institute, 1973).

Sources

Finally, trolling requires the right sources. Sometimes the right sources are not the most obvious ones, as a young Milwaukee lawyer learned. He was trying to get information from the Veterans' Administration, and kept running into a brick wall. He was the third junior associate in the firm to be given the job of trying to pry loose some medical records for which there was a proper waiver, but which the Veterans' Administration was inordinately reluctant to give up.

Instead of trying to get them as veterans' records, he decided to try them as Army records. A simple letter to the judge advocate general (that said nothing about the difficulty with the Veterans' Administration) got the records in a matter of days—directly from the Veterans' Administration.

Lawyers are accustomed to getting emergency room records and weather and motor vehicle reports. On the other hand, tow truck drivers, ambulance drivers, paramedics, and other emergency service people are sometimes overlooked.

Credit bureaus are good sources of information on people and businesses. State employment offices may have records showing that someone who claims to be out of work is now being paid by some other employer, and police radio logs and blotter reports can show if the happy domestic scene described in a deposition has required police intervention to keep the peace.

Newspaper morgues are treasure houses, and lawyers seem to forget that many public libraries have reference librarians that offer service over the telephone.

Lawyers are learning that computerized legal research tools like Westlaw and Lexis can be used for more than just finding cases. The computerized search can, for example, help track down the courtroom background of an expert witness as well as tell you whether your opponent has tried similar cases.

In products liability cases, competitors are often excellent sources of information. There is a good chance they know all about the product and are more aware of its shortcomings than the university professor who has only studied the product to prepare for testifying in this particular case.

In patent cases, 10K forms filed with the Securities and Exchange Commission often make very different representations about an invention than does the patent claim itself—even if they were both written by the same law firm.

Most personal injury lawyers know that insurance companies are members of index bureaus that keep records on all claims filed, and can assemble comprehensive claims histories. The bureaus work for the benefit of insurance companies and their lawyers, so that plaintiffs' lawyers usually cannot have direct access to the files.

Less well known than the index bureaus are the insurance company pool files. These are pools of information that the insurance company has about its own policy holders, and are often extensive.

Telephone books and street directories (that list people and their telephone numbers by their addresses) are essential law office tools. The *National Directory of Addresses and Telephone Numbers* (Concord Reference Books, 1982) can be useful for businesses and governmental offices.

One of the most remarkable reference books is Harry Philo's *Lawyer's Desk Reference: Technical Sources for Conducting a Personal Injury Action* (Lawyer's Co-op Publishing Co. 6th ed., 2 vol. 1979). While it is designed for plaintiffs' lawyers, it is useful for the defense as well. Furthermore, its scope of information and suggestions for sources will serve as an inspiration to search similar channels, even if your case has nothing to do with personal injury.

But most important of all, you will learn, is your own personal network that you will develop over the years—your friend at the newspaper, the officer at the bank, other lawyers, accountants, doctors, business people, and the like. They are your window to the world.

Finally, if you start trolling, you will find a new bias developing. Instead of turning to a formal hearing or written demand when you want to learn something, you will ask yourself whether there is some other way to get this information. When you do that, you will have the right approach.

CHAPTER 3

Depositions

The young lawyer was concerned.

He was working as a "litigator," with the largest firm in town. Six months ago he had passed the bar examination, and since then had sat in on some trials and depositions. Now he was setting out to do his first deposition on his own.

The senior partner with whom he was working had given him the file and a form with a list of 150 standard questions he was to ask.

"Just fill in the blanks in the questions from the file, and you will be ready to conduct the deposition without any trouble," said the partner. "I would go with you, but I have a hearing in federal court, and I couldn't get the setting of either the hearing or the deposition changed, so you'll have to cover for me. It's a straightforward case, and you won't have any trouble."

The young lawyer was not so sure.

He knew he would have no difficulty adopting the form questions to suit the case. What bothered him was even more fundamental. He wondered if the firm practice made any sense; whether this was the right way to go about taking depositions.

He even began to wonder whether there was an economic benefit to the firm in treating depositions like cost-plus profit products in which there was no incentive to save the client any money at all.

He realized that there are a number of reasons for the discovery explosion of the past several years.

One of the recent trends is to treat depositions as doctors have come to treat x-rays—something you have taken automatically, whether it is a good idea or not.

Perhaps the worst part of this trend is to approach all depositions the same way—assign them to the juniors in the office and have them ask every possible question, with the organization of the contents and even the form of the questions being dictated by the firm's standard set of questions that came from a form book.

What could be wrong with that?

Plenty.

First, there is expense. Many cases that might be tried do not justify the cost of extensive depositions. Second, informal discovery is often more effective than are depositions for finding out what happened. Depositions were not designed so much for discovery as they were for preserving testimony. It should not be surprising that they work best for their intended purpose.

Third, depositions often create information that is damaging to the side that conducts the deposition. Many answers are never thought of until the question is asked. Taking a witness's deposition is an excellent way to prepare him for testifying at the subsequent trial.

Because it is troubling to think that you are preparing your opposition's witnesses for trial, it is a task you do not want to undertake unless you are going to get something in return that makes it worthwhile.

While caution will lead many lawyers to take the deposition of every witness no matter what, that does not mean it is tactically wise. In fact, Alan Morrill suggests that you consider *not* taking depositions in the following circumstances:

- Do not depose a friendly witness unless it is necessary to preserve testimony for trial. The deposition will only serve to commit the witness to minute details. Then if he later deviates from them, your opponent is armed with impeachment evidence he would not otherwise have.
- Do not take a deposition when the cost outweighs the benefit.
- Do not take the deposition of a hostile witness who already has given you a detailed statement that is helpful to your case. The deposition gives the witness a chance to dilute some of the impeaching possibilities of the prior statement. Often a deposition offers a better opportunity for a witness to retreat from a damaging statement than would the actual trial.

24

- Do not take the deposition of a hostile witness who is elderly or gravely ill. It is your opponent's job to preserve his witness's testimony—not yours.
- Do not take depositions when it is obvious that the other side is not preparing for trial. Starting to take depositions can wake a sleeping opponent.

See A. Morrill, *Trial Diplomacy, Selected Text* 181 (Court Practice Institute, 1973).

Informal discovery is something to do whether or not you elect to take the deposition of any particular witness. But informal discovery is not a complete substitute for depositions. While you can talk to any witness you want without notifying the opposing lawyer, it is improper to talk with the opposing party without the consent of his attorney. CODE OF PROFESSIONAL RESPONSIBILITY, DR7-104.

There are other weaknesses in informal discovery. Suppose you personally take a witness's statement. Later, in trial, he denies making it. Then you may be in the difficult situation of being a witness (and perhaps having to withdraw from representation) in the case. On the other hand, if an investigator takes the statement and needs to take the stand to prove that the statement was made, his employment as an insurance investigator—or as a private investigator—is admissible in cross-examination on the issue of bias. In some jurisdictions, the court will give an instruction that the testimony of a private investigator must be viewed with caution.

Of course it is always a good idea to confirm oral statements in writing, provided the witness is willing to do it. If not, you should at least make detailed notes of what the witness said, and strongly consider using a deposition to nail down the witness's testimony.

Requests for admissions and written interrogatories are a sort of halfway house between informal discovery and oral depositions. Because of this, it is natural to start with informal discovery, move to requests for admissions and written interrogatories, and finish up with full depositions.

There is a danger in doing this. As Kenny Hegland points out, interrogatories can subtly educate your opponent about the theory of your case, and help shape his testimony at a deposition. K. Hegland, *Trial and Practice Skills in a Nutshell* 257 (West Pub. Co. 1978). This means that if your opponent's lawyer is a procrastinator in witness and client preparation, you should consider holding your interrogatories until after the deposition.

There are a number of good reasons for taking a witness's deposition.

- Preserve the testimony of the witness who may not be able to appear at trial because of age, illness, or distance.
- In states where it is permissible, record the testimony of witnesses who—like some experts—would much rather not testify in open court. Sometimes such witnesses make it clear that if compelled to appear at trial, their testimony will not be nearly as favorable as during a deposition scheduled at their own convenience.
- Make sure that a witness will not change what he has already said, or establish limits to his testimony in certain areas.
- Evaluate the witness (and the opposing lawyer, too).
- Establish your credibility as a competent lawyer with your opponent and his witnesses (they evaluate you).
- Encourage a settlement by demonstrating how strong your case is or how much the witness can be made to squirm under your cross-examination.
- Seek basic information—the discovery deposition.

The kind of information sought and the way it is pursued depend on the purpose of the deposition.

Take the discovery deposition as an example. It is astonishing how many lawyers do a full discovery deposition when they ought to do something else. If the only thing needed is to gently contain the witness in one or two areas, it is an error to do a discovery deposition and educate your opponent about your theory of the case and teach the witness how to deal with some difficult questions.

The form of questions asked is another matter. Many lawyers assume that narrow, carefully phrased questions are saved for the trial, while depositions are the time for open-end questions or why questions that invite unlimited explanations.

That may be true for discovery depositions, and not true for others. Why?

One reason is the purpose behind the deposition. If it is for investigation, then the full explanation is something you are willing to put up with in return for the information you gain. On the other hand, if you already know what the answers are from your informal discovery, then permitting explanations is too high a price just to contain the witness to his present position.

Part of this cost is demonstrated by Rule 106 of the Federal

26

Rules of Evidence—the rule of completeness that applies in most jurisdictions. When a lawyer tries to use a discovery deposition to impeach a witness, he finds that the explanation comes into evidence along with the damaging statement. The opponent who invokes Rule 106 does not even have to wait for redirect examination to get the explanation into evidence.

On the other hand, there are times when discovery depositions are essential. Suppose that a witness absolutely refuses to answer your calls, meet with you or your representatives, or even talk to you without a court order.

Is he within his rights?

Absolutely.

Is there anything you can do about it?

Send him a subpoena and take his deposition.

Then, because you are in search of information, you are justified in asking every question and inviting every explanation.

It can be summed up like this: do not take a discovery deposition unless you have to. The discovery deposition is like a doctor giving penicillin for a cold. It is prescribed out of habit. It probably will not do any good, and it runs the risk of causing real harm.

Knowing why you are taking a deposition will make a difference with other sorts of depositions as well. Preserving the testimony of a witness is a good example. Typically this sort of examination is done in anticipation of the witness not being available at trial. This means that nearly everything should be done as if the jury were right there in the room. Pay particular attention to foundations and preliminary questions. Typically only matters of form are waived if not objected to, so you cannot count on your opponent's silence as meaning the evidence will be admissible. It is too late to fill in the gaps after the witness has become unavailable.

In these testimonial depositions, you should have the reporter mark the exhibits that are referred to by the witness. Be sure to read into the record all gestures, nods, and other forms of nonverbal communication, just as if you were in trial. It may be even more important to have this information for the jury than it is for an appellate court. Even so, the printed page—no matter how meticulously complete—can never communicate as effectively as a live witness. This is a good reason for considering a videotape deposition if it is permitted under your rules.

When you are taking a deposition to make sure that a witness will not change what he has already said or to establish limits to his testimony in certain areas, the approach is different. Now there is no general need to be complete, to lay full foundations, or to read things into the record.

If the effort is to contain the witness in a few areas, you may wish to start with seemingly harmless generalities, and gradually lock the witness in. But be careful not to take it too far. Just as in cross-examination, it is dangerous to ask one question too many in a containment deposition.

Evaluating the witness is something to do in every deposition you take. The problem is, it can be difficult unless you have a system for doing it.

If you depose the witness alone, it is hard to concentrate on the impression he would make at trial unless there is something outstanding—either good or bad—about the way he comes across. You will be too busy thinking about your next question. This means that it is a good idea to debrief yourself immediately on returning to the office. It is a good time to record your impressions of the witness's physical appearance, voice, demeanor, education, knowledge of the facts, temperament, and especially whether he seems sympathetic and sincere.

It is easier if you have an assistant evaluating the witness while you are asking questions. It is still worth doing the debriefing, though, no matter how many assistants you have.

One of the things you should do—unless you want to lull your opponent into complacency—is to give both the witness and your opponent the idea that you are diligent and competent. One exception to this may lie in the case of the expert witness. This is not to suggest that if you are a Manhattan personal injury lawyer, you should try the ''poor country boy'' routine on a Boston doctor. On the other hand, it usually is not a good plan to try to convince the witness that you are a genuine expert in his own field. You will only guarantee that he will be well prepared for trial.

Take this idea a little further. Normally you do not want to attack a witness or even the opposing party during a deposition. There may come a time, however, when you want to convince your opponent that it would be wise to try to settle. One way to do that is to conduct a bit of real cross-examination in the deposition.

Even when you are encouraging settlement, you will not want to fire all of your guns during the deposition. Generally, you should start or end (or maybe both) with about five minutes of high pressure examination that is designed to let both the witness and the lawyer know what can happen at trial. Then conspicuously avoid attacking in some obvious areas so they will get the impression that they "ain't seen nothin' yet."

No matter what kind of deposition it is, there are some general rules worth following. At the very beginning of the deposition, read into the record who you are, and what is going on. Have the witness respond that he understands what is being done. Tell him not to answer any question if he does not understand it. Invite him to ask for a clarification whenever necessary. Do not worry. Your opponent has already told him this, and the witness will forget it anyway—but it will help with impeachment if he later claims he was confused by your questions.

Similarly, at the end, you should ask the witness whether he understood the questions, whether he answered every question truthfully, and whether he would like to change the answers to any questions.

Although it is rare, witnesses sometimes challenge the accuracy of the transcript of a deposition. If you follow the custom that exists in many states, the witness will be excused from reading and signing the deposition if you agree to the "usual stipulations." Probably no one knows completely what is included in the phrase, the "usual stipulations," especially because it varies from state to state. Typically, however, it includes a waiver of a reading and signing of the deposition by the witness.

When you waive a reading and signing of the deposition, it can still be used for impeachment even if the witness disputes its accuracy at trial—but it will have a lot less impact.

For this reason, some lawyers do not like to make the "usual stipulations" (or even just waive the reading and signing) even though there may be pressure from other lawyers in the community to do it. By the way, it is obviously more difficult for the witness to claim that the transcription is wrong if the original of the deposition is available on audio or videotape.

Short questions are just as important in a deposition as they are in a trial. They are particularly valuable if the deposition is going to be read to the jury, either as a substitute for the live witness or to impeach him.

There are some disarming questions worth asking at a deposition, especially if the witness is a party that you suspect has not been well prepared. "Who do you think was really at fault?" will sometimes bring astonishing results such as, "Why, both of us, actually."

One of the problems sometimes encountered in depositions is

the obstreperous opposing attorney who answers questions for the witness, makes speeches instead of objections, or instructs the witness to refuse to answer proper questions.

Even if the lawyer who does this ultimately pays for his actions with coins taken from the purse of reputation and good will, you still must deal with him at the time.

In those jurisdictions where depositions can be taken before a clerk, court commissioner, or some other judicial officer empowered to make rulings in depositions, the problem is much simpler—schedule the deposition in front of such an officer as well as the court reporter.

Sometimes that option is not available. Then you have to know other remedies. Sometimes it is stopping the deposition to get an order that the witness must answer a question, or that the lawyer refrain from answering questions. Sometimes it will simply be your reading an objection into the record.

In other cases it may be an instruction to the court reporter to bracket each speech made by your opponent, coupled with the promise to bill him for all comments on the record that go beyond proper legal objections.

Sometimes your opponent will tell the reporter that something is off the record even though you want it on. Normally it is a dangerous practice to go off the record except for matters that are unrelated to the case. You may wish to give standard instructions to the court reporters you hire that nothing is off the record without your approval.

Finally, you should think about the order in which you will take your depositions. As Hegland notes, parties often like to testify last at trial, to avoid little conflicts between their testimony and what their witnesses say. Since you are the one scheduling the deposition, it may pay to deny your opponent the advantage of going last and take his deposition first, "before you depose his supporting cast of ruffians and ne'er-do-wells." K. Hegland, *Trial and Practice Skills in a Nutshell* 257 (West Pub. Co. 1978).

CHAPTER 4

The Horse Shed

It was in this room and in this old courthouse [in White Plains, New York] that William J. Fallon began the practice of law as a member of the firm of Hunt, Fallon & Smith. It was concerning this court that James Fenimore Cooper coined the phrase: "Horse-shedding the witness." There were carriage sheds near the courthouse in Cooper's day, where attorneys lingered to rehearse witnesses. Mr. Hunt could remember the sheds right well, and if he had had a mind to do so, could have told of indulging in no little "horse-shedding" himself.

Gene Fowler,
The Great Mouthpiece:
A Life Story of William J. Fallon 93 (1931).

So *that* is where the term came from. Most trial lawyers are familiar with it even though they find it a little awkward. It is difficult to use when talking to those who have not heard it before. Good taste demands that it be spoken with unusual precision, and it is often accompanied by a short explanation, just to make sure the listener did not misunderstand. And for that very reason in some states it is called "wood-shedding" while in others it is known as "sandpapering the witness."

If "horse-shedding" is a clumsy anacronism, then why use it? Because it is so much more expressive than "witness preparation." "Witness preparation" sounds like a dull, routine thing to do, while "horse-shedding" has an exciting almost conspiratorial

31

ring to it, describing an activity that may at times come close to the limits of ethical conduct.

Either term—"witness preparation" or "horse-shedding"—is different from factual investigation. They do not apply to the process of the lawyer gathering information, but rather to how the witness is prepared for testifying. By the time the case is ready for the horseshed, the lawyer should know more about the case than *any* of the witnesses.

Witness preparation begins early on in the history of a case. In fact, one of the most important kinds of witness preparation is getting ready for depositions. In many cases, the deposition *is* the trial. Just because no judge is present does not mean it is not a trial—the witness is being evaluated by one of the most important fact finders, the opposing counsel.

This means that failure to prepare witnesses for depositions is a genuine professional disservice. Of course depositions are different from trials, but most of the techniques of witness preparation are easily adjusted to suit depositions as well.

Taking witness preparation seriously makes great demands on time. It leads some trial lawyers to turn the job over to paralegals or junior lawyers in the office, while some sole practitioners rely on handouts that explain some of the fundamentals to witnesses.

In some ways witness indoctrination may profit from this sort of efficiency. On the other hand, actually going over the testimony with the witness is something that most good trial lawyers want to do themselves.

One useful system is to record your basic indoctrination talk on a cassette, and have the witness listen to it in your office. The beauty of the tape recording is that it does not forget. Furthermore, it is not as cold and forbidding as a pamphlet. If you use a system like this, it is best to follow it up with a personal question and answer period.

One of the early steps in witness preparation is something a tape recording cannot do—visit the scene with the witness. (Usually there is at least one scene, even in business litigation.) Visual stimulus has a striking effect on people's recollections. Going to the location can bring back details that would otherwise remain lost. Even if you know every possible detail, going to the scene is worthwhile. It will spark language from the witness that would otherwise remain dormant, and the testimony will seem more vivid as a result.

What to Wear

The most fundamental rule about dress is that the witness should be clean and well groomed. But be careful. It is a mistake to dress anyone up beyond their ability to handle it. While dark business suits with neckties and white or light blue shirts can help create a nice impression, some people cannot wear those clothes without looking stiff and uncomfortable. Flashy clothes—of whatever style—are unwise. You should discuss attire with every witness. While you are talking about clothing, remember to caution every-one not to wear any jewelry other than functional watches and wedding rings if they are married.

Why so much caution? It is a genuine shock to see your police officer show up in court in blue jeans and a Hawaiian shirt be-cause you forgot to tell him to wear his uniform. Imagine, if you will, the distress of a new assistant United States attorney in Texas whose principal witness (a secretary with a federal agency) appeared in federal court dressed like Minnie Mouse—complete with short red skirt, long black tail and mouse ears. It was the day before Halloween, and her supervisor had ordered everyone in the office to come to work in costume. Because the attorney had not told her what to wear, she had not brought a change of cloth-ing with her to work.

When the witness is your client, even more care and attention is called for. Under the appropriate circumstances you should pick out what your client will wear, and you should certainly see what it is before trial.

How to Act

The basic principal is to behave naturally. Witnesses (and espe-cially clients) need to be instructed not to smoke in or around the courtroom, to avoid chewing gum, to rise whenever the judge comes in or goes out, and to avoid discussing anything with the lawyers or other witnesses in a way that might make it appear that they are making up testimony—jurors can be very suspicious. It is a good rule not to whisper to your client, expert witness or associ-ate during the course of the trial. Tell these people that if they need to communicate with you they should write you a note. Keep a legal pad and pencil for this purpose. If anyone does write you a note, do not be too quick to dispose of it. You can do that later if need be.

Some witnesses need to be told not to give anyone any dirty

33

looks. This is especially true for defendants in criminal cases. Criminal defendants (and some others) also need to be told to look at the jury at appropriate times—especially when on the witness stand—but not to stare at the jury during the entire trial. It is particularly dangerous for an intense young man with dark eyebrows and a piercing gaze who is charged with a triple axe murder to stare fixedly at the jury during the whole trial.

Voice

Very few witnesses speak too loudly, but there are always plenty that do not speak loudly enough. Telling people to speak up will not cure everyone, but it will help some, so everyone needs to be told. They also need to be told to speak distinctly and to look at the jury when they answer questions.

Some courtrooms have fine acoustics and some others have microphones for witnesses. But there are many courtrooms in which it is difficult to be heard, and your advice to the witness about keeping his voice up will not be effective. Provided you are not the victim of some needless local rule that keeps you seated at counsel table or chained to a podium, you can still overcome this problem by standing close to the furthest juror from the witness. Instinctively the witness will speak up so you can hear him, and you will be able to tell if the testimony is loud enough for the jury to understand what he is saying.

Verbal Habits

Some speech patterns are truly unfortunate on the witness stand. ''I've got to be honest with you,'' or ''let me be honest about this'' carry the strong implication that the rest of the testimony might not be honest, or that honesty is a matter of casual choice for the witness.

A more insidious problem is the habit of the witness saying ''O.K.'' after each question, before giving the answer. The overt message is, ''very well, I understand the question.'' The danger is that some jurors will read it as meaning that the witness is signaling that he remembers the question, has been working on his testimony, and knows what he is supposed to say.

There are some people who have verbal habits that do not reflect on their credibility, but which still keep them from being effective witnesses:

''Do you know what I mean?''

34

You must be careful in dealing with such habits. If they are not extreme, you should consider not mentioning them, lest you make the witness unnecessarily self-conscious. On the other hand, if they are serious, then deal with them with some warmth and understanding:

> John, do you know what? You do something I used to do. You say 'I mean' all the time. I didn't even know I was doing it until a court reporter pointed it out to me. I guess she got tired of typing 'I mean' so many times. Anyway, I got rid of the habit by just putting 'I mean' on a little 3 x 5 card and drew a cross through it. I put the card on my mirror where I would see it every day, and in less than a week I stopped saying 'I mean.' I didn't even have to think about it. Just seeing the card put my subconscious mind to work and 'I mean' went away.

Physical Habits

You need to watch for physical mannerisms, and use discretion in dealing with them as well. Some witnesses chew their nails, stare at their feet, pull at their clothing, twist their rings, or play with their glasses. When you spot something like this, you must decide whether you can do something to make the person a more effective witness.

Occasionally you will have a witness who has a genuine impairment, one that is either temporary or permanent. People—including judges and juries—want to shield themselves from others who make them feel uncomfortable. Unless the impairment is part of the damages, you do not want to risk having the jury draw the emotional curtain that will protect them from the witness with a handicap.

The question is what to do about it.

The answer is to have the one with the handicap bring it out in the open. But how? Certainly not by complaining.

Perhaps the best approach is that taken by a young lawyer who had been in a serious automobile accident a few weeks before trial, and was unable to get a postponement even though her jaws were wired shut. She could speak well enough, but it sounded like she was clenching her teeth. Her method for dealing with it was classic:

> Before we start, ladies and gentlemen, I want to tell you that I was in an automobile accident a few weeks ago, and the doc-

35

tors wired my jaws together. I thought they did it because they found out I was a lawyer, but they claim it is because my jaw is broken.

The result is I talk a little funny. Anyway, I want you all to know that I am not in any pain and I am not at all uncomfortable, and if you won't let it bother you, then I won't let it bother me.

Impartiality

Few things are more damaging than a witness who tries to be too helpful. All witnesses need to understand that they should not exaggerate or overstate anything. The careful witness makes a much better impression than one who is trying to be impressive.

It is natural for people to identify with one side or another. It is also understandable that witnesses want to stay in court and see the rest of the trial after they have been excused. Do not let them do that.

Tell all witnesses—except the expert who is part of the trial team or the client or personal representative—to leave the courthouse (not just the courtroom) after they are excused so the jury will not think they have an interest in the outcome of the case.

Prepare for Direct Examination

First go over previous statements and depositions with the witness. Be careful what you choose to review. Under Rule 612 of the Federal Rules of Evidence, if a witness uses a writing to refresh his recollection before testifying, then the court has discretion to require that it be produced so that the adverse party may inspect it, cross-examine the witness on it, and introduce it in evidence. The thorny problem that results—to what extent does refreshing a witness's recollection in preparation for trial destroy the traditional work product privilege?—is discussed in J. Weinstein and M. Berger, 3 *Weinstein's Evidence* ¶ 612[04].

The lesson is clear to the thoughtful lawyer. Do not use your personal strategy notes to refresh the witness's recollection if his deposition or some other writing already in the possession of the opposition will do the job.

Care also requires that you have the witness read all of his depositions and statements to which the other side has access. You should already be familiar with whatever ambiguities and inconsistencies can be found, and you should call them to the witness's attention, explaining how he can be impeached with prior inconsistent statements. Help the witness understand that if he made a mistake and an earlier statement is incorrect, it is much better to admit it frankly than to deny the statement was made or offer an implausible explanation for it.

Use this same session to discuss the probable testimony of other witnesses. Now is the time to deal with problems and conflicts in the testimony—not in the middle of the trial.

After going over the basic facts and ironing out wrinkles, it is time to get into a rehearsal of the testimony and to decide what form it is going to take. By now you have seen the witness in several different settings. Can he be turned loose with a short introduction and a question calling for a narrative, or will you have to develop everything with traditional questions and answers? Now is the chance to try out each method. With nervous or inexperienced witnesses, do your rehearsal in a courtroom to familiarize them with the surroundings.

It may be that you are planning to save some powerful bit of evidence for the end of the witness's testimony. If so, you will need to tell the witness so that he will not blurt out the climax at the very beginning.

Resist the temptation to give the witness the precise order of questions or their exact wording. (There is an exception to this rule for expert witnesses, who should help you work out the wording of a few key questions. Doing this is an insurance policy against an expert suddenly deciding that based on your question he does *not* have an opinion to a reasonable degree of medical probability as to the cause of the plaintiff's condition.) It is much better for there to be a little awkward spontaneity than the impression that everything is canned.

Sometimes a witness will come up with a marvelous answer during a rehearsal session, and you find yourself wondering what to do to make sure that the witness says the same thing at trial. One way to make it stick in the witness's head is to ask *him* to help *you* remember.

What was it you said about Mr. Brendle's arm—what it looked like?

It looked like his arm had been caught in a giant egg beater. Long strips of flesh were ripped off his arm and were just hanging to it.

That's it. Do me a favor and help me remember that. (Having heard that description there is no chance you could forget it. You just want to make sure the witness will have it burned in his mind as well.)

After you have done all this there is a serious question: How do you keep everything fresh until trial? Certainly one of the things that has changed since James Fenimore Cooper saw the carriage house in White Plains is the length of time between when a case is filed and when it actually comes to trial.

Keep in touch with the witnesses. People move, change their telephone numbers, go on vacation, find new jobs or just plain disappear. The lawyer has to accept the responsibility of keeping track of the witnesses as time goes on. Even though you tell the witnesses to call you if they move, keeping you up to date is not going to be their first priority. If you call or write them periodically, it will help keep things fresh in their minds.

One way to undercut good pretrial preparation is to call a witness twenty months after you last talked to him and say, "I need you in court on Monday morning." It is much easier for the witness to arrange taking off from work if you notify him three or four months in advance. Planning ahead will also give you an opportunity to have a brief refresher session shortly before the hearing.

Do not forget the logistic details such as the date, time and place. Make sure the witness is told where to park or what bus or subway route to take to arrive at the courthouse. Give the witness the name of the judge as well as the courtroom number. Then, if the hearing is moved to another courtroom, some clerk will know where to find the judge, but would be unlikely to know where to find you. If you are really thoughtful about these details, you will put them in a letter as well as in a telephone conversation.

Prepare for Cross-Examination

There are some rules you can give witnesses for cross-examination that are nearly absolute:

1. Pause after every question before giving the answer. There are at least three good reasons for this. First, it will help the witness be careful. Second, it will give you a chance to object if necessary. Third, it will give the witness a chance to turn back toward the jury. The chances are that the cross-examiner will position himself so that the witness must look away from the jury to see him. Pausing just a second or two will let the witness look at the jury.

2.   Answer the questions that are asked. It is a mistake to try to avoid questions or give cute answers. Witnesses should let the lawyers argue the case at the end of the trial.

3.   Do not add anything that is not called for by the question. Volunteering information or explaining away apparently damaging material is a sure sign of partisanship that detracts from credibility.

4.   Do not argue with the cross-examiner. As Gerald Chattman from Cleveland, Ohio, tells witnesses, there are two main traps to avoid. The first is anger. Some lawyers will try to bait you into losing your temper. If the witness sees what is happening and remains polite, the lawyer will be hurt, not the witness. The second pitfall is the ''nice guy'' trap. Witnesses need to remember that the lawyer for the other side is trying to win, so they should stick to their testimony, not change it to please that friendly lawyer.

5.   Do not be embarrassed to admit that you do not know the answer to a question. If you do not know, say so.

6.   Do not guess. It is not a lay witness's job to give opinions.

7.   Do not be too flexible, especially when the cross-examiner is asking ''if it is possible.'' Anything is possible, but that does not change what happened.

8.   Beware of ''Have you talked to anybody about your testimony?'' There is nothing wrong with talking about the case before trial. How else could it be properly prepared? Expert witnesses should similarly be warned about ''How much are you being paid for your testimony?''

After going over all these points, the witness is ready to be cross-examined—not by the opposing counsel, but by you. If you do not want to cross-examine the witness because you think it might injure your relationship with the witness, have it done by a friend or associate while you are present.

Signals

Some witness is bound to wonder what signal system you use, so you need to tell all witnesses that you do not use any system at all. It is amazing how many jurors study lawyers and their clients— especially in criminal cases—to see if they can ''break the code.''

The most important thing for the witness to understand is that he should not look to the lawyer for help in answering any question or for aid in an uncomfortable situation. Let the witness know that this will make the jury think there *is* some signal system even though there is none. Witnesses should understand that they do not need to worry how they are doing, and that if there is any difficulty you will deal with it by a proper objection.

Tell the witnesses that if you object, they should stop testifying at once. Any time you object, the witness should put his mind in high gear and mouth in low gear.

After an objection the witness may not remember the question. It is usually a good idea for the witness to ask to have it repeated.

Witnesses should not worry if the questions are proper. With the exception of personal privileges belonging to the witness, the job of objecting belongs to the lawyer and not to the witness.

Witness Coaching

The most intriguing problem has been saved for last. Up to now everything has been witness preparation. What about the real business in the horseshed? Where is the line between developing testimony so it will be effective and suborning perjury by telling the witness what to say?

The English barristers have an easy answer. It is improper for them to talk directly to clients or witnesses under most circumstances. See Sir William Boulton, C.B.E., *A Guide to Conduct and Etiquette at the Bar of England and Wales* 8, 14-15 (Butterworths, 6th ed. 1975). That rule, of course, simply takes the problem away from the barrister and puts it in the hands of the solicitor.

Because we act as both barristers and solicitors, the problem is hard to avoid. According to James W. Jeans, our duty to our clients and our ethical obligation to avoid participation in a fraud on the court put us squarely in the middle:

> Where do good ethics lie? Who is the candidate for disbarment—the lawyer who advises his client accused of a crime to 'just tell the policeman all you know' or the one who says, 'If you want to get out of this alive take my advice and say you shot in self-defense.' In both instances the role of the lawyer has been profaned and each of the erring advocates should have his ticket torn from the wall. The true advocate will seek the golden mean. He can neither passively sit by while his charge spills his guts nor can he write the script for his pliant client. He must acquaint his client with the legal facets of the case, tell him of the significance of his testimony and then let the truth come forth.

J. Jeans, *Trial Advocacy* 18 (West Pub. Co., 1975).

Sometimes the "golden mean" may be hard to find, particularly if you try to "acquaint your client with the legal facets of the case and tell him of the significance of his testimony." Consider these different questions, each designed to find out what the client would say about the speed of a vehicle:

How fast would you say it was going?

You think it was going 30 or 35? The other witnesses say it was more like 45 or 50. Are you sure it was only going 35?

The other witnesses say the car was going 45 or 50. What do you say?

The speed limit on the Shore Drive is 35 mph. If the other car was speeding, that would help our case. How fast would you say he was going?

Perhaps the surest way to find the "golden mean" is to understand that the duty to client and the duty to our profession come up against each other, and we are more likely to do the job properly if we are aware of both duties.

To some extent the problem of witness coaching is self limiting. The witness who is told what to say is the one who is likely to blurt out, "That's what the lawyer told me to say" when he is attacked on cross-examination.

More than that, the witness's very testimony can become its own impeachment. Perhaps the best example is the testimony of Kate Alterman, the state's star witness in *People v. Harris and Blanck*, the case of the famous "Triangle Shirtwaist Company Fire" in New York.

It was Kate Alterman who testified about the horrible fire that swept through the ten-story loft in Greenwich Village on March 25, 1911, killing hundreds of young immigrant seamstresses, and it was Max Steuer on behalf of the defendants in the case—a criminal action—who conducted the cross-examination.

There was something about Kate's direct examination that did not ring true to Steuer. The words she used, the dramatic images, and her development of the facts did not go with the grammar and accent of a barely literate young immigrant.

What Max Steuer heard the first time became obvious to everyone when he asked Kate to go over her story again and again. Each time she told the story it sounded like the needle had been dropped into the same groove on the record, and all the while she insisted she had not discussed her testimony with anyone. Once when she skipped a part, Steuer reminded her that she had missed something and she was able to pick it up from there and go to the end.

Max Steuer's son, Aron, comments on the effect of the cross-examination in *Max D. Steuer, Trial Lawyer* 108-109 (1950).

> No fact in the story was contradicted, nor was the character of the witness called into question. And yet her value was destroyed. The case, instead of ending on a note of drama, concluded in an atmosphere of ridicule. Whether the girl was coached in her story or whether she made it up herself became immaterial. The high-flown imagery set in the crude grammar was, of course, the key to the realization that the account was not of her recollection but at best a touched-up version of what she remembered.

There it is. Too much time in the shed, and the testimony is bound to smell just a little like horse.

PART II

Starting the Trial

CHAPTER 5

The Theory of the Case

The young lawyer was flushed with victory. The cross-examination-his first—was going marvelously. The witness was an important one for the other side, and the young lawyer's senior partner let him take the witness on cross-examination.

The high point for the young lawyer was his impeachment of the witness with a prior inconsistent statement. First, the witness was committed irrevocably to his direct examination statement that was inconsistent with his deposition. It was not until the witness himself unwittingly cut off each avenue of escape that the young lawyer closed the trap and confronted the witness with the inconsistent deposition.

That was the crushing blow, and it is easy to imagine the young lawyer's surprise on seeing the tight-lipped expression on the face of the senior partner.

"What is the matter?" asked the young lawyer in the hall during a recess. "I thought you would like that impeachment. It is just what you taught me to do."

"Oh, it was classic," replied the senior partner. "It was a textbook example of exactly how to impeach a witness with a prior inconsistent statement. I could not have done better myself. There is only one difficulty. You should not have done it."

"What do you mean?" asked the young lawyer.

"What I mean," replied the senior partner, "is that although you impeached that witness, by the time you finished, the jury accepted the prior statement rather than his testimony on direct examination. The problem is they now think our client was going fifteen miles per hour faster than when you started your cross-examination.

"Your technique was perfect. What happened was, you committed the cardinal sin of doing something that is inconsistent with the theory of the case."

There it is. One of the most fundamental rules in trial practice. It comes before the rules of evidence, techniques of persuasion, impressive demonstrative evidence, and sophisticated touches of eloquence. It is simple, understandable, and nearly absolute:

Never do anything inconsistent with your theory of the case.

Just what is meant by the theory of the case is a study all itself. First, it includes the legal theories of the claim or defense, but it is not so narrow. A plaintiff can recover for negligence that causes harm, but that does not tell us very much.

Then there is the factual theory. It might be the plaintiff's factual theory that the defendant ran into him because he was not paying enough attention to where he was going as he drove down the street.

That tells us something more, but not much.

What is the theory of the case, then?

The theory of the case is the basic, underlying idea that explains not only the legal theory and factual background, but also ties as much of the evidence as possible into a coherent and credible whole. Whether it is simple and unadorned or subtle and sophisticated, the theory of the case is a product of the advocate. It is the basic concept around which everything else revolves.

A good theory of the case is the very heart of advocacy, since it provides a comfortable viewpoint from which the jury can look at all of the evidence—and if they look at the evidence from that viewpoint, they will be led ineluctably to decide in your favor.

Little wonder that the theory of the case is a sort of home cave to be defended at all costs unless utter disaster commands that it be deserted in favor of some unfamiliar place further up the hill.

What is the theory of the case?

It is what the advocate creates out of the legal theories and the facts.

That your knowledge of the facts will influence your choice of legal theories is obvious.

That your knowledge of the legal theories will influence which facts you investigate and develop is evident on reflection.

What is impermissible is to let the legal theory change any fact—a fundamental principle that shows why the defense law-

48

yer's lecture on the law to his client in Travers's *Anatomy of a Murder*, reprinted in Legal Lore, LITIGATION, Vol. 4, No. 3 at 39 (1978), pushed (if not stretched) the ethical line.

There is more to it than choosing the legal theory that will be easiest to prove with the available facts. The applicable statute of limitations, the kinds of permissible damages, whether there is a right to a jury trial, whether the case is in state or federal court, and even the state where the case is filed—all bear on the theory of the case.

One of the distressing things about the theory of the case is that you are permitted to have more than one.

Through the magic of the law, they are even allowed to conflict. As Irving Younger says, at common law you are entitled to reply to a plaintiff who claims his cabbages were eaten by your goat:

> You had no cabbages.
> If you did, they were not eaten.
> If they were eaten, it was not by a goat.
> If they were eaten by a goat, it was not my goat.
> And if it was my goat, he was insane.

Does this mean you should never have inconsistent theories? Surprisingly, there are instances when it may actually make sense to present conflicting claims or defenses. The problem is discussed in R. Keeton, *Trial Tactics and Methods*, 280-285 (2d ed. 1973). But be careful. The usual result of inconsistent theories is disaster.

Sometimes the law itself is an obstacle to presenting conflicting theories of the case, but usually that is not so. Usually, the reason to avoid presenting conflicting theories is simple credibility.

Lawyers, like salesmen, must believe in their products. The effective argument is usually the one that conveys the lawyer's belief in his client to the jury.

In fact, if you do not believe in it yourself, it is virtually impossible to convey the necessary confidence in your client's case.

Why?

If you do not believe in what you are arguing, your body language will give your insincerity away, even if your words do not.

Please understand that this is not a suggestion that a lawyer ever *tell* a judge or jury that he personally believes in the justice of his client's cause. That is specifically forbidden by the Code of Professional Responsibility, DR 7-106 (C). The ethical prohibition

49

forbids saying you believe in your client. Effective advocacy suggests you actually believe in your client.

It is a point worth remembering.

If you ask for more damages than you believe in, it will show. Cut the case down to a size you can honestly argue.

If it means dismissing the case against a party you are unable to believe is responsible to your client, do it.

If there are things you do not like about your client, do not hide them—bring them out.

It can even turn a terrible weakness into a telling strength.

The story is one told by Judge Gerald T. Wetherington of Dade County, Florida, to a group of students at the 1978 National Institute for Trial Advocacy in Boulder, Colorado.

A lawyer's client lost his leg when it was run over by the defendant's streetcar. The difficulty with the case was that the plaintiff was a derelict, with no visible means of support. He was mainly known for rambling through town, begging the price of a cheap bottle of wine.

A more experienced lawyer friend was consulted on how to go about cleaning up the plaintiff to make a good impression at trial.

The friend was all in favor of having the plaintiff be *clean*, but argued against trying to dress him up or trying to make him look like something other than what he really was.

That advice resulted in a theory of the case that produced a classic final argument:

> Clean sheets he never knew, but did they have to take his leg? A warm meal he seldom had, but did they have to take his leg? An education, a good job, fine clothes—all were strangers to him—but did they have to take his leg?

What you believe in is not the only test. Your sincerity helps persuade the jury, but except in the rarest cases, will not lead them to accept things they feel are implausible.

Plausibility—what the jury feels is more likely true—is a constant advocate. The closer your case is aligned with basic probabilities, the better.

A simple example makes the point.

A lawyer was getting ready to defend a trucking company in an unfortunate accident involving one of its trucks and a young child who did not cross at the walk. It is the sort of case called a "child run-down" by plaintiffs' lawyers, and a "child dart-out" by defendants.

50

Because of the jurisdiction's approach to contributory negligence and the tender years of the child, contributory negligence was not a defense. Still, the lawyer realized that the plaintiff had to show that the defendant's driver was causally negligent in the first place.

He was discussing his plan to call some witnesses who would help give the impression that the truck driver was driving slowly immediately before the accident.

His friend advised another approach:

> John, for heaven's sake, don't try to slow that truck down too much. People will never believe it was going that slow. And if they do, they will surely think that the driver should have been able to stop in time. Don't try to slow down the truck—speed up the kid. He didn't stroll into the middle of the street—he ran.

What is the point? Either way the lawyer can believe in his client. The more telling theory is the one the jury is likely to accept as probable.

The next step is to make it simple.

Surprisingly enough, simplicity is often achieved by taking into account as many of the facts as possible. The more facts your theory of the case explains—that is, the fewer facts there are that do not fit your case—the simpler and more believable it will be. Achieving simplicity takes work, but it is worth the effort.

Suppose, for example, that an unbiased eyewitness is called by your opposition. You have two equally attractive theories (something that can only happen in hypothetical cases). One requires you to attack the unbiased witness as a liar. The other theory explains how the witness believes she is telling the truth, but is understandably mistaken. Chances are, the second theory is better than the first.

Your own sincerity and a simple, plausible theory are marvelous assets, but it is possible to want even more.

A truly superb theory of the case will fit comfortably into the value scheme of the judge and jury.

Good trial lawyers tend to be voracious readers, watchers, and listeners. They crave information about the world around them. One of the interests that trial lawyers tend to share is a desire to understand the values of the communities in which they try cases. Indeed, one important reason for conducting a jury voir dire examination is to take the opportunity to study the members of the jury to see what sorts of people they are.

Why?

To adjust unconsciously the way questions are asked and arguments are constructed to make them fit the fundamental values of the jurors.

As between two equally simple, plausible theories that are both presented with equal sincerity, the one that more comfortably fits community values is more likely to be accepted.

That proposition sounds good as an abstraction, but does it work in real life?

Certainly.

Take the difference between charity and paying a debt. As Craig Spangenberg demonstrated in his excellent article, *Basic Values and the Techniques of Persuasion,* LITIGATION, Vol. 3, No. 4 at 13 (1977), Americans tend to think people should pay their debts. In fact, some of the best plaintiff's jurors are those who feel that paying a debt—and paying it on time—is an important part of their lives.

Charity, on the other hand, is an important value according to Spangenberg, but not so high with many people as paying the debt. The man of wealth satisfies his conscience with a quarter in the Salvation Army bucket at Christmastime.

It follows, then, that in a personal injury action a theory of the case that is articulated as an obligation owed because of the wrong that was done—rather than as an appeal for pity because a person got hurt—is more likely to bring an adequate award.

To be sure, there are times when you may not have the luxury of a theory. But they should be rare—just as rare as the times when you have a professional obligation to assert a theory in which you have no confidence.

In criminal practice there is even a name for this uncomfortable situation. It is called the cockroach defense. That is when there is no real defense, and all the advocate can do is act like a cockroach, and crawl all over the other side.

Does that work?

Sometimes.

More often, it is just a long drawn-out guilty plea.

When it works, it is usually because there is a more credible underlying theme. Often it is that the government's proof simply is not good enough to justify conviction, and under our system of justice, that means the jury should acquit.

Once you have a solid theory of the case, it will help throughout the trial.

Take the opening statement. Sadly, too many lawyers use the first minutes of their opening statements to lecture the jury about the function of the opening statement.

It is an unfortunate waste.

During the first few minutes of the opening statement, the jury is highly attentive, and accordingly receptive. They are eager to learn what the case is all about.

It is the perfect time to give them your theory of the case.

That is exactly how an opening statement should begin. Instead of some standard words about opening statements, give them the theory of the case—carefully distilled into a memorable theme which will stay with them and shape their understanding throughout the trial.

The theory of the case helps decide which witnesses to call. Often a difficult choice whether to call a particular witness can be answered from the perspective of whether it will really advance the theory of the case.

It also helps decide the order of witnesses. Start strong and end strong, to be sure, but let the order in which they testify be one that helps explain your theory of the case.

Once the witness is on the stand, the principle still applies. Certainly, there are important background matters and bits of foundational information that must be presented. But beyond that, the rule is simple: Limit your questions to those asking for information about your theory of the case, or those tending to attack your opponent's theory.

As with our beginner who unfortunately wound up accelerating his own client's car, it is probably easiest to forget about the theory of the case during cross-examination. For that reason, more care is needed in cross-examination than anywhere else.

Final argument is the time for the theory of the case to triumph.

The troubling thing for some lawyers is to commit the case to one theory.

Even in a simple negligence case, the defense might be:

> We were not negligent.
> If we were, you were contributorily negligent.
> Even if we were negligent and you were not contributorily negligent, you were not hurt.
> Even if you were hurt, you were not badly hurt.

You will notice that it is more than a little like the crazy goat.

The problem is either to articulate these ideas so they do not detract from each other, or to abandon those defenses that are not seriously arguable.

Why?

The signal you send when you refuse to put very many eggs in any one basket is that you do not trust the basket.

Surely, the point in constructing a theory of the case is to get a basket big enough and strong enough to carry all the eggs you need.

CHAPTER 6

Humanizing the Client

What do you want most to convey to the judge or jury about the person you represent?

That he is paying for your services?

Call him your "client."

That there are criminal charges against him?

Call him "the accused."

That he is a party to the case and he has certain procedural rights?

Call him "the plaintiff" or "the defendant."

On the other hand, if you would like the judge or jury to understand that you are representing an actual human being with senses and emotions, memories and anticipations, duties and obligations, who is entitled to fundamental dignity and a rightful place in the world, then you might consider using his name.

Actually, that is a good place to start in thinking about "humanizing the client."

How about calling your client by name—not only by his last name, but his first as well?

In *Trial Diplomacy—Selected Text* at 4-5 (Court Practice Institute 1973), Alan Morrill suggests that you can call any client by his first name.

Maybe so. But not everyone is comfortable calling a client by his first name. Furthermore, there are some occasions when first names seem out of place—even downright offensive. On top of that, one even hears of some trial judges who will not permit lawyers to use their clients' first names in contested hearings.

Of course, if there is a local rule, you must follow it (until you succeed in getting it changed). Assuming there is no rule against first names, you should use them, keeping in mind some sensible limitations dictated by good taste.

It is usually wise to start out the trial talking about your client with his full name—for example, "Mr. Ronald Carlson." As the trial progresses, you start referring to him as "Ronald Carlson" or "Ron Carlson" and then finally just "Ron."

This natural progression helps the jury feel they are becoming acquainted with someone rather than having familiarity thrust upon them.

Does it work?

Henry Rothblatt, speaking at a seminar in New York City in the spring of 1979, told about a case he tried on the Eastern Shore of Maryland in which this progressive familiarity was so successful that when the jury returned its verdict, the foreman announced, "We find Bobby not guilty."

But when your client is older than you, using his or her first name may be a signal mistake. This is especially true if a juror might think you were condescending toward your client or toward some racial or ethnic group by using your client's first name—no matter how friendly you might be with your client outside of court. Indeed, in some parts of the country it may be more appropriate for a woman litigator to call her male client by his first name than it would be for a male litigator to call his female client by just her first name.

The point is not to suggest that anyone adopt a superficial dual standard in speech. On the contrary, good litigators, both men and women, need to be sensitive to the society in which they try cases and learn to express themselves effectively in ways that will not give offense.

There is more to the first name question than age, sex, and minority status. There is the virtually absolute principle that you should never do anything inconsistent with your theory of the case. What sort of feeling do you want the jury to have about your client? It is a question that can only be answered from the vantage point of your theory of the case. The answer will help you choose the degree of formality you want to surround the person you represent.

It is possible to overdo the first name technique. Some defense lawyers are ready to expose the use of the plaintiff's first name. It can be a dangerous attack (no matter which side makes it) if the target has the presence of mind to respond in rebuttal argument:

Well, of course I have called John Milliken by his first name. Since he contacted me after the defendant's truck smashed into his car, John and I have spent literally hundreds of hours together working on this case, getting ready for trial, since we knew that the defendant was going to try to deny responsibility for the wreck he caused.

Considering all the time we have spent together, it would be rather strange if I didn't get to know John pretty well, to like the man, and to call him by his first name.

Notice that what otherwise might have been improper argument is permissible because the opposition has opened the door.

But what you call your client is just the start.

Take, for example, how the judge and jury first meet the person you represent. To be sure, the judge may introduce the lawyers and clients and everyone else at the beginning of jury voir dire, but that hardly counts.

How does the typical lawyer introduce his client? Something like this.

My client (you already know better) in this case, ladies and gentlemen (pointing vaguely toward the other side of the room) is that man seated at the counsel table.

There is no rule against doing it right:

Ladies and gentlemen, I would like you to meet Mr. Tom Read, the man who was crossing the street when the defendant's truck came crashing through the light (as he walks toward where his client is seated). Tom, would you stand up, please? (And Read rises—having previously been told that when he stands, he should get *all the way up*—not just lift his backside from the chair an inch or two—and looks at the jury.) Ladies and gentlemen, this is Tom Read. (Then to the client) Thank you Tom, you can sit down again.

While you are instructing your client how to stand when he is introduced, there are some additional rules to pass on:

- Every time the judge comes in or goes out of the courtroom, rise fully. The jury is always watching the lawyers and clients, and they may take even unintentional lapses in protocol into account.
- During the selection of the jury, turn your chair so you

are looking directly at the jury panel. In many courts the jury starts out behind the bar during jury selection, and it is a mistake to sit with your back to them.

- If you have something to tell me during the trial, write it down. I will give you a legal pad and a pencil. For heaven's sake, do not whisper to me if you can avoid it. Strange as it may seem, the jury may think we are concocting some testimony if we are seen whispering to each other.

Do you doubt this? Television and movies always seem to show lawyers and their clients whispering to each other, and like it or not, we often unconsciously mimic the movies. If you are tempted to whisper to your client, restrain yourself. Nearly every lawyer is familiar with the print by Honoré Daumier showing a lawyer whispering in his client's ear while the client is picking his pocket. The next time you look at that print, try to imagine what the lawyer is saying.

If you really want to look disreputable, whisper in your client's ear at the same time you look at someone else in the courtroom.

There are a number of other rules for clients to follow, especially about how they answer questions on direct and cross-examination, but most are matters better saved for a discussion of witness preparation. Those instructions should include the firm direction to look in the jurors' eyes when answering questions, and not at you, lest it seem that the client is seeking instructions in what to say, rather than merely looking for comfort in an alien setting.

Next comes dress.

Supposedly, all trial lawyers know that they should be careful about what their clients wear. It is a good idea to have your client (and all your witnesses, for that matter) come to your office a day or so before trial wearing exactly what they plan to wear to court, so you can make appropriate adjustments.

John T. Molloy's, *Dress for Success* (1975), has generally solid, if somewhat conservative, notions about what you should wear, and many of the ideas are worth passing on to your clients as well. I leave to you the decision whether to choose dark colors and whether to accept V. Hale Starr's suggestion, reported in the *ABA Journal*, Vol. 66, No. 1, at 21 (1980) that businessmen and expert witnesses should wear ''good, honest brown.''

Be particularly careful about jewelry. Mike Schmidt suggests that even in Dallas, Texas, both men and women should wear *no* jewelry other than wedding rings and functional watches. That means remove other rings, pins, bracelets, necklaces, and other bits of decoration other than lapel pins for noncontroversial civic organizations.

The effort to make your client attractive and presentable is worthwhile. A number of studies cited in Michael J. Saks and Reid Hastie, *Social Psychology in Court* (Van Nostrand Reinhold Co. 1978), pp. 156-160, indicate that attractiveness is "important on its own"; that attractive individuals were found guilty less often and sentenced less harshly in criminal settings. Similarly, "loving and warm" individuals were treated more leniently than those described as "cold and unapproachable."

So far we have lawyers talking about their clients by name, making certain they are well dressed and taking a few moments to introduce them properly. It is surprising how much difference these little touches will make, and yet, when you think about it, they still do not tell the jury very much about your client.

Suppose that you wanted to convey the general impression that you represent a decent person who is worthy of belief. Since you obviously cannot turn to the jury at some point in the trial and say, "See here. The man I represent is a decent person who is worthy of belief," you will have to think of some other way of getting this idea across.

The answer is, if you cannot say it, then do it. If you act like your client is an ax murderer, you are likely to convey that impression. On the other hand, if you believe in your client, then you should be able to put an avuncular arm around his shoulder—especially in a criminal case, as if to reassure and protect him from the misguided charges that are leveled against him. In other words, if you believe in your client, do not be afraid to touch him or her. Of course, it should be unambiguously platonic, and should, like the use of names, take into account all the dictates of good taste and the relationship between you and your client.

A warning. Do not fake it. If you do, it will backfire. Some unconscious body set, expression or movement will give you away, and the jury will understand that you are not being sincere.

There is another little technique, brilliant in its simplicity and effectiveness, that was done by Craig Spangenberg of Cleveland, Ohio, during a demonstration opening statement at The Litigation Forum at Case Western Reserve University School of Law in March, 1979.

One or two minutes into his opening statement, Spangenberg was uncertain of a minor detail—one of the things his client was going to pick up at a convenience store:

He was going to get some ice cream, some soda for his children, and, uh, one other thing which I have forgotten right now. . . .

Then just about thirty seconds later, almost interrupting another thought, Spangenberg said, turning toward his client and pointing his finger at him:

Oh, yes, now I remember. You were also going to get a quart of milk.

Instinctively, his client nodded a silent "yes." Satisfied, Craig turned back to the jury and went on with his opening statement.

What had happened?

Did the client testify or even say anything not under oath?

No.

Did Craig Spangenberg improperly state his personal belief in the justice of his client's cause?

No.

Yet, the totality of this interpersonal transaction reflected that the lawyer had absolute trust in his client. He had just relied on him to verify a fact.

The message? When this person takes the stand, he can be believed.

So clients can be humanized with dress, introductions, names, and some sign from you that they are credible people. "But wait," you say. "There must be more to it than that."

You are right.

So far everything has been preliminary. When we actually get into the case, what do you say about your client? And when he takes the stand, what do you have him say about himself?

Obviously, what the judge and jury learn about your client is limited by the strictures of relevance. But that should not be at all troublesome to you. In the first place, reasonable amounts of personal background are admitted for all witnesses, essentially on the basis that it is important for the jury to know who is talking to them. Within the discretion of the trial court, somewhat more time for such background information is permitted for parties.

In the second place, personal information that amounts to a plea for sympathy is likely to backfire anyway.

Very well, then. Within the guidelines of relevance, what do you choose?

Back to the theory of the case, then a quick trip to the art museum.

In a personal injury action, for example, where the plaintiff has lost the use of one hand, it makes a difference that she used to play the piano for the kids at Sunday school. If on the other hand, you are representing a truck driver who is charged with negligence, you might deal with his limited background (and, by implication, his difficulty getting another job should he lose this one) in the following way.

Q: Would you tell us, Mr. Sullivan, what you do for a living?

A: I am a truck driver, with Simplex Trucking Company.

Q: And how long have you been a driver, Mr. Sullivan?

A: All my working life—ever since I was eighteen. Let's see—that's almost twenty years, because I will be thirty-eight in November.

Q: Have you ever worked at any job other than truck driving, Tom?

A: No, sir. Driving's all I've ever done, and all I know how to do.

Do not think that personal injury cases are the only kind that justify some humanizing details about the litigants. Does it matter in a patent infringement suit that the inventor claiming the infringement worked in his basement workshop for five years perfecting the invention? Does it matter in a construction contract dispute that the plaintiff started his company from scratch some fifteen years ago?

Certainly—if it fits your theory of the case.

Now to the art museum.

Except in unusual cases, the humanizing details are not the points on which you can spend the most time. You must, therefore, make a little information do a lot of work. Picasso once did a drawing with just one line and produced striking results. The line looks like a gracefully curving J with no horizontal line across the top.

Try it yourself. As you draw the vertical line of the J, gently curve the line first to the left and then back again before making the large curve at the bottom of the J. If you do it right, it will not be a Picasso—but it will unmistakably be a woman's derriere.

The point is that there is an artistry in choosing the kinds of details that will epitomize the characteristics you want to convey about your client. They will not all be as deft as Picasso's single line, but if they are chosen with some thought, they will make a difference in the case.

"Fine," you say, "but none of this really applies to me. I usually represent fictitious clients—corporations. Believe me, if you think you can humanize one of my clients. . . ."

It is on this notion that too many members of the defense bar surrender creativity to their counterparts who represent plaintiffs.

Can you humanize a large corporation?

Let us take a specific example.

Suppose you represent the largest bakery in the world—ITT Continental Bakeries. That should do for a large, impersonal corporation.

Now suppose they are charged in a private action with having committed violations of the antitrust law in achieving their commanding market position. Is there *anything* you could do to humanize the client in that case?

This is exactly the problem that was faced by Patrick E. Higginbotham, now a United States District Judge for the Northern District of Texas.

The starting point for solving the problem of humanizing the client was the theory of the case. Patrick Higginbotham's basic idea was that ITT Continental became the world's largest bakery by doing a good job selling bread—not by breaking any antitrust law.

Who, then, was chosen as a representative of the corporation to sit at counsel table during the trial? Pat Higginbotham rejected any number of bright, young executives from New York.

The man he finally chose was a big, red-faced, smiling Irishman with "hands like hamhocks," who started out delivering bread to stores in Alabama, and who had worked his way up to district sales manager in Missouri by the time of trial. He was a salesman, and he knew how to sell bread: Be a pleasant, outgoing person who likes his customers, make prompt deliveries, help out with special problems, pick up stale merchandise—salespeople who do all that get good rack space in the stores and sell a lot of bread.

This was not a person who would explain the theory behind successful sales with statistics and graphs—other witnesses

62

could do that if necessary. This was a person who lived the theory and made it happen.

Pat Higginbotham's point was a good one: representing a corporation does not make it impossible to humanize your client. It may be a greater challenge, but like making ordinary people seem more real, it is surely worth the effort.

CHAPTER 7

The Credibility of the Lawyer

Sanctus Ivos erat Brito, Advocatus et non latro, Res miranda populo.
Saint Ives was a Breton, a lawyer and not a thief, a thing of wonder to the people.

A federal court of appeals judge was sitting as a district judge in a small North Carolina town 20 years ago. He was hearing a moonshine case tried to the bench. The defendant on trial was not charged with brewing the stuff—just having trafficked in it somehow.

Even I, a first-year law student literally walking into a federal court to see what it looked like, could tell that it was a ragtag defense. The lawyer, specializing in moonshine cases, was no stranger to the federal court, but he was a stranger to the rules of evidence and was not even on speaking terms with the canons of ethics.

The cross-examination of the apprehending officer was devastating—the lawyer was torn apart. The lawyer then tried to get some snapshots of the scene of the still into evidence, but no one could authenticate them, so the lawyer just told the judge he had taken the pictures himself, and the judge let them in.

The capper was final argument.

Good old country stories?

No.

Clever weaving of facts and law?

No.

Procedural obstacles or constitutional stumbling blocks?
No.
Impassioned eloquence?
No.
It took less than a minute to deliver:

> Your Honor, this boy ain't no criminal. He ain't no moonshiner. He just happened by mistake to be there buying some lightning when this raid took place.
>
> I know he ain't guilty, Your Honor, because when he paid me my fee, he paid it in all little bills—ones and fives that he had borrowed from friends and neighbors. If he'd have been a moonshiner, they'd have been big bills, Your Honor.

The defendant was found guilty. Maybe the judge figured that a *dealer* in moonshine would have plenty of ones and fives.

But there is a lesson in this argument, even though the lawyer lost the case, did not know any evidence, and obviously violated the ethical rule that it is absolutely improper to state your personal belief in the justice of your client's cause.

The lesson is one of credibility.

Not the client's credibility or even the witnesses' credibility, but the lawyer's credibility.

Strangely enough, it is not entirely a negative example.

That lawyer knew something that some of the rest of us sometimes forget. Underlying every trial is a simple progression:

I am honest.

You should believe me.

I believe in the justice of my client's cause.

Therefore, you should decide for my client.

Do you doubt this really underlies what happens during a trial?

Consider. In most criminal cases, juries think that the defense lawyer really knows whether the defendant is guilty, and they watch the lawyer for subtle clues that will give the truth away.

During the voir dire examination of the jury (or during opening statement if the judge conducts the voir dire), the jury is sizing you up at the same time you are sizing them up. Kenney F. Hegland, *Trial and Practice Skills in a Nutshell* (West, 1978) at 101. As Hegland says (at 83), during those long recesses when the jury is not supposed to be talking about the case, they are talking about the lawyers.

But what about the ethical rule? It is wrong to tell the jury or judge that you personally believe in your client's case. In ethical matters you are usually supposed to go one step further and avoid even the appearance of evil. Does this mean that you should be at pains *not* to believe in your client, lest your inner feelings show?

No.

The ethical rule forbids that you *say* you personally believe in your client's cause. It does not forbid you actually to believe in it or to show that belief in ways other than words.

Of course, there is no contrary rule either. We are fortunate there is no requirement that we believe in everything our clients do.

So long as you are not participating in a fraud or a crime, or bringing a baseless action, there is generally nothing to keep you from arguing a case in which you have no faith whatever. You may even occasionally win such a case.

But usually not.

Usually the case you do not believe in is the case you do not win. Usually, the most effective thing you can do as an advocate is believe in your case.

Do not think this means that the quest for effective advocacy is a search for ways to convey a belief that is not there.

On the contrary.

The real function of body language is to betray the inner feelings. As John Stefano said in *Body Language and Persuasion,* 3 LITIGATION, No. 4 at 31, 54 (1977):

> If, on the other hand, you do not know what you are doing, or you do not believe in it, or you are afraid of revealing what you feel, your body and voice will betray you, no matter how you attempt to manipulate them.

The starting point, then, is to frame your case so you can believe in it. It is an essential step that was discussed more fully in Chapter Five, *The Theory of the Case.* But that is not the message of this chapter. This time we start from that point and go on. Now we are concerned with how the credibility of the lawyer transcends mere belief in the case. Here, the emphasis is on how the lawyer's credibility is a concern that touches all levels of trial techniques.

In other words, the question, "How will this affect my credibility as an advocate?" is a good vantage point for examining everything you do during the course of a trial. It is an excellent starting point for any serious self-evaluation.

You undoubtedly remember hearing warnings about not promising too much during opening statement. One way to look at the danger is that the jury may actually believe it must find everything you promised to return a verdict in your favor.

Maybe there is a better explanation. After all, a judge in a bench trial is not likely to be misled into thinking that each promised fact is an element of a case, and still it is dangerous to overstate your expected proof in a trial to the court.

Why?

Your credibility.

When you state what you anticipate the evidence will be and then do not deliver, your case is damaged even though it is technically as valid as ever. Your believability has suffered, and your case along with it.

Direct examination presents special problems of the lawyer's credibility. That may seem puzzling at first, because a good direct examiner does not intrude himself needlessly on what the witness has to say. If it is a good witness, who has been well prepared, the direct examiner should seem almost unobtrusive.

How, then, is there a problem of the lawyer's credibility?

Theater people call it the challenge of re-creating the first impression. Obviously you know (we hope) what the answers to all of the questions on direct examination should be. Everyone knows that you spent a considerable amount of time preparing for trial. Nothing—well, almost nothing—should be a surprise.

The trouble is, if you do not show any response to the testimony, something seems wrong. You must respond to the evidence almost as if you were hearing it for the first time. This does not mean you need to go to acting school to be a trial lawyer. On the contrary, any attempt to act will get in the way. Instead, you must feel free to respond as a normal person to what you are hearing.

What is the best way?

Listen to the answer.

You are told by Irving Younger to listen to the answers on cross-examination, lest you miss something astounding.

Now you are told to listen to the answers on direct examination so your response will be a normal, human one—not something that fails to mesh with what is going on in the courtroom.

As you become accustomed to thinking about *your* credibility, some of the standard bits of advice about trial behavior make even more sense. It is important to be deferential to the court. Why? Lawyers who respect obvious authority figures are the kind more

67

likely to be thought of as credible themselves. Surely there are exceptions, occasions when the lawyer must attack authorities, but they are rare.

It is important to be fair to your opponent. Why? Certainly it is obvious that well-mannered people who make the jury feel more at ease are more likely to be effective. But it goes even further. Hostility may lead you to act as if you have something to hide, with the resultant damaging message about your credibility.

Follow the standard amenities. Cite to the pages of the documents you refer to, show your opponent exhibits before you offer them. Not only does it seem open and fair, it cuts off any opportunity your opponent may have to make an objection which suggests you are trying to get some evidence in without giving him a chance to see what it is.

That suggests a related point.

Judge Robert E. Jones of Oregon conducted an interesting, informal survey when he was on the trial bench a few years ago. He wanted to know, among other things, what juries liked best and what they liked least about the trials they heard.

What they liked least is revealing: bench conferences.

It should not be too surprising. After all, if two people whisper to each other, and it is clear they are doing it for the purpose of excluding *you*, then you will resent it.

When lawyers have a sidebar discussion, it is obvious to the jury that it is done to exclude them. Naturally, they resent it.

What does that mean to you?

Do not ask for a bench conference if you can avoid it. Asking for a bench conference is a signal you have something to hide from the jury, and they will resent it.

It will damage your credibility.

Instead, anticipate evidentiary problems with a motion in limine or motion to suppress, as it is often called in criminal practice. Talk about things in chambers or during recesses, but avoid asking to approach the bench.

Of course, there are times when a bench conference is the only possible remedy. Just be aware that each time you ask for one, it is likely to be charged against your credibility.

The point goes even further. Needless objections should be avoided. Each time you object, you run the risk of looking like you are trying to keep some essential truth from the jury.

Often, however, there is a good reason for making the objection, one which, if the jury understood it, might keep them from feeling you were trying to keep reliable information from them by interposing technicalities.

The trouble is, if you were to turn to the jury and start explaining things in the middle of the case—the way they used to in the movies—it would be only moments before you were held in contempt.

On the other hand, there is no rule that forces us to make objections incomprehensible. It is possible—and entirely proper—to make objections stated to the judge that are also understandable to the jury.

For example, a typical objection might be, "Objection, Your Honor, the question calls for inadmissible hearsay."

In about the same amount of time, counsel might say this instead:

"Objection, Your Honor, the jury can't tell whether this unknown person who is not on the witness stand was telling the truth. This is hearsay."

There it is. In five seconds, the underlying basis of the hearsay rule is exposed so it does not look as if a mindless technicality is being used to withhold truth.

Obviously, the technique has its limits. First, some judges frown on "speaking objections"—an unfortunate vogue in a few jurisdictions. It is apparently in response to lawyers who use objections as a launching pad for protracted jury arguments. Second, not every objection should be made understandable to the jury. When the objection is that a gory picture will inflame them, the argument is better made outside their presence. Third, it is almost impossible to articulate objections so they are understandable to the jury if it is done extemporaneously. They need to be worked out in advance, something that is surely worth the effort.

To be sure, juries expect some contentiousness from lawyers, and it may help to have the judge give the standard instruction that the lawyers are just doing their job when they object. Still, the reason why the instruction is given is the tendency for juries to deduct objections from a lawyer's credibility account.

One more point before leaving objections. A lawyer concerned about his or her credibility avoids asking objectionable questions in the first place. When you do something that results in a sustained objection, the jury is likely to think you violated the rules on purpose. The net result is that the objection gets charged against your credibility—even though it may also work against the one who objected.

If you are serious about your trial advocacy skills, you have thought about cross-examination. It commands attention partly because of some of its dangers. We guard against asking questions when we do not know the answers, letting a witness explain, asking why, or asking one question too many.

But what we are not warned about is the stupid attack. It ought to be the first rule of cross-examination. Do not make a stupid attack.

Why?

Because of the lawyer's credibility.

"But wait," you say. "I do not want to appear naive, but what do you mean by a 'stupid attack'?"

A good question. Let us take, as an example, one of the oldest cross-examination stories, the one that everyone has heard about the cross-examiner who asks one question too many and is rewarded with the answer that the witness is sure the defendant bit off the victim's nose because he saw the defendant spit it out.

That story, according to the pundits, is an example of asking one question too many.

Humbug.

It is an example of *a stupid attack*.

Suppose we retry the case. The cross-examiner, who has been laughed at for hundreds of years, now has a chance to avoid that last question, and he does. Now there is the inference, decently clear from that refined cross-examination, that the witness should not be believed, because he did not have an adequate opportunity to see what happened.

Rejoice for the defense counsel! He had it to do all over again, and he has done it the way everyone says it should be done.

We will even make the prosecutor so ignorant that he asks no questions on re-direct examination, which is often a good time for asking what would have been one question too many on cross.

Now what will happen?

Is there any real possibility when the victim takes the stand that the jury will conclude that his nose just fell off one day?

The lawyer has made a stupid attack on cross-examination. He tried to undercut a witness with questions designed to show that he did not have an adequate opportunity to see what happened. The trouble is, the witness was right, and when that becomes obvious, then the lawyer's credibility is in grave danger. So what is a stupid attack? One that can be exposed as incorrect,

70

misguided or dishonest. Any time a stupid attack is exposed, the party making it is worse off than if the attack had never been made.

Reading your own transcripts can be a painful thing to do, especially if you are looking for good grammatical structure, which is almost always a misguided effort.

Mercifully, most court reporters edit out many of our little verbal infelicities such as "um" and "uh." On the other hand, they tend to leave in our longer, needless phrases such as "let me ask you this question," which is roughly translated as meaning, "I am trying to think of another question."

One of the more dangerous habits is responding to every answer the witness gives on cross-examination with "O.K." If you do it, you probably mean nothing more than, "I have heard and understand."

The danger, however, is that some of the jury may interpret your "O. K." as meaning "I accept that." At best, it seems to be a set of mixed signals, one attacking the witness, the other accepting what he says, while at worst, the jury may believe you and accept what the witness says is true.

Closing argument is another part of the trial in which the credibility of the lawyer is a chief concern. A well chosen analogy can help convince the jury. If it draws on your own background, it is likely to ring true. Apt analogies can be powerful.

On the other hand, be certain they fit the case and are not susceptible to being turned against you by your opponent. If you are going to use analogies, use only one or two during final argument. One reason for this is that if metaphors or analogies are too quick, they tend to appear clever, and they detract from rather than add to your believability.

Another danger is reading your final argument. One way to look at the difficulty of reading an argument or statement is that it is almost impossible to recreate the exact emotion that was present when the words were written. The result is an artificial feeling about the entire case.

The point was recently refined by Kenneth A. Albers, the head of the Theater Department of Case Western Reserve University, who cotaught an advanced workshop in Trial Advocacy Techniques, not as an acting coach, but as an expert in communication skills. Mr. Albers told the student:

When you are reading facts to me, I can accept that as a

juror. You want to make sure you have got your details right. It looks like you are trying to be careful, trying to be accurate.

But when you are talking to me about what those facts mean, that is different. If you have to get your argument from something you wrote down, it looks to me like you don't believe it.

Finally, having a reputation with the judges and lawyers in the community for being scrupulously fair and honest, as well as being thought of as one who truly knows the law, is more valuable than rubies. A judge is sometimes called the thirteenth juror. No matter if the local rules forbid the judge from commenting on the weight of the evidence. If the judge thinks you are honest and fair, it will show in subtle little ways that will influence the jury throughout its deliberations.

CHAPTER 8

Voir Dire

Let us start hypothetically.

A young lawyer is about to try his first case. On the eve of trial it suddenly occurs to him that there is more to trying the case than direct and cross-examination, opening statement and final argument. He must conduct a jury voir dire as well.

Too late to sign up for any special trial advocacy course, he consults a more experienced practitioner in the firm.

"Voir dire," says the older lawyer. "A fascinating topic. That we should call it voir dire is a study all itself. The words themselves mean almost nothing to us; they are quaint relics of Anglo-French and translate into something like 'to speak the truth.' "

"Fine," responds the young lawyer, anxious to get on with the practical part of the lesson.

"It interests me because how we talk about something is profoundly connected with what we think about it, and how we do it," said the older lawyer.

"Take the historical sense of voir dire as the starting point. We use the term today to refer to two very different procedures—the questioning of prospective jurors, and the preliminary cross-examination of witnesses to determine if they are qualified to testify.

"A little thought shows why the two different practices travel under the same name. Each one is a preliminary examination of someone to determine his qualifications—either as a witness or a juror. The term, voir dire, as it turns out, does not refer to the actual examination, but to the oath that is administered before the examination begins."

"Listen," interrupted the young lawyer, "I really am afraid I am imposing on you—perhaps if you had a book I could borrow, maybe I could—"

"Oh, don't think of it," replied the experienced practitioner. "As I was saying, the point of this is not just an academic exercise. First, we distinguished the preliminary cross-examination of witnesses from questioning jurors. Now down to business. Voir dire, as a term, has almost no intrinsic meaning to us. Yet it is true that how we talk about something is profoundly connected with what we think about it, and how we do it."

"In other words, since the words in themselves are meaningless to us, what lawyers do in conducting voir dire is meaningless, right? I gather you are telling me it does not make any difference what I do tomorrow," said the young lawyer.

"That may be true, but I hadn't thought of that," said the older man. "I had something else in mind. How we think of something *is* influenced by how we speak of it. Voir dire is a term that needs translation. There are at least three different ways to translate it, and which one you choose will have a profound effect on what you do.

"What I mean is absolutely practical in every respect. Take the first translation of voir dire as an example. Never mind for the time being its literal meaning. I refer to a working translation of the term. What does it mean in the trial of a case, forgetting as we have agreed to do, the preliminary cross-examination of a witness?"

"Well, how about jury selection?"

" 'Jury Selection,' that's fine. And that, for most people, is what voir dire means, the chance to pick a jury."

"I am with you so far, but I don't know what it proves."

"Well, once you start thinking about picking a jury, that is what you are going to try to do.

"If you think of voir dire as jury selection, you will start thinking about the use of psychological data to determine what sort of jury you need for any particular case.

"Of course, the most famous examples come from criminal cases, as in the defense of Angela Davis, or, more recently, Joan Little. In fact, there is a fascinating article about the whole thing, McConahay, Mullin & Frederick, *The Uses of Social Science in Trials with Political and Racial Overtones: The Trial of Joan Little*, 41 LAW & CONTEMP. PROB. 205 (1977).

"Certainly it is easier to get a broad-ranging voir dire examina-

74

tion in a criminal case than in a civil action, but that does not mean you can only use clinical psychologists in criminal cases. There are a number of personal injury lawyers in the country who regularly consult with clinical psychologists to develop profiles of the jurors they want and those they want to exclude.

"One of the best systems uses a scoring method, since the whole purpose is to enable the lawyer to make intelligent choices between prospective jurors in the exercise of peremptory challenges. With the point count system, you and the psychologist carefully go over the entire case, identifying those factors that seem likely to be psychologically significant.

"For example, in a personal injury case, the age, sex, race, religion, marital status and educational background of the plaintiff may all make some difference on the kind of juror you want. You and the psychologist may decide, for example, that it is worth 5 points on your scale to have a married juror, and 7 points if the juror has children. Taking variables like that into account, you develop a complete point count system to fill out for each juror.

"Having done that, you have thought out—with the benefit of the clinical psychologist—how to weigh apples against oranges. In other words, you have come up with a system that at least makes a stab at comparing, for example, the advantage of having a married juror with the advantage of having one who went to college, or one who is the same religion as your plaintiff.

"Obviously, a separate scoring chart must be created for each case.

"The beauty of the method is that once it is done, the lawyer can fill out the questionnaires himself during voir dire without the psychologist having to be present during the trial.

"The danger, on the other hand, is that with all those numbers you may think you are being truly scientific, when in reality, you are not. If the clinical psychologist you consult is any good, he will tell you that what you come up with is not a substitute for your judgment about jurors, but only a helpful supplement to it.

"If you use this system, the best advice is, if you have a juror you really do not like, then challenge him, no matter how high his score.

"Obviously, this psychological profile is based on the notion that people will decide issues based on fundamental aspects in their own backgrounds. It is a supposition that trial lawyers have had for a long time. There is, in fact, a well-developed courthouse lore about types of jurors, and it is based almost entirely on superficial stereotypes relating to sex, race, ethnic background, economic class and education.

"As it happens, no less a trial lawyer than Clarence Darrow wrote an article for *Esquire* back in 1936, entitled *Selecting a Jury*. The reason I know is that it is reprinted in James W. Jeans, *Trial Advocacy* 167-172 (1975). It is so outrageous in its biases, it is quaint. Nevertheless this kind of lore is tenacious. There are a number of trial lawyers who insist that plaintiffs should be careful to strike very wealthy or very poor jurors. They reason that the best plaintiffs' jurors are upwardly bound middle class individuals who make enough money so they are not shocked by large amounts, but who do not have established wealth they need to protect.

"There still are, moreover, lots of trial lawyers who claim that some ethnic backgrounds produce better plaintiffs' or defendants' jurors than others.

"More important than these stereotypes is how individual jurors seem to respond to you and your client.

"Most of this will be expressed in 'body language.' As Professor Ray Birdwhistle put it, more than half of all human communication is nonverbal. Facial expressions, body positions and eye contact tell us things as well as the spoken word. If you study how to 'read' body language, it will be a help. You might, for example, look at *Body Language* by Julius Fast (1970).

"Actually, you already 'read' body language. You—and everyone else—are accustomed to taking other people's nonverbal communications into account subconsciously. It means if you or your client sense that someone on the jury does not like you, you should use one of your peremptory challenges to get him off the jury, because what you think of as 'instinct' or 'hunch' is probably an accurate reading of nonverbal communication."

"Well," said the young lawyer, starting to rise, "this is great. I knew somehow you could give me a hand. Now I know what I need to do. Thanks a lot!"

"Wait," said the older lawyer.

"You mean there is more?"

"I mean there is more."

"But I really think I have a good idea of what I am supposed to do to pick a jury."

"But suppose you do not want to pick a jury."

"What do you mean?" said the young lawyer.

76

"I mean that picking a jury is just one way to look at jury voir dire. There is another way to translate the term. Not a literal translation, to be sure, but a translation nonetheless."

"I'm listening," said the young lawyer.

"Suppose you decide it is wrong to think of voir dire as jury selection. After all, there are eighteen veniremen on the panel. Unless there is something unusual, controversial or highly publicized about the case, there will not be many challenges for cause. Say that each side gets three peremptory challenges in an ordinary case. A total of six are challenged. And those challenges were largely on the basis of superstition (the stereotypes), hunch (subconscious body language) or educated guess (clinical psychologist and jury profiles).

"Who are the twelve who will sit on the jury? Are they people you chose? Hardly. They are the majority who are left after you exercised your superstitions, hunches and educated guesses. They are the people who were already there by the luck of the draw. It is a serious exaggeration to call that 'jury selection.'"

"So what should you do," asked the young lawyer, "just take the first twelve who come along?"

"No, look out for that one," replied the older lawyer. Lyndon Johnson used to say, 'Anytime someone says he's "just an unsophisticated country boy," I put my hand on my wallet.' It is the same way with taking the first twelve jurors. Whenever you hear that line, watch out. The chances are you will be in a small town on some local lawyer's turf, and he is personally acquainted with everyone within a fifty mile radius.

"No, a hunch or a guess may be better than no challenge at all. But the point goes deeper than that. Here you have this opportunity to conduct voir dire. But there is really not that much *choosing* you can do. So if you are not going to use that time and effort for choosing, why not use it for something else?"

"Like what?" asked the young lawyer.

"Like using the time to sell your case to the jury."

"But I thought you couldn't do that. I thought you were supposed to wait until opening statement and final argument to sell your case to the jury."

"Of course. It would be entirely improper for a lawyer to stand up in front of the jury and deliver a final argument before the case ever began. But, on the other hand, I suppose you agree with me that if you ask some potential juror a question, it would be perfectly all right if that question and the answer to it incidently had the effect of committing the juror to a fundamental principle that is on your side.''

''I am not sure about that one. What do you mean?''

''Well, suppose that a juror was on a panel that was to hear a criminal case. Further, suppose that the juror feels that it is morally reprehensible ever to charge anyone with a crime, no matter what the evidence shows. Would the prosecutor be entitled to strike that juror for cause?''

''Certainly,'' said the young lawyer.

''Well, then, I guess that the prosecutor must be entitled to question jurors about basic things like that during voir dire.''

''I agree again,'' said the young lawyer.

''Fine. Then suppose that the prosecutor feels that a lot of people really hesitate to say the word, 'guilty.' It would be a great help if he could get everyone on the panel to say ''guilty'' before the trial started.''

''A great help for him—not for the defendant,'' said the beginner.

''What do you think the judge would do,'' asked the older lawyer, ''if the prosecutor said to the jury during voir dire, 'I want each of you to say the word, ''guilty,'' before we go any further. Mr. Jones, would you please say the word, ''guilty?'' ' ''

''Simple. The judge would hold the prosecutor in contempt.''

''And rightly so,'' replied the older lawyer. ''But now suppose it would be possible to get that same answer from all the potential jurors by asking questions that relate to their ability to follow the judge's instructions and return a verdict of guilty in a proper case. Here is how a prosecutor might do that:

'' 'Now, ladies and gentlemen, you understand that because this is a criminal case, the defendant, Tom Read, should not be convicted unless he is proven guilty beyond a reasonable doubt.'

'' 'By the same token, if he is proven guilty beyond a reasonable doubt, then do you understand it is your duty as citizens to *find* him guilty . . . whether or not you feel sorry for him or think he should be given another chance?'

'' 'Mr. O'Connor (one of the veniremen), if the state proves Tom Read guilty of arson beyond a reasonable doubt, will you be able to set aside whatever sympathy you may feel for him and decide the case according to the evidence?' ''

'' 'Yes.' ''

'' 'And if the state proves that Tom Read is guilty of arson beyond a reasonable doubt, what will your verdict be?' ''

" 'Guilty.' "

"And then," continued the older lawyer, "the prosecutor goes down the entire list, calling every potential juror by name, asking each one what his verdict will be if the state proves guilt beyond a reasonable doubt—and every juror says the word, 'guilty,' before a single witness takes the stand."

"My God! Am I a babe in the woods? You mean that there are prosecutors who actually do that? Why, they are virtually conditioning those jurors to return a guilty verdict before they have heard any evidence at all. Can they get away with that?"

"The answer is," said the older lawyer, "that there are lawyers all over the country who use that technique every time they pick a jury. And there is nothing wrong with it, even though there are some courts that do not permit it. After all, the defendant can use the same technique.

"Furthermore, there is nothing limiting the practice to criminal cases. In fact, Alan E. Morrill gives some fine examples how the juror commitment technique can be used in civil cases in his book, *Trial Diplomacy—Selected Text* 1-21 (1973)."

"I take my hat off to you," said the young lawyer. "I was all set to select a jury, but now I've changed my mind. I am not going to pick a jury tomorrow—I am going to commit them. I am thoroughly convinced. By the time I get through, those veniremen will be so completely programmed, they will say 'We find for the plaintiff' in their sleep for the next month. And by the way, thanks again. I've got to get going."

"Not so fast," said the older lawyer.

"But I really have got to get home for. . . ."

"It can wait another minute. You are all set to commit the jury to your side tomorrow, right?"

"I am sold."

"Because that is the way you think voir dire should be translated?"

"Like you said, it may not be word for word, but it describes what I want to do."

"But suppose," said the older lawyer, "that is *not* what you want to do?"

"Then I have the feeling I have been here before. Go ahead," said the new lawyer as he sat down again.

"You do not strike me as extraordinarily vain," said the more experienced colleague.

"Well, I mean, I uh, I hope not."

79

"Then why do you think you are so amazingly persuasive as an advocate?"

"I don't. I came here to ask your advice, didn't I?"

"Certainly. Just my point. Then you can hardly suppose you will convince 18 people—or at least 12 out of 18 people—whom you have never seen before—to set aside their beliefs built up over a lifetime by giving them a five minute exhortation and asking a few questions."

"Do you mean . . ."

"I mean there are plenty of lawyers who are not worried about their opposition trying to 'condition' the jury, because they feel it simply is not very effective. They feel that whatever it does, it is not enough to make up for having a weak case to begin with."

"All right," said the young lawyer, "I will bite one more time. If I am not going to select a jury, and if I am not going to commit a jury, then what am I going to do tomorrow morning—sit there and look at them for half an hour?"

"Not badly put."

"Wait a minute," said the new lawyer, "I thought I was being sarcastic."

"*You* were. *I* am not. One of the very best things you can do tomorrow is study that jury. Learn as much about it as you possibly can."

"Study it? What for? Why should I study them if I am not going to select them and I am not going to commit them? What would be the point of it?"

"I think," said the experienced lawyer, "you will be able to answer that in a second. But first, tell me what kind of case you have tomorrow."

"Well, just a personal injury action. Morris Jones, who is now about 67, just retired last year, and shortly afterward was injured when he ran his car into a bridge abutment. His brakes failed, and he ran into the abutment to avoid hitting a child who was crossing the road."

"Who is the defendant?"

"The manufacturer. The brakes were defective in design. I have both a local mechanic and a nationally recognized engineer willing to testify—although I do not want to pay for the engineer if I can avoid it. There are only $37,000 in special damages. Morris had a good recovery, and there are absolutely no lost earnings. Well, the net result is, I do not want to eat up any verdict with big witness expenses if I can avoid it."

80

"That makes sense. So which witness are you going to call—the engineer or the local mechanic?"

"I don't know. I was going to talk to you about that."

"So let's talk about it. Suppose you decide to study the jury tomorrow, and your study of the jury convinces you that they are not impressed by big authority figures—that in fact they tend to reject what they say. If that happens, which one will you call?"

"Hey, wait a minute. I think I see something here. If I study the jury carefully, I will pick up on how they react to basic things like that. And that means that I can change how things are put to suit them."

"That's it, my friend. As John A. Burgess says, there is a much better chance to adjust your case to suit your audience than there is to adjust your audience to suit your case."

"You mean that when you are 'selecting the jury' or 'committing the jury,' you are really trying to change your audience to suit your case, but when you study the jury, you do it so you can change how you present your case so as to suit your audience?"

"Well, something like that, yes."

"Now, hang on just a second. I have already fallen for your routine two times. I have the strange feeling I am missing something. Is this system really good for anything besides helping pick which witness to call?"

"Absolutely. As it happens, it is probably more useful for shaping arguments and opening statements than it is for picking witnesses. In fact, the beauty of the system is that often it works best when you are least aware of it."

"What," asked the younger lawyer, "is that supposed to mean?"

"Well, once you become a student of juries, you start craving knowledge about the people you will be trying to convince. You will find that you will make unconscious decisions that are based on the information you gather. What I mean is, if you study that jury tomorrow and decide they do not like authority figures, you probably would have decided which witness to call without having to run through the choice in your mind on a conscious level. You just would have done it.

"The same is true in argument, but even more so. You are naturally aware of the persons you are talking to. Your adjustment is automatic, and there is nothing put-on about it."

"I'm not sure I agree."

"I bet you do. You talk 'law' to me, right? On the other hand, I am certain you have an entirely different vocabulary when dealing with the gas station attendant or a clerk at the store. You have another vocabulary when talking to your friends, yet another for judges—and the list goes on. The point is, you are completely natural with all these individuals, even though you have a different vocabulary for each one. It simply stands to reason that once you know about the jury, you will automatically use a vocabulary suitable to them even though you are entirely unconscious of doing that.

"The reason I say it works better when you are not aware of it is this: start talking to your garage mechanic some day. In the middle of your conversation, consciously say to yourself, 'This is a man of limited education. He probably did not get past the fifth or sixth grade. I must choose only words he will understand.' What do you think will happen?"

"Well," said the younger lawyer, "without meaning to, I will probably start condescending—and he will notice it. He probably will not pick it up on a conscious level, but he *will* notice it, because people really do react to condescension."

"Bravo! Now you are on the track. Learn as much as you can about the jury. Be aware of what they are like. You should feel as if you are getting to know them. It will have an influence on how you try your case, and you should let this happen, but you should not let it make you talk down to them.

"The effect is not limited to picking witnesses or choosing vocabulary, either. It extends to all levels of argument and persuasion. It touches everything we do as advocates. It influences the pace of our words, the examples we pick, the arguments we emphasize and the values we identify with our clients. We naturally adjust what we do and how we do it to suit our audience—but only if we know our audience."

"Well," said the young lawyer, getting up, "it took a while, but I finally got there. I really appreciate. . . ."

"No, no. Don't go yet."

"You don't mean I've left too soon again?"

"Maybe just a few minutes," responded the older lawyer. "I know you are in a hurry, so I will not take too long with this, but it is important.

"So far we have been talking about what you do. Perhaps even more important is how you do it. I told you about James W. Jeans, *Trial Advocacy* before. In his chapter on voir dire, especially at pages 188 to 196, he has some very good suggestions on how to ask jurors questions.

"But there are some other things as well. Sometimes you run across a really delicate subject matter—oh, say, like sexual or intimate physical subjects on which people may have strong biases, yet find it difficult to speak. Just imagine how long and difficult that could make voir dire.''

"I can see that," said the young lawyer.

"Robert Maynard of Cleveland, Ohio, came up with an excellent device for speeding up jury voir dire in that kind of situation. Obviously, he did not want to pry into the jurors' personal, intimate experiences in conducting voir dire. Instead, he wrote up a detailed written questionnaire. With the judge's and the opposition's consent, he had every venireman fill out that questionnaire. Then when the answers on the written questionnaire required, potential jurors were examined individually in chambers.

"One more thing before you go."

"Yes?"

"You realize you only have three peremptory challenges, don't you?"

"That's right."

"That means that if you find a juror you do not want, you will first try to challenge him or her for cause?"

"Exactly my plan."

"If the challenge for cause does not work—that is, if the judge does not think that what you have developed is sufficient to remove the juror—then you will use a peremptory challenge?"

"I could not have said it better."

"I thought not. Now, as I remember, kinship with one of the parties, interest in outcome and enough bias or prejudice so that the juror could not render a 'fair and impartial verdict' are grounds for challenging jurors.

"You need not worry about kinship or interest. The judge will take care of that automatically. But I am troubled by something. Suppose you ask the entire panel tomorrow this question: 'Is there anyone here who cannot be fair and impartial? If there is, would you raise your hand, please?' How many hands would you get?"

"I think I would get approximately zero people who would raise their hands."

"You are right. Yet there are thousands of lawyers who ask almost exactly that question—not once (which may make some sense as a sort of catch-all), but time after time with slightly different language. They cannot seriously believe that people think of themselves as unfair, but that is what that question says.

"The most amazing thing is that you will hear lawyers use a question like that to destroy what was a perfectly good challenge for cause, and by the time they are finished, they have so offended the juror that they are *forced* to exercise a peremptory challenge.

"Take a case like the one you will start trying tomorrow. The lawyer representing the plaintiff is examining the panel, and learns that one of the jurors, a Mr. Maguire, has a son who is an automotive engineer.

"Think what that means to the plaintiff. It is probably worse than if the man himself were the automotive engineer. The reason is, if the juror were the automotive engineer, he would have a healthy understanding of the kind of mistake that these people can make. He may well have a high level of professional pride (he feels that *he* would never make a mistake like this) and hold the defendant to a stricter standard than the law requires. This is all suppositional, of course. There still is the very real danger that if the juror were an automotive engineer, he might feel too much sympathy for the defendant—but not necessarily.

"But take the father, on the other hand. He does not really understand engineering, but he thinks he does. He is proud of his son, and thinks he is a fine person. He is terribly loyal, and thinks that any attack on an automotive engineer is an attack on his son.

"To be sure, there is a chance that the father of the automobile engineer is more impartial than that. Nevertheless, there is too strong a possibility of unreasoning loyalty to let this go. So what will the average lawyer do? Unfortunately, once he develops the facts that come close to justifying a challenge for cause, the average lawyer will literally talk the juror into saying he can be impartial. Here is what he will do:

" 'Mr. Maguire (that's the juror), you said your son is an automotive engineer.'

" 'Yes, that's right.'

" 'You realize that in this case there will be testimony that the plaintiff's brakes were not properly designed.'

" 'My son does not design brakes.'

" 'What does he design?'

" 'Diesel engines.'

" 'Nevertheless, he must work with people who do design brakes?'

84

'' 'I suppose he does. He never said, one way or another.'

'' 'Well, despite the fact that your son probably works with individuals who design automobile brake systems, do you think you could be fair and impartial in deciding this case?'

'' 'Yes, I think I could.' ''

"What," asked the younger lawyer, "was wrong with that?"

"I will tell you," the older lawyer responded, "and I want you never to forget. There is a fundamental principle. You will almost never get someone to admit he or she is unfair. Instead, it is much more effective to appeal to their fairness—not their unfairness—in challenging them for cause."

"Oh, come on," said the younger lawyer, you expect me to say to someone, 'please be fair and leave the jury?' ''

"Almost. Let's go back to Mr. Maguire, and question him the right way.

'' 'Mr. Maguire, I understand your son is an automotive engineer, is that correct?'

'' 'Yes, that's right.'

'' 'You must be very proud of him.'

'' 'We are. He graduated from State Tech with honors.'

'' 'Well, Mr. Maguire, there are going to be some witnesses in this case who will testify that some automobile engineers didn't do their jobs properly. You understand they will *not* be talking about your son or his company, don't you?'

'' 'Yes, I understand.'

'' 'Nevertheless, that testimony might make you just a little uncomfortable for a moment or two, as proud as you are of your son.'

'' 'Oh, I suppose. Just for a minute or two. But (smiling a big smile) I think I could handle it.'

"(Now, at this point, whatever you do, do not agree. Instead, go on.) 'And if you were one of the parties in this case—either the plaintiff or defendant—you might feel even more uncomfortable, knowing someone with your relationship to an automotive engineer was on the jury?'

'' 'I guess so' (the smile fades).

'' 'Not knowing you personally, it might *look* to them as if the jury was not as impartial as it ought to be, is that it?'

'' 'Yes, that's it.'

'' 'In view of that, do you think *you* might feel more comfortable sitting in judgment on some other case that did not involve questions that come so close to your family interests?'

"Now you see," went on the older lawyer, "what you are in a position to do. Here is when you should approach the bench to suggest a challenge for cause if the judge has not already picked it up. Even if you must make the challenge in open court, you are not attacking Mr. Maguire, you are helping him avoid the appearance of bias:

" 'Your honor, in fairness to Mr. Maguire, I suggest it may be better if he were excused from this panel, so that he could sit on some other case.'

"See what that does for you," said the older lawyer. "The judge may well grant the challenge for cause. Even if he does not, things are still working to your advantage. Suppose you decide to use your precious peremptory challenges on apples that are even more bruised and suspicious looking than Mr. Maguire. You are not forced to use a peremptory challenge on Mr. Maguire, because you have not attacked his capacity to be fair. Instead, you have supported him.

"If you are forced to keep Mr. Maguire on the jury, you do not have an enemy, but a friend. He may well bend over backwards the entire trial to prove his fairness to you. And even if he does not, his bias has been exposed gently to the other jurors, who are likely to discount what he says in support of automotive engineers."

"I see what happened," replied the younger lawyer, "but I am not sure there was anything to it other than simple good manners."

"No, I told you there was a principle, and there is. This challenge for cause is called the *Trial Notebook* Two-Step.'

"Here are the two steps that come after you find out there are some facts that might support a challenge for cause: First, have the juror look at his bias from the eyes of the parties. It will give the juror a chance to recognize that the *appearance* of unfairness can be as troublesome as unfairness itself. That is a pretty sophisticated step for a juror, but it can all be done with the question, 'It might *look* to them as if the jury was not as impartial as it ought to be?'

"The second step is as important as the first. That is to take the juror back into himself and ask if, in view of the appearance, he would feel 'more comfortable' sitting in judgment on some other case.

"Interestingly, this challenge for cause never has the juror openly admitting he cannot be fair. In fact, logically, he admits no unfairness at all. Yet the development of the appearance of unfairness is accepted by lawyers and judges, in part because the CODE OF PROFESSIONAL RESPONSIBILITY stresses not only avoiding evil, but also avoiding the appearance of evil.

"Furthermore, in a sense there is an admission of possible unfairness. There is an acknowledgment that the background facts create the feeling of unfairness. On top of that, we should not strip off the social mask entirely just for a challenge for cause; jurors must be permitted to save a little 'face.' "

"I like that. I really like that," said the younger lawyer. "And I learned one other thing."

"What's that?" asked the older lawyer.

"Not to try to leave before you're finished. I am going to wait until you tell me you're done."

"Well, I guess I am done for now, even though there is a lot more, especially in the area of technique. I know you need to get home. Just one final question before you take off. Which of the three are you going to do tomorrow: select a jury, commit them or study them?"

"I guess I am going to do the only thing I think makes sense other than have you pick the jury. I am going to do all three, but mainly I am going to study that jury."

"Marvelous. You heard everything I said after all."

"Certainly. And thanks again, dad."

"Don't mention it, son. See you at home."

CHAPTER 9

Opening Statements

The typical opening statement is delivered by a lawyer who learned how by watching and listening to someone else—and the unwitting teacher was not very good at making opening statements. Sadly, most opening statements are thrown together almost as an afterthought, even by lawyers who pride themselves as being good litigators. They use techniques and verbalizations that have been made part of the tradition of trials with little thought about whether they are effective. And this should not be so. The opening statement is such an important part of the trial that it has a good claim to considerable care and thought in its preparation.

The uncomfortable fact is that juries often start to make up their minds on hearing opening statements. And thoughtful trial lawyers have known for a long time that when juries make up their minds, it is difficult to change them. It means that the opening statement is so important that it should almost never be waived, and that it is nearly unforgivable (in the absence of a contrary rule) merely to read the pleadings to the jury instead of making an opening statement.

It suggests to defense counsel in either civil or criminal cases that the opening statement usually should be made as soon as possible in the case instead of waiting until the plaintiff or prosecution rests, lest the case already be decided. It even suggests that, if you represent the defendant in a case where the only real issue is an affirmative defense, you should strongly consider admitting the plaintiff's nominal case so that you will have the right to open first, as well as have the first and last words in final argument. Without question it suggests that any trial lawyer bent on winning a trial should take the trouble to make a very good opening statement.

Just what you do in an opening statement depends largely on the jury selection process. In a jurisdiction where lawyers are permitted wide ranging voir dire examinations, some of the functions of the opening statement have already been performed by the time for opening. Because jury voir dire varies so greatly from jurisdiction to jurisdiction and even from court to court, the litigator must be ready to adjust the voir dire and opening statement to accomplish all of his objectives. This discussion is based on the assumption that the trial court has done most of the voir dire examination and that the opening statement is the lawyer's first real opportunity to talk to the jury.

The opening statement should introduce you and your client and tell the jury what the case is all about. While that sounds simple enough, what that means and how it should be approached takes thorough analysis. The starting point for deciding what to do is the psychological notion of ''primacy,'' or the importance of what is said first. The first minute or so of the opening statement (or of any argument, for that matter) is the most important. Your listeners, unless they are instantly hostile or embarrassed for you, are at their most receptive stage, and it is a mistake to throw away that opportunity. In that first minute you should convince the jury that justice lies on your side. The challenge is to state the essential nub of your case in that time in a way that will impel the jury to view everything that happens after that—everything they hear and see—in your favor.

The litmus test for a good introduction to an opening statement is this: if the jurors heard it, and nothing else at all, would they understand what the case is about, and would they want to find in your favor? This does not mean that, if you were able to ask the jurors those questions at the end of the introduction, they would tell you just that. Their sense of fair play would obviously make them say they wanted to hear both sides. What you are after is that sort of convincing predisposition that makes them look at the other side through your eyes.

The sort of introduction that meets this demanding test takes time to work up and is easily worth an hour or so of effort. The first step is to develop a theory of your case that explains as much of the uncontroverted evidence as possible in your favor. The theory that you develop will, of course, be the basis for your entire trial strategy and the keynote of your closing argument. The second step is to create from that theory a theme or phrase that is striking, even memorable, which epitomizes the theory.

Some examples are in order. Assume the case of an injured workman whose back was seriously and painfully hurt when a load of plywood, which had been placed on the roof of a house on which he was working, slipped off and fell on him as he was bending over. Liability is not in serious question. Damages are a difficulty, however, because the plaintiff's new job brings him far more income than he earned as a construction worker. Lost wages, one of the most tangible damage issues, is simply not there. Viewing this as one of the most difficult problems, one leading trial lawyer who represented such a plaintiff began his opening statement as follows:

> Ladies and gentlemen: This is a case about a person who is less than a man—and more than a man. Less than a man because for him each day starts and ends with agonizing pain which cannot be made to go away with medication or medical treatment. More than a man because despite what he suffers from because of another man's carelessness, he is actually able to provide more for his wife and children than before he was injured. This case is about Joe Warren, who used to work, until one day, as a carpenter . . . .

The problem created by the aggravation of a pre-existing injury is different, where the "more than a man, less than a man" theme will not do. Dealing with a pre-existing injury can be tricky. If the pre-existing injury is concealed by the plaintiff, the jury may get the impression that the whole case is fraudulent when that injury is revealed by the defendant. To prevent the defendant from capitalizing on the pre-existing injury, the plaintiff should make it part of his opening statement. It even offers the possibility for a strong theme. Consider the following:

> Ladies and gentlemen, every one of us probably knows or at least knows of someone who has been able to overcome a great handicap in life—the kind of handicap that would have stopped a lesser man or woman. This case is about a man like that; a man who had managed to overcome the crippling effects of an industrial accident, and had begun to once again lead a normal and happy life only to have his last chance

taken from him by a young woman driving a car one day who was just too preoccupied to bother with a turn signal.

Warm, engaging themes are not limited to personal injury cases. Take the following ordinary breach of a commercial contract action as an example:

Ladies and gentlemen, as I was driving my six-year-old boy to school this morning before coming down to the courthouse, he asked me what this case was about. I knew I really could not tell him about options and sales and breaches of contract, so I put him off. Well, he persisted. 'What's it about Daddy?' So I tried to think of a way to explain it to him, and I finally said, 'Son, this is a case about two men who both gave each other their word, and now one of them wants to break it'.

The defendant needs a good theme just as much as, if not more than, the plaintiff. Sometimes it is appropriate to focus on the defendant, as in the ''he did the best he could'' type of situation. In other cases, the theory of the case may call for a theme which points to some flaw in the plaintiff's actions. Consider a commercial case where the plaintiff is a prime contractor who sought bids from subcontractors for a paving job and, in reliance on those bids, submitted a winning bid to the city for a paving contract. Then he finds himself unable to obtain materials from the subcontractors at the prices they bid. Basing his case on the doctrine of promissory estoppel, he brings an action against one of the sub-contractors. The sub-contractor bases his defense on the plaintiff's efforts to buy materials for a lower price than the defendant's bid before finally calling on the defendant to honor his bid. The focus on the defendant is almost compelling. ''Ladies and gentlemen, this is a case about a man who would bind someone else, but is unwilling to bind himself; a man who asks you to let him have his cake and eat it too.''

There are occasions when the defendant does not want to announce his theory of the case too clearly at the beginning of the trial. Usually the only good reason for this is to prevent the opposition from learning about impeaching materials. The question for the opening statement is how can you take advantage of the value of first impressions without educating your adversary too much? Unfortunately, there is no one best answer, because the task is to convince the jury that there are two sides to the story without telling them what the other side is. It means that the theme statement must be an appeal to the jury to keep their minds open until they have heard all the evidence. But rather than do that in so many words, it may be effective to do it by a short analogy which forces the jury to come to the conclusion themselves that they must reserve judgment. That process—making the jury join in the thought progression—is one of the great tools of the advocate. Whenever a juror thinks of something on his own, he holds the conclusion more strongly than if you merely told him what it is. The difficult job is to lead him to the point where there is only one way to go and still let him take the last step himself.

It is essential to make the theme fit the facts well enough so that this memorable phrase at the beginning of the trial is not turned against you. One of the best solutions is to develop the theory of the case first and then choose an appropriate theme, rather than trying to start with a catchy theme which you hope will fit the facts. The other important step is to try to turn it around any way you can; in other words, to look at your theme from your opponent's point of view.

The statement of the theme is as close to argumentation as you ought to come in this part of the trial. There is no place in the opening statement for comparing, except in a general way, the credibility of the witnesses, commenting on what testimony is believable or exhorting the jury to find in your favor. First, most judges do not allow it and may even stop you on their own if you try to argue during opening statement. Second, there is the possibility of having an adverse jury reaction to blatant argumentation in an opening, since they have not yet heard the evidence and may be suspicious of arguments that seem too zealous at this point.

The development of a good theme in the first minute of the opening statement is so important that it ought to be considered before working out how you are going to introduce yourself and your client. The customary way to begin an opening statement, if you have not already been introduced to the jury satisfactorily during voir dire, is to introduce yourself, your client, and, depending on the sense of etiquette in the community, your opposing counsel as well. But there is an argument that the custom ought to be altered slightly. Although it is not the sort of practice that will suit everyone, opening statements with delayed introductions can be very effective. If the opening begins with the theme and is followed by a short chronology which leads up to how you were contacted by your client, stating your name to the jury can come slightly after the theme quite comfortably. Whether you introduce yourself at the very first or wait a minute or two, the theme should be one of the first things the jury hears.

Another custom in making opening statements is even more deserving of re-examination: the remark that the opening statement is "only lawyer's talk." The practice which has developed among many lawyers is to discount the opening statement while making it, saying something like this:

> Nothing I tell you now or what Mr. Randolf is going to say is evidence in this case. Instead, what you must pay attention to and the only thing you are justified in basing your verdict on is testimony you hear from that witness stand.

James Jeans argues that this practice is an example of "mimicking mediocrity," and that no one who wants to tell a convincing story should start out by asking his audience to disregard what he is saying. Jeans, *Trial Advocacy* 205-06 (1975).

The most that can be said for this "lawyer's talk" routine is that it is an anticipatory defense to the opposition saying much the same thing and carrying the suggestion that you were somehow trying to convince the jury that what you were saying *was* evidence. But self-protection does not need to be so negative. Instead, as you progress into the body of your opening statement, you can refer to the testimony and other evidence which is to come. You can make the point affirmatively that the evidence will justify the verdict without running down what you are doing.

Just how detailed you should be in discussing what testimony the jury will hear is another problem. The danger is that of overstatement. If you make specific promises to the jury, you may be embarrassed to hear them thrown back at you at the end of the case if you do not produce the evidence as promised. This can raise the possibility of the jurors concluding that you were careless about your case, that you tried to mislead them, or that you have failed to prove an essential element of your case, even though that is not at all true. If you promise to prove something, the jury may think you have to prove it to win. The problem of how detailed an opening statement should be is discussed further in Keeton, *Trial Tactics and Methods* 270-72 (2d ed. 1973).

On the other hand, one of the most important functions of an opening statement is to let the jurors know what is coming, and alert them to what they should look for as the trial unfolds. Because you cannot always call witnesses in the order you would like and the flow of direct examination will be broken up by objections and cross-examination, it is essential to give the jury an understandable picture of what you expect the evidence to show. Moreover, it can be crucial not to be too cautious in what you say so that you do not tell the jury enough. If it is evident from your opening statement that you do not have a case, some jurisdictions permit the trial court to grant a directed verdict after the opening statement. The lesson is straightforward enough: be certain to state a prima facie case or defense in your opening.

While the opening statement is a good point for the plaintiff to start establishing liability, it may not be a good place to discuss the amount of damages sought, particularly in personal injury cases where you are seeking large awards. Convincing a jury that the plaintiff should receive, for example, two or three hundred thousand dollars takes time, and even talking about that amount of money with them before they have seen the justification for it is dangerous.

Finally, you should use the opening statement to start a process that will continue through the entire trial: making your client a real person rather than a procedural entity like a client, plaintiff or defendant. Those are terms you reserve for the other side. Referring to an individual litigant by name is easy, natural and too often neglected. Making a corporation come alive is harder, but worth the effort. The words you choose, the person you select to sit at counsel table with you, as well as your other actions, should all add up to making the jury think of the corporation as the very real person sitting next to you.

PART III

Evidence

CHAPTER 10

A Quick Review of the Federal Rules

The very idea that there would be Federal Rules of Evidence was exciting. Evidence suddenly became more important—not just a loosely knit group of ideas that federal courts casually adopted from the locals (and which necessarily varied from state to state). Federal Rules could bring reform, simplicity, and uniformity.

They could provide inspiration—a standard the states could look to for guidance in preparing for the year 2000 and beyond. It was in this spirit that the Supreme Court turned to the proposed rules to give definition to the requirements of the Fourteenth Amendment in *Chambers v. Mississippi,* 410 U.S. 284 (1973).

New rules of evidence suggested an opportunity for rethinking old ideas; creating new intellectual models that would not only cause us to reexamine an entire subject, but would let us borrow the new ideas for an exciting sort of legal cross-fertilization.

Some of all of that—but not nearly enough of any of it—turned out to be true.

Working with the rules has made us lower our expectations. The Federal Rules of Evidence are not a code. They are not self-sufficient. Many of the rules only make sense against a detailed understanding of the common law. A number of the provisions are fragmentary, leaving the gaps to whatever was already in place or to subsequent judicial development. Moreover, some areas were simply left out.

Do not let that give you the wrong impression. It is a worthwhile contribution to write a restatement of evidence that covers most of the main points. The Federal Rules do that and more.

Nowhere in the Federal Rules has there been a great conceptual departure from the common law, but some rules, such as expert witnesses and the best evidence rule, have been significant steps forward, while some of the tricky parts have been taken out of character evidence.

It is not a great reformation, yet the rules set the new standard for the admissibility of prior convictions used to impeach witnesses—especially defendants in criminal cases.

In the years since their adoption, trial lawyers have not only lowered their expectations for the rules, they have changed their attitude toward them somewhat. What once looked intriguing may now appear to be a wrinkle or a wart while some blemishes have seemed to fade. Here are some of the warts and gleams of the Federal Rules:

Hearsay Definition

Consistency may be an overrated virtue, but inconsistency can be a genuine vice.

Rule 801 defines hearsay as a "statement, other than one made by the declarant while testifying at the trial or hearing offered in evidence to prove the truth of the matter asserted."

It is—for a set of rules—decently short and clear. Two things are required:

1) an out-of-court statement
2) that is offered for its truth.

The authors of the rules successfully avoided the more arcane academic pronouncements about hearsay and used the working definition that most trial lawyers prefer instead.

That was commendable. The next step was not.

Faced with a definition of hearsay, most lawyers would think that if evidence fits the definition it should be called hearsay, and that to be admissible it should have to qualify as an exception to the hearsay rule. That simple pattern is the approach of the common law, one that is easy to apply in the pressure of a trial.

But consistency ran out. Instead, Rule 801 contains—as part of the definition of what is hearsay—a number of important exceptions to the hearsay rule. Why did the drafters do that when there were two rules specifically set aside for hearsay exceptions?

There is an answer, but it is not a very good one.

Admissions are a common-law exception to the hearsay rule. But in the Federal Rules they are called "non-hearsay." In the

Advisory Committee notes, the drafters say that admissions are "excluded from the category of hearsay on the theory that their admissibility in evidence is the result of the adversary system rather than satisfaction of the conditions of the hearsay rule."

It is not very compelling logic. Admissions are out-of-court-statements. We admit them for their truth. In other words, they fit the definition of hearsay in the Federal Rules. That they do not share the unreliability of other hearsay is reason enough to make admissions admissible in evidence. That there may be different good reasons for admitting them that are not shared by other hearsay exceptions does not mean they should be called "non-hearsay."

Not content with admissions, the authors also declared that some prior consistent and inconsistent statements are non-hearsay as well—but admissible for their truth. They gave statements of prior identification the same treatment—admissible for their truth, but non-hearsay. They also chose the definition of what is hearsay as the place to put the foundation for prior consistent statements, The foundation for prior *inconsistent* statements, however, is in Article Six, Witnesses.

In short, the drafters did not stick with their definition, but garnished it with rules of admissibility and exclusion that belong in other parts of the hearsay section or in entirely different articles.

Should that matter? The result is the same—the evidence is either admissible because it is non-hearsay or admissible because it is an exception to the hearsay rule. What difference does it make where it is located, especially if its location satisfies some deep-felt academic need?

Major exceptions to the hearsay rule—especially ones that have been recognized for hundreds of years—do not belong in a rule that defines hearsay. It makes the organization harder to use and gives no genuine reward in return.

Like the medieval scholar who stayed up too late, the definition of hearsay in the Federal Rules smells of the lamp. And what pleases the scholar at night may frustrate the lawyer during the day as he tries to find the right rule in the middle of trial. A system of organization is not much help if you have to know where the rule is before you start to look for it. That may not bother lawyers who use the rules every day, but it is a trap for those who only get occasional trials.

Having seen the practical annoyance caused by the Federal Rules, New York did something different in its proposed code of

101

evidence. It took admissions, prior identification, and prior statements back out of Rule 801 and made them exceptions to the hearsay rule. That is a sensible improvement.

Privileges

Some of the most important work done by the drafters of the Federal Rules was in the field of privileges. But in the early 1970s, privileges—particularly *governmental* and *executive* privileges—suddenly became unpopular. The specific rules were dropped and a general provision was enacted instead. It says that federal courts should be "governed by the principles of the common law as they may be interpreted by the courts of the United States in the light of reason and experience." To avoid forum-shopping problems, the rule defers to state law "with respect to an element of a claim or defense as to which State law supplies the rule of decision."

It was an understandable accommodation to the times. But Watergate is over, and we still do not have any real section on privileges in the Federal Rules.

The gap has not been unnoticed. The Supreme Court recently took advantage of it nearly to destroy the familiar rule that let a defendant in a criminal case keep his spouse from testifying against him unless that spouse was the victim of the crime. In *Trammel v. United States*, 445 U. S. 40 (1980), the Court held that the privilege no longer belonged to the defendant, but only to the spouse who had been called as a witness.

Other Crimes or Wrongs

The theory is easy to state. Only evidence tending to show that a defendant is guilty of the crime charged is supposed to be admissible in evidence. If a defendant in a criminal case has committed other crimes, they are not admissible to show that he is guilty of the one he is charged with now.

This is not because the evidence has no probative value. On the contrary. Experience is one of our few guides to the future. Other acts do have probative value. Failure to pay attention to the other acts of a person can easily constitute negligence. The driving record that would be inadmissible against the operator of a car can be offered against the owner to establish negligent entrustment. *Guedon v. Rooney*, 160 Ore. 621, 87 P.2d 209, 120 A.L.R. 1298 (1939).

So when evidence of prior acts is offered against the defendant in a criminal case, it is not excluded because it lacks probative value, but because the danger of misuse by the jury is too great. In the language of evidence, its probative value is outweighed by its unfair prejudicial effect.

But do not conclude that evidence of other crimes or wrongs is completely inadmissible. It may not be admitted to show that the defendant is the sort of person who would commit this crime. But if evidence of other crimes or wrongs is relevant to prove something else, it is admissible.

That is the starting point for understanding what the Federal Rules do with other crimes and wrongs. Rule 404(b) gives a decently accurate restatement of the common law. It provides:

> Evidence of other crimes, wrongs, or acts is not admissible to prove the character of a person in order to show that he acted in conformity therewith. It may, however, be admissible for other purposes, such as proof of motive, opportunity, intent, preparation, plan, knowledge, identity, or absence of mistake or accident.

The similarity between this rule and the common law is perhaps its biggest problem. A few examples should show why that is so.

In our first case, the defendant is charged with robbing a federally insured bank. Because it is a federal crime, he is being tried in federal court. Stealing a car that is not taken across state lines is not a federal offense. But evidence that the defendant stole a car to serve as a getaway vehicle would be admissible because it showed preparation or plan.

That is how the rule is supposed to work. Evidence of other crimes is admissible when it is relevant for some purpose other than poisoning the well. But now consider this second case:

The defendant is charged with the burglary of a woman's apartment. He is acquitted, then charged with another burglary. Evidence tending to show he was guilty of the crime for which he had been acquitted was offered in the second trial on the issue of "intent."

Just to make sure you have it straight, the two burglaries were not similar enough to be evidence of identity, nor did one provide the motive for the other. The only excuse for offering the evidence is that burglary is a crime of intent.

As it is. But intent was not really in issue. The only real question was identity, but this evidence did not go to that point.

103

Would a prosecutor attempt such a transparent way around the general rule?

Certainly. Could both a trial and an appellate court accept the evidence without critical injury?

Without a doubt. See *People v. Massey*, 196 Cal. App. 2d 230, 16 Cal. Rptr.402 (1961). The case is representative of the way in which many courts treat evidence of other crimes or wrongs—the principle is often stated but seldom honored.

The drafters of the Federal Rules had an opportunity to attack this problem, but did not. Professor Kenneth W. Graham's reaction sums it up: ''[T]his is a topic deserving of some statutory ordering. Lamentably, the Advisory Committee chose to leave the law in its messy state; Rule 404(b) does nothing to clarify the issues, and may in some respects have muddied the waters even more.'' 22 C. Wright & K. Graham, *Federal Practice and Procedure: Evidence* ¶ 5239 (1978).

Subsequent Remedial Measures

The tenant falls through the front steps and sues the landlord for his injuries. After the fall (but before the suit), the landlord fixes the steps. Now the landlord claims that he was not negligent in the way he maintained the steps, so the tenant wants to use evidence of the repair as an admission of the defective condition.

Enter the rules of relevance.

It used to be thought that subsequent remedial measures had no probative value—that is, they did not raise a valid inference that there had been any negligence. *Columbia and Puget Sound R. R. Co. v. Hawthorne*, 144 U.S. 202 (1892). Later we came to realize that the more sensible reason for the rule is that we want to encourage remedial measures—or at least we do not want to discourage them. The result is that we do not permit evidence of repairs to prove fault.

But because it is a rule of evidence, it is riddled with exceptions. Subsequent repairs are admissible to show almost anything except negligence. Once again, the Federal Rules restate the law. Rule 407 provides:

When, after an event, measures are taken which, if taken previously, would have made the event less likely to occur, evidence of the subsequent measures is not admissible to prove negligence or culpable conduct in connection with the event. This rule does not require the exclusion of evidence of subsequent measures when offered for another purpose,

104

such as proving ownership, control, or feasibility of precautionary measures, if controverted, or impeachment.

So if our landlord argued that he had no obligation to repair the steps, or that they could not have been made safer than they were, the repairs would be admissible.

There it is—a judge-made rule enacted by Congress as part of the Federal Rules of Evidence. Perhaps that is its difficulty. To understand why, we turn to a recent California case, *Ault v. International Harvester Co.*, 13 Cal. 3d 113, 528 P.2d 1148, 117 Cal. Rptr. 812 (1974).

In the *Ault* case, two men were riding in an International Harvester Scout. Suddenly it went out of control and plunged to the bottom of a 500-foot cliff. Both of them developed retrograde amnesia about the accident. In the wreckage it was found that the steering gearbox—the housing that holds the gears that transmit control from the steering wheel to the front wheels—was broken. The box was made out of an aluminum alloy.

The plaintiffs claimed that a defect in the box caused the Scout to go out of control and plunge down the cliff. International Harvester, on the other hand, claimed that the fall to the bottom of the cliff broke the steering gearbox.

To prove their point, the plaintiffs wanted to introduce evidence that International Harvester had stopped making steering gearboxes out of aluminum alloy and had gone back to what other auto manufacturers used, malleable iron.

It turned out to be important evidence. The case was tried twice. In the first trial, the judge excluded the evidence and there was a hung jury. In the second trial the evidence was admitted and the jury found for the plaintiff.

On appeal, the Supreme Court of California had to interpret a statute nearly identical to Federal Rule 407. It held that in products liability cases, proof of subsequent remedial measures was admissible to prove a defective condition—on the dubious notion that making a defective product was not "culpable conduct." In other words, evidence of the switch back to malleable iron in manufacturing was admissible even though it did not fit any exception to the basic rule.

Some jurisdictions have followed the *Ault* holding, while others have rejected it. Lawyers who have thought about the problem tend to line up depending on the interests they usually represent.

Perhaps the most interesting aspect of the controversy is the stunted role played by the Federal Rules. Because Rule 407 was written before the *Ault* case was decided but was enacted by Congress a year afterward, the rules have provided no real guidance for dealing with the competing interests. But that does not mean that Rule 407 has not played a part.

There is the real possibility that Rule 407—the rule about subsequent remedial measures—is based on a false notion of human behavior. Perhaps landlords are going to repair their steps whether or not the evidence is admissible. If that is the case, then we are sacrificing relevant evidence and getting nothing in return. But there is little that federal judges can do about that now. Making the rules of evidence an act of Congress has limited judicial action to tinkering with definitions—like the Supreme Court of California did in the *Ault* case.

Business and Public Records

One of the astonishing things about the history of hearsay is that the business records exception was created by statute only about 50 years ago. Before that, commercial litigation had to struggle along under the old shopbook rule. See *McCormick on Evidence*, 2d Ed., 717–19 (E. Cleary, ed. 1972).

For the most part, the Federal Rules version, Rule 803 (6), tracks the ideas—if not the language—of the early business records statutes. See Read, *The Business Records Exception: Something Less Than Revolutionary*, 2 LITIGATION, No. 1, at 25 (Fall 1975).

Like most state business records statutes, the Federal Rule is intended to have broad application. Rule 803 defines business as "business, institution, association, profession, occupation, and calling of every kind, whether or not conducted for profit." That definition is broad enough to include governmental activities of any sort.

The problem is that the Federal Rules also have a public records exception, Rule 803(8). And it overlaps with the business records exception. The public records exception has an important limitation, intended to protect defendants in criminal cases. Rule 803(8)(B) provides that "matters observed by police officers and other law enforcement personnel" are not admissible against the defendant in a criminal action.

The question is whether a prosecutor can avoid the protection given criminal defendants by choosing the business records rule rather than the public records exception. In *United States v. Oates*, 560 F.2d 45 (2d Cir. 1977), the court said no.

Prior Convictions

Anytime a witness takes the stand to testify, his credibility becomes an issue. That suggests a number of important things.

One of them is the right to attack the witness's credibility with prior convictions. The typical way to proceed is to confront the witness with the conviction on cross-examination. If he denies the conviction, it can be shown by extrinsic evidence—ordinarily by introducing a certified copy of the conviction.

This is the practice that most jurisdictions follow. Some of them permit a witness to make a brief explanation of the conviction on re-direct examination, while some states do not permit a witness to deny guilt. A few states apparently permit the explanation to be avoided by permitting the impeachment with documentary evidence after the witness has left the stand.

Instead of seeking uniformity on such minor problems, the authors of the Federal Rules concentrated on more important matters. Unfortunately, they did not get all of those, either. Yet what they accomplished was considerable.

Under the common law in most states, a witness could be impeached with a conviction for any felony or for a misdemeanor of "moral turpitude." Some states imposed the "moral turpitude" limitation on felonies as well, but only a few jurisdictions had a prohibition against using old convictions to impeach.

Rule 609 makes a significant change in this practice. It permits impeachment with any felony or misdemeanor of dishonesty or false statement. Other convictions can be used only if they are felonies and the trial court specifically determines that the probative value of the conviction outweighs the prejudicial effect to the defendant, a test adopted from *Luck v. United States*, 348 F.2d 763 (D.C. Cir. 1965). The other major change is the ten-year limit on convictions that may be used. Time is calculated from the date of conviction or release from confinement, whichever is later.

These are valuable changes, to be sure—yet they leave out something important. To understand just how important, you must picture yourself in preparation for trial in a criminal case. The person you are representing has two prior convictions—both less than ten years old—and neither involving dishonesty or false statement. Your defendant tells you he is not guilty and says he wants to testify on his own behalf.

Now you see the problem. What do you tell the defendant? Your entire strategy is determined by whether he testifies. And your advice on whether he should take the stand will hinge on the admissibility of the convictions. The difficulty is that the situation falls in the gray area in which the judge weighs probative value against prejudicial effect, so the trial judge might decide either way. What you need is a ruling before trial.

Rule 104(c) offers a little help, but not enough. It says that when the accused is a witness, he has the right to a hearing on preliminary matters outside the presence of the jury. That is fine for the middle of trial, but does nothing to help advance planning. You can make a motion to suppress in advance of trial, but the rules do not require the judge to hear it.

Instead of leaving it to the whim of the particular trial judge, New York's proposed evidence code makes pretrial determination of the admissibility of convictions a matter of right for a criminal defendant.

But the protection for the defendant in a federal criminal case who needed to decide whether to take the stand was undercut by the Supreme Court. In *United States v. Luce*, 105 S.Ct. 460 (1984), the defendant asked for—and got—a pretrial ruling of the admissibility of his prior convictions. The judge said they were admissible, so the defendant stayed off the stand.

On appeal, the defendant said the trial judge was wrong. The United States Supreme Court concluded that the defendant had no standing to attack the adverse ruling (which had shaped the entire strategy) because he had not taken the stand and been impeached. They said he had to testify—and actually get impeached—to be able to complain that the judge's ruling was wrong. It is this kind of decision that could only be made by a panel of judges who never spent much time trying cases as lawyers.

Learned Treatises

Experienced trial lawyers know that impeaching expert witnesses with learned treatises is difficult. If the expert is properly prepared, it will be difficult to get an agreement that a particular treatise was relied on in forming the opinion—or is even regarded as authoritative in the field.

The Federal Rules make that unnecessary. Getting the witness to admit that a book or article is authoritative is just one of the ways to lay the foundation for a learned treatise. The others are

108

having some other expert establish that the work is authoritative in the field, or having the court take judicial notice that it is authoritative.

Take just a moment to let the effect of this rule sink in. You are cross-examining a witness. You have a leading article in his field that contradicts him. The witness refuses to admit that the article is authoritative. At common law, that would be the end of it. But under the Federal Rules you can go ahead and impeach the witness anyway.

Unless the work is widely known outside the field, do not count on the judge taking judicial notice. Instead, have your own witness testify that the work is authoritative. But suppose your witness will not testify until later in the trial. Is there anything you can do?

Certainly. You are an officer of the court, and you can tell the judge you will provide the necessary foundation later. It is called "promising to connect up later."

Now then, where would you expect to find a rule that permits you to do all this? In Article Six, which deals with witnesses? In Article Seven, which covers experts and opinions?

It is part of Rule 803(18), which makes learned treatises an exception to the hearsay rule.

The common law rules in most jurisdictions did not admit learned treatises for their truth, but just to impeach. Rule 803(18) changes that and makes them admissible for their truth, but there are limitations. Not only must the treatise be recognized as authoritative, it is only admissible "[t]o the extent called to the attention of an expert witness on cross-examination or relied upon by him in direct examination. . . ."

No Privity Admissions

One of the consequences of squeezing major exceptions to the hearsay rule into the hearsay definition is that something is likely, to be overlooked. That is apparently what happened to "privity admissions"—statements made by a predecessor in interest that were considered admissions at common law. A perfect example is provided by a recent case.

The plaintiff, Mrs. Huff, brought an action for wrongful death of her husband, who had been fatally injured driving a truck manufactured by the defendant, White Motor Corporation. While her husband was in the hospital before he died, he told a witness how the accident took place. The defendant offered the evidence as an admission, or alternatively under the catchall exceptions to the hearsay rule. The trial court excluded it.

The court of appeals reversed, holding that privity admissions could be admissible under Federal Rules 803(24) and 804(b)(5)—the catchall exceptions. *Huff v. White Motor Corp.*, 609 F.2d 286 (7th Cir. 1979). While the result makes sense, the difficulty the court goes through to reach a decision does not. It would be unfair to create a derivative cause of action that could be freed of the derivative admissions that might accompany it. Privity admissions make sense, and a court should not have to treat each one as an original question under an exception to the hearsay rule that was intended for unusual cases.

Two Identical Hearsay Exceptions

When the proposed Federal Rules of Evidence went to Congress, there were two different catchall exceptions—one in Rule 803 and the other in Rule 804. The exceptions in Rule 803 are admissible in evidence whether or not the declarant is available as a witness. The exceptions in Rule 804, on the other hand, require that the declarant be unavailable. As originally drafted, there were some minor differences between the two catchall exceptions in addition to the availability of the declarant.

But not after Congress had finished. In a master stroke of legislative equality, Congress made the two exceptions identical. The result is that now the only difference between them is that one requires a showing that the declarant is unavailable, while the other does not. And if you talk to those who watched the rules go through Congress, they will admit in private that it makes no sense to have both.

But there are some who think the emperor is well dressed. They insist there is an advantage to having the same catchall in two separate lists of hearsay exceptions.

Some of the states that have adopted the rules have been fooled as well. Ohio was not. It refused to adopt either one, apparently on the idea that judges had no rightful place in the continuing development of judge-made rules.

New York, on the other hand, saw the value of the catchall exception, but realized it needed only one. It kept the one in Rule 804, with some modifications. The result requires a showing of nonavailability of a declarant before catchall hearsay is admissible. In view of the general policy favoring live testimony, that makes good sense.

CHAPTER 11

Opening the Door

The trick was in knowing when to make his objection. The defendant was flirting with an improper line of argument, and timing would be everything in dealing with it.

If he did not wait long enough, his objection would seem technical, premature, unjustified. There would be a good chance that instead of ruling in his favor, the judge would reprimand *him*.

But if he waited too long, the moment would be gone. The judge would no longer see the reason for the objection, and his reaction would be just as bad. At best, the judge would rule the objection was waived—at worst, he might grant a mistrial. There was no question the improper argument was deliberate and that the defendant did not want to be caught at his game. The plaintiff saw the defendant take a quick look at him over at counsel table, trying to read whether he was listening and knew the argument was improper. The plaintiff decided that the best way to look like he was missing it was to look tired, and that was not hard to do.

So the defense made the mistake of going on.

The defendant was a chiropractor whose defective examining table had collapsed twice before. The third time it let go, it dumped the plaintiff, Mrs. Knapp, on the floor—injuring her already deteriorating spine. The improper argument was the subtle implication that the 74-year-old chiropractor—Dr. Suggs—would personally have to pay any judgment himself, now that he was retired.

Of course there was insurance in the case—at least three policies—but the plaintiff knew that was inadmissible, reversible error even to mention insurance in front of the jury.

It was when the defense lawyer started talking about how unfair it was that a claim like this should come to hunt the man down in his retirement that the plaintiff made his move:

> Your honor, I object. Defense counsel is trying to suggest the doctor would have to pay this claim himself, when the fact is he would not have to pay a penny of the plaintiff's damages out of his own pocket.

> Sustained! I was beginning to wonder when you were going to object. To defense counsel and the jury: The defendant's argument is improper and misleading. The jury is instructed to disregard counsel's implications. Counsel, confine yourself to proper arguments.

Even though the plaintiff never used the word insurance, his objection got the idea across. And it was perfectly proper because the defendant had opened the door to the otherwise improper comment by his own argument.

That is the idea of opening the door, fighting fire with fire. Something happens that justifies retaliation with evidence or an argument that otherwise could not be used.

Not surprisingly, the scholars have an awkward term for it, curative admissibility. See 1 Wigmore, *Evidence* Sec. 15.

But trial lawyers call it opening the door, which may turn out to be a better term.

The reason is simple. Curative admissibility deals with the question of when improper evidence justifies retaliation with other improper evidence. But opening the door is broader. Trial lawyers use it to mean that something triggers the admissibility of evidence that would otherwise be inadmissible. If you wonder whether there is any difference, this is it:

Scholars talk about curative admissibility when *illegal* evidence triggers the admissibility of other *illegal* evidence. But the law is filled with situations where perfectly legal evidence opens the door to a rebuttal that would otherwise not be available.

An example will demonstrate the difference.

The defendant is charged with burglary. He does not take the witness stand himself because of his three prior convictions for burglary and armed robbery. Instead he calls his mother, who is his alibi witness. She testifies that her son could not have committed the crime because he was at home watching television that night.

She has been carefully instructed not to talk about anything other than what her son did that evening. By no means is she to say anything about what kind of person her son is. But on the witness stand she cannot help adding, "And besides, he is such a good boy and he has always taken care of me. He would never do anything like this."

A case for curative admissibility?

Absolutely not.

There was nothing wrong with her testimony. While it was a tactical disaster, it was legally proper. A defendant in a criminal case can use his character as a defense, FED. R. EVID. 404(a)(1). And Rule 405(a) of the Federal Rules of Evidence specifically permits opinion testimony to prove character when it is admissible.

Not being improper, there is no need for illegal evidence to rebut other illegal evidence.

But did it open the door?

Oh, yes.

The defendant has "put his character in issue." The mother's testimony is admissible to show that her son is not the kind of person who would commit this crime. This kind of character testimony is usually not admissible in civil actions—except assault and battery cases, where a peace-loving or violent character is particularly important. But in criminal cases, we permit defendants to do what civil litigants cannot. We let them offer evidence of their good character to show they would not do what they are charged with.

But the price is high, and it is marked right on the outside of the package.

When the defendant puts his character in issue, it lets the prosecution cross-examine his character witnesses about his criminal background. It also lets the prosecution put on its own character witnesses to testify about the defendant's character, FED. R. EVID. 404(a)(1).

In other words, it opens the door.

Before we go on, is there nothing that can be done for this defendant whose case was just turned inside out by his well-meaning mother? Just maybe. Suppose two different situations. One:

> Q: Tell us, Mrs. Morris, what did your son do that night?
> A: He was at home all night with me. We were watching television. And besides, he is such a good boy and has always taken care of me. He would never do a thing like this.

The part of her answer that opens the door is non-responsive.
If he is on his toes, the defense lawyer can have the extra information stricken for that reason. That will close the door again. But
wait. Can the lawyer who asks the questions have non-responsive answers stricken? As a matter of fact, the questioner is supposedly the only one who can make that objection. *Hester v.
Goldsbury*, 64 Ill. App.2d 66, 212 N.E.2d 316 (1965).

Two:

> Q: Tell us, Mrs. Morris, why do you say your son is not
> guilty?
> A: He was at home all night with me. We were watching tel
> evision. And besides, he is such a good boy and has al
> ways taken care of me. He would never do a thing like
> this.

Same answer, different question. But now the answer *is* responsive, and the defendant is stuck with it.

That is opening the door. Curative admissibility is different.

Curative admissibility is when improper evidence is used to
open the door to other improper evidence. And because courts
are dealing with ''illegal evidence''—evidence that is sometimes
genuinely prejudicial—they are sometimes reluctant to follow
simple rules that can be counted on to apply in any given situation.

Even though the trial judge has considerable discretion (no surprise) and appellate courts often decide the issues on a case-to-
case basis, McCormick says the decisions tend to fall into four basic patterns:

1. When the improper evidence is not prejudicial and is not
   material, then (to save time and avoid confusion) the
   judge will refuse to let the other side respond.
2. When the improper evidence is relevant and damaging—
   or irrelevant and prejudicial—and counsel has properly
   objected, he should also be given the right to answer the
   evidence. He tried to prevent the error, and he should be
   given the chance to meet the improper evidence and
   even out the trial.
3. When counsel fails to object, the right to answer the evidence is in danger. Some cases say the court should consider whether a cautionary instruction will do the job,
   while others let counsel respond.
4. But whether or not counsel has objected, if the improper

> evidence is so prejudicial that an objection or motion to strike could not erase the harm, then some cases give counsel the right to respond anyway.

See generally, *McCormick on Evidence* Sec. 57 (3d Ed. 1984).

But courts do not always find it easy to deal with whether improper evidence or conduct justifies retaliation with similar medicine. Look at the difficulty the Supreme Court had in dealing with *United States v. Young*, 45 CCH S.Ct Bull. B1090 (February 20, 1985).

Billy G. Young was charged with doctoring fuel oil to make imitation crude—a violation of lots of federal regulations.

In final argument, Young's lawyer got over-exuberant. The argument—hardly a novelty—was to attack the prosecution. But he did not stop with charging unfairness or even intimating that the prosecution had withheld evidence that would show Young's innocence. The capper was when Young's lawyer pointed at the prosecutor's table and said, "I submit to you that there's not a person in this courtroom, including those sitting at this table, who think that Billy Young intended to defraud Apco."

The prosecutor did not object.

He bided his time until rebuttal. Then he said, "I think (defense counsel) said that not anyone sitting at this table thinks that Mr. Young intended to defraud Apco. Well, I was sitting there, and I think he was. I think he got 85 cents a barrel for every one of those 117,250.91 barrels he hauled, and every bit of the money they made on that he got one percent of. So I think he did. If we are allowed to give our personal impressions, since it was asked of me."

The prosecutor did not stop there, either. He also defended the integrity of the prosecution with his personal opinions.

Defense counsel did not object.

But on appeal Young raised the point that the prosecutor had stated his personal belief in the justice of his cause—improper argument and a violation of professional ethics.

The court of appeals reversed Young's conviction on the ground that the prosecutor's remarks were so bad they amounted to plain error—the only practical way to get around the defense counsel's failure to object. The court was annoyed that the prosecutor had taken retaliation into his own hands. "[T]he rule is clear in this Circuit that improper conduct on the part of opposing counsel should be met with an objection to the court, not a similarly improper response." 736 F.2d 565, 570 (10th Cir. 1983).

115

The Supreme Court did not like it, either. Chief Justice Burger said that "the kind of advocacy shown by this record has no place in the administration of justice and should neither be permitted nor rewarded."

Was the prosecutor's response really that bad? If it was, it should certainly amount to plain error. But the court held it was not. And in the tangled prolixity that has marked Supreme Court opinions in the past decade, the court upheld Young's conviction, 5 to 4.

The result makes more sense than the reasons or the rhetoric. Stating your personal belief in the justice of your cause is wrong. But if there ever was invited error, this was it. Instead of seeing that the situation wound up decently balanced from an adversarial standpoint, the Supreme Court seemed to harbor the amazing idea that an instruction from the trial judge could have made the poison of the *defense* counsel's improper invitation just go away.

So curative admissibility is sometimes difficult to handle. But thinking about what opens the door rather than whether a given set of facts qualifies for curative admissibility broadens and simplifies analysis just when you need it most—in the middle of trial. It often has more predictable results:

Bias

The plaintiff was walking back across the street after picking up a pizza and was hit by a car. While he was in the hospital, an agent for the defendant's insurance company got a statement from the plaintiff.

Insurance is normally not admissible in evidence. And if the defendant simply uses the statement in cross-examining the plaintiff—and if the plaintiff admits making the statement—insurance is still not in the case.

But if the plaintiff contests the accuracy of the statement, and the defendant calls his insurance investigator to the stand to show the statement is valid, the investigator's employment is now in issue—not to prove liability, but to show the bias of the witness on the stand. *O'Donnell v. Bachelor*, 429 Pa. 498, 240 A.2d 484 (1968). Putting the investigator on the stand opens the door to insurance.

Some courts do not go quite so far. Instead they only let the jury hear that the investigator was "hired by an agent for the defendant." The idea is to admit the fact of bias without letting the

116

jury know there is money to pay a judgment. The problem with this practice is, insurance tends to show the *degree* of the witness's bias.

Rule of Completeness

Rule 106 of the Federal Rules of Evidence has its counterpart in virtually every state: ''When a writing or recorded statement or part thereof is introduced by a party, an adverse party may require him at that time to introduce any other part or any other writing or recorded statement which ought in fairness to be considered contemporaneously with it.''

The first idea is that one part of a document may open the door to some other part, or even some other document. Offering part of something may open the door to the rest.

The surprising part of the rule is that it recognizes that rebuttal is not always enough. You do not have to wait two weeks or two months until it is your turn to offer evidence again. The rule of completeness lets you *force* your adversary to offer your rebuttal evidence *at the same time* he is offering the part he wants. That is a point to remember.

Prior Convictions

The prosecution is ordinarily not entitled to introduce the defendant's prior convictions. The arsonist with five prior barn burnings to his credit only has to worry about the evidence that says he set this one on fire. But if he takes the stand, he opens the door to prior convictions.

Why?

They are now relevant on the question of his credibility as a witness. Under Rule 609 of the Federal Rules of Evidence, the convictions must be either crimes of dishonesty or felonies in which the probative value of the conviction outweighs the prejudice to the defendant. And under the Federal Rules, the prior convictions are subject to a 10-year time limitation.

Hearsay

When hearsay is offered, the witness on the stand is often not the one whose credibility is in question. Sure, you can cross-examine the witness who is in court, but what about the one whose words are being repeated for their truth?

Hearsay opens the door, Rule 806 FED. R. EVID. The declarant's credibility may be attacked (and then supported) just as if he had

testified as a witness in the case. And if the hearsay is contradicted with a prior inconsistent statement, there is (thankfully) no
need to confront the declarant with the inconsistency.

Deadman's Rebuttal

The old Deadman's Statute worked to bar oral testimony of an interested party to a transaction with someone who is now dead. It
was a rule founded in superficial notions of equality: ''Death having sealed the lips of one party to a transaction, the law will seal
the other's.''

Some states hated the rule and cut it back, while others gave
expansive readings to what it covered. Some states even called an
automobile accident and the statements prompted by it a ''transaction.''

Many states recently abolished their Deadman's Statutes when
they adopted their versions of the new Federal Rules of Evidence.
So the dead man's statements come in, and the surviving party
can testify to them.

Fearing frauds, Ohio wrote a new rule. When the interested
party takes the stand and testifies to the transaction, it opens the
door to other statements made by the dead man even though they
would normally be inadmissible hearsay. OHIO EVID. R. 804(b)(5).
While this is the law in Ohio by rule, other jurisdictions could
adopt this idea by common law developments or the hearsay
catchall of FED. R. EVID. 803(24).

Confessions

The police slip up and forget to read the defendant's rights to him
properly. His confession is not admissible.

But if the defendant takes the stand and testifies that he is not
guilty, that opens the door to use his confession to impeach him
as a witness. *Harris v. New York,* 401 U.S. 222 (1971).

The Victim's Character

The defendant who pleads self-defense may offer testimony
about the victim to prove his case. It works two ways. First, the
victim's violent character may show the victim started the fight.
Second, if the defendant *knew* about the victim's character, he
may have thought he needed to use great force to protect himself.

Either way, the victim's character opens the door to rebuttal
from the prosecution, showing the victim had a reputation for be-

ing peaceable. Under Federal Rule 404(a)(2), any testimony that the victim was the first aggressor also opens the door to the victim's good character in a homicide case.

Repairs

Logically, repairs are an admission that something needed fixing. But we want potential defendants to fix things without worrying whether the repairs might be used against them in court. Otherwise the stairs or the gearshifts or the shut-off valves might not get fixed, and more folks might wind up being injured. So we have a rule that makes the repairs inadmissible.

Just claiming that the condition was defective does not open the door to the repairs—but lots of defenses will. Under Rule 407, FED. R. EVID., subsequent remedial measures are admissible to prove "ownership, control, or feasibility of precautionary measures, if controverted, or impeachment."

This means that if the defense counsel just says in his opening statement that the defendant had done "as good a job as he could" in maintaining his stairway, that may be enough to open the door to later repairs.

Attacking Credibility

As soon as any witness takes the stand, an important door is opened. His believability is now open to question. And timing is important. Credibility of a witness is not normally open to question until he *is* a witness.

By the same token, a witness's credibility cannot be supported until it is attacked. It is a timing rule. It is simple, but it is surprising how often lawyers and judges forget it.

Just as important is what happens when certain kinds of attacks are made. Suppose on cross-examination the lawyer suggests a witness made up his testimony because of recent developments. Today in court the witness said the light was red. Before trial, he said the light was green. The cross-examiner points to something that happened last month, implying that it made the witness change his testimony.

That can be effective cross-examination. It can also open the door to a prior consistent statement in which the witness said the light was red—just like he did on direct examination.

That prior statement was not admissible for its truth at common law, as it only went to the witness's credibility.

Under Federal Rule 801(d)(1)(B), prior consistent statements offered to rebut an implied or express charge of recent fabrication are even admissible for their truth. The notion is that since the witness is already on the stand and available to be cross-examined about it, we might as well let the prior consistent statement in evidence without an instruction from the bench that would not be understood anyway.

Witness Preparation

Preparing a witness for trial with his own statement makes sense. It encourages consistency. It also makes sense that the statement used to prepare the witness could be discovered by the opponent.

But what about other statements—say memos written by the lawyer, reflecting what is normally called "work product," or, say, the statement of another witness?

Preparing the witness with *any* statement throws the door wide open—to discovery, to using the document in cross-examination, and even to offering relevant portions of the document in evidence, FED. R. EVID. 612.

Now let us take a step back for a moment. If you look back over these examples of opening the door, you will see that most of them illustrate what happens when the other side does something that unlocks the evidence you want. If you are not careful, they may seem like illustrations of a series of little rules that are nice to know but that all fit into separate niches in the law of evidence.

There is a better way to look at them.

They are all part of the law of *relevance*. The idea behind opening the door is that what was not relevant before is relevant now. When you think of it that way, your notion of what opening the door is will become even more creative. It will occur to you that you will not always have to wait for your opponent to open the door. Sometimes you can do it yourself:

- Your plaintiff was injured by a drunken truck driver with a history of driving while intoxicated. If you sue the trucking company for the driver's negligence, his driving record is not admissible. Generally, you cannot use evidence of someone's character to show that is the way he behaved this time.

   But if you sue the trucking company for negligent entrustment of a vehicle to someone they should have known was untrustworthy, you have opened the door to

120

his driving history. *See Snowhite v. State,* 243 Md. 291, 221 A.2d 342 (1968).

- If you base a products liability case just on strict liability, evidence proving negligence in making the product should normally not be relevant. But if you also allege negligence, you have opened the door to proof of fault— an important psychological factor in the outcome of the case.

If you think of opening the door in its broader sense, it will also occur to you that there are things you can do to close the door.

- You represent an employer whose talkative employee drove the truck that injured the plaintiff. Under the Federal Rules of Evidence, statements an employee makes about a matter within the scope of his employment— made during the existence of the relationship—are now admissible in evidence as admissions. Rule 801 (d)(2). So if the defendant fires its employee, that closes the door to further admissions. (But on the other hand, firing him may guarantee a very uncooperative witness at trial.)
- You represent the defendant in a personal injury case, and liability is clear. Damages are in dispute. If you admit liability, you are ordinarily closing the door to proof of fault that might otherwise be used as an emotional basis for increasing damages. On the other hand, if the plaintiff is asking for punitive damages, that opens the door to fault again, since the degree of wrongdoing is relevant to punitive damages.

Take a step back one more time. What does it all mean? Probably that opening the door is a helpful way for a trial lawyer to look at the law of evidence.

CHAPTER 12

Character Evidence and Impeachment

While it is obviously a good idea to research as many anticipated evidence questions as possible before trial, lawyers do not always have time to do that. For novel questions, debatable points or even mundane matters that promise to be pivotal issues in important litigation, there is no substitute for a well-documented memorandum ready to be produced when the question comes up. But for other matters, litigators must rely on their general knowledge of the law of evidence.

For most trial lawyers, this includes a general sense of relevance, an understanding of hearsay and a handful of exceptions, the best evidence rule, the requirements for authenticating documents and telephone calls, the magic litany for a number of foundations and the rules that regulate the forms of questions.

There may be other things in this bag of common tricks, but the chances are that a solid knowledge of character evidence is not one of them.

Part of the problem is sheer complexity. Another is the illogical but somehow workable interrelationship of permissible thrusts and parries that has defied all but superficial tinkering in the Federal Rules of Evidence. Mr. Justice Jackson—one of the few members in the history of the Supreme Court to have any real feeling for the law of evidence—was speaking of character evidence when he said, ''To pull one misshapen stone out of the grotesque structure is more likely simply to upset its present balance between adverse interests than to establish a rational edifice.'' *Michelson v. United States*, 335 U.S. 469, 486 (1948).

Moreover, for some lawyers, character evidence seems to have a value in inverse proportion to the complexity of the rules. Like picking the meat out of a lobster's legs, the harder it is, the less it seems worth doing.

But character evidence is important. Credibility, the central factor underlying many of the rules, somehow manages to be an issue in nearly every contested case. Because character evidence continues to win and lose cases, this discussion is intended for those trial lawyers who want to add an understanding of it to their regular bag of tricks. But a word of warning: Since character evidence is complex and this is an outline, it is necessarily incomplete and in a sense somewhat inaccurate. Nevertheless, it should help.

1. One may not impeach his own witness.

The common law prohibits a party from impeaching the witnesses he calls and examines. Actually eliciting testimony is required; merely taking a witness's deposition does not make him your witness to prevent impeachment at trial by you unless you introduce the deposition into evidence.

The common statement that a party is ''bound by his witness's statement'' is misleading, because the rule does not prohibit contradiction by other witnesses on relevant matters. Instead, the rule prohibits impeachment by the use of prior convictions, prior inconsistent statements, bias, interest or bad reputation.

Fortunately, many jurisdictions have an important exception to the rule. A party may impeach his own witness with a prior inconsistent statement if two conditions are met: First, the party calling the witness must be surprised at the change in the witness's story, and second, the testimony must be affirmatively harmful—which means actually adverse, not that the witness merely forgot what he had said before. When the witness cannot remember, you are free to try to refresh his recollection, but *not* attack his credibility.

In a number of states, the rule against impeaching one's own witness does not apply when the adverse party is called as a witness. The only surprise is that this rule does not apply everywhere.

Similarly, the rule does not apply to attesting witnesses or others who are required by law to be called.

Most important, the rule does not prohibit revealing damaging information yourself when you are not seeking to discredit your witness. Usually the best way to deal with your opponent's attack on your witness is to draw out the harmful material yourself, rather than trying to explain it away on redirect examination. In other words, it is often best to try to steal the thunder from the other side. Since this is not impeachment—far from it—the rule against impeaching your own witness has no proper application to this situation, a distinction which escapes some trial judges.

2. Under the Federal Rules of Evidence, a party may impeach his own witness.

In a delightful stroke of simplicity, the Federal Rules of Evidence, Rule 607, adopted the minority American rule, which permits any witness to be impeached by any party. For a more thorough discussion of the rules prohibiting impeaching one's own witness, see Ladd, *Impeachment of One's Own Witness*, 4 U. CHI. L. REV. 69 (1936).

3. A witness may not be impeached on collateral matters.

While one may, within the limits of discretion, ask about collateral matters on cross-examination, this rule forbids contradiction by other witnesses on these side issues. Once again, the traditional statement of the rule is misleading. It does not prohibit questioning about collateral issues, forcing the witness to admit he made a mistake or even impeaching a witness with a prior inconsistent statement, provided the witness authenticates it himself. What the rule does is forbid calling another witness to contradict testimony that is not directly relevant to the case.

When a collateral matter is so important that it provides a good test for the accuracy of disputed relevant testimony, then contradicting witnesses may be called. A classic example of this exception comes from *Stephens v. People*, 19 N.Y. 549 (1859), where the defendant was charged with murder by poisoning with arsenic. The defendant's witnesses testified that the arsenic bought by the defendant was used on rats in a cellar where provisions were kept. The court held that it was permissible to show that no provisions were kept in that cellar.

Even more important, there are some matters which are not issues in the case, but which are never collateral. These include bias, interest, conviction of a crime or lack of opportunity for the witness to have knowledge of what he has testified to. See *McCormick on Evidence* 97-100 (2d ed. 1972).

4. Any witness may be impeached with prior convictions.

When a witness takes the stand, his character for truth and veracity (the standard legal redundancy) is the issue. Prior convictions are a proper subject for cross-examination, and if the witness denies the convictions, they may be shown by extrinsic evidence—usually by certified copies of conviction records.

In some states, magic words are required on cross-examination, such as, "Are you the same Harold Morgan who was convicted of arson on October 15, 1977?"

Nearly everywhere it is only proper to inquire into the fact of the conviction and not aggravating details, except in some states it is permissible to ask about the sentence imposed.

On the other hand, many states permit the conviction to be briefly explained on redirect examination, although some jurisdictions do not permit the witness to deny guilt, apparently to avoid retrying the impeaching case.

Putting this together in a simple example, it would be improper to ask, "Weren't you convicted for aggravated assault because you beat a 58-year-old lady with a leather whip as she lay helpless on the floor of the World Trade Center?" but permissible for the witness on redirect examination to explain, "Yes, but the victim was my mother-in-law."

There is disagreement about what sorts of convictions may be used to impeach a witness. Many states permit the use of all felonies and also those misdemeanors which involve "moral turpitude." A small minority imposes the moral turpitude restriction on felonies as well.

The Federal Rules of Evidence change this practice. Under Rule 609, a witness may be impeached with any crime involving dishonesty or false statement. If the crime is not one of dishonesty or false statement, it must be a felony, and the trial court must find that the probative value of the conviction outweighs the prejudicial effect "to the defendant," a balancing test adopted from *Luck v. United States*, 348 F.2d 763 (D.C. Cir. 1965).

Furthermore, Rule 609 imposes a ten-year time limit on convictions that may be used, calculated from the date of conviction or release from confinement for it, whichever is later. That ten-year limitation may only be circumvented by advance written notice of the intent to use the conviction to impeach and by an express finding that the probative value of the conviction outweighs its prejudicial effect.

While the rule permitting impeachment with prior convictions applies to all trials, it is most commonly used in criminal cases, where it is a favorite weapon of prosecutors cross-examining recidivist defendants. Partly because of this, one of the difficult judgments for a defense counsel is whether to call a defendant with a prior conviction to testify on his own behalf.

The Federal Rules of Evidence ease this problem a bit. Under Rule 104(c), when the defendant is a witness, he has a right to a hearing outside the presence of the jury on any preliminary issue, apparently including the admissibility of prior convictions. If this procedure is used before trial, it helps defense counsel plan in advance whether to call the defendant as a witness. For a more complete discussion of this issue and others concerning the use of prior convictions to impeach, see Burleson, *Rule 609: Impeachment with Prior Convictions*, LITIGATION, Vol. 2, No. 1 at p. 14 (1975).

5. A witness may sometimes be cross-examined about bad acts for which there has been no conviction.

When the purpose of the cross-examiner is to cast doubt on the witness's credibility—and not to bring out facts otherwise relevant—there are at least three prevailing views:

    a. The previous bad acts must have some relation to credibility.

    b. The previous bad acts need only show bad moral character.

    c. Previous bad acts may not be used on cross-examination.

These are not the only rules, just the most prevalent ones. Irving Younger lists six different rules in *Three Essays on Character and Credibility Under the Federal Rules of Evidence*, 5 HOFSTRA L. REV. 7, 12 (1976).

The Federal Rules of Evidence, Rule 608(b), permit cross-examination on prior bad acts in the discretion of the court if they are probative of truthfulness. The Federal Rule also makes it clear that while these matters may be inquired into, electing to testify does not in itself waive the privilege against self-incrimination about prior bad acts.

Besides the question of what sorts of acts may be the subject of cross-examination, there is another difference between convictions and bad acts for which there is no conviction. If the witness denies the conviction, it may be shown independently. On the other hand, if the witness denies the prior bad act, the cross-examiner may not use extrinsic evidence to prove the witness did it. Thus it is said that the questioner is "bound by the witness's answer."

Even though extrinsic evidence of bad acts is not permitted, there must be a reasonable basis for asking questions about them. The trial court may require a cross-examiner to show his adversary what evidence he has that the witness committed the act. It may even be possible for the adversary to put the offending attorney on the witness stand to show the question was asked without any basis. *Cf. United States v. Pugliese*, 153 F.2d 497 (2d Cir. 1945).

6. A witness may not be asked about his arrests to impeach his credibility.

While a witness may be asked about prior convictions and prior bad acts, an arrest or a charge does not establish that a person has done anything wrong. Although arrests may affect *reputation*, witnesses ordinarily may not testify about their own reputations. The easiest rule of thumb, therefore, is never ask a witness about his own arrests unless they are relevant for some purpose other than impeachment.

7. A witness's credibility may not be supported before attack.

The rule is a sensible one designed to make trials go more quickly. After all, the attack may never be made. On the other hand, the rule can be irksome, especially when it requires later recalling witnesses to rebut what you know must come. The rule prohibits showing prior consistent statements before impeachment with prior inconsistent statements, testimony of a witness's good character for truth and veracity before attack, and the like.

It is a general rule, subject to exceptions. Evidence of a rape victim's fresh complaint to corroborate her testimony is a common example. For others, see *McCormick on Evidence* 102, n. 73 (2d ed. 1972).

8. A witness may be impeached with bias, prejudice, or interest.

Bias, prejudice, and interest are not collateral. This means they are so important their use is not limited to cross-examination; they also may be proved by extrinsic evidence. As with impeachment with prior inconsistent statements, however, a majority of jurisdictions require a foundation for extrinsic proof of bias or prejudice to be laid on cross-examination, confronting the witness with the impeaching information. This foundation is not always required, however, especially where indisputable matters such as kinship with a party are involved.

9. A witness may be impeached with a prior inconsistent statement.

One of the most effective devices in the cross-examiner's arsenal is the prior inconsistent statement.

Under the hearsay rule, a prior inconsistent statement is not admissible to show that the prior statement is true unless the witness adopts it during the trial. Instead, it is thought to be relevant only to the credibility of the witness. Federal Rule 801(d)(1)(A) is *contra,* admitting a statement to prove its truth if it was made "under oath and subject to the penalty of perjury at a trial, hearing, or other proceeding, or in a deposition." The Federal Rule thus makes it possible for a prosecutor to introduce grand jury testimony not just to impeach, but to prove its truth. See McDaniels, *Rule 801: More Than a Definition,* LITIGATION, Vol. 2, No. 1, pp. 17, 19 (1975).

The rule in *Queen Caroline's Case,* 2 BROD. & BING 284, 313, 129 Eng. Rep. 976 (1820), requires that a witness be confronted with particularity on cross-examination concerning the prior statement to permit proof of it by extrinsic evidence. Federal Rule 613 modifies this requirement. Under it, the witness must merely have some opportunity to explain or deny the statement, and the court has the discretion to waive this requirement.

When the witness is a party, the prior statement will be an admission, and no confrontation on cross-examination is required. It will also be admissible to prove its truth, even when it is principally used to impeach the party-witness.

10. A witness may be rehabilitated with a prior consistent statement.

After a witness has been impeached with a prior inconsistent statement, there is the possibility of rehabilitating him with a prior consistent statement. The requirement for admissibility of these prior statements varies according to jurisdiction. A few states permit them just so long as they were made before the impeaching prior inconsistent statement. Apparently all states, however, permit prior consistent statements that were made before an alleged motivating factor for recent fabrication. See *McCormick on Evidence* 106 at n.93 (2d ed. 1972).

As with prior inconsistent statements, prior consistent statements are not admissible to prove their truth, but rather are considered as going to the credibility of the witness. Federal Rule 801(d)(1)(B) is *contra* once again, admitting prior consistent statements to prove their truth. To be admissible, they must be offered to rebut an express or implied charge of recent fabrication, competent to prove the truth of the matter asserted.

11. A witness may be impeached by a character witness familiar with his reputation for truth and veracity.

After any witness testifies, the way is clear to attack his veracity, not only with the means already given but with an additional type of testimony as well. A character witness may be called to testify that he is familiar with the reputation for truth and veracity of the witness being impeached and that it is bad.

The difficulty is there is another sort of character witness who testifies similarly, and it is easy to get the two mixed.

Character witnesses may be called in any case, civil or criminal. They testify about the reputation of any witness for truth and veracity in the community in which he lives and works.

The other sort of character witnesses may only be called in criminal cases. They do not testify about the reputation of someone as a witness but about the reputation of the defendant as having a character inconsistent with the crime charged.

In most states, a character witness can only testify about reputation; the witness's personal opinion about the believability of the witness who is being impeached is inadmissible. The Federal Rules of Evidence continue the common-law prohibition against using specific acts in the direct examination of character witnesses, but do make a sensible reform. Rule 608(a) permits character testimony in the form of either reputation or personal opinion—which is what character witnesses really testify to anyway.

12. Character witnesses may be contradicted with other character witnesses.

A witness's credibility may not be supported before attack, but after an attack everything is changed. One permissible rebuttal is to call other character witnesses who are familiar with the reputation for truth and veracity of the witness whose credibility is under scrutiny and who say that that reputation is good. Like character witnesses who are used to attack a witness, these witnesses are limited to reputation (or opinion under Federal Rule 608(a)) and may not testify on direct examination to specific instances of conduct.

13. Character witnesses may be cross-examined with specific instances of conduct.

Part of the point of limiting the direct examination of character witnesses to reputation is to keep trials short. But on cross-examination of these witnesses, whether they testify that another witness's reputation for truth is good or bad, specific instances of conduct are permissible.

One of the important oddities of the law of character and impeachment concerns the sort of information that may be used on cross-examining these witnesses. Because they have testified to someone's reputation for truth and veracity, it is relevant to test their knowledge of that reputation.

Now recall that arrests are not admissible to impeach. While an arrest may make us suspect that the person arrested actually was guilty of something, we know that the danger of prejudice from this information outweighs its probative value so much that we say arrests are simply not relevant to character.

On the other hand, we also recognize that reputation is a fragile thing. Even illogical, baseless rumors can ruin reputations. While arrests do not show bad character, they may well affect reputation. Thus in maddeningly syllogistic logic the law has concluded that arrests as well as convictions and prior bad acts with no convictions may indeed be inquired into during the cross-examination of a character witness—not to prove character, but to test the witness's knowledge of the person's reputation.

This logical consistency goes on. Because knowledge of reputation is being tested, and actual character is being shown only indirectly, it is not proper to ask a character witness whether he "knew" that the witness being impeached had been arrested. That is error. It is perfectly proper, on the other hand, to ask whether the reputation witness "has heard" of the arrest, a distinction made for the benefit of juries who are unlikely ever to appreciate the difference involved.

Do the Federal Rules of Evidence change all that? Do they wipe away this illogical testing of reputation, now that Rule 608(a) permits character witnesses to testify to their actual opinions instead of masking those opinions in the form of reputation testimony? They do not.

Instead, Federal Rule 608(b) permits the cross-examiner to ask the character witness whether he "knew" of the arrest, abolishing the requirement to ask "have you heard." Thus does reformation become superficial tinkering.

Judge Jack B. Weinstein, on the other hand, argues that Rule 608 can be given a more restrictive reading. Even though neither the rule nor the Advisory Committee Note to it mentions arrests or charges, he asserts they should not be permissible lines of questioning under the Federal Rules because they are not "specific instances of conduct" mentioned in Rule 608. J. Weinstein and M. Berger, 3 *Weinstein's Evidence* § 608[06] at 608-36 (1976).

14. A criminal defendant may call character witnesses to show he is not the sort of person who would commit the crime charged.

So far character evidence has centered around the rules that are applicable in all sorts of trials concerning the believability of witnesses. Now comes a series of rules bearing some resemblance to the ones that have gone before, but differing in two ways: First, they apply only in criminal actions, and second, the purpose for which the evidence is admitted is different.

One of the basic beliefs that permeates our system of criminal justice is that a defendant may be proven guilty only on evidence that tends to show he committed the crime charged. Consider what that means.

A prosecutor may not show that a defendant has committed crimes in the past to show the defendant is an evil person who should be found guilty now. Unless there is some additional relevance for other wrongs, they are not admissible to show guilt of the crime for which the defendant is now on trial.

It is not that other bad acts have no relevance whatever. Instead, we fear that a jury might well give disproportionate (call it prejudicial) weight to this kind of evidence.

It might seem consistent to prohibit a defendant from showing he led a blameless past, but that is not the rule.

Because the risk of prejudice is gone, the defendant may start something the prosecutor may not. He may "put his character in issue." This is a misleading phrase, because a defendant's character does not become an element of the crime that the prosecutor must prove. It simply means a defendant may use his good character as circumstantial evidence that he did not commit this crime.

He does this by calling character witnesses.

Like other character witnesses, these are also limited in their direct testimony to the reputation of the defendant in the community in which he lives and works. But under the majority rule, at least, it is a different kind of reputation. Instead of believability, it is a reputation for having a character inconsistent with the crime charged—being peaceable, for example, if the charge is murder.

As with other character witnesses, the Federal Rules of Evidence permit these to give their personal opinion of the defendant as an alternative to his reputation. Rule 405(a).

15. Character witnesses used to defend may be contradicted with other character witnesses.

Now comes the meaning of the phrase "putting character in issue." While the prosecutor may not show the bad character of a defendant as part of his case in chief, once the defendant raises the issue, his hands are not tied. He may now call other character witnesses to testify that the reputation (or the witness's opinion under Federal Rule 405(a)) of the defendant is that his character is consistent with the offense.

16. Character witnesses may be cross-examined with specific acts of the accused.

The process here is (thank goodness) pretty much like cross-examining other character witnesses. There are exceptions, of course. Under *People v. Hannon*, 381 Ill. 206, 44 N.E.2d 923 (1942), a character witness called by the accused may only be cross-examined about prior arrests or charges similar to the present charge. Although it appeals to our sense of relevance, it is the minority view and was rejected in the famous case, *Michelson v. United States*, 335 U.S. 469 (1948).

17. A criminal defendant may show the violent reputation of the victim to aid his claim of self-defense.

In a homicide case when the defendant claims he acted in self-defense, the general rule is he may call character witnesses to show the violent or turbulent nature of the victim.

This evidence can be relevant in two ways: First, if the defendant shows he knew of the victim's violent reputation, it can support the reasonableness of the defendant's belief he was in danger. *State v. Blair*, 305 S.W.2d 435 (Mo. 1957). Second, the violent reputation of the victim can show that the victim was probably the first aggressor. *State v. Wilson*, 235 Iowa 538, 17 N.W.2d 138 (1945).

18. The prosecution may rebut testimony of the violent reputation of the victim and may sometimes show the defendant's violent reputation as well.

The prosecution may not prove the peaceable nature of the victim as part of its case in chief. However, when the defendant opens the door to the victim's reputation, it is well-established that the prosecution may rebut this evidence with other character witnesses who testify to the peaceable reputation of the victim. *State v. Brock*, 56 N.M. 328, 244 P.2d 131 (1952). Under Federal Rule 404(a)(2), in homicide cases, the prosecution may show the peaceable nature of the victim in response to any defense evidence that the victim was the first aggressor.

The problem is whether the prosecution may do anything else as well. A few cases have held that testimony of the victim's violent reputation opens the door to the *defendant's* reputation for violence as well. *See Note*, 99 U. PA. L. REV. 105 (1950).

19. A civil litigant may not ''put his character in issue.''

The situation is simple. Defendant is charged with larceny. He may ''put his character in issue'' by showing his good reputation that is inconsistent with theft. Charged with the same act in a civil action for conversion, he may not show his good reputation.

While this is the general rule, a growing minority of states permits reputation evidence in civil cases that in effect charge crimes involving moral turpitude. See *McCormick on Evidence* 459 (2d ed. 1972).

In civil assault and battery cases involving self-defense, the law is more liberal, following rules about reputation like those in homicide cases. See. e.g., *Linkhart v. Savely*, 190 Ore. 484, 227 P.2d 187 (1950).

Of course this rule does not operate to bar evidence of habit and custom in civil and criminal cases, a subject that lies outside character evidence and impeachment.

20. The prosecution may show a defendant's prior bad acts if they are relevant for something other than impeachment.

A final rule lying on the ragged edge of character and impeachment is the use of prior bad acts to show the defendant's guilt. The rule is unequivocal that the prosecution may not introduce evidence of prior bad acts as part of its case in chief if the purpose is to show that the defendant is an evil person who ought to be convicted.

133

But suppose a man stole a car, then robbed a bank. The two crimes are unrelated. When charged in federal court with the robbery of a federally insured bank, the theft of the car—a state offense—is irrelevant. The defendant does not take the stand. There is no opportunity to use this other act, even in cross-examining the accused.

But if the car was stolen to serve as a getaway vehicle, the theft is now admissible—not to show that the defendant is a bad person, but because it is part of the overall transaction of robbing the bank.

McCormick on Evidence 448–50 (2d ed. 1972) lists ten different theories justifying the proof of other crimes that are not charged to support the prosecution's case in chief.

The Federal Rules of Evidence also admit evidence of other crimes or wrongs in what is a good summary of the general law. According to Rule 404(b), ''Evidence of other crimes, wrongs, or acts is not admissible to prove the character of a person in order to show that he acted in conformity therewith. It may, however, be admissible for other purposes, such as proof of motive, opportunity, intent, preparation, plan, knowledge, identity, or absence of mistake or accident.''

A *final note.* Like the hearsay rule, the law of character evidence and impeachment often presents situations where evidence is admissible for one purpose but not for another. The unhappy solution to this problem is the usually meaningless (if not actually harmful) limiting instruction.

Is it worth asking for?

The trouble is, if you do not, the evidence is typically ''admitted generally,'' to prove whether it logically tends to show. *Hatfield v. Levy Bros.*, 18 Cal.2d 798, 117 P.2d 841 (1941).

Finally, this outline on character and impeachment deals with the difficult issues presented when character is used as circumstantial evidence, usually to prove conduct. But there are numerous situations where character is actually an issue in the case, as in defamation actions or in child custody cases where the question is who is the better parent.

When character is truly an issue—when it is an element of the case or defense—then the rules in this outline do not apply, and the tendency of the law of evidence is to admit proof of specific acts as well as opinion evidence. Rule 405(b), Federal Rules of Evidence.

CHAPTER 13

An Outline on Hearsay

Make a nationwide survey of experienced trial lawyers and judges. Ask them to characterize the hearsay rule in a few words. You know the kind of responses you would get: ''baffling,'' ''amazingly complex,'' ''impossible to apply.''

The results might lure you into conducting another survey of the same group, this time inquiring about the value of the rule to our adversary system. The responses would be almost as consistent. Some might call it ''outmoded,'' or even ''archaic,'' but most would grudgingly admit it is necessary. Some might even be eloquent: ''The hearsay rule protects the fundamental right to cross-examination.''

And there you have it: vilified, ridiculed, misunderstood, and misapplied, the hearsay rule and the exceptions by which it is known stand as a grotesque guardian of a treasured right. Surely it is a rule that justifies at least a working knowledge by serious trial lawyers.

The starting point is cross-examination. The right to cross-examination can help identify what is hearsay. There is a question to ask that helps focus the inquiry: Whom do you want to cross-examine to test the reliability of challenged evidence, the witness on the stand or the person who originally said what is now being repeated? If you want to cross-examine the witness on the stand—that is, if cross-examination of the witness is adequate to test the reliability of the evidence—then the out-of-court statement is not hearsay. If, however, testing the evidence would require cross-examination of the person who originally made the statement, then it is hearsay.

It is a useful test, because it points to what is called the scholarly definition: *Hearsay is evidence that depends for its probative value on the veracity of an out-of-court declarant.* Since cross-examination is the test of veracity, the definition spots the very interest to be protected—whom do you want to cross-examine?

But there the advantage ends. The scholarly definition suffers from a serious fault. It is not merely cumbersome; it is almost incapable of easy application in the heat of trial. Because of this, the common law—trial lawyers and judges and appellate courts—has evolved a definition susceptible to more convenient use in contested hearings: *Hearsay is evidence of an out-of-court statement offered to prove the truth of the matter asserted.* Even though it has more words than the first definition, it is easier to apply because it breaks down into two elements:

1. An out-of-court statement.
2. Offered to prove the truth of the matter asserted.

Although many writings and judicial opinions use the words "offered to prove the truth of the matter asserted," that idea can be conveyed by even simpler words, "offered to prove its truth."

Trimmed down to fighting weight, the definition is finally easy to use:

1. An out-of-court statement,
2. Offered to prove its truth.

This definition of hearsay has been adopted in virtually every jurisdiction. It will lead to the same results as the first definition in nearly every instance with one exception: when the out-of-court declarant is also the witness testifying to what he said out of court. Then the first definition would lead to the result that the statement is not hearsay; it would still be hearsay under the second.

This difference in definitions was on the brink of merely academic interest until the most important event in evidence law in the past fifty years, the Federal Rules of Evidence. While seeming to adopt the simple, two-element definition, the drafters of the rules actually created a complex admixture of the two.

According to Federal Rule 801 (c), " 'Hearsay' is a statement, other than one made by the declarant while testifying at the trial or hearing, offered in evidence to prove the truth of the matter asserted."

It looks just like the second definition, and it is. The difficulty is that under Rule 801 (d), some previous statements by witnesses—prior inconsistent statements made under oath and subject to the penalties of perjury, prior consistent statements, prior identifications, and admissions—are *not* considered hearsay. Nevertheless, they can still be admissible to prove their truth.

Why is this so? The answer cannot be found in the hearsay definition in Rule 801 (c). Without ever saying so directly, the drafters chose the first, scholarly, definition of hearsay for admissions, prior consistent and inconsistent statements and prior identifications. They called these statements non-hearsay because they do not depend for their probative value on the veracity of out-of-court declarants. Thus, they are not hearsay under the scholarly definition.

Does this mean that the Federal Rules proclaim one definition but really use another? Unfortunately, they are not even that consistent. The scholarly definition is not applied to all prior statements of witnesses. Present sense impressions, excited utterances, statements of physical condition and other out-of-court statements that are recognized as exceptions to the rule against hearsay in Federal Rule 803 may be testified to in court by the original declarant when they meet the qualifications for those exceptions. They may be admissible, but they are hearsay, even under the Federal Rules.

What is the trial lawyer who is intent on learning a basic definition of hearsay to do—throw up his hands in disgust? No. Learn the simple definition of hearsay, an out-of-court statement, offered to prove its truth. Then just remember that admissions, prior consistent and inconsistent statements as well as prior identifications are all called non-hearsay by the Federal Rules (whether we like it or not).

Abstractions are always difficult, and the definitions of hearsay are no exception. A few examples will help show how easy the two-element definition of hearsay is to apply. Remember that both requirements must be met, an out-of-court statement, offered to prove its truth. In each instance the witness is repeating from the stand what someone said outside of court:

''I heard a bystander say that the light was red.''

Offered to prove the light was red, hearsay. Offered to prove the bystander was awake, not hearsay.

''I heard a mechanic tell the pilot the rudder on the airplane was not working right.''

Offered to prove the rudder was not working right, hearsay. Offered to prove that the pilot was on notice of a defect in the plane, not hearsay. Since it might well be relevant for both purposes, a limiting instruction would have to be granted if requested.

"I heard donor say to recipient, 'John, this money is for you,' as he handed him a hundred dollar bill."

Suppose the recipient offers this as a defense in a debt case, as proof that the hundred dollars was a gift, not a loan. This is hearsay, is it not?

No.

Is it not being offered to prove the truth of the statement? No. It is being offered to prove it was said. The law does not care about a donor's secret intentions, but rather how his intentions appeared to a reasonable man or woman. These words of donative intent constitute one of the elements of a completed gift. The statement, then, is a verbal act.

The problem with this case is that while the words are not being offered to prove their truth—because of the objective theory of gifts and contracts—they may look to some as if they are hearsay. The statement that donor was giving the money to recipient is being used to prove that donor was giving the money to recipient.

If verbal acts—words of legal significance—give you trouble, there is a hypothetical situation which will always work to clear it up.

Lotta Beakers, a laboratory technician, defames Harold Morticutt M.D., a leading pathologist. She says, "Doctor Morticutt is a lying, thieving, no-good son of a bitch who would steal anything that is not nailed down." In Morticutt's action against Beakers, a witness is called to the stand who heard her say this to a group of fifty other people.

When Beakers challenges the witness's testimony as hearsay, Morticutt's response is a telling one:

> Your honor, when the witness testifies that Lotta Beakers said, 'Doctor Morticutt is a lying, thieving, no-good son of a bitch who would steal anything that is not nailed down,' that is not hearsay. I am not offering it to prove I am a lying, thieving no-good son of a bitch who would steal anything that is not nailed down. On the contrary. I am merely proving that those words were spoken.

The words have legal significance. They are part of the cause of action. They are not offered for their truth. So it is with words which create a gift or a contract, even though admitting them in evidence may sometimes make them come true.

Spoken or written words are easy to identify as statements. So are actions that are intended substitutes for words, such as prearranged signals like flares or lights in an old church tower. Actions—conduct—intended to be a substitute for words can qualify as hearsay. If someone nods instead of saying "yes," it is hearsay.

Trouble is encountered, however, when conduct is not intended to convey an idea when it is done, but is later offered to prove the truth of the assumptions on which it rested. While this sounds complicated, it is not.

The leading case, *Wright v. Doe d. Tatham,* 7 Adolph. & E. 313, 112 Eng. Rep. 488 (Exch. Ch. 1837), involved letters written to a testator, each one on the assumption that the testator was sane. When the letters were offered to prove that the testator was sane, they were rejected as hearsay. The letters were in effect offered to prove the truth of the implied statements, the belief on which they rested.

This is called "non-assertive conduct," because it is conduct that was not intended as an assertion, even if it is later used as one.

The concept is rejected in some states and by the Federal Rules of Evidence. Rule 801 says "A 'statement' is (1) an oral or written assertion or (2) nonverbal conduct of a person, if it is intended by him as an assertion."

Put it another way: non-assertive conduct is not hearsay under the Federal Rules. This does not mean non-assertive conduct is automatically admissible under the Federal Rules. Instead, it means that it will be tested under the general standards of relevance set out in Rule 403, rather than under the more specific rules of hearsay.

That takes care of the basic rule, but what about all those exceptions?

There are, depending on how particular you want to be, up to 100 recognized exceptions to the hearsay rule. The Federal Rules of Evidence list 29 exceptions, which really add up to only 28, since Rule 803 (24) and Rule 804 (b)(5) are virtually identical. On the other hand, the Federal Rules make admissions non-hearsay as well as admitting prior identifications, consistent and inconsistent statements as non-hearsay, so even that count is off.

Of all the exceptions, there are a dozen or so that trial lawyers need to recognize instantly in their daily practice. While one might quibble about some that ought to be on this list, most litigators would agree that the following should be included.

Admissions

An admission is any act or statement of a party inconsistent with the position he now takes at trial. One way or another, this exception appears in most trials. It has some notable features:

1. First-hand knowledge is not required.
2. It may be in opinion form.
3. It need not be against the interest of the declarant at the time it is said or done.
4. Confrontation is not required—the whole trial is a confrontation. This means that when the opposing party testifies, he may be impeached with an admission without following the confrontation requirements from the Rule in *Queen Caroline's Case*, 2 Brod. & Bing 284, 313, 129 Eng. Rep. 976 (1820).
5. Silence *may* be an admission—but beware. Too many courts are lax about this situation, letting in evidence of silence under doubtful circumstances. See Note, *Tacit Criminal Admissions*, 112 U. Pa. L. Rev. 210 (1963).

Vicarious admissions (admissions made by someone acting for a party) are also admissible. At common law, the vicarious admission of an employee was not admissible unless it was in the scope of employment for the employee to make the statement. Under Federal Rule 801 (D) (2), an employee's statement is admissible if the statement relates to the scope of employment, a signal change from the common law.

Statements by predecessors in title to property, made while they were in possession, were considered admissions at common law, when offered against one holding title through the individual who made the statement. *Du Bois v. Larke*, 175 Cal. App. 2d 737, 346 P.2d 830 (1959). Except to the extent that such a statement may qualify as a declaration against interest, this exception is apparently not included in the Federal Rules.

To avoid confusion, do not speak of "admissions against interest." The phrase is misleading because the statement need not be against the declarant's interest at the time it was made, and because it can cause confusion with the next exception, declarations against interest.

Declarations Against Interest

These consist of:

1. A statement;

2. against the pecuniary or proprietary interest of a non-party declarant;
3. who knew it was against his interest at the time he made it; and
4. who is unavailable to testify.

At common law, only money and land were important enough. Statements against the penal interest of the declarant were not admissible. Under Federal Rule 804 (b) (3), declarations against penal interest are admissible, but they require corroboration if offered in a criminal trial to exonerate the accused. In effect this rule applies to state criminal trials as well. *Chambers v. Mississippi*, 410 U.S. 284 (1973). See Federal Rule 804 (a) for a liberal list of what constitutes ''unavailability.''

Dying Declarations

These consist of:
1. A statement;
2. by one who was aware of immediate impending death;
3. who had abandoned all hope of recovery;
4. who in fact later dies;
5. concerning the cause or circumstances of his impending death;
6. offered in a homicide case concerning the death of the declarant;
7. to inculpate or exculpate the accused.

The common law rule is thus restricted. Federal Rule 804 (b) (2), however, extends dying declarations to civil cases and takes away the requirement of abandoning all hope of recovery and the necessity of dying to make the statements admissible. On the other hand, unavailability of the declarant is still required.

Excited Utterances

This exception used to be put in the garbage can of hearsay, *res gestae*. That was once a useful label but now is not nearly precise enough because it contains so many different exceptions and even covers some non-hearsay. Res gestae includes verbal acts, bodily condition, state of mind, excited utterances and present sense impressions. Most trial lawyers now use these separate categories, but when modern argument fails to strike a responsive chord, they can still bring themselves to say, ''It is part of the res gestae, your honor.''

As Irving Younger explains in his lectures at the National Institute for Trial Advocacy, it is easy to recognize excited utterances: They all start with "*My God,*" and all end with an exclamation mark. There are four elements:

1. A statement;
2. prompted by an exciting event;
3. explaining or related to the event;
4. made without opportunity for conscious reflection.

The last element was often said to be "made at or near the event," until the law professor's dream came true in *Cestero v. Ferrara*, 57 N.J. 497, 273 A.2d 761 (1971), and the excited utterance was made in a hospital some time after the accident, as soon as the plaintiff regained consciousness.

Federal Rule 803 (2) is similar, requiring that the statement be made "while the declarant was under the stress of excitement caused by the event or condition."

Present Sense Impressions

Closely related to excited utterances is another exception to the hearsay rule. The leading case is *Houston Oxygen Co. v. Davis*, 139 Tex. 1, 161 S.W.2d 474 (1942). There it was held error to exclude a driver's contemporary description to her passengers of how an overtaking car was being driven—hardly an exciting event. There is a rough parity between this and excited utterances, however. What is lacking in excitement is somewhat compensated for by limiting the time between the event and the description. There are three elements:

1. A statement;
2. describing an event or condition;
3. made while perceiving it or immediately afterwards.

Until Federal Rule 803 (1), *Houston Oxygen* was a distinct minority rule.

Professor Jon R. Waltz argues that the federal rule should have an added safeguard: the opportunity for someone to check the accuracy of the statement immediately after it is made. See Waltz, *Present Sense Impressions and the Residual Exceptions: A New Day for "Great" Hearsay?* LITIGATION, Vol. 2, No. 1 p. 22 (1975).

Bodily Condition

There are four things to keep in mind:

1. Statements of *present* bodily condition are admissible as exceptions to the hearsay rule, no matter to whom made.
2. Involuntary cries, groans and grimaces are circumstan-

tial evidence of bodily condition, and not even hearsay, unless they are feigned (in which case they are not involuntary).

3. Statements of *past* bodily condition (medical history) are admissible if made to a practitioner of the healing arts (doctor, if you prefer), only if consulted for the purpose of treatment. They are only admissible to the extent pertinent to treatment. The majority rule was that such statements were only admissible to ''explain'' the doctor's opinion. A substantial minority, on the other hand, admitted the statements as a complete exception to the hearsay rule.

4. Rule 803 (4) of the Federal Rules of Evidence admits statements made for the *purpose of medical diagnosis or treatment.* This simple phrase makes the rule different from the common law in two important ways: First, the statements need not be made directly to the doctor. Second, the statements need not be made for treatment, meaning that the distinction between treating and non-treating doctors is abolished.

Take a moment to think about what that means. You are not required to call a treating doctor to prove medical history—a non-treating expert can do the job.

State of Mind

Declarations of present state of mind are admissible as an exception to the hearsay rule. There is no difficulty in admitting them when state of mind is an issue in the case. Thus if a person's hostility to the plaintiff is relevant, his statement, ''I hate John Martin,'' is admitted without problem.

Notice that if the individual had said, ''John Martin is a lousy person,'' the statement would not be considered hearsay, if offered to prove the declarant's hostility to him. Why? Because it is *circumstantial* evidence of the declarant's state of mind. Similarly, if, instead of the statement, an act of hostility toward John Martin—such as letting the air out of his tires or throwing a brick through his window—were testified to, this also would be circumstantial evidence of the person's state of mind, and not hearsay.

In other words, non-assertive conduct is not considered hearsay in the state of mind area. Why is that so? Because the actor's deeds point directly to the state of mind, a thing itself in issue. There is no need to construct an implied statement from that circumstantial evidence.

The difficulty with state of mind as an exception to the hearsay rule arises when state of mind is not in issue, but is rather used as circumstantial evidence of some other fact. In the famous case, *Mutual Life Ins. Co. of New York v. Hillmon*, 145 U.S. 285 (1892), a statement—I am going to Crooked Creek—was admissible to prove that the person who said that later went to Crooked Creek. To put it in abstract terms, a declaration of state of mind was admissible to prove that the declarant subsequently acted in conformity with it. In simpler terms, state of mind is admissible to show that someone did what he said he was going to do. Thus state of mind can "look forward" in time.

In *Shepard v. United States*, 290 U.S. 96 (1933), before she died, Mrs. Shepard said, "Dr. Shepard has poisoned me." The statement did not meet the requirements of a dying declaration, and so was offered under the state-of-mind exception. The Supreme Court held that her statement was inadmissible to prove that Dr. Shepard had poisoned his wife. The Court's principal analysis was that declarations of state of mind should not look backwards in time. Perhaps more important is that fact just barely noted in Justice Cardozo's opinion—the statement related not to the actions of the one who spoke, but to someone else.

State-of-mind declarations are admissible when they look backwards in time in wills cases to prove that someone wrote or revoked a will, to show its terms or to identify it. In other cases, backward-looking statements are generally not admitted.

State of mind that looks forward in time is not admissible to show the actions of someone other than the declarant. *People v. Alcalde*, 24 Cal. 2d 177, 148 P.2d 627 (1944) (dissenting opinion). Federal Rule 803 (3) is in conformity with this discussion.

Former Testimony

The hearsay rule is designed to protect the right to cross-examination. There are some situations where that right has already been exercised, and hence they qualify as exceptions to the rule. Ordinarily, former testimony fits this description.

The simplest example is the retrial of a case. Because there is a strong preference for live (*viva voce*, if you like) testimony, the transcript from the first trial is not admissible unless a witness is not available. But if a witness is unavailable, then the former testimony is admissible.

In addition to unavailability, other elements usually listed include a unity of parties and interests and the right to cross-examine.

In some situations these requirements have been stretched rather thin. The leading case is *Travelers Fire Ins. Co. v. Wright*, 322 P.2d 417 (Okla. 1958), where the former testimony of a subsequently unavailable witness—given in the criminal trial against one brother-partner—was admitted in a civil case brought by the other brother-partner concerning the same transaction.

Prior Identification

Early cases tended to admit prior identification only to corroborate in-court identification. *United States v. De Sisto*, 329 F.2d 929 (2d Cir. 1964), however, permitted prior identification to be admitted as an exception to the hearsay rule. First proposed as part of the Federal Rules, then removed by Congress, and finally reinstated, prior identification is admissible under Rule 801 (d) (1) (c). Although it is admissible to prove the truth of the matter asserted, it is considered non-hearsay under the Federal Rules.

Past Recollection Recorded

First distinguish past recollection recorded from present recollection refreshed. Everyone has temporary lapses, which can be overcome with any number of reminders—words, pictures, memos, even odors or other sensory stimuli. When a witness has a lapse and then is reminded of what had been temporarily difficult to recall, that is called present recollection refreshed. The things used to refresh recollection are not hearsay, because they are not offered into evidence to prove their truth. (Indeed, they need not be offered into evidence at all, and if offered may be objected to as hearsay.)

Past recollection recorded is different. For it you need:

1. A writing (a term of art—any system of recording will do);
2. made at or near the event (close to the time it occurred or was perceived);
3. by someone with first-hand knowledge (by the person, at his direction, or adopted by him at the time);
4. who has no present recollection (the writing must first be used in an effort to refresh recollection);

5. but who can give a "voucher for correctness" (that is, testify that the writing was accurate when made).

Under Federal Rule 803 (5), the second element is relaxed, so that the writing need only be made "while the matter was fresh in his memory," and it may be read into evidence but not received as an exhibit unless it is offered by the opponent.

This latter limitation, not followed in every jurisdiction, is to prevent a witness from claiming his recollection was not refreshed in an effort to get a document into evidence that the jury may look at later, heightening its impact over other testimony.

Business Records

The predecessor to the business records exception was the shop book rule, which was really just an adaptation of past recollection recorded.

Business records statutes, enacted in virtually every jurisdiction, admit properly authenticated business records (usually by the custodian of the records) as an exception to the hearsay rule. To be admissible under the typical statute, in addition to being made at or near the event, the record must be made in the ordinary course of business and it must be in the ordinary course of business to make the record. These two requirements sound redundant, but they are not. "Made in the ordinary course of business" relates to how and when the record was made. "In the ordinary course of business to make the record" means that the record must relate to the business conducted.

Other objections, including the lack of first-hand knowledge on the part of the one who made the record, go to the weight, not the admissibility of the record.

There are some important cases in the interpretation of the business records statutes. The first is *Johnson v. Lutz,* 253 N.Y. 124, 170 N.E. 517 (1930). In that case, a police report which obviously qualified as a business record was not admissible to prove the truth of statements of bystanders to the policeman who was investigating an accident. The situation was different from that impliedly contemplated by the statute because the bystanders had no "business duty" to report to the policeman. There was, in effect, hearsay within hearsay, and the business record was competent to cure the overall hearsay problem of the business record, but not the inner hearsay in the police report, for which there was no exception.

This analysis explains the otherwise apparently inconsistent

146

case, *Kelly v. Wasserman*, 5 N.Y.2d 425, 158 N.E.2d 241 (1959), where the business record was a welfare worker's report. It contained a statement made to the welfare worker that had not been made under any business duty, but which amounted to an admission. Since there was a separate exception for the "inner" hearsay, the report was held admissible.

The third important case is *Palmer v. Hoffman*, 318 U.S. 109 (1943), which held that a business record (a railroad's accident investigation report) made with a view toward litigation was inadmissible. *Palmer v. Hoffman* is generally followed, but statements made with a view toward litigation are often admitted if there are strong indications of reliability. *Yates v. Bair Transp. Inc.*, 249 F. Supp. 681 (S.D.N.Y. 1965).

Dean Frank T. Read analyzes Federal Rule 803(6) as following the doctrines of both *Johnson v. Lutz* and *Palmer v. Hoffman* in *The Business Records Exception: Something Less Than Revolutionary*, LITIGATION, Vol. 2, No. 1, p. 25 (1975).

Learned Treatises

At common law, an expert witness could be impeached with learned treatises—but only as if they were prior inconsistent statements. In other words, the witness had to rely on the treatise in forming his or her opinion, or at least acknowledge that it was authoritative in the field. Like prior inconsistent statements, the contents of learned treatises were only admissible to impeach, not to prove the truth of their contents.

In practice, impeaching experts with learned treatises proved difficult since experts would often refuse to concede that even very standard works were authoritative.

Federal Rule 803(18) makes learned treatises admissible as an exception to the hearsay rule. They may be established as authoritative by the witness being impeached, by some other witness, or by judicial notice. They are admissible not only to impeach, but also to support direct examination. Like past recollection recorded under the Federal Rules, however, they may not be received as exhibits. Furthermore, they are only admissible to the extent called to the attention of a witness on cross-examination or relied upon on direct examination. This means that even though you may authenticate a treatise by judicial notice, an expert witness is still required to make it admissible.

Other exceptions to the hearsay rule, such as family pedigree, ancient documents, and even ancient tombstone markings can be important as well as the dozen discussed above. Usually they are known sufficiently in advance of trial to permit more leisurely consideration. That is also the reason why the new "catchall" exceptions in Rules 803(24) and 804(b)(5) have more bark than bite.

It will not do to first suggest in the middle of trial that one of the "catchall" exceptions will work if some other foundation fails. The "catchall" exceptions each require advance notice of intention to use the statement, including the content of the statement and the name and address of the declarant.

CHAPTER 14

Learned Treatises

The witness had more courtroom experience than the cross-examiner, and it showed.

He was a medical examiner—a coroner—with a national reputation among pathologists and law enforcement officials. Direct examination had been vivid—and unsettling. The witness had testified in a criminal trial about the cause of a young woman's death. He said his autopsy showed she was severely beaten, and the blows to her head so traumatized her brain that it started to swell. The pressure inside her head became so great that it damaged her brain stem and caused her to stop breathing.

Under the circumstances, the cross-examiner thought it would be a good idea to talk about something other than the trauma to the victim's head. It was his theory that the woman had drunk enough alcohol to accomplish chemically what the witness said was done by violence.

Imagine, then, the cross-examiner's shock as the cross-examination started:

Q: Doctor, I would like to ask you some questions about alcohol. You had a blood alcohol test performed on Alicia Baxter, correct?

A: That's true, counsel, but I really cannot tell you much about alcohol, because I am not a toxicologist.

Q: You are a medical doctor, are you not?

A: Yes.

Q: And you are a pathologist?

A: Yes, but toxicology—the study of how some substances

have a toxic effect on humans—is a separate field of specialization. Of course I studied about alcohol in medical school, but detailed questions about the effect of alcohol are outside my field.

[The defense had its own expert that it would call in another day or so. But it made all the difference whether this witness (the official medical examiner, who had made such a dramatic impression on the jury) could be cross-examined effectively. Understandably, the cross-examiner persisted, but it did not do any good. The thrust of every telling question was first blunted by a gentle impression that the witness thought the cross-examiner was mistaken, followed by the observation that he was sorry he could not be more helpful, but he was not a toxicologist, and his opinion that in any event, Alicia Baxter was beaten to death. That is when the cross-examiner decided to play his last card, and the witness threw down his trump on top of it.]

Q: Tell us, please, are you familiar with Dr. Maurice Victor's article, *The Effects of Alcohol on the Human Nervous System?*

A: Counsel, I told you I am not a toxicologist. I have heard of Dr. Victor, of course, but I am not familiar with that article.

Q: Well, Doctor, even though you are not familiar with it, do you recognize that article to be authoritative on the subject of the effects of alcohol?

A: Certainly not.

[The doctor, who was sure he had cut off any further discussion of alcohol, was a little surprised when the lawyer continued.]

Q: Well, since you are not familiar with Dr. Victor's article, perhaps you'd like to take a look at it now. I am handing it to you, and I would appreciate it if you would turn to page 32.

State's Attorney: Objection, your honor. This is entirely improper. The witness has not even recognized this article—wherever it came from—as authoritative, much less said that he relied on it in forming his opinion.

[That was what *both* the witness and the state's attorney thought was the law. But it was their turn to be shocked when the defense lawyer took out his copy of the rules of evidence and replied.]

Defense Counsel: If I may be heard, your honor. Under the new rules of evidence, Rule 803(18), the witness does not have to recognize a learned treatise or article as being authoritative to be cross-examined on it. We will do that through another witness. The defense is going to call its own expert in this case. We already know that *he* regards Dr. Victor's article as authoritative—as do many others. I am asking permission to cross-examine this witness about the article, subject to our promise to connect up later.

The Court: Objection overruled. Counsel, you may proceed.

And now we will leave the good doctor, caught in the very trap of legal complexities he had intended for the cross-examiner. He had been right about what used to be the law. Learned treatises were (except in Alabama, Kansas, and Wisconsin) not admissible as exceptions to the hearsay rule. They were admissible only to impeach expert witnesses, and only under limited circumstances. To use a learned treatise in cross-examination, the expert first had to admit he had relied on it in formulating his opinion, or in some jurisdictions, acknowledge that it was authoritative in the field.

That made escape easy. All the expert had to do was deny that the treatise was authoritative, and then it could not be used in cross-examination. Understandably, a lecture on the law of impeachment became a regular part of preparing any expert witness to testify.

To counteract disingenuous testimony that books and articles were not authoritative, lawyers had to devise methods that would push witnesses into admitting during deposition that at least some writings were recognized in the field:

Q: Doctor, after all that schooling—four years of college, four years of medical school, then internship and residency—you probably never have to look at another book again.

A: (Sensing it would be a mistake to admit he does not keep current) No. What do you mean? Of course I have to look at books.

Q: You mean a medical expert of your stature has to consult the professional literature to keep current?

A: Certainly.

Q: Well, Doctor, could you tell me some of the books and articles that have crossed your desk in the past year or so?

Under Federal Rule 803(18), it is no longer necessary to get concessions like that in advance of trial (but it still can help). Since the Federal Rules became effective in 1975, a number of states have adopted their own versions. Even though they have been around for a long time, some rules continue to hold surprises. The rule on learned treatises is one of them:

> To the extent called to the attention of an expert witness upon cross-examination or relied upon by him in direct examination, statements contained in published treatises, periodicals, or pamphlets on a subject of history, medicine, or other science or art, established as a reliable authority by the testimony or admission of the witness or by other expert testimony or by judicial notice [are exceptions to the hearsay rule]. If admitted, the statements may be read into evidence but may not be received as exhibits.

Take just a moment and skim through that rule again. Notice that nearly everything in it (except a short definition of learned treatises that requires publication) is procedural. It explains how the treatise can be used on direct and cross-examination. It lists three ways the treatise can be authenticated. It says it can be read to the jury but not received as an exhibit.

So what?

Just this. The major change brought by Rule 803(18) is not that learned treatises are suddenly admissible for their truth (one of Wigmore's campaigns), but rather how they can be used in trial. Because the drafters were intent on economy of words, they took the rules about confrontation and reliance (which would have fit nicely in Article 6, Witnesses) and authentication by an expert (which might have gone in either Article 6, or Article 7, Experts) and put them in an exception to the hearsay rule. That is no great sin against those who are regulars in the courtroom. They can be expected to know the rule, or at least know where to find it. But for those who only occasionally get to court, it can be hard to find the rule in the heat of battle.

The location of Rule 803(18) has done more than make the rules of confrontation and authentication hard to find. It has also influenced our perception of what the rule does. Because it is an exception to the hearsay rule, a number of writers and analysts have assumed that the hearsay exception was the most important part of the rule. They have paid more attention to learned treatises being admissible for their truth than to the flexibility given to direct and cross-examiners.

Normally it does not make much difference that learned writings are a hearsay exception under the Federal Rules. That is because Rule 803(18) only makes them admissible to the extent they are called to the attention of the expert on cross-examination or relied on by him on direct. In other words, under the Federal Rules, a learned treatise is admissible to corroborate and contradict expert witnesses who take the stand, not supplement or serve as a substitute for them.

Put it another way. On direct examination the book or article is treated as if it were an admissible prior consistent statement. It reinforces what was covered on direct. It is only admissible if it was relied on by the witness in formulating his opinion. On cross-examination, on the other hand, the learned treatise need not be relied on, but it must be specifically brought to the witness's attention.

Confrontation is different from authentication. There are three ways to establish that the writing is authoritative: through the statement of the witness on direct or cross-examination, through the testimony of some other expert witness, or by judicial notice.

Finally, the only part of the writing that is admissible is what is actually read into evidence. The writing itself is not received as an exhibit. This, by the way, does not excuse you from offering into evidence what has been read to the jury. See *Maggapinto v. Reichman*, 481 F.Supp. 547, 550 (E. D.Pa. 1979), which says that a formal offer is still required.

The idea behind 803(18) was to make the direct and cross-examination of experts more flexible, avoid limiting instructions that the jury would not understand (the principal effect of making learned writings admissible for their truth), but not dispense with expert witnesses. No matter how the writing is *authenticated*—by this witness, another witness, or judicial notice—there still must be a witness on the stand who relied on the book in forming direct testimony or who is confronted with it on cross-examination. No witness, no book.

Now the question is how to use learned treatises effectively.

Start with direct examination. One advantage of the learned treatise exception is that it lets the witness show—before any attack has been made—that his opinion is supported by the major writers in the field. This is how it works:

Q: Doctor, are you alone in this position, or are there any others in the field who agree with you?

A: As a matter of fact, in the past two years there have been five important studies that support this conclusion. The first was reported in the *New England Journal of Medicine*.

Q: Is that the article I asked you to bring with you today?
A: Yes.

Then you have the witness read the pertinent part into the record. The result is you are able to support your expert witness before he is ever attacked. Contrast that with the rule about prior consistent statements: not admissible until a cross-examiner suggests the testimony on the stand is a recent fabrication. Rule 803(18) lets you multiply the effect of an expert's direct examination without multiplying witnesses.

But wait a minute. Is it permissible to offer treatises that the witness found *after* he formed his opinion? Yes. The rule says learned treatises are admissible to the extent "relied upon by him in direct examination." It does not say "relied upon by him in forming his initial opinion." When a witness reads the professional literature and it corroborates an opinion he has already reached, it strengthens his opinion. So it is fair to say that expert literature which has been read in preparation for testimony was relied upon by the expert in direct examination.

Then comes cross-examination. Usually it is dangerous to try to meet an expert on his own grounds. But impeaching with a learned treatise—while surely not risk free—is more attractive than taking the expert on in a free-form give and take. If you have done your homework right, the treatise helps keep your attack within manageable grounds.

If it is going to work, there are some rules to follow:

- Pick something understandable. Most professional writing is nearly indecipherable by the layman. Because you are using it to attack the witness, it hardly makes sense to have the witness translate the writing into understandable English. That would send the message that, despite the attack, you rely on this individual to explain complex ideas to the jury. If you must pick a passage that is hard to understand, you do the translation, forcing the witness to agree. But since each explanation is an additional opportunity for the witness to quibble, you are better off picking something that is easy to understand to begin with.

- Set it up properly. The first step is to create the necessary contrast. Here is where many lawyers make a mistake by having the witness repeat his direct examination several times and in various ways, to dramatize the difference between it and what is in the book.

The problem with that is it drives home the witness's testimony, not the learned treatise. So instead, frame your set-up questions from the book, not the witness's direct examination. Use the book's very words, if you can. Write them in your notes instead of picking up the book at the start. There is no sense in telegraphing your punch unless you deliberately want a mild impeachment.

- Do not be unfairly selective. If you take something out of context so that its meaning is changed, you will be exposed. Under Rule 106, the Rule of Completeness, the missing context can be read into evidence simultaneously with the part you offered. The net effect will be to impeach *your* credibility.

- Read the treatise out loud to the witness so the judge and jury can hear it. The rule requires that you confront the witness with the writing. It does not require that the witness read the treatise to the jury (he will do a bad job). It does not require that he first be given a chance to read it silently to himself (he will dream up some reason why it does not apply in this case). It does not require that you ask him whether he agrees with it (he will say no). It only requires confrontation, and you can do that best yourself.

Perhaps the most effective way to confront is to give a copy of the treatise to the witness and have him follow along as you read out loud. When you have finished, ask the question, "Did I read that correctly?" That is the one question to which you know he must answer yes.

A word of warning. Be sure you can pronounce every word properly. You do not want the witness to correct your reading. When the prisoner tells the hangman how to tie the knot, it makes you wonder if there will be an execution.

- Pick something that matters. If you only impeach the witness on some peripheral point, no one will be fooled but you.

- Pick unimpeachable treatises. The treatise is an exception to the hearsay rule (I know you already know that, but watch what happens). That means the author is a hearsay declarant. That means that when the treatise is offered in evidence, the author's credibility can be attacked just as if he had testified as a witness. Rule 806,

Federal Rules of Evidence, another rule that still holds some surprises.

Just what does that mean? Reputation for truth is at issue, and if the author is in bad professional repute, that is admissible. Bias and prejudice are relevant, and if the article was written by someone who had an ax to grind, it is admissible, too. Inconsistencies are relevant, and Rule 806 specifically abolishes any requirement of confrontation for hearsay declarants. "Evidence of a statement or conduct by the declarant at any time, inconsistent with his hearsay statement, is not subject to any requirement that he may have been afforded an opportunity to deny or explain."

Take special note of the words, "at any time." With hearsay exceptions, it does not matter whether the inconsistent statement was made before or after the statement being attacked. Either one can be used. If the witness is impeached with the second edition of a book and the third edition is inconsistent, it is admissible. When your opponent unleashes an unfair attack with a spurious learned treatise, you are not limited to redirect examination in trying to draw the poison.

CHAPTER 15

The Cleveland Exception to the Hearsay Rule

Trial lawyers know that two of the three most popular specific evidentiary objections are not even taught in law school. If you were inclined to do a nationwide study to determine the three most common specific objections (not counting, of course, the simple general objection), here are the results you would probably get:

1. Leading;
2. Asked and answered;
3. He's badgering the witness.

Not a very impressive array. Of this group, only leading is taught in law schools with any regularity. The other two are left for what may be the ultimate clinical-legal course, the practice of law.

But on the other hand, it is not a very dangerous omission, either. The intellectual challenge offered by "asked and answered" and "badgering the witness" can usually be overcome in about a minute of real study.

The results are, however, symptomatic of a more serious problem.

Make another nationwide survey. This time question litigators, those with courtroom experience ranging from one to thirty or forty years. Ask them just two questions:

1. Where did you really learn evidence?
2. In what subject do you feel most deficient as a trial lawyer?

Do you know what answers you would most frequently receive? They would seem strangely inconsistent:

1. I did not really learn what evidence was all about until I started trying cases. I learned it in the courtroom.
2. Of all the subjects I use the most, I feel weakest in evidence.

Answers like those ought to give legal educators some pause, and they do. Within the past decade there has been a tremendous increase in intellectually solid trial advocacy and evidence courses that are designed actually to teach some of the practical skills needed in making and meeting objections in trial.

But learning evidence does not end with law school.

The education in evidence that comes from trying cases will continue no matter what is done in formal courses, during or after law school.

In the supercharged pressure of trial, objections are made, met and ruled upon, often without the opportunity for legal research of any sort by any of the participants—including the judge.

This system has produced its own customary law—a body of working rules, some of which are marvelously out of step with any statute, case or published rule of court.

A good number of these "rules" of evidence are fortunately confined to just one area. Take for example, the inexplicably bizarre Maryland practice concerning documents. If your opponent uses a document—no matter how—and you ask to see it, it can automatically be introduced into evidence.

There are other aberrant "rules," however, that have gained wider currency. In fact, the customary law of erroneous evidence rules is, in a sense, like the Federal Rules of Evidence. Although not expressly adopted in many states, they seem to be persuasive authority in most.

The purpose of this discussion is not to stamp out these deviancies. Like weeds, if they are cut off at the ground, they may grow back even stronger.

On the other hand, good trial lawyers know that knowledge is power, and that given the right arguments, they can sometimes overcome the forces of darkness. What follows are some typical evidentiary mistakes to which lawyers are prone, and which judges are likely to accept. Of the list of perhaps hundreds of potential candidates, I have picked only a handful. If you conducted yet a third survey, they might not even turn out to be the most common. But they are among my favorites.

The Document Speaks for Itself

The setting could be nearly any trial in which a document is offered in evidence. To keep the problem uncluttered, let us assume a simple commercial case. At issue is whether Aaron Stryker, president of the defendant corporation, agreed to supply the plaintiff, Michael Herman, with 5,000 cubic yards of concrete mix. The market price has risen, and the plaintiff is asking for $100,000 in damages—the difference between what he had to pay for the concrete mix he finally was able to obtain and what he says the defendant promised to charge.

Hoping for a sympathetic ear in a time of crushing inflation, the defendant demanded a jury trial.

To prove the disputed contract, the plaintiff offers the original letters he and the defendant's president exchanged two years ago. Going through the appropriate steps, plaintiff's lawyer has them marked, identified and authenticated before offering them into evidence. Recognizing the letters are verbal acts of legal significance—and thus not subject to hearsay rule—the trial judge overrules the defendant's objections to their admissibility.

Then the plaintiff picks up Plaintiff's Exhibit Number 5. It is a three-page letter, signed by Aaron Stryker (the president of the defendant corporation) and already in evidence. Of the entire letter, only the date, the signature and one sentence are really important. That sentence reads as follows:

> We agree, then, to supply you with 5,000 yards of #3 commercial concrete mix, delivered to your Hopewell construction site during the month of May, 1976, for a total cost of $112,118.50.

The plaintiff's lawyer would like this sentence read to the jury, and the following exchange takes place:

PLAINTIFF'S COUNSEL: Your honor, I request permission to have the witness read to the jury from Plaintiff's Exhibit 5.
DEFENSE COUNSEL: Objection, your honor, the document speaks for itself.
THE COURT: Sustained.

What has happened? The plaintiff's lawyer, well schooled in the theory of evidence (but not the local lore) is at first confused.

Could he have forgotten something? Did he leave out some essential part of the foundation? But then he remembers the document has already been admitted. By now, objections to the foundation have been waived. With some composure, then, he rises to clarify things.

PLAINTIFF'S COUNSEL: Your honor, if I may be heard for a moment. Plaintiff's Exhibit Number 5 has already been admitted into evidence. It is the letter of October 12, 1976, from Mr. Stryker—the defendant's president—to the plaintiff, Mr. Herman. It is the letter in which the details of the agreement are spelled out.

THE COURT: I understand that counsel, and I have sustained the defendant's objection.

PLAINTIFF'S COUNSEL: Well, since the letter is in evidence, your honor, I request permission to have a portion of it read to the jury.

DEFENSE COUNSEL: Your honor, we stand by our objection; the document speaks for itself.

THE COURT: Sustained. Plaintiff's counsel, proceed with the direct examination of this witness.

Ruffled but not shaken, plaintiff's counsel decides he has pushed the judge enough, so he goes on to other matters.

Plaintiffs counsel lost that skirmish, but was determined not to lose the battle. So after the court recessed for the day, he went to the county law library to see if he could figure out some way to get that letter before the jury.

Initially he was discouraged, since no index he consulted had any reference to documents speaking for themselves.

On the other hand, he did discover that when documents have been admitted into evidence, the trial court has discretion to permit all or part of them read to the jury.

Would he be able to convince an appellate court that the trial judge abused his discretion in refusing to permit part of the document read to the jury? Not likely, since the document was in evidence it could be given to the jury for their examination, referred to during final argument and taken by the jury to the deliberation room at the end of the trial.

Thus, from a practical standpoint, he realized it would be hard to show real prejudice from the judge's ruling.

Still, it would help to be able to read that sentence to the jury now. Was there some way he could convince the judge to reverse his ruling? When he came across the Best Evidence Rule in *McCormick on Evidence*, §§ 229–243 (2d ed. 1972), he formulated a plan.

The next morning he rose to address the court before the jury was brought in.

PLAINTIFF'S COUNSEL: Your honor, as you will recall, yesterday I asked for permission to have a portion of a lengthy document read to the jury, and the defendant objected on the grounds that the document speaks for itself. I confess that I did not meet that objection squarely when I attempted to respond to it, and I would like permission to do so now.

There is no question that you have discretion to permit any document admitted in evidence read to the jury. *Poole v. Life & Cas. Ins. Co. of Tenn.*, 47 Ala. App. 453, 256 So.2d 193 (1971).

The defendant's objection that the document speaks for itself is a misunderstanding of the Best Evidence Rule. That rule forbids secondary evidence to prove the contents of a document unless the original is accounted for. But, your honor, we *have* accounted for the original—we introduced it into evidence.

If I had asked Mr. Herman to *interpret* the letter, that might present some Best Evidence problem, as well as a Parol Evidence Rule problem. But I did not ask him to do that. I asked him to read part of it.

When Mr. Herman reads from this letter, he is not violating the Best Evidence Rule, he is just saving all of us time, letting the jury hear what is pertinent in that letter without forcing them to wade through the entire thing.

Finally, your honor, your power to permit the witness to read the document is implicit in Rule 106 of the *Federal Rules of Evidence*, which is the Rule of Completeness. If the defendant wants any other part of the letter read to the jury, he is welcome to do it.

THE COURT: Defense counsel, the plaintiff's position seems to make sense. Do you have any authority for your objection?

DEFENSE COUNSEL: Why, uh, your honor, no I don't have any cases, but I have always heard that the, uh document speaks for itself, and I. . . .

THE COURT: I'll permit you to read that letter. Bring in the jury.

161

That's Not the Best Evidence

Does it happen?

Every day.

Perhaps the most delightful instance was when the objection was made in response to the offer of a photograph of a locomotive.

The more usual case goes something like this:

DEFENSE COUNSEL: Tell us, please, what the weather was like on December 19, the day of the accident.

PLAINTIFF'S COUNSEL: Objection, your honor. If counsel wants to prove what the weather was like, he should offer the weather report. The witness's recollection is not the Best Evidence.

The notion that the Best Evidence Rule requires the best possible evidence is an idea at which (given the name of the rule) only lawyers could laugh. That is why scholars—including the drafters of the *Federal Rules of Evidence*—have been at such pains to try to change the name of the rule. McCormick calls it "The requirement of the Production of the Original Writing," *McCormick on Evidence* 559 (2d ed. 1972), while Rule 1002 of the *Federal Rules of Evidence* is entitled "Requirement of Original."

The difficulty is, the early writers *did* assert that producing the "best evidence" was a general requirement, see *McCormick on Evidence* 559–560 (2d ed. 1972), and some modern cases follow that notion. *Padgett v. Brezner*, 359 S.W.2d 416 (Mo. App. 1962).

In the great majority of jurisdictions, however, the Best Evidence Rule simply means that to *prove the contents of a document,* you must produce the original or give a satisfactory explanation of why you cannot.

It means that when a witness has firsthand knowledge of something, he can testify to that fact—even though there is also some document containing that information.

A good example is *Herzig v. Swift & Co.*, 146 F.2d 444 (2d Cir. 1945). In that case it was held reversible error to refuse a witness permission to testify to partnership earnings of which he had firsthand knowledge, even though there were business records also containing the information. The point is the witness was not going to testify to what he read in the business records, but give his firsthand knowledge. If, on the other hand, his information had come from the books, then the Best Evidence Rule would have been violated.

162

The test, in other words, is not whether the information happens to be *in* a document, but whether it comes *from* the document. In our hypothetical situation, it does not matter that there is a weather report. So long as the witness is testifying from his own knowledge—and not from having read the weather report—there is no violation of the Best Evidence Rule.

Objection, Your Honor, That's Non-Responsive

Now we have another suppositious case. Robert Jennings brings an action against John Homer for injuries he received in an altercation during half-time while the two were watching the Super Bowl on television. Jennings was a guest of Homer, and the two former friends were arguing about the relative merits of various professional quarterbacks when the fight started.

Counsel for the plaintiff, Jennings, has called an eyewitness, Ms. Carol Simmons, to testify how the fight began:

> PLAINTIFF'S COUNSEL: Now then, Ms. Simmons, where were you when the half-time program started?
>
> MS. SIMMONS: Well, I saw John Homer just pick up a heavy glass ash tray full of cigar butts and turn it upside down over Bob Jennings's head.
>
> DEFENSE COUNSEL: Objection, your honor, that's non-responsive. I move to strike the response, and I request that you instruct the witness to answer only the questions that are asked.
>
> THE COURT: The objection is sustained. The jury is instructed to disregard the witness's last answer. Ms. Simmons, you are not the lawyer in this case. You are to answer only the questions put to you and not volunteer any additional information. Is that clear?

Now what could be wrong with this? The witness has certainly been non-responsive. That is a basis for objecting, is it not?

It is. But the objection of non-responsiveness may only be made by the one who asks the questions, not the opponent. See *Hester v. Goldsbury*, 64 Ill. App.2d 66, 212 N.E.2d 316 (1965). Why should this be so?

The lawyer asking the questions is entitled to develop the information he wants, when he wants. Non-responsive answers interfere with that right.

Probably the greatest value of the objection is in controlling hostile witnesses on direct or cross-examination, who might otherwise use every question as an excuse to argue their points to the jury.

Its use is not limited to hostile witnesses. It is available in any situation—but only to the one who is asking the questions.

What about the opponent? Will non-responsiveness do nothing for the other side who is trying to keep out inadmissible evidence?

While the opponent does not have the objection of non-responsiveness as such, a non-responsive answer does do something. Recall that ordinarily an objection must be made as soon as the grounds for it are reasonably apparent. That usually means an objection must be asserted when the question is asked and before the answer is given. Otherwise the objection is waived. *Cheffer v. Eagle Discount Stamp Co.*, 348 Mo. 1023, 156 S.W.2d 591 (1941).

When an answer to a proper question is non-responsive, it is not apparent whether there are grounds for an objection until *after* the answer is given. That means that a non-responsive answer permits what you may think of as an after-acquired objection. If there are grounds for objecting to an answer (other than non-responsiveness) which did not appear when the question was asked, the opponent may assert them *after* the answer.

Even though this is a sensible enough rule, habitual non-responsiveness does invade a legitimate interest of the opponent—that is, the one who did not ask the question. The rules of evidence contemplate screening testimony *before* it comes. Thus a judge should be free to caution a witness to answer responsively in the future, even though his admissible (but non-responsive) answer is permitted to stand.

But many judges and lawyers do not know these are the rules. Instead, they think either party may have an answer stricken because it is non-responsive.

With that in mind, let us return to the hypothetical *Jennings* case. This time, change it a little. The same question is asked, but the answer is different.

> PLAINTIFF'S COUNSEL: Now, then, Ms. Simmons, where were you when the half-time program started?
> Ms. SIMMONS: Well, I heard Maggie Conlon tell me that John Homer dumped an ash tray full of cigar butts over Bob Jennings's head.

The answer is obviously hearsay. Because it is non-responsive, the defense counsel would be permitted to make his hearsay objection after the answer, and it would not have been waived.

Take the case a little further. This time the question and answer are the same as they were at the beginning:

PLAINTIFF'S COUNSEL: Now, then, Ms. Simmons, where were you when the half-time program started?

Ms. SIMMONS: Well, I saw John Homer just pick up a heavy glass ash tray full of cigar butts and turn it upside down over Bob Jennings's head.

DEFENSE COUNSEL: Objection, your honor, that's non-responsive. I move to strike the response, and I request that you instruct the witness to answer only the questions that are asked.

The court is about to rule on the objection, and the plaintiff's counsel has just a few seconds to respond. Assume that he—unlike many others—knows that the defendant is not permitted to make the objection of non-responsiveness. Should he tell that to the court? Assume that if he does the court will rule correctly and allow the answer to stand.

What would happen?

The jury would hear the answer and that would be an end to it.

But suppose he makes no response.

Naturally, the court tells the jury to disregard the answer. Then the plaintiff's counsel continues:

PLAINTIFF'S COUNSEL: I'm sorry, Ms. Simmons, perhaps I did not make myself clear. I asked where you were when half-time started during the telecast of the Super Bowl.

Ms. SIMMONS: Oh, I was right there, in the living room with John Homer, Bob Jennings and Maggie Conlon.

PLAINTIFF'S COUNSEL: Were you able to see what happened?

Ms. SIMMONS: Everything.

PLAINTIFF'S COUNSEL: Tell us what you saw, please.

Ms. SIMMONS: Well, I saw John Homer just pick up a heavy glass ash tray—it must have weighed four or five pounds, and it was full of smelly cigar butts—and turn it upside down over Bob Jennings's head.

Now what has happened? The answer was responsive and it is admitted. The difference is that this time the jury has heard the information twice.

Why is it not improperly repetitious?

Because the first time they heard it, it did not count. The judge said so himself.

Without question, the jury is more likely to remember the testimony. Furthermore, they may even resent the first objection, sensing it was just some sort of lawyer's technicality, since when the questions were changed just slightly, the answer was permitted to stand.

What is the lesson in all of this? If your opponent knows what he or she is doing, you should not object to an answer to your opponent's question just because it is non-responsive. You do not want to risk the chance that the judge will make a mistake and rule in your favor.

It's Not Offered for Its Truth, Your Honor

This time assume a criminal case, a crime of passion. Like most such instances, it is essentially simple. Last February 11, Linda Mosely, a 27-year-old married woman, was found stabbed to death in her home. Her husband, William Mosely, is on trial for murder.

The prosecutor has a letter in his file. It was written by the victim to her mother, Mrs. Clara Zimmerman. It was sent just three weeks before Mrs. Mosely died. Here is the pertinent part of that letter:

Bill has started drinking again, and that really worries me. He gets so violent, I fear for my safety.

After calling Mrs. Zimmerman, the victim's mother, to the stand, the prosecutor has this letter marked for identification and proceeds.

PROSECUTOR: Mrs. Zimmerman, I am showing you what is marked Prosecution Exhibit 7 for identification. Are you able to recognize it?

MRS. ZIMMERMAN: Yes, I am.

PROSECUTOR: Are you familiar with the handwriting on this letter?

MRS. ZIMMERMAN: Yes, it was my daughter's.

PROSECUTOR: How do you know that?

MRS. ZIMMERMAN: Linda wrote to me at least once a month ever since she left home. Ever since she was 17.

PROSECUTOR: Is there any question, Mrs. Zimmerman, whether that is your daughter's—Linda Mosely's—handwriting?

MRS. ZIMMERMAN: None at all.

PROSECUTOR: Now, then, Mrs. Zimmerman, would you tell the judge and jury whether you have seen Prosecution Exhibit 7—this letter—before?

MRS. ZIMMERMAN: Yes. I got it in the mail at the end of January; just about two-and-one-half weeks before Linda died.

PROSECUTOR: (Giving copy of letter to defense counsel and original to judge) Your honor, the state offers Prosecution Exhibit 7 for identification into evidence.

DEFENSE COUNSEL: Your honor, may we approach the bench?

THE COURT: Certainly.

DEFENSE COUNSEL: (At the bench) Your honor, the defense objects to this on the basis of hearsay.

PROSECUTOR: But your honor, this is not hearsay. We are not offering this to prove the truth of the matter asserted.

DEFENSE COUNSEL: We think it is hearsay, your honor.

THE COURT: I am going to admit the exhibit.

DEFENSE COUNSEL: May we have a limiting instruction, your honor?

THE COURT: You may.

There it is. Other than missing the objection altogether, this is probably the most frequently encountered hearsay problem. To sort it out properly, we must start at the beginning.

The more formal definition of hearsay is evidence that depends for its probative value on the credibility of an out-of-court declarant. Decently accurate, that definition is difficult to use in trials. There is a simpler definition which breaks down into two elements: Hearsay is an out-of-court declaration, offered to prove the truth of the matter asserted.

Notice the two elements:

1. Out-of-court declaration.
2. Offered to prove the truth of the matter asserted.

Actually, it can be made even simpler and still be as accurate, so long as you remember that statement means any kind of assertion:

1. An out-of-court statement.
2. Offered to prove its truth.

Look at the implied thrust of the prosecutor's reply to the defendant's objection. He said he was not offering the letter to prove its truth. What he was saying was shorthand for this:

For hearsay, your honor, two elements are required. First, an out-of-court statement. We admit this letter satisfies that requirement. But another element is required. The statement must be offered to prove its truth. We are not offering it to prove its truth. That means the hearsay rule cannot keep it out of evidence.

It has a seductive appeal, but it is all wrong.

Why?

If this letter is not being offered to prove that William Mosely started drinking again and Linda Mosely was in fear for her safety, then what *does* it prove?

Merely saying that an out-of-court declaration is not offered to prove the truth of the matter asserted does not make it admissible. The non-hearsay purpose must be relevant to some issue in the trial.

Very well. The letter is hearsay. Let us return to the trial and give the defense counsel another chance.

DEFENSE COUNSEL: (After hearing the prosecutor's response that the letter is not offered to prove its truth) Your honor, we must challenge that offer. If this letter is not being offered to prove the truth of what it says, then we fail to see its relevance to this case.

PROSECUTOR: That's easy, your honor. This goes to show the state of mind of the declarant.

DEFENSE COUNSEL: That does not mean it is not hearsay, your honor.

PROSECUTOR: Then, if it is hearsay, it falls within the state of mind exception to the hearsay rule.

DEFENSE COUNSEL: Do I understand the state to be offering only the statements that Mrs. Mosely was worried and feared for her safety, without reference to Bill Mosely's alleged drinking and violence?

PROSECUTOR: No, your honor. The other statements are necessary to explain her state of mind.

THE COURT: I am going to admit the exhibit.

DEFENSE COUNSEL: May we have a limiting instruction?

THE COURT: Certainly.

What was accomplished?

Nothing.

The argument was longer, and the prosecutor responded that the letter fits the state of mind exception. The limiting instruction does not help the defendant. In fact, it will probably make things worse, underscoring the damaging information.

But the defense counsel still missed the point. The victim's state of mind is not an issue in the case. Thus the *Mosely* trial parallels a leading California case, *People v. Talle,* 111 Cal. App. 2d 650, 245 P.2d 633 (1952). There, the murder victim prepared a statement that was to be given to the District Attorney if anything happened to her. Naturally, the statement implicated the accused. Admitted on the theory that it showed the victim's state of mind, the case was reversed on appeal because the victim's state of mind simply was not an issue in the case.

Of course, there are times when the victim's state of mind may be relevant. One example comes from the famous case, *Shepard v. United States,* 290 U.S. 96 (1933). In that case the defendant claimed that his wife had committed suicide. At issue was the admissibility of her statement (which did not qualify as a dying declaration) that ''Dr. Shepard has poisoned me.''

The prosecutor argued to the jury that the statement showed Dr. Shepard's actions. In other words, he used it to prove its truth. The Supreme Court reversed the conviction, but not without noticing that the statement was admissible for the limited purpose of showing that Mrs. Shepard did not intend to take her own life.

Our hypothetical *Mosely* case, however, has nothing like that in it. It follows, then, that Mrs. Mosely's state of mind is not an issue, and the letter is not admissible. Saying that an out-of-court statement is not offered to prove its truth does not make it so. An out-of-court statement must be relevant to some issue in the case before it can be admitted as non-hearsay or as an exception to the hearsay rule.

But Your Honor, This Goes to Intent

The principle is easy to state. Under the Anglo-American system of justice, a defendant may only be convicted by evidence that tends to show he is guilty of the crime charged.

Put it another way: evidence is inadmissible if its only relevance is to show that the defendant is a bad person, likely to commit a crime.

Because it is a rule of evidence, however, it is riddled with exceptions. All of them fall under one general umbrella: if evidence of other crimes or bad acts besides the ones charged is relevant for some other purpose—besides showing the defendant is a bad person—then it is admissible.

Rule 404(b) of the Federal Rules of Evidence gives a good summary of the law:

> Evidence of other crimes, wrongs, or acts is not admissible to prove the character of a person in order to show that he acted in conformity therewith. It may, however, be admissible for other purposes, such as proof of motive, opportunity, intent, preparation, plan, knowledge, identity, or absence of mistake or accident.

A few examples will show how the rule is supposed to work:

1. Motive. Defendant rapes a 6-year-old girl who cannot identify him. An eyewitness to the event, however, threatens to do so. Defendant kills the eyewitness to keep him from testifying, and is charged with murder. In the murder trial, evidence of the rape as well as the threat to testify is admissible on the issue of motive. Take away the fact that the murder victim saw the rape and made the threat, and evidence of the rape is inadmissible in the murder trial.

2. Intent. Defendant passes a bad check. It is drawn on his account, but the check is for $5,000, and he has no funds whatsoever in the account. Evidence that just one month before he wrote on his account three other checks that were returned marked ''insufficient funds'' is relevant to the issue of intent, even though he is not charged with those acts in this trial.

3. Preparation. Defendant is charged with robbing a federally insured bank, a federal offense. In preparation for the crime, he steals a car to serve as a get-away vehicle. The car is not taken across state lines. The theft of the car may be shown in the federal trial to prove preparation even though it is not a federal offense and may not be charged.

4. Identity. Defendant is highly skilled at the art of disconnecting sophisticated burglar alarms, which he always does with a combination of electromagnetic devices and self-expanding plastic foam to silence alarm bells. His modus operandi is virtually his signature. Evidence of other burglaries committed by him using this technique is admissible on the issue of identity.

Other examples that demonstrate the remaining theories are easy to work out. They share a common thread. In each instance the evidence of other wrongs is highly relevant to something that goes beyond proving the defendant is a bad person. Finally, when the evidence is admitted, the defendant is entitled to a limiting instruction (if he thinks it will do any good) that the evidence is only to be used for the narrow purpose for which it was admitted.

With all of that in mind, let us consider another case.

The defendant, Harold Parker, is charged with burglary. Specifically, it is alleged he broke into the victim's house and stole the silverware and a color television set. He has a prior conviction—two years old—for an earlier burglary of the same type.

Knowing what is in the prosecutor's file, defense counsel advises Parker not to take the stand on his own behalf. He is not an effective witness, would probably be severely damaged on cross-examination, and besides, testifying would permit the prosecutor to impeach the defendant with that prior burglary conviction.

It is not bad advice, especially since the prosecution's case is rather thin on the issue of identity. Furthermore, there was nothing distinctive enough about the former burglary to qualify it on the issue of identity.

While not exactly complacent, Parker's lawyer is suddenly shocked to see the prosecution starting to introduce evidence of Parker's prior burglary conviction during the prosecution's case-in-chief. Fortunately, he is able to head things off before the jury has any idea what the evidence is, and makes his objection out of the presence of the jury.

DEFENSE COUNSEL: Your honor. We object to any evidence of this prior conviction. The defendant has not taken the stand. This thing is not admissible on the issue of identity. There is nothing distinctive about the prior burglary. It is highly prejudicial, your honor, and it is simply not relevant.

THE COURT: Prosecutor, do you want to be heard before I rule on this?

PROSECUTOR: I do, your honor. Burglary is a crime of intent. It is necessary to show a specific *mens rea*. About the only way that can be done is through circumstantial evidence. The problem is, this defendant has committed a covert crime. We can hardly introduce direct evidence of what was in his mind. That means we have to do it circumstantially.

What it boils down to is this, your honor. The prior burglary necessarily shows the defendant's state of mind. The

171

fact of the prior crime shows that this one he is charged with now was no accident. We are not offering this to show identity, your honor. We are offering it on the issue of intent.

THE COURT: The objection will be overruled. You may have a limiting instruction if you wish.

DEFENSE COUNSEL: Thank you, your honor.

THE COURT: (To the bailiff) Bring back the jury.

How about it? Is the ruling right? Of course not—in principle, at least.

Breaking into a house and stealing silverware and a television set is no accident. All the necessary intent may be fairly inferred from the nature of the crime itself. Despite the necessity of proving the element of intent, it is not really an issue in the case.

This means that the evidence will be used by the jury not for the purpose for which it was offered, but for its inadmissible purpose—to show the defendant is a bad person—no matter what the instructions say.

Do prosecutors nevertheless offer such evidence? Every day.

Do trial judges nevertheless admit such evidence? All the time.

Do appellate courts reverse convictions for the trial court's failure to test the relevance of such prejudicial evidence? Not often enough.

Surprisingly often, the problem can be traced to defense counsel's failure to argue the matter properly. It is, after all, one of those issues that can usually be anticipated in advance of trial. For those in criminal practice the problem arises often enough to justify having a stock memorandum ready to submit in support of the objection.

To be sure, most jurisdictions have cases that reflect a shameful lack of critical analysis about the relevance of prior bad acts offered to show intent. See, e.g., *People v. Massey*, 196 Cal. App. 2d 230, 16 Cal. Rptr. 402 (1961).

On the other hand, some federal courts of appeals have started insisting on a strong showing of relevance of the prior bad act to some issue in the case. *See United States v. Benedetto*, 571 F.2d 1246 (2d Cir. 1978).

The Cleveland Exception to the Hearsay Rule

As a final vignette, assume the facts in one more criminal case. The defendant, Michael Dorsanio, is charged with assault with intent to commit rape. The defense is alibi, and misidentification is a key issue.

Briefly, the victim, Ms. June Knickerson, claims that Michael Dorsanio attacked her outside the rear entrance to ''The Bucket,'' a local discoteque popular with young singles.

Ms. Knickerson says that about 25 minutes after the attack she and her older brother, Carl Knickerson, went into ''The Bucket'' and confronted Michael Dorsanio, who was seated at a table with three other young men. The examination of Ms. Knickerson's brother, Carl, is in progress:

> PROSECUTOR: Mr. Knickerson, how long were you in 'The Bucket' before you saw the defendant, Michael Dorsanio?
> MR. KNICKERSON: Only about one or two minutes.
> PROSECUTOR: What did you do?
> MR. KNICKERSON: June and I walked over to the table where he was sitting.
> PROSECUTOR: Now, then Mr. Knickerson, did your sister say anything to you at that time?
> DEFENSE COUNSEL: Objection, your honor, hearsay.
> THE COURT: Was it said in the presence of the accused?
> MR. KNICKERSON: Yes.
> THE COURT: Objection overruled. Proceed.

That is the Cleveland Exception to the Hearsay Rule. According to it, anything said in the presence of the accused is admissible in evidence.

Actually, there has been some confusion concerning the proper name of this rule. In North Central Texas, for example, it is known as the Dallas Exception to the Hearsay Rule. In Massachusetts, it is called the Boston Exception. William E. McDaniels even claimed it was really the Philadelphia Exception in *Rule 801: More Than a Definition*, 2 LITIGATION No. 1, p. 17 (1975).

The difficulty is that it sort of has a claim to legitimacy. In some instances, for example, the out-of-court statement may be offered not for its truth, but for its effect on one who hears it. Interestingly, that comes perilously close to a hearsay exception—admission by silence.

Here is the idea: an admission is anything a party says or does that is inconsistent with the position he now takes at trial. If someone is accused of a crime and does not deny it, it can be an admission.

The problem is that it is not a complete foundation for an admission by silence. According to a thoughtful student note, *Tacit Criminal Admissions*, 112 U. PA. L. REV. 210 (1963), courts have generally required *seven* elements before admitting statements that are thought to be adopted by the silence of an accused: (1) made in the presence of the accused; (2) within his hearing; (3) he must have understood it; (4) it must have dealt with facts within his knowledge; (5) he must have been able to speak; (6) he must have been psychologically free to speak; and (7) the circumstances must naturally call for a reply. See also, *United States v. Alker*, 225 F.2d 851 (3d Cir. 1958).

Just establishing the first of these factors is not a sufficient foundation. Even more obviously, evidence of the post arrest silence of a defendant after a Miranda warning is a violation of due process, *Doyle v. Ohio*, 426 U.S. 610 (1976).

What about our case in which Michael Dorsanio is finally convicted after the receipt into evidence of whatever it was June Knickerson said to her brother Carl? Will it be reversed on appeal? Probably not. It will be judged by the rule that underpins all of the customary law of erroneous evidence, the doctrine of harmless error.

PART IV

Foundations and Objections

CHAPTER 16

Making the Record

It is rare for a deposition to become famous, but it can happen. Twenty years ago—when Governors Island, New York, was an army installation—there was such a deposition.

A soldier was charged with having committed a crime in Germany. Because the United States Army has worldwide jurisdiction, it can try a case anywhere, and this soldier was being tried in the United States. One of the principal witnesses against him appeared by deposition. The defendant and his lawyer had travelled to Germany and attended the deposition, and they heard the witness testify.

Of course the court-martial trying that soldier did not see or hear the witness. They heard only the deposition, read out loud in court.

That is when the defense counsel's tactics became evident. He had used a simple—but devastating—technique: Every time the witness moved during the deposition—no matter how slightly—the lawyer read the movement into the record with scrupulous accuracy:

Let the record reflect that the witness has pulled on his left ear with his right hand before answering the question . . . Let the record reflect that the witness shifted from side to side in his chair after answering the last question . . . Let the record reflect that as he answered the question, the witness rocked his body back and forth in his chair . . .

So it went all throughout the direct and cross-examination of the witness. And when the deposition was read to the members of the court trying the defendant, the effect was remarkable. The witness appeared to be a fidgeting, uncomfortable liar.

Making the record means something more pedestrian to most lawyers. They use the term to mean that you should prove all the essential facts in your case and make sure they are properly recorded on the transcript. And that is a good starting point. It is obvious—painfully so to the ones who do it—that there are some lawyers who are great at getting verdicts but who cannot keep them on appeal.

There are times when the proof is simply not there, even though there are plenty of legal doctrines designed to help that problem. Modern discovery, judicial notice, placing the burden of proof on the party who has the best access to the facts, dispensing with proof of negligence in products liability cases, and res ipsa loquitur are all examples of rules that ease the burden of proving a case. They make it easier to make the record because there is less of a record that needs to be made.

The kinds of cases to worry about are those in which the proof was available, but was not presented because of human error in the heat of battle.

The best way to avoid that kind of mistake is the trial notebook system of trying cases. It involves carefully planning the theory of the case and preparing outlines of direct and cross-examination and proof check lists. They are all put in an actual notebook from which you try the case. See Chapter 1, *The Trial Notebook*.

But making a trial notebook is not making the record—it is preparation for trying the case and making the record. This discussion is about actually doing it. And there is more to making a record than making sure the reporter gets everything that happened—a point that becomes obvious when you look at the list of things included in the record of a case:

- Pleadings;
- Motions and supporting briefs;
- Orders of the court;
- Exhibits received;
- Exhibits marked and offered but not received;
- Verbatim transcript;
- Proposed jury instructions;
- Verdict form or answers to special interrogatories;
- Findings of fact and conclusions of law.

Looking at the list is instructive. Many are things that can be done in the sanctuary of the office. That is important, because it can minimize the opportunities for error. Findings of fact and conclusions of law are an excellent example. Many judges—particularly in state courts—give prevailing counsel the job of drafting their proposed findings and conclusions. It is a grand opportunity to protect a favorable verdict with careful writing. On the other hand, if you are on the losing side, you should take a close look at what your opponent prepares for the judge's signature.

Studying the list also helps you understand why the transcript (and the things related to it) get such emphasis. It is something you have to deal with—through another person—on the spot—as it actually happens.

Dealing with the transcript is important enough to justify learning something about it. Verbatim transcripts are relatively recent. If you read about an old trial from several hundred years ago, the chances are you will have only bits and pieces that are actual quotations. Verbatim transcripts came into vogue with shorthand. The popular shorthand systems were invented around the late 1800s. And there are probably some court reporters who still take notes by hand.

But not many. It is hard to take ordinary shorthand faster than 80 words a minute, and average conversation is about 140 words per minute. Enter the stenotype machine. It was invented in Dallas, Texas, in 1910. It permits stenographers to take about 200 words per minute (the typical requirement for courtroom work) and whizzes to do more than 280. It is currently the most popular system. Audio and video tapes are gaining in popularity because of their reduced costs. Some stenotype operators have electronic machines that make ordinary paper tapes and also cassette tape recordings that can be read by computers to transcribe the electronic notes.

All systems have their own peculiarities and all produce some errors. There is almost always the possibility for mistakes such as ''fatal'' being substituted for ''vital'' or ''not'' being typed for ''now.'' While most errors in transcripts are harmless and easy to spot, some are tricky and dangerous. When exact wording is important, it is worthwhile proofreading and correcting the transcript.

Understanding that it is a tough job to be a court reporter, there are some things to remember that will help the transcript be more accurate.

Speak Clearly

The court reporter is not the only reason for clear speech in court. Many judges and jurors are elderly and do not hear as well as younger people. In fact, it is a good idea to get the court reporter to help you if you think you have a problem being understood. Tell the reporter about your concern and have him raise his hand if your voice drops too low. Some—but not all—will do this automatically.

Do Not Talk Too Fast

Easy to say, but harder to do for those who are fleet of tongue. If people tell you that you talk too fast, there are at least two things that will help: First, listen carefully to a good national news announcer—what is now called an anchor. They usually speak at a pace that is close to the optimum for interest and comprehension. Second, learn to use pauses. Jurors and court reporters alike have built-in buffers. People can hear a string of fast talk and then figure out what it means—provided they have occasional periods to absorb what they have heard. Using pauses effectively is one of the first steps to gaining control over the pace of your speech.

Spell

Everybody knows that witnesses should be asked to spell their names so the reporter can write them down accurately. In fact, many clerks and bailiffs who swear in witnesses include a request for name, address, and spelling of last name as part of their initial litany. So this is a suggestion that you have witnesses spell other things besides their names—such as the names of people they refer to, or technical terms they use in their testimony.

In fact, when it is worth asking for an expert to explain a term to the jury, it is often a good idea to ask to have it spelled as well. ''Doctor, you have told us that 'parenchyma' is a word that means the body of an organ—would you mind spelling that for the court reporter?'' But be careful. You do not want to embarrass your experts with a spelling test. If you know you will be using a number of technical terms during the trial, you should consider making a glossary for you and the court reporter.

Be Careful with Numbers

The problem is ambiguity. Street addresses are usually clear enough, but technical numbers may not be. So when reading numbers in which there is a decimal point, be sure to put it in.

Otherwise the reporter (and the jury) will not know the difference between 5201 and 52.01 when you say "fifty-two-oh-one."

Side-bar Conference

Important rulings take place up at the bench during side-bar conferences. Unless they are invited, some court reporters will stay in place (and miss what is whispered between judge and counsel). It is not hard to have the court reporter there. The typical stenotype machine lifts off its tripod with a quarter turn and can be carried to wherever it is needed.

Perhaps the most difficult question is when to have a transcript. The answer should not be automatic. There is a constant tension between need and the expense that requires a thoughtful trial lawyer to approach the question from a fresh viewpoint for every case. Look at the different stages of the trial and you will see why. It is universal practice to have a transcript for only one of the stages on the list—testimony in open court.

1. Pretrial hearings
2. Jury voir dire
3. Opening statements
4. Testimony in open court
5. Side-bar conferences
6. Oral motions and requests for instructions
7. Final Argument
8. Instructions
9. Verdict
10. Polling the jury

While there is no "school answer" to the problem, there are some considerations worth taking into account.

Error can happen at any point in the trial. When it happens is when it is important to have a transcript. Having the reporter take notes does *not* mean you have ordered the transcript, which is a big part of the expense.

If you do not trust your opponent or the judge, you should generally have more of the proceedings recorded.

Jury voir dire, opening statements, and final argument are good candidates for being on the record. They offer lots of opportunities for counsel to misstate the evidence, inject improper issues, or commit other errors. Moreover, in your own final argument, you may sometimes want to quote a promise your opponent made during his opening statement.

It is usually a mistake to go off the record in a side-bar argument or in a hearing outside the presence of the jury. If the judge insists that something be off the record, you should make it a point to make a statement *for* the record if something happened that you want recorded.

There are times when the forum you are in is so hostile that you will need your own independent court reporter. When you do, there is no need to be unpleasant about it—just do it. It is one of the best cures for the few judges in the country who deal with error after the fact by selectively "correcting" the transcript.

Now that you have thought about how and when it is all taken down, it is time to talk about how to do it.

Being Eyes for the Appellate Court

The transcript is part of the adversary process. Making sure that it contains everything you want is up to you. Normally the court reporter only takes down what people say—not what they do—unless you do something about it. Think of yourself as being the eyes for the appellate court, and read what you see into the record:

1. Gestures and other non-verbal communication. "Your honor, may the record reflect that the witness held his hands about two feet apart?"

2. Require audible responses. If you get a grunt, nod, "um-hmm," or any other non-verbal response from a witness, it is up to you to straighten it out. "May the record show that the witness nodded his head, indicating 'yes'? And, Mr. Malone, if you would please, answer my questions out loud, so the court reporter can take down your testimony."

3. Be ready to estimate distances in the courtroom in any case that involves distances between objects. The best way to do this is to *know* in advance what the distances in the courtroom are, and have a long tape in your briefcase should you be challenged. How, you ask, will your knowledge get on the record? The simplest way is by stipulation:

> Q: Mrs. Jackson, how far away was Mr. Butler standing from you when you first saw him?
> A: Oh, I would say about from where I am to the flag.
> Q: (To your opponent) Counsel, can we agree that the witness has estimated a distance of approximately 12 feet?

And if the other lawyer is foolish enough to disagree, you can have the witness measure the distance and testify to the results.

4. Record improper conduct of the judge, opposing counsel, or

witness. It is not a popular thing to do, so the key is to be polite. It is common for lawyers to make little speeches about how long-suffering they have been in waiting to object, something that probably does not help: "Your honor, we have been *most* patient in putting up with the antics of opposing counsel, but the time has finally come when we feel we must object to his constant harassment in crinkling papers and slamming books." It is usually better to be direct: "Your honor, I am making a formal objection, and want the record to reflect that four times during the last few minutes counsel for the defense has deliberately crumpled paper and slammed books on the floor." The same goes for improper conduct of the judge. Be polite, but read it into the record.

Introducing Stipulations

Stipulations can be troublesome. In civil cases the agreement is between counsel, whereas in criminal cases it is common to have the express consent of the defendant as well. Either way, the stipulation puts some issue or question of fact to rest—if it is introduced in evidence. A stipulation is not like a pleading that automatically limits the scope of a trial. If a defendant in a civil case admits liability in his answer, and only contests damages, then the trial is about damages—not liability (except to the extent that facts that prove liability may also prove damages). On the other hand, if that same defendant agrees in a stipulation that some fact is true, that does not put the question to rest until the stipulation is offered into evidence.

It is wise to get stipulations in writing, in advance of trial. Then during your case in chief you can read them to the jury. Giving a written copy to the court reporter gets a bit of gratitude—it is a chance to rest his hands for a few moments while you read. You should also get the court to give a short instruction on the meaning of the stipulation—how the jury should accept the stipulated facts as true without any further proof.

There is still more to watch out for. A stipulation to a fact serves to settle that fact. But a stipulation that someone would testify to a fact is only an agreement that the person would testify that way—not that what they would say is true. Such a stipulation lets the other side offer testimony in opposition to it. And if you think that is tricky, it gets worse.

A stipulation that someone would testify to a fact is not an agreement that the facts are even relevant or admissible in evidence—only that the person would say those if the court permitted.

"Your honor, we have agreed that if Mr. Kaplan were in court, he would testify to a change in the speed at which we permit our busses to travel. But, your honor, even though we agree he would testify to that if he could, the evidence is simply inadmissible under Rule 407 of the Federal Rules. And your honor, there is nothing improper about our position—if they brought Mr. Kaplan here to court right now, it would change nothing. The evidence would still be inadmissible."

When you think about it, it is not unfair. A stipulation that someone would testify in a certain way is a convenient way to avoid having to call a witness. It is a time saver. But it does not put a party in any better position than if the witness were called to the stand. Nevertheless, relying on this kind of technicality is the sort of tactic that can get you a reputation for sharp practice. Besides, you may lose. The judge may decide you waived your objection, depending on how the stipulation is worded. If you agree to a stipulation and want to reserve the right to object on some particular grounds, you should spell out your reservations in the stipulation rather than springing them on your opponent in the middle of trial.

Many stipulations are not worked out in advance, but are rather spur-of-the-moment affairs in the middle of trial. Two quick words of advice about that kind of stipulation: If you are the one getting the stipulation from the other side, make sure his statement in agreement is on the record. On the other hand, if you are the one making the concession, put the agreement in your terms (or at least put your terms in the agreement) so that you do not inadvertently agree to more than you intend.

Laying Foundations

Proving preliminary facts is an essential part of making the record. It is also too important a topic just to be part of this chapter which is why it is treated separately. See Chapter 18, *Foundations*.

Introducing Exhibits

While many exhibits are premarked and preadmitted, you must know the steps to go through in introducing exhibits in trial. You need to know them so well that you can concentrate on laying the proper foundation rather than worrying what is the next mechanical step to take. Here they are in summary:

1. Ask the reporter to mark the exhibit for identification.
2. Show the exhibit to the opposing counsel. As you do it, say something like, "I am showing counsel for the defense what has been marked plaintiff's exhibit 14."
3. Show the exhibit to the witness and lay the proper foundation.
4. Offer the exhibit into evidence. "Your honor, I offer plaintiff's exhibit 14 into evidence." Sometimes you will hear lawyers offer evidence by moving that it be admitted. Doing that is unnecessary and may cause confusion. Just offer the exhibit in evidence.
5. Simultaneously with the offer, show the exhibit to the trial judge.
6. Now is the time for any objection from your opponent, and any questions of the witness in aid of the objection—called a voir dire examination of the witness.
7. Wait for the ruling from the judge admitting or excluding the exhibit.
8. Put on testimony about the exhibit. Up until the time the exhibit is admitted in evidence, it is improper to have testimony about the exhibit, except to the extent necessary to lay the foundation for its admission in evidence.
9. Publish the exhibit to the jury. It is traditional to ask the court's permission to do this.

For a more complete discussion, see Chapter 17, *Steps in Introducing Exhibits.*

Objections

The immediate purpose in objecting to evidence is usually to keep improper information from going to the jury. Making the record is just as important. Here are some points to remember:

1. Object promptly. The time to object is as soon as the basis for the objection is reasonably apparent. Otherwise the objection is waived. Normally that means you must object as soon as the question is asked—but not always. If the question is proper, but the answer contains something objectionable, then the grounds were not reasonably apparent until the answer.
2. Make the objection specific enough (you may think that is equivocating, but it is not). General objections are fine so long as they are sustained. If you rise and only get as far as "I object, your honor. . ." before the judge cuts

you off, you have been specific enough, and it would be foolish to say any more. You might show the judge that he was wrong in sustaining your objection, and convince him to change his mind. On appeal, a general objection will be sustained if there were any valid grounds for the objection—even if neither the judge nor the lawyer thought about them at the time.

On the other hand, if the objection is overruled, then it must be specific. But then it is too late to be specific, right?

Wrong.

When the judge gives the first hint of overruling your objection, that is the time to ask, "May I be heard, your honor?" And then you make your specific objection.

If you sense there is a difficulty with specific objections, you are right. They only preserve the errors they mention.

3. Make running objections. A running objection is a convenient way of making the record without continually making the same objection that has been repeatedly overruled. Here is the way to do it: "Your honor, we understand that there will be a substantial amount of testimony about the meeting held on September 28. It is our position that all of that testimony is inadmissible on the grounds of relevance, and we understand that you have ruled the other way. We would appreciate it, your honor, if we could have a running objection to *all* the testimony about the meeting, so we can keep from continually jumping up and wasting everyone's time."

Just be careful to make your running objection specific enough and broad enough to cover all the times you plan on remaining seated. Some appellate courts have been foolishly strict in interpreting running objections, which are devices that ought to be encouraged.

4. Get a ruling. Some judges are masters of evasion. They like to respond with ambiguities. When you make an objection, you are entitled to a ruling—but it is up to you to make sure you get it. So what do you do if the court is evasive? Say, "Your honor, would you kindly rule so we can go ahead with the trial"? No. The right way is easy and obvious. "I am sorry, your honor, I did not hear the court's ruling." Even more direct is, "Your honor, may we have your ruling?"

188

Offers of Proof

In the middle of one of your direct examinations, your opponent raises an objection. The objection is sustained. You are sure the judge is wrong in excluding the evidence. But unless you make the record, you cannot raise the issue on appeal.

No matter what it is called—proffer, bill of exceptions, or offer of proof—it is the way to put on the transcript the evidence that has been excluded by the court's ruling. If it is already clear from the context what has been kept out, then a formal offer is not required. Rule 103(a) (2) of the Federal Rules of Evidence does a good job of paraphrasing the common law: an erroneous evidentiary ruling may not be raised on appeal unless, ''In case the ruling is one excluding evidence, the substance of the evidence was made known to the court by offer or was apparent from the context within which questions were asked.''

Usually the transcript gives a good idea of what was excluded—but not always. Particularly if the objection is argued at side-bar and the court reporter is not present, there is a real chance that the record will not be sufficient.

Now for a bit of irony that should help drive the point home. Unless the court directs otherwise, counsel can make the offer of proof in any form he sees fit. Although a few old cases suggested otherwise, it is usually not necessary to make the offer of proof by questioning the witness on the stand.

So what? you ask.

So, all that is necessary to make an offer of proof is to make a statement as an officer of the court what evidence you expected to introduce that was excluded by the court's ruling.

So why is there any irony? you ask.

Because the lawyer who can simply make a statement for the record at trial cannot do the same thing once the case is on appeal. Then he is bound by the record, and it is too late to make a statement.

Just because you can make an informal offer of proof by making a statement for the record does not mean it is the best way to do it. When you make your offer, the judge will be listening as well as the court reporter. And the judge will be wondering how the offer will look to an appellate court. If you are actually content with the court's ruling (and you may be, having decided to make the record on this error just as a little insurance policy), then you may not want it to sound too impressive. On the other hand, if you would like the court to change its ruling, then you want the offer to be noticed.

The easiest way to do that is to put the witness on the stand outside the presence of the jury, ask the questions, and get the answers. If the trial court prefers, it can require that the offer be done that way. Fed. R. Evid. 103(b) and Federal Rule 103(c) follows the common law practice of having offers of proof outside the presence of the jury: "In jury cases, proceedings shall be conducted, to the extent practicable, so as to prevent inadmissible evidence from being suggested to the jury by any means, such as making statements or offers of proof or asking questions in the hearing of the jury."

Now for a quick aside. Take another look at Rule 103(c). There are some federal district judges who claim that this rule—which the advisory committee note shows was directed toward offers of proof—also requires lawyers to make all objections at side-bar, so they cannot be heard by the jury. The judges who give the rule this broad interpretation have either not paid enough attention to the limitation, "to the extent practicable," or just want to make the lawyers come up to side-bar anyway.

Back to offers of proof.

If you make a verbal offer of proof, you can always follow up with a written offer of proof and a short memorandum showing why the excluded evidence should be admitted. It is hard work in the middle of trial, but it is the kind of effort that makes a difference.

One final problem. Suppose the judge wants to make things difficult for you. The easiest time to make an offer of proof is at the time of the adverse ruling. But the judge may not want to let the jury go at that time, and may direct you to make the offer at the end of the session. That is when you will be tired and have your mind on other things. Caught up in the problems of the moment, you may decide that what seemed important at 9:15 A.M. can be skipped at 4:45 P.M.—or you may simply forget.

Both are serious mistakes.

If the judge seems to be making it hard for you to make your record, you ought to be doubly careful to do it.

It is rare, but judges have sometimes forbidden counsel the opportunity to make an offer of proof. Is there anything that can be done?

Just to make it clear, first the interchange between court and counsel, and then the transcript:

THE COURT: I said the objection was sustained, counsel.

COUNSEL: Your honor, may I approach the bench?

THE COURT: You may not. Call your next witness.

COUNSEL: Your honor, before I do that, I respectfully request the opportunity to make an offer of proof.

THE COURT: Counsel, I have ruled on the matter, and I do not want to hear any more about it.

COUNSEL: Well, your honor, may the record reflect that I have requested the opportunity to make an offer of proof on this matter, and the court has refused to let me do so.

THE COURT: The record will reflect nothing of the kind. Counsel, call your next witness, or I am going to have a contempt hearing.

COUNSEL: Very well, your honor. The plaintiff calls Ernest Droner to the stand.

That was the exchange. Here is the transcript:

THE COURT: I said the objection was sustained, counsel.

COUNSEL: Very well, your honor. The plaintiff calls Ernest Droner to the stand.

There is a technique for dealing with the problem. It is called the Bystanders' Bill of Exceptions, and it is specifically recognized by statute in some states. *See* TEX. R. CIV. P. 372(j). It is a mechanism for putting improper conduct on the record when the judge forbids it. In Texas the supporting affidavit must be signed by three unbiased eyewitnesses. If the procedure is not known in your jurisdiction, an affidavit of counsel attached to the record on appeal ought to be sufficient, although the signatures of unbiased observers would surely help.

Limited Offers

Evidence worth fighting over is often not completely admissible or inadmissible. Usually part of it is admissible—or it is admissible to prove one thing but may not even be considered to prove something else.

If you were not a lawyer, this might make you laugh. But you are a lawyer, and you know that over such quiddities whole appeals are won and lost.

When evidence has limited admissibility, it can tangle everything into knots. Even with an offer of proof explaining what was excluded, it is possible to miss making a proper record for appeal. So there is a rule about limited admissibility that you must commit to memory.

191

It is up to the losing party to suggest the proper limitation. Remember, it does not matter who offers the evidence and who opposes it. What matters is who loses the objection. Two simple examples will show how this rule works:

1. The plaintiff offers evidence of a conversation that is relevant for two purposes: one to show someone had notice of a fact, the other to show what was said is true. The defendant objects on the grounds of hearsay, and the judge sustains the objection. It is up to the plaintiff to point out the admissible, non-hearsay purpose of the evidence—not because he offered it, but because he lost the objection.

2. In the same case the plaintiff offers a hospital record that contains both admissible and inadmissible information. The defendant objects, and the plaintiff points out why the record is being offered. The court overrules the objection. The defendant does not request that the inadmissible information be kept from the jury. The defendant did not adequately make his record. He should have asked to have the improper material redacted (which is trial technique school talk for "cut out").

The principle is valid. It is up to the loser to make sure his point is on the record. See C. McCormick, *Evidence* 117 (2d ed. 1972) (who puts it a bit differently).

If you think about it, you will realize that it is not simply a negative rule. It is even more useful put affirmatively: Be ready to make a limited offer or a limited objection whenever evidence is only partly admissible. You will be more likely to win your point at trial, and if you do not, you will have preserved it for appeal.

Be an Advocate

There is a tendency for some lawyers to think of themselves as advocates only when they are talking directly to the jury. They tend to view the formal requirements of the law—laying foundations, making and meeting objections, reading things into the record—as mechanical items to be handled like chopping wood.

It is the wrong approach.

First, technical competence can help win the judge and jury's respect as a credible source. Second, just making the record can be persuasive.

Almost everything you do during the course of the trial has some potential for factual and emotional persuasion. Making the record is not a technical hurdle—it is an opportunity to be a trial lawyer.

CHAPTER 17

Steps in Introducing Exhibits

It is essential that the trial lawyer be thoroughly acquainted with the necessary procedural steps for introducing exhibits into evidence. Yet this routine trial procedure is for many litigators—particularly those with less experience—a troublesome task. The result is often confusion and delay, preventing some lawyers from taking full advantage of the effective use of demonstrative evidence. The procedural checklist set forth below is suggested as a guide for avoiding confusion and delay.

1. Ask that the exhibit be marked for identification

Counsel should make the request as follows: "I request that this be marked as (plaintiff's) (prosecution's) (defendant's) exhibit for identification." Technically, identifying the object or document in more than very general terms violates the rule against unsworn testimony. While you may or may not be challenged by the opposition, it is improper to identify the exhibit as, for example, "a picture of the plaintiff's car taken after the collision." Further, you should permit the reporter or clerk to assign the appropriate exhibit number or letter. That is his domain, and he may well resent any intrusion on it. Of course, if he makes a mistake, it should be called to his attention. Typically reporters or clerks keep a list of the numbers or letters used, and are less likely to make a mistake than you are.

When the case is one with a large number of exhibits, especially where they are similar in nature, it is often wise, as part of the pre-trial order, to agree to the numbering and lettering of exhibits in advance, and even to stipulate to their admissibility. There are many situations, to be sure, when you do not want your adversary to know you have a particular document or exhibit, particularly if its chief value is for impeachment. It is essential, therefore, to know the entire process well for use at trial.

2. Let opposing counsel examine the exhibit

Professor Keeton suggests that the exhibit be offered into evidence before it is shown to opposing counsel. R. Keeton, *Trial Tactics and Methods* 63 (2d ed. 1973). However, waiting until that time is an invitation to a pointed request from the other side to see the document, which can be embarrassing.

3. Lay the foundation for the exhibit

Failing to lay a complete foundation for an exhibit (or for other testimony, for that matter) is a typical failing of even experienced trial lawyers. Unless one is blessed or cursed with total recall, the best method is to have a foundation checklist in the trial notebook for each type of exhibit you plan to use. While the subject of foundations justifies an entire volume, a few of the more typical problems are covered here.

For a photograph of a scene, all that is required is the statement of a witness that the picture is a true and accurate representation of the scene, and testimony that the scene is relevant to the case. The simplest way to lay such a foundation is through an ordinary fact witness. There are instances, however, when one is not available for this purpose. Then the photographer can establish at least part of the foundation, describing the technical details of his photographic process to help show that the picture is a true and accurate representation of the scene it portrays. Laying this foundation does not guarantee the admissibility of the picture, however, because its probative value may be outweighed by some prejudicial aspect of it. But the foundation is an essential step to its admissibility.

Models and charts are somewhat simpler. For example, in a head injury case, a plastic model of a skull and brain might make a neurologist's testimony more understandable. The proper foundation for the use of such an exhibit is that the object is an accurate reproduction of the human skull and brain for the purpose of illustrating the testimony of the witness. Absolute accuracy is not the test, and the model or chart need only be as detailed and accurate as required by the function it is to serve. Some courts take a relaxed approach to such exhibits and do not even require a foundation to be laid to permit their use. Others, however, insist on their being marked, a foundation laid, and formal introduction into evidence. This is an important step to have a complete record and to allow the exhibit to be taken to the jury room. Thus, it is often the better practice to take the trouble to make a formal introduction. With the court's permission, a description or picture can be substituted for the exhibit for inclusion in the record at the close of trial.

When something is used to refresh a witness's recollection, it is not itself introduced into evidence. Nevertheless, some courts require such items—typically documents—to be marked for identification, and it often is best to do so. This is especially true since the foundation for the admissibility of past recollection recorded includes the inability of the witness to have his recollection refreshed by the document. Stated briefly, the requirements for the admissibility of past recollection recorded are: (a) a writing, (b) made at or near the event by the witness or someone acting under his direction and control, (c) no present recollection by the witness as to the matters recorded and sought to be introduced, and (d) a "voucher of correctness" or statement that the witness is certain that the information recorded was accurate at the time made.

With real evidence—such as murder weapons, defective machinery in a products liability case and other such exhibits which are the things themselves—the foundation is complicated by the necessity to show a chain of custody. The requirement is to show from whose custody the object is produced, who had custody in a continuous chain from the relevant time, and that the object is in the same condition as when originally received. The trial court has discretion, when the object is readily identifiable and not subject to easy tampering, to admit the object on merely a foundation that it is in substantially the same condition as at the relevant time. The court, however, can require a meticulous chain of custody when the object is subject to change, is not easily identifiable, or may easily have been tampered with.

When one cannot establish a chain of custody, all is not necessarily lost. The trial court may exercise its discretion to admit a model or duplicate for the purpose of illustrating testimony. The object which fails to pass the chain of custody test *may* qualify for these purposes. For a short but adequate discussion of the chain of custody problem, see *McCormick on Evidence* 527–30 (2d ed. 1972).

195

4. Offer the exhibit into evidence

Too often this step is overlooked, with the result that the jury cannot take the exhibit to the jury room with them, or they do so improperly. It can be a fatal omission.

The offer should be as follows: "Defense exhibit 14 for identification is offered into evidence." Some courts prefer all exhibits to be offered into evidence at once, usually near the time the party rests. This practice saves time and makes an accidental omission less likely. This procedure, however, keeps the exhibit from the jury until admission or blinks at the prohibition against testimony concerning an exhibit—as opposed to testimony authenticating it—until it is formally admitted in evidence. Arguably, therefore, it is the better practice to offer the exhibit directly after authentication and examination by opposing counsel whenever you want the jury to view the exhibit right away or when there is to be additional testimony concerning it.

5. Give the exhibit to the trial judge for his inspection

If the judge does not already have a copy of the exhibit, the right time to show it to him is simultaneously with the formal offer into evidence.

6. Voir dire examination of the witness, objection and argument by opposing counsel

Because it is possible to have laid a prima facie foundation for the admissibility of an exhibit which is nonetheless inadmissible, opposing counsel can conduct a preliminary examination of the witness on the apparent foundation. Whether such an examination will be permitted usually lies within the discretion of the trial court.

When done properly, this form of examination is not preliminary cross-examination of the witness generally, but only as to those matters which relate to the apparent foundation which is being tested. Moreover, it is usually better not to ask for a voir dire examination unless you feel there is a good chance that the exhibit will be excluded as a result. Should the court rule that the objection goes to the weight rather than to the admissibility of the exhibit, there is the danger that the jury will interpret the ruling as a statement that your attack was legally without force and should be ignored. Therefore, unless you feel you can exclude the exhibit, it is better to save your attack for cross-examination.

While some trial lawyers feel to the contrary—that two cross-examinations of a witness are better than one—use of the voir dire examination of a witness for that purpose is impermissible. And while some judges have never heard of a voir dire examination of a witness, others know the procedure well and are quick to cut off examination which goes beyond its appropriate scope.

7. Ruling from the court

If the judge forgets to make a ruling, it is probably a good idea to ask for one.

8. The testimony concerning the exhibit

Any testimony about the exhibit not necessary as a foundation to its introduction should only come after it has been admitted into evidence.

9. Give the jury the exhibit or copies of it

Trial courts usually permit copies of pictures and documents to be distributed to the jury. When you want the jury to look at something during the testimony concerning it, it is useful to have a copy for each juror or an exhibit large enough for all jurors to see at once. Giving the jury exhibits is important, since they are permitted to take them into the jury room for use during their deliberations—a procedure which heightens the impact of demonstrative evidence considerably. However, testimonial exhibits, such as depositions, are usually not permitted in the jury room, on the theory that the jury will give disproportionate weight to that testimony. For a good general discussion, see H. H. Spellman, *Direct Examination of Witnesses* 98–107 (1968).

If only a portion of an exhibit is relevant, such as one entry in an entire log or record, it is customary to request the court's permission to read from the exhibit, identifying what excerpt is being called to the jury's attention. The rule of completeness, the antidote to unfair selectivity, permits the opposition to present explanatory or modifying materials from the same exhibit.

CHAPTER 18

Foundations

The trouble with foundations is that they lurk everywhere, waiting for a chance to trip you up. Usually, it seems, the gods of litigation save the most complex and arcane foundations for times when your client is at your side and your opponent makes an obscure objection that is sustained by a trial judge whose dual determination is to force you to turn some square corner and to refuse to tell you what it is.

Part of the problem is due to the usual law school courses in evidence, which are organized around abstract conceptual progressions rather than proof of facts at trial. Even if you check as helpful a book as *McCormick on Evidence* (2d ed. 1972) and look under "Foundations" in the index on p. 930, you will be referred to "Preliminary questions and particular topics." If you then turn to "Preliminary questions of fact" on p. 935, you will find only eight entries.

Why?

Probably because nearly everywhere you look in the law of evidence there is something you have to introduce first before you can prove what you are really after. In other words, you can, if you like, view the whole law of evidence from the question: What do I have to prove first?

The results are worth the effort. Evidence will begin to fall in place. Instead of a disjointed collection of rules, a pattern will emerge that will help change evidence from a troublesome hurdle to a commanding strength in the courtroom. For a trial lawyer, a reputation for knowing evidence is beyond price.

First, there is a checklist of basic points. Not many foundations have all these requirements. On the other hand, if all these points are accounted for, the chances are nearly any foundation will be complete:

- Witness qualification
- Authentication
- Relevance
- Best evidence rule
- Hearsay and appropriate exceptions
- Procedural prerequisites such as confrontation, corroboration, attack or notice, and
- Magic words.

Obviously, this checklist is useful only if the terms mean something. While they are all familiar words, each of them is worth some discussion.

Witness qualification heads the list for two reasons: because it usually comes first in time and because it is often forgotten. Experts are not the only witnesses whose qualifications need to be established. There is a basic requirement that any fact witness must be shown to have firsthand knowledge about the matter to which he is about to testify.

Experienced trial lawyers usually solve the problem out of habit:

Q: Were you able to hear whether Mr. Bladen said anything in return?

A: Yes, I heard him.

Q: What did he say?

It is important to lay this foundation of personal knowledge at the beginning of any witness's testimony, and to reestablish it from time to time as the examination goes on. It will forfend that objection usually intended just to break up the pace of examination: "Objection. If he knows, your honor."

Most foundations can be waived by failing to assert them promptly, but this is not completely true with firsthand knowledge. If there is no testimony on direct examination about the ability to observe and no objection is made, the testimony may yet be attacked. If on cross-examination it develops that the witness does not have firsthand knowledge, it is still proper to strike the testimony. See *McCormick on Evidence*, 21 (2d ed. 1972).

The requirement for firsthand knowledge is not merely a restatement of the rule against hearsay. Someone who testifies to impermissible opinions violates the rule as well. But between the

199

hearsay rule and the opinion rule, the requirement for what Rule 602, Federal Rules of Evidence, calls "personal knowledge" seems pretty well covered. Why then a separate rule? Perhaps the best reason is for the very purpose of requiring the customary foundation of firsthand knowledge before any substantive testimony is received.

Next on the basic checklist is authentication. This requirement is best understood with a rule of thumb that is very nearly true: The law of evidence takes nothing for granted. If you want to prove that a signature was written by the person whose name it depicts, or that the person who made a telephone call is the man he said he was, something more is required.

How to authenticate signatures and telephone calls will come a little later. Here these examples illustrate a more general proposition: In laying the foundation for real evidence and in some other situations, it is necessary to prove that the thing is what it purports to be. Usually this can be done by any chain of circumstantial evidence that makes sense—but it must be done.

Then comes relevance. After qualifying the witness and establishing that something is what it purports to be, the next step is to show that the evidence has some rational tendency to prove a fact in issue. Of course, we use relevance to mean more than that. We use relevance to describe the evidentiary balancing where probative value is pitted against competing interests. For now, however, it is enough to think about showing that the evidence will have something to do with the case.

One of the common stumbling blocks is to go too far when you are merely laying a foundation. Suppose the plaintiff in a personal injury case wants to introduce the picture of his injured leg six weeks after it was injured. It is a necessary part of the foundation to show it is a picture of his leg taken six weeks after his injury. But it is improper (before the picture is introduced into evidence) to have testimony on how the picture shows the size of the scar, or how it illustrates a temporary limitation of movement.

The best evidence rule is the next stopping point on the general checklist. It is a problem limited to documents—and in some jurisdictions, photographs and X-rays as well. While writers and law reformers have tried valiantly for years to change the name of the rule to the "original writing requirement," the old name has stuck, even though it is misleading because it suggests a general preference for the best proof obtainable for any contested fact.

There are three important things to remember about the best

evidence rule. First, it only applies to proving the contents of a document. If a witness has firsthand knowledge of facts that also happen to be contained in a document, the rule does not bar the witness's testimony. Second, in most jurisdictions, the rule happily does not apply to documents that are collateral to a case, only those central to the main issues. Third, the best evidence rule does not require that an original always be produced. Secondary evidence is admissible if the original is properly accounted for. Even if its disappearance is inexplicable, testimony of a thorough search will make secondary evidence admissible. But beware. It is not enough to show that the opposing party has the original unless a prior demand for its production has been made.

Now for the most difficult of the exclusionary rules, hearsay. Any time you offer evidence of a written or oral statement made outside court, you must be ready to do one of three things: show that it is relevant for some purpose other than proving the truth of the out-of-court statement, show that it is a verbal act (like the words of offer and acceptance in a contract case, or the words of defamation in a libel suit) or establish all the foundation requirements for one of the exceptions to the hearsay rule.

After hearsay are some procedural prerequisites that are found in a variety of foundations. Confrontation is the most important of these. It is most familiar as a prerequisite to impeachment with prior inconsistent statements. Confrontation is also a prerequisite to impeachment with evidence of bias, unless the evidence of bias is virtually incontrovertible, such as kinship with a party.

Attack usually arises in foundations for character evidence. Prior consistent statements for example, are usually admissible only after a witness has been impeached, or his credibility at least attacked with the suggestion of recent fabrication. This, of course, is nothing that the proponent of a prior consistent statement can do. It must be done by the other side. On the other hand, it is useful to think of it as part of the foundation, since if it is not there, the evidence cannot be admitted over challenge. It means the proponent of a prior consistent statement must be ready to identify the conduct of the other side that has triggered the prior statement's admissibility.

Notice can also be a foundation requirement. The demand on the other party to produce an original document is a common law requirement that comes close to notice. There are two important notice requirements in the Federal Rules of Evidence. The first is found in Rules 803(24) and 804(b)(5)—identical hearsay ''catch-

201

all'' exceptions that require advance notice to use "reliable" hearsay that is not admissible under some other exception. The second is found in Rule 609, which requires advance notice to offer evidence of a conviction more than ten years old.

The final entry on the general checklist is magic words. When you go through the steps to introduce an exhibit or lay a foundation, there is often some special language you should use. While these words need not be said as precisely as an incantation that accompanies mixing eye of newt and toe of frog, still they have their particular value. They signal that a proper foundation is being laid. With minor variations from state to state (and even from court to court), judges are accustomed to hearing and acting on these magic words. It usually makes sense to take advantage of these trained reflexes.

When, for instance, you are laying the foundation for a photograph, it is customary to ask the witness whether it is a "fair and accurate representation" of something important to the case. As traditionally put, it gently leads the witness in a fashion which is almost always permitted. You may even wish, as Harlan Heller of Mattoon, Illinois suggested at a recent session of the National Institute for Trial Advocacy, to expand our usual redundancy: "Would you tell us, please, whether that photograph is a true, fair, accurate and complete picture of that street corner as you saw it?" No one will complain about the addition of "true" and "complete" to the list, and they do make the foundation more impressive.

Having gone over this general checklist, you can see how it applies to some of the more common foundations.

Photographs

Contrary to what some lawyers think, it is not necessary to have the photographer lay the foundation for a photograph. In fact, calling him as a witness usually tends to inject needless detail about the way in which the picture was taken—camera and lens selection, film and shutter speed, developing, enlarging and printing techniques—all of which will only tend to undercut the foundation either by confusing the jurors, or worse, making them unnecessarily suspicious.

Of course, should the integrity of a photograph be seriously questioned, then it is entirely appropriate to call the photographer. Moreover, if you really think that a photograph will be seriously attacked, it is probably better to lay an expert foundation in advance rather than try to prop it up later.

But those are unusual situations. In the ordinary case—the kind that arises in daily trial work—any witness familiar with what the picture portrays should be able to give a proper foundation.

Running down the basic checklist, there are five points to cover: witness qualification, authentication, relevance, best evidence rule and magic words.

Suppose we have a simple landlord-tenant case. The tenant claims he was injured when he tripped on a loose step on a common stairs. A neighbor who lives in the same building is on the stand.

Q: How long have you lived in the Gardner Apartments, Mrs. Randolph?

A: Two years.

Q: Do you ever use the back stairs that lead to the alley?

A: Yes. I use them nearly every day.

Q: Are you familiar with the condition they were in on the twelfth of August last year?

A: Yes.

Q: I ask the reporter [or clerk] to mark this as a plaintiff's exhibit for identification.

Reporter: This will be plaintiff's exhibit number 7 for identification.

Q: Thank you. Counsel [showing exhibit to defense counsel]. Now, Mrs. Randolph, I show you what has been marked as plaintiff's exhibit 7 for identification and ask you to examine it. Can you tell us what it is, please?

A: Yes. This is a photograph of the back stairs of the Gardner Apartments.

Q: Mrs. Randolph, turning your attention once again to those stairs as they were last August twelfth, are you able to tell us whether plaintiff's exhibit 7 for identification is a fair and accurate picture of the stairs as they appeared at that time?

A: Yes. Yes, I would say it is.

Q: Thank you, Mrs. Randolph. Your Honor [handing exhibit to the judge], we offer what has been marked as plaintiff's exhibit 7 for identification into evidence and ask permission to show a photographic enlargement of it to the jury so they can all see it during Mrs. Randolph's testimony.

That is enough of a foundation. How long should it take? Two or three minutes; certainly no more.

How does it meet the five points from the basic checklist? The first few questions dealt with the witness's familiarity with a relevant scene, thus covering both witness qualification and some of the relevance problem. Then the witness examined the picture and told the jury what it showed. That and the magic words (which also helped finish the relevance chain) established its authenticity. The only point left is best evidence—a problem that was avoided by not asking any questions that would tend to describe just what the picture showed until it was in evidence.

Maps and Charts

There are exhibits for which the "fair and accurate" magic words used for photographs simply will not do. Sketches, models, charts, maps and all sorts of specially prepared demonstrative evidence often fall into a category where they are incomplete and inaccurate, yet may be perfectly fair and very helpful to the jury in understanding what a case is all about.

The foundation for these exhibits is much like that for photographs; it draws on the same points from the basic checklist. The difference is, the magic words are changed. Now the question should be whether the exhibit is "sufficiently accurate to illustrate" the testimony of the witness to the jury. Obviously the answer to the question is "yes," especially if the exhibit was prepared by the witness.

Some lawyers prefer to ask whether the exhibit will "help the jury understand" the witness's testimony. Others avoid this, on the theory that suggesting the jury needs help understanding something is unnecessarily demeaning—an idea that probably carries a useful concern too far.

Real Evidence

Fond as we are of exhibits that look like a scene, explain an event, or demonstrate something, we know that everyone is fascinated by the real thing—the actual bullet that pierced the victim's heart, the very ropes used to tie up the carton that fell apart, the crystalized metal arm that caused an airplane's landing gear to freeze. This is real evidence.

When real evidence is introduced, the points on the basic checklist are the same as with demonstrative evidence, with one exception: Best evidence is no longer even a theoretical problem, because there is no possibility of trying to prove the contents of a writing. There is, however, something more. Depending on the type of case and importance of the exhibit, more evidence is needed to satisfy the requirements of authenticity and relevance. We satisfy these additional requirements with evidence of a chain of custody.

A chain of custody is established by showing from whose custody the exhibit is produced, who had custody in a continuous chain from the relevant time, and that the exhibit is in the same condition as when originally received.

When the exhibit is readily identifiable and not subject to easy tampering, most courts are willing to relax the requirement for a detailed chain of custody. On the other hand, where the precise nature of the exhibit is essential to the case, as in a prosecution for selling illicit narcotics, then a meticulous chain of custody will be required.

What happens if a chain of custody cannot be established? All is not necessarily lost. The court has discretion to admit the exhibit as demonstrative evidence, and it can be used as a model to illustrate the testimony of a witness. If so, it is necessary to make it clear that the exhibit is no longer being offered as the thing itself.

For a short discussion of chain of custody, see *McCormick on Evidence,* 527–530 (2d ed. 1972).

Telephone Conversations

Once again the basic checklist provides the key for a proper foundation. The witness must be qualified, the call must be authenticated, it must be relevant, and the hearsay hurdle must be cleared.

Obviously the central problem is authentication. Authentication usually comes through circumstantial evidence, virtually any sort of circumstantial chain that makes sense.

The first is where the witness is already familiar with the voice on the other end of the line. This is enough. It may also be sufficient if the person on the other end of the line has knowledge of facts that only the proper person would have. *Gutowsky v. Halliburton Oil Well Cementing Co.,* 287 P.2d 204 (Okla. 1955); *but see Smithers v. Light,* 305 Pa. 141, 157 A. 489 (1931).

There are other ways, of course, such as dialing a listed number and talking to someone who identified himself as the person in question, or receiving a telephone call in response to a properly addressed letter.

Letters

Like telephone calls, writings received in the mail present special problems of authentication that usually can be solved fairly easily. Probably the most common way to authenticate a business letter is to show that the recipient is familiar with the signature it bears or that it is in response to some other communication and was received without undue delay. *Winel v. United States*, 365 F.2d 646 (8th Cir. 1966).

The whole business can be done in a short time. Suppose the defendant in a contract case is on the stand, and his counsel wants to introduce a letter he contends was sent by the plaintiff. The defendant has already testified that he talked to the plaintiff on the telephone.

> Q: After your April 19th telephone call to Mr. Robinson, when you offered to sell the printing press for $15,000, did you hear anything further from him?
>
> A: Yes. About a week later I got a letter from him saying . . .
>
> Q: Pardon me, Mr. Blattner, but before you tell us what is in the letter you received, it will have to be introduced in to evidence. Your honor, we ask that the reporter mark this as a defendant's exhibit for identification.
>
> Reporter: This will be defendant's exhibit G for identification.
>
> Q: Thank you. I give counsel for the plaintiff a Xerox copy of what has been marked as defendant's exhibit G for identification. Mr. Blattner, I show you defendant's exhibit G for identification, and ask you to examine it. Can you identify it for us, please?
>
> A: Yes, this is a letter I received.
>
> Q: In the mail?
>
> A: Yes.
>
> Q: Do you remember when you received it?
>
> A: Yes, about a week to ten days after I called John Robinson. Let's see, that would be about the 27th or 28th of April.
>
> Q: Without going into the details of what this letter says, could you tell us whether or not the letter responds to the offer you made on the telephone to Mr. Robinson?
>
> A: Yes, it does.
>
> Q: Can you tell us what date this letter bears?
>
> A: Yes, it is dated April 24, 1977.
>
> Q: And what name is at the bottom of the letter, please?
>
> A: John Robinson.

And there you have it, a sufficient authentication of the letter even though the recipient never saw the sender sign his name, never saw any other letter signed by him or even ever met him in person.

Copies of Letters

Copies of letters can be a little more difficult than the letters themselves. The case comes up every day. The plaintiff was insured with the defendant insurance company, but failed, the defendant says, to pay his premiums on time. As it always seems to happen, just two days after the cancellation became effective his car was totally wrecked. The plaintiff contends he never received any notice, and the defendant's job is to introduce a copy of the letter into evidence.

Returning to the checklist gives the answer again. Witness qualification and authentication will probably not be very difficult. The witness (an employee of the defendant insurance company) will not have any trouble saying this is a copy of a letter he signed, and it is properly addressed to the plaintiff.

But relevance becomes more acute. It makes no difference that the witness signed a letter unless there is some evidence that it was sent to the plaintiff (from that, its receipt may be inferred). Once again circumstantial evidence is the answer, this time through business habit and custom.

The witness has no idea whether the letter was actually mailed or not; he signs hundreds just like it every day. But he can testify to the office routine for handling outgoing mail.

In some jurisdictions this is not enough, and there must be "corroboration," usually from testimony that there was no reason to deviate from the established routine on the day this letter was mailed. Thankfully, this added little fillip has been disposed of in Rule 406 of the Federal Rules of Evidence.

Because a copy is being offered into evidence and the contents of a writing are at issue, the best evidence rule returns, and with it an interesting little problem. The rule requires that the original be produced or its absence explained. It is not enough to claim that the original is in the hands of the other party unless a demand for its production is made. *Padgett v. Brezner*, 359 S.W.2d 416 (Mo. App. 1962). But where the plaintiff has alleged in his pleadings that he never received the original, the matter would seem to be settled. *Cf. McCormick on Evidence*, 572–74 (2d ed. 1972).

Finally hearsay is not a problem because the letter is a verbal act, which goes to determine the rights of the parties.

Business Records

Now for the bête noire of beginning commercial litigators, business records. Approached from the wrong end, it can take an agonizing half hour or so just to get them in evidence. On the other hand, going back to the business records statute and the general checklist to lay everything out, the whole thing can be done in well under five minutes of trial time.

First the statute itself. Most states that have not yet adopted a version of the Federal Rules of Evidence have statutes very much like the old Federal Business Records as Evidence Statute, 28 U.S.C. § 1732(a):

> In any court of the United States and in any court established by Act of Congress, any writing or record, whether in the form of an entry in a book or otherwise, made as a memorandum or record of any act, transaction, occurrence, or event, shall be admissible as evidence of such act, transaction, occurrence, or event, if made in regular course of any business, and if it was the regular course of such business to make such memorandum or record at the time of such act, transaction, occurrence, or event or within a reasonable time thereafter.
>
> All other circumstances of the making of such writing or record, including lack of personal knowledge by the entrant or maker, may be shown to affect its weight, but such circumstances shall not affect its admissibility.

Broken down into its elements, the statute requires:

1. A writing or record . . .
2. Of an act, transaction, occurrence or event . . .
3. Made in the regular course of business (a regularly kept record) . . .
4. And in the regular course of business to make the record (it must relate to the business), and . . .
5. It is the business routine to make such records at the time of the event or within a reasonable time afterwards.

Now go back to the general checklist. The witness needs to be qualified to testify to the elements required by the statute. It may happen that no single witness can do this, but in the usual situation one properly prepared witness should know enough about the business routines to establish the entire foundation.

Before the business records acts, it was the common-law rule to require the testimony or establish the unavailability of every witness who participated in the chain of making the business record. The business records acts were obviously designed to do away with such wasteful formalisms. Still, some writers suggest that courts may occasionally require such detailed proof. See *McCormick on Evidence*, 729–730 (2d ed. 1972).

On the other hand, many business records statutes, like Federal Rule 803(6), make it clear that the entire foundation may be established by the "custodian or other qualified witness."

Authentication is the next point, and the witness must certainly be able to testify that this exhibit is the record in question.

Relevance is always a requirement. Ordinarily the importance of the record will be clear on its face, but occasionally additional testimony or even another witness will be necessary to tie it into the case.

The best evidence rule may give you some pause at first. What about records of records? Do the original sales slips or notations have to be offered? Fortunately not. Records of other records—so long as they meet the requirements of the statute—may be admitted. *See, e,g., Garves v. Garvin*, 272 F.2d 924 (4th Cir. 1959). Some statutes go even further and specifically approve of photographic, photostatic, microfilm or other accurate reproductions. *See* Vernon's Ann. Tex. Civ. St. art. 3731(b). Moreover, under Federal Rule 1003, duplicates (such as Xerox copies) are admissible to the same extent as originals unless there is a genuine question about the authenticity of the original or some other reason why admitting the duplicate would be unfair.

Hearsay is the next issue. The business records statutes provide an exception to the hearsay rule, but only as to the overall record. If there is hearsay within hearsay, as when the record contains a statement made by someone not connected with the business, then there is another problem. The business record may be enough to prove the statement was made, but some other exception to the hearsay rule will be necessary to prove that the statement is true. See *Johnson v. Lutz,* 253 N.Y. 124, 170 N.E. 517 (1930), requiring a "business duty" to report information contained in a police record, and *Kelly v. Wasserman,* 5 N.Y.S.2d, 425, 158 N.E.2d 241, 185 N.Y.S.2d 538 (1959), admitting a statement made without any "business duty to report" where the statement qualified as an admission by the opposing party. Finally there is the problem of opinions, especially in hospital reports that contain medical diagnoses. Here the law has been in disarray from state to state but seems to be moving toward the position taken by Federal Rule 803(6), which specifically admits evidence of "acts, events, conditions, opinions, or diagnoses."

Now we are ready to put it all together in its proper order:

- Put the custodian of the records on the stand.
- Have him explain his duties.
- Establish his general familiarity with the business routines.
- Make it clear that it is the business custom to make records at the event or shortly afterwards.
- Have the business record marked for identification and show it to the other side.
- Have the witness identify it as a record of which he has custody.
- Show that this record was made in the ordinary course of business.
- Establish that the record relates to that business.
- Have the witness tell who provided the information on the record and that it was his duty to gather the information and pass it on to the witness or the person who made the record.

That does it. Unless there are additional matters such as hearsay within hearsay or opinions that need to be accounted for, the next step is to offer the record into evidence.

Lay Opinions

After business records, lay opinions are easy. The main point from the basic checklist is to establish the witness's qualifications.

There is a whole group of lay opinions that are traditionally admissible. These include estimates of speed, time, distance, weights and measures, sanity and sobriety and other matters that (as Federal Rule 701 puts it) are rationally based on the perceptions of the witness and helpful to the finder of fact.

Understanding that, the principal foundation is that the witness had an adequate opportunity to observe the things that give rise to his opinion.

Suppose you have a witness who is prepared to testify that the plaintiff was drunk at the crucial moment. There are two basic ways to approach the problem. First is the shorthand method:

Q: How long were you able to see the plaintiff, Mr. Reynolds?

A: Oh, I would say for about four or five minutes.

Q: Were you able to tell what sort of condition he was in?

A: Yes.

Q: What was that?

A: He looked like he was drunk.

At that point you may be ready to go on to something else, hoping the cross-examiner may stumble into more damning details. If you think your opponent will not conduct such an artless cross-examination, you may want more details in the foundation:

Q: How long were you able to see the plaintiff, Mr. Reynolds?

A: Oh, I would say for about four or five minutes.

Q: Were you able to see how he walked?

A: Yes.

Q: How did he walk?

A: Not very well. He was staggering and stumbling.

Q: Were you able to see his eyes?

A: Yes.

Q: How did they look?

A: Red. Bloodshot is the word, I guess.

Q: Did you hear him talk?

A: Yes.

Q: How did he talk?

A: Well, his speech was slurred and mumbling.

Q: Could you understand what he said?

A: Not really. Everything was rambling and disjointed.

Q: Can you recall anything he said?

A: No, not really. No, none of it made any sense.

Q: Could you smell his breath?

A: Yes.

Q: What did it smell like?

A: Alcohol. Like he had been drinking.

Q: From these things were you able to tell what condition he was in?

A: Yes. I would say he was drunk, virtually falling down drunk.

The advantage of this rapid-fire (but more complete) foundation is that it makes the final conclusion more impressive. By the time you ask the last question, the jury has already concluded that the plaintiff was drunk.

211

There is, however, a danger in this sort of tactic. If you take it too far—and especially if you take too long—you may be met with the objection that the jurors can draw the conclusion perfectly well themselves without the aid of the lay opinion. In other words, a more complete foundation opens the door to the argument that the opinion is no longer helpful to the jury.

There are responses that should work. One is that since the plaintiff may well argue that something else caused these conditions, the opinion is still helpful to the jury. Another tempting reply is to say, "Your honor, if I understand plaintiff's counsel to say that the only reasonable conclusion any jury could reach based on this witness's testimony is that the plaintiff was drunk, I will be happy to withdraw the question. Otherwise, your honor, I think they are entitled to the witness's opinion." But watch it. You do not want your response to be too slick.

Expert Opinions

Expert witnesses are professional explainers. They are called for the very purpose of interpreting data, whether it comes directly from them or from other witnesses in the case. Understanding that, we can look back at the general checklist again to see what sort of foundation is required for the testimony of an expert.

Recall that the very first entry on that list is witness qualification. Certainly the witness must be established as an expert in his or her field.

But that is not enough. Something else is needed, even before we get to the witness's qualifications. That extra ingredient is a special sort of relevance. It is not merely that the testimony will have something to do with the case. It is even more basic than that. The expert's field must be an area of expertise that will be helpful to the jury.

When the field of expertise is ballistics, chemistry, engineering, electronics, fingerprinting, medicine or any of a host of studies of obvious value and recognition, then this basic need for establishing the usefulness of the expert's field is not even mentioned.

On the other hand, new scientific fields—such as suicidology—or studies that seem to exist solely for the purpose of litigation—such as accidentology—may require a showing that the field is one that can actually help the jury understand and decide the case.

The first two steps, then, are to show that the field of expertise can help the jury and that the witness is qualified in the area. What comes after that? The facts or data on which the opinion will be based.

Remember that experts are explainers. This means they may or may not have any facts or data of their own to tell the jury. Either way, those facts come next under the common law. If the expert testifies to information he will later interpret, now is the time for those facts. On the other hand, if he has no facts or data himself, the requirement must be met some other way.

The device the common law created for doing this is the hypothetical question. It permits the examiner to recite the facts or data on which the opinion will be based so the jurors can understand just what is being interpreted. This is to give them a chance to reject the opinion—even if they think the opinion itself is sound—if they do not believe the facts on which it is based.

Of course counsel may not just make up the facts recited in the hypothetical question. They must be based on the testimony of other witnesses. The ordinary expectation is that these foundational facts will be testified to before the expert witness who will interpret them ever takes the stand.

If the hypothetical question anticipates some testimony that is yet to come, it is objectionable because it "assumes facts not in evidence."

Because things do not always move smoothly and expert witnesses often have to be called out of order, the counsel who asks a hypothetical question without first proving all the facts it recites is able to meet the objection by promising to "connect up later" with subsequent testimony.

By this time we have shown that the expert's field is a worthy one, established the witness as a decent enough expert in that field, and put forward—either through his testimony or a hypothetical question—the facts he is going to interpret. Are we now ready for the opinion itself?

No.

There is one last step before the actual opinion. There is a tradition, considered foundational in some jurisdictions, to put another question to the witness. That question is whether the witness has an opinion to a reasonable degree of probability in the field of his expertise.

Assuming a doctor is examined with a hypothetical question in a personal injury case, this next-to-the-last question would go like this:

"Now Doctor Allen, based on the facts I have asked you to assume are true, do you have an opinion, to a reasonable degree of medical probability as to the cause of this person's condition?"

At this point, the expert will want to give his opinion. But it is still to soon. The right answer to the question—and the witness must be properly instructed before trial—is "yes." Then it is finally time for the opinion itself.

Much of this common law tradition has been changed by the Federal Rules of Evidence. Under Rule 705, hypothetical questions are no longer needed unless the trial court specifically requires them. Under Rule 703, the facts or data need not even be admissible in evidence if they are reasonably relied on in the field. Even the traditional magic words apparently can be dispensed with, since Rule 702 permits experts to testify in forms other than opinions, a provision that logically leads to the point that it would be unnecessary for an opinion to be held to any particular degree of probability. For a more complete discussion, see Chapter 30, *Expert Witnesses and the Federal Rules*, and Chapter 31, *Qualifying Experts*.

Prior Inconsistent Statements

A few years ago a survey was conducted in Oregon to see what jurors liked most about trials. The results were impressive. The most enjoyable thing, at least for Oregon jurors, was not final argument, impressive demonstrative evidence or even flashy expert witnesses. What they liked best was watching a witness squirm when being impeached with a prior inconsistent statement.

This surely means that it is worth doing well, and that means we must go back one more time to the basic checklist. Witness qualification is not a concern. Authentication and the best evidence rule, however, may be important if the prior inconsistent statement is in writing. Hearsay, on the other hand, is taken care of so long as you remember that any prior inconsistent statement made by a party will be an admission, and other prior inconsistent statements are not offered for their truth, but rather just to impeach the witness.

Rule 801 of the Federal Rules of Evidence changes this, making prior inconsistent statements non-hearsay which are admissible for their truth if they were made under oath and subject to the penalty of perjury at a trial, hearing, other proceeding or in a deposition.

The essential foundation is confrontation. Under the rule in *Queen Caroline's Case*, 2 Brod. & Bing 284, 313, 129 Eng. Rep. 976, (1820),to introduce any prior inconsistent statement, written or oral, the witness must first be confronted with particularity concerning the prior statement. In other words, the witness must have his attention directed to the time, place and circumstances under which the prior inconsistent statement was made and then asked if he made the statement. Only if the witness denies making the statement may it be proven by extrinsic evidence—meaning evidence outside the cross-examination. Moreover, if the statement is in writing, the witness must be shown the document and given an opportunity to read it.

Only the English sense of fairness could create such a rule. Only the American sense of scholarship could lead to its adoption in this country, largely after it had already been abrogated in 1854 by parliament. 17 & 18 Vict., c. 125, § 24 (1854).

The difficulty with the rule is obvious: How can a cross-examiner make a witness squirm if he first must say, in effect, "See here. You said something different before you came to testify, and I am now giving you an opportunity to think of a good explanation before showing the jury just what you said"?

The answer lies in two words: commit and confront. First commit the witness irrevocably to the story he has given on the witness stand, and then confront him with the prior inconsistent statement.

How you confront is important. The best advice is to do it clearly, firmly and completely. The witness's attention must be directed to when, where and under what circumstances the statement was made, and to what other people who were present. After this, if the prior inconsistent statement is a writing, you can have the witness first authenticate it by directing his attention to the date it was made, having him agree that his signature is at the bottom of the page and then having him read the statement out loud.

Finally, there are some bits of general advice worth following:
- Avoid having to lay foundations during trial. Take care of them in advance by pretrial conference requests, stipulations or requests for admissions. Impeaching materials should be saved for trial.
- Make all foundations quick, simple, and complete.
- Use the magic words.
- Checklists can be invaluable. While it is usually a mistake

to read written questions—except hypotheticals put to expert witnesses—it is better to have a foundation written out in advance than to have the evidence excluded.

- Do not try to get too much from any one witness. If it is stretching things too much to get an entire foundation from one witness, do it with two.
- Do not offer evidence until the foundation is complete. Certainly there are exceptions when you must be ready to connect up later.
- If you promise to connect up later, do it. If you do not, the evidence will be subject to a motion to strike.

CHAPTER 19

Making and Meeting Objections

The ability to make and meet objections well is one of the hall-marks of superior litigators. Sadly, it is infrequently seen. Too often trials are larded with drawnout and confused objections which bring chaos instead of understanding, where lawyers argue points only marginally related to the real issues using terms which leave the jury with the correct impression that something is being kept from them. Furthermore, the testimony becomes fractured and disjointed, making it difficult for the jurors to piece things back together. Then the whole process is sometimes capped by the judge telling the jurors to forget something they had almost forgotten, but now are sure to remember. Poorly framed objections and responses are one of the causes for trials often being boring affairs, where lawyers literally put to sleep the very people they later ask for million-dollar verdicts.

One reason for this is the number of conflicting purposes—legitimate and illegitimate—for which objections are made. Understanding them is a good starting point in becoming skilled in making objections.

The most basic reason for objecting is to shape the testimony heard by the fact finders. It is for that purpose, after all, that the rules of evidence exist. At this first level, it should be obvious that objections must be handled entirely differently in judge and jury trials. No matter what is said, judges are no more able than anyone else to disregard what they hear, although they may rule in spite of it. So the purpose for objecting in judge trials is to test the sufficiency of the case—to prevent your opponent from establishing an action or defense through your failure to object. The first purpose for objecting in jury trials, on the other hand, is to control the information the jury actually considers.

The second reason for objecting, fully as important as the first, is to preserve the record for a directed verdict, a motion for judgment non obstante veredicto, a motion for new trial or appeal. This requires great care, planning and attention to detail. In considering when and how to object, the attorney should also make an effort to keep from annoying the jury with incessant obstructions and interruptions.

Balancing these legitimate objectives is difficult enough for anyone. Unfortunately, objections are sometimes also used for a variety of other purposes, such as coaching a witness or giving him a breather, getting improper information before the jury, throwing opposing counsel off stride, confusing the jury and even using a trial as a public podium for social or political speeches. Except for the most flagrant instances of improper objections and the few but notorious instances of ''political trials,'' the grievance sanctions of the canons of ethics and more recently the Code of Professional Responsibility have been ineffective to deal with most such practices. Enforcement is left to the tactical judgment of opposing counsel and the control by the judge of the course of the trial. It means that litigators must be ready to defend their positions not only by making but also meeting objections.

A favorite tactic of some wily trial lawyers is to try to catch their less experienced adversaries between two seemingly overlapping objections. If the beginner constantly leads a witness—as is often the case—repeated and successful objections to the leading questions can cause the young lawyer (who is rapidly becoming flustered) to give up on the question-and-answer process and ask instead that the witness simply tell his story in his own words. If an objection to a question calling for a narrative response is then sustained, because the objector has convinced the court that he will be deprived of the right to object until it is too late, the young adversary feels whip-sawed between the two objections and may, in his confusion, fail to establish a crucial line of testimony.

The antidote to this ploy cannot come from the bench unless the judge is to become an unwitting participant (and fortunately, many judges take a somewhat protective attitude towards young counsel). Rather the answer is that counsel must know how to ask questions without leading, posing multiple questions, being argumentative or offending any of the other testimonial rules of evidence when the occasion demands.

Making objections to get improper information before the jury, like asking improper questions for the same purpose, is clearly forbidden by EC 7-25 of the Code of Professional Responsibility, but once again is not usually enforced by disciplinary measures. This tactic is probably best met in advance whenever possible, by a motion in limine, usually called a motion to suppress in criminal practice. Furthermore, it often carries its own punishment by opening the door to rebuttal information which otherwise would not be admissible.

Sometimes the need for keeping a tightly controlled courtroom, motivated by knowledge of such doubtful tactics or just part of the old fire horse syndrome, will lead a trial judge to enter the fray unnecessarily. The sua sponte objection by a judge to an improper question which you are nevertheless delighted to have answered can present a real problem. The statement, ''The defense has no objection to this line of questioning, your honor,'' or the response, ''No, you do not,'' to the inquiry from the bench, ''Do I hear an objection to that question?'' should always be honored by the court—although sometimes it unfortunately is not. More importantly, such intrusions by the trial court may alert your opponent to a vital tactic you preferred to keep in the background at the time.

Even more difficult is the judge who still fancies himself a trial lawyer and cannot resist extensive questioning of every witness. Attempting to restrain such a judge without giving offense is difficult. At some point it may be necessary to say, ''I have no objection to your trying the case, your honor, so long as you do not lose it.''

On the other hand, one must have some sympathy for trial judges. They have a difficult balance to strike, finding the right point between too much interference and not enough, especially because the point varies radically depending on the quality of the lawyers in the case.

There are some important rules to follow in making objections:

1. Rise whenever you object. Doing so will rarely offend even the most informal judges, while failing to do so may incur the wrath of a great many.
2. Make objections specific. If a general objection is sustained, the law typically is that the matter was properly determined if the appropriate objection lies within the

general objection. On the other hand, an overruled general objection is insufficient to preserve error in most jurisdictions. It is unnecessary to, except to a trial court ruling in most jurisdictions. Criminal trials in Texas are a notable exception.

3. Object to improper information even if you do not think the witness is credible. Failing to object to a line of questions put to one witness will often "open the door" to the same line of questions put to a more convincing witness.

4. Make running objections to avoid the necessity of constantly jumping up for each similar question. It is customary to define the subject matter you want covered and ask the judge for a ruling which dispenses with the obligation to reassert it.

5. Never make an objection without a good reason for it. A trial is not an evidence examination. Needless objections increase the risk of jury alienation.

6. Unless it is necessary to preserve the record, it is usually unwise to object unless you think it will be sustained. When an objection is overruled, the attention of the jury is more clearly focused on the answer than it might have been, and the jury is more likely to resent your attempted interference.

7. Make objections in advance whenever possible. This can be done through a motion in limine or a pretrial order. The tough tactical question is when should you do this? Making a preliminary motion educates your adversary, while failing to make such a motion may put you in the position of trying to rebag the cat. Another advance tactic is to conduct a voir dire examination of a witness to destroy an apparently proper foundation which your adversary has attempted to establish. Obviously this cannot always be done without revealing what you want excluded, so there is the possibility of conducting the voir dire out of the presence of the jury. This procedure is usually discretionary on the part of the trial court, except in *Miranda* warning hearings, when it is required.

8. Use supporting memoranda whenever possible. Their use usually creates a favorable impression with the trial court if they are short, well written and accurate. Moreover, since many trial lawyers do not use them, they can

be devastating to opposing counsel. It is a good idea to start a file of these memoranda for commonly encountered objections—such as one refuting the typical notion that anything said in the presence of the accused in a criminal case is an exception to the hearsay rule.

A more advanced and valuable technique to develop is to learn to make objections understandable—even appealing—to the jury. It is true that objections are supposed to be made to the bench, not to the jury or opposing counsel. In fact, addressing either your adversary or the jury is an invitation for a reprimand from the judge. On the other hand, there is no rule against making objections so that the jurors understand the basis for your objection and perhaps even sympathize with your position, rather than concluding that you are pulling some lawyer's trick to keep them from hearing the whole truth.

Essentially the idea is to state a legally sufficient objection—one that is specific and accurate—which a layman can understand and appreciate, and do it in five to ten seconds. For example, "Objection, leading," may win a "sustained" from the judge, but will not really help the jury understand what you have done. "Objection, your honor, leading. Counsel is putting words in his witness's mouth," lets the jury see that your adversary has been doing the testifying.

The time limitation is very important, since if you take too long, you are inviting attack for making a speech. With some work, even the most difficult concepts can be understandably compressed in a short time. Instead of saying, "Objection, hearsay," you might say "Objection, your honor, the jury can't tell whether some casual bystander this witness overheard was telling the truth. This is hearsay." This statement, which takes about seven or eight seconds to say, may be just a little long. But it does have the advantage of focusing on the underlying difficulty with hearsay, and hopefully will be persuasive to the court and understandable to the jury.

It is a mistake to think that the superior trial lawyers who make well-phrased objections do it all extemporaneously. The wording must be worked out in advance in ways that suit you and make sense to the judges and juries you confront. An ideal place to start programming yourself is with the more common objections: leading, multiple questions, asked and answered, hearsay, best evidence rule and the like. Later, a more complete list, which can be found in Keeton, *Trial Tactics and Methods* 210–15 (2d ed. 1974), will be helpful. Having worked them into your personal bag of tricks, you should review your transcripts to check your performance. After this effort at self-programming, it is surprising how well the unconscious retrieval system works during the pressure of trial.

CHAPTER 20

Speaking Objections

It was a mistake, and he knew it just as soon as the older lawyer started to answer his objection. The trouble was, he did not know what to do about it.

Here is how it happened:

The young lawyer was representing Metropolitan Security, a company that provided security guards to local businesses. Metropolitan Security was the defendant in a personal injury case. The plaintiff was a customer in an all-night convenience store who was shot by one of Metropolitan's security guards.

The young lawyer thought his defendant had a pretty good case. At least three witnesses said the plaintiff jumped the security guard, started the fight, and tried to grab the guard's gun.

The trouble with the defendant's case was the particular security guard. We can call him Mike Conley. He had two prior convictions for assault, and the young lawyer was worried about them coming into evidence. So he made a motion in limine, and the trial court said Conley's convictions were too old to impeach him if he took the witness stand, and too remote to prove he was the first aggressor in the fight.

The young lawyer thought he was in great shape—until the trial.

It happened when the owner of Metropolitan Security was on the stand. The older lawyer representing the plaintiff started asking the owner about the guard's criminal convictions:

    Q: You investigated Mike Conley's background?

A: Certainly. I check on all my guards before they are ever hired.

Q: Did you find out about Mike Conley's past trouble with the law?

That is when the young lawyer jumped up and objected. Secure in the protection of the court's pretrial ruling, he challenged the older lawyer:

''Your honor, I have been most patient with counsel, but I must object. Frankly, I do not see what Mr. Conley's background has to do with this case.''

The older lawyer responded, and that is when the young lawyer knew he had made a mistake.

''Your honor,'' said the older lawyer, ''this evidence is what this case is all about. A security guard company—a rent-a-cop company—puts deadly weapons in the hands of untrained men and women so they can go out and shoot innocent customers in stores. That's bad enough. But this case is much worse. It boggles the mind. This rent-a-cop, this Metropolitan Security outfit, puts a .38-caliber police special revolver on the hip of a man who has had no training in its use, and now it turns out he has a criminal record. This is not just corporate negligence, your honor, this is corporate irresponsibility, and the jury is entitled to hear about it, so they can put a stop to it . . . (the older lawyer did not stop there, but we will, even though it will not deaden the pain the young lawyer felt).

As he thought about it later, the young lawyer realized he had made more than one error.

First, he should have known that evidence inadmissible for one purpose might still be let in for some other reason. While evidence of an employee's prior history might not be admissible to show that is the way he acted on *this* occasion, it might still show the defendant was negligent in hiring him or keeping him on the job. *Cleghorn v. New York Central & H. River R.R. Co.*, 56 N.Y. 44 (1874).

Second, once the older lawyer started fulminating, the young lawyer should have asked to approach the bench right away. The rules of courtroom decorum do not let you talk directly to the opposing counsel in the middle of a hearing, and it was out of the question to walk over and put his hand over the older lawyer's mouth. But that did not mean he just had to sit there and take it.

The third was his biggest sin. The young lawyer was aware that he had invited his opponent's speech. When he realized the response was virtually a miniature summation was when he began to suspect that his older opponent had been waiting for just such an opportunity. That is when he figured out that whenever you make an objection that challenges your opponent to explain why evidence is relevant, you are likely to get what you ask for.

What the older lawyer did is what judges often call a speaking objection. Of course, it was not. It was a speaking response, which may be why the trial judge did not do anything to help the young lawyer. He had invited the problem.

Most judges do not like speaking objections because they have a tendency to get out of hand. The result is, some judges even have written rules forbidding them, which is usually not necessary if the judge pays attention to the trial. (That may sound like a gratuitous poke at trial judges, and it is not. Many judges listen to trials with only one ear, and a number of fine trial judges will confess they like jury trials because they give the judge an opportunity to get routine paper work done on the bench.)

With two good trial lawyers and one good judge, there is no need for an absolute rule. On the other hand, the lawyers have to be ready to protect themselves. As Federal District Judge Herbert Stern of New Jersey says, ''Speaking objections are like gas warfare. They are against the rules, but the best defense is not some umpire sitting on the sidelines. It is the threat of retaliation—sending your own attack of lethal gas back over the trenches—that keeps your opponent in line.''

The attempt at a miniature final argument in the middle of trial is one way to get a hostile reaction from the bench. And there is something that is even more likely to get a judge annoyed. That is when you turn directly to your opponent and start arguing with him, leaving the court out of it entirely.

It is understandable why some lawyers try to make speeches in the middle of trial. The law of evidence imposes a heavy obligation on lawyers. With everything happening at once, they suddenly have to object to the improper questions (or answers) coming from the other side. If the objection is not sustained, the lawyer has to be ready to state legal grounds that are specific and timely, otherwise the objection is not sufficient to preserve a complaint about an improper ruling for appeal.

Furthermore, there is a good chance that all of these timely, legally sufficient objections will be taken by the jury as attempts to use legal technicalities couched in meaningless jargon to keep them from hearing part of the truth.

They are right.

That is exactly what the rules of evidence are supposed to do—screen out evidence. That there may be perfectly good reasons for keeping the evidence out (with which the jury might even agree) does not occur to them or even many lawyers.

This is why some lawyers try to state their objections in ways that are understandable to the jury. They do not want the jurors holding their objections against them. For that reason, some lawyers explain during jury voir dire (and some judges give preliminary instructions) that lawyers are expected to make objections during the trial.

This is where a few judges (especially those who have not tried cases themselves) do not understand. They feel that any objection that is not limited to legal terms is improper. And they are wrong. There is no rule—and no good social purpose—that requires objections to be unintelligible to jurors.

An example is in order. "Objection, leading" may be sustained, but "Objection, counsel's question tells the witness what to say" lets the jury see there is a good reason for the objection.

The plain language objection may be related to the speaking objection, but it serves a different purpose. The speaking objection is an attempt to argue the case in the middle of the trial, or interrupt the proceedings to give a rattled witness a chance to collect his wits. The plain language objection puts the legal basis for the objection in terms the jury can understand. Its point is not to try to argue the case at the wrong time, but rather to minimize the animosity the jury may feel toward the lawyer who objects.

Think of it this way: When the trial starts, both lawyers have a limited goodwill account with the jury. Given the attitude toward lawyers, it is not a very large account, but it is there nevertheless. Lawyers do some things that make deposits in the account. Mostly, they make withdrawals. Plain language objections make smaller withdrawals than the legalistic kind.

There is a serious difference between the plain language objection and the harangue. The plain language objection gives the legal grounds quickly and accurately—it just does it in terms the jury can understand.

Now that you have the idea what to do, it would be a mistake to think that you can just walk into your next trial and make all your objections in ways that are palatable to the jury. It will not work that way. The words will just not come that neatly and quickly. You will have to work out the way you are going to make objections in advance. Otherwise, what you intend to be five-second statements will become one-minute speeches, and you will be in bad trouble.

So what do you do, memorize somebody's list of snappy plain language objections? Almost. But instead of somebody else's list, make it your own. Use the following as examples for what you can do yourself. That way you will not be taking someone else's language that may not fit your style.

LEADING—Objection, your honor, counsel is putting words in the witness's mouth. This is leading.

HEARSAY—Objection, your honor, the jury cannot tell if someone who is not a witness was telling the truth. This is hearsay.

BEST EVIDENCE—Objection, your honor, it's not fair for the defendant to talk about what is in that letter and not let the jury see it. Not the best evidence.

Christopher J. Munch, Chief Deputy District Attorney in Denver, Colorado, is a lawyer who has developed a whole series of plain language objections. Here are some of his:

ARGUMENTATIVE—Objection. It's improper to ask a witness to agree with your little theory or argument. You're supposed to ask questions about the facts.

IRRELEVANT—Objection. That has nothing to do with the things this jury has to decide.

SPECULATIVE—Objection. He's asking the witness to guess. Witnesses are supposed to tell us what they know, not speculate.

HEARSAY—Objection. The witness should only be asked what he knows, not what somebody else told him.

BEYOND THE SCOPE—Objection. This is getting off the subject. It is beyond the scope of direct examination and violates Rule 611(b).

INSUFFICIENT FOUNDATION—Objection. Without more background there is no way to tell whether this is reliable enough to even be considered, much less believed.

NARRATIVE—Objection. He's asking the witness to give a speech instead of answering questions. The witness might accidentally say things that are improper and he shouldn't be put in that position.

Finally, there is another kind of objection that does not have as good a claim to propriety as the plain language objection, but which you will hear in every part of the country. If you want a name for it, call it the quick dig, and everyone has his favorite. Here are a few:

JACK CURTIN, Boston, Massachusetts: He's getting close to that legal problem, your honor.

JOHN KAPLAN, Stanford Law School: That's unfair, your honor!

JON WALTZ, Northwestern University Law School: That's unfair, your honor, and he knows it!

BOB HANLEY, Denver, Colorado (In response to protracted leading): I've been listening to Mr. McNamara for half an hour, your honor, and if he persists in testifying, I'll have no alternative but to mark him and offer him in evidence.

FAUST ROSSI, Cornell Law School: Incompetent, irrelevant, and immaterial . . . and against the interests of justice . . . and just no good.

IRVING YOUNGER, University of Minnesota School of Law: He's getting on dangerous ground, your honor.

TOM MCNAMARA, Grand Rapids, Michigan: Objection, your honor. Counsel knows that's totally improper.

JIM BROSNAHAN, San Francisco, California: Judge, could we get on with something that has to do with this case?

HAMILTON BURGER, Perry Mason's traditional opponent: Objection, your honor, that's highly unusual.

Of all of them, perhaps Burger's is the best. Certainly it got consistent rulings from the judge: Yes, that's highly unusual, Mr. Mason, highly unusual.

PART V

Examining Witnesses

CHAPTER 21

The Language of Examination

You will not believe you do it yourself, so go listen to someone else examine a witness. Pick any trial, civil or criminal; any jurisdiction, large or small; any court, state or federal. It should be a case in which you are not involved, so you can concentrate on the questions instead of the answers. If you listen with careful ears, you will be astounded. You will hear questions that are convoluted and obtuse. They will be stilted, unnatural assemblages of words infrequently used in normal conversations. They will be larded with meaningless phrases of over-caution, endlessly re-used. They will sound as though they were asked by lawyers.

If you do as I say and become aware of the problem, you will ask three questions: What are we doing? Why do we do it? How can we stop? Believing that critical self-evaluation can help, this chapter of *Trial Notebook* is an effort to answer those questions.

First is a list—in no way complete—of the sorts of unhappy words and phrases we use instead of simple, vigorous language, followed by some possible translations.

State what, if anything, unusual happened on that occasion.

What happened then? or What did you see?

How long have you been so employed?

How long have you worked for Mr. Jensen?

Would you relate to the jury what occurred subsequent to your seeing the vehicle in question?

What happened after you saw the yellow car?

Would you indicate, please, at what distance the plaintiff's motor vehicle was from yours when you first observed it?	*How far away [or near] was the other car when you first saw it?*
In your previous statement you indicated . . .	*You said before that . . . or A minute ago you said . . . .*
Did the victim ever attempt to initiate a conversation with the defendant?	*Did Mrs. Morgan ever say anything [or try to talk] to Ronald Tunmore?*
For what period of time did you maintain surveillance over the subject in question?	*How long did you watch him?*
Did you have occasion to . . . ?	*Did you . . . ?*
What was the information he gave you regarding the condition of . . . ?	*Did he say anything about . . . ?*
And a time came, did it not, when you occasioned to observe the defendant departing from that building?	*You saw Mr. Jacoby leave the building?*

Rare examples of inept questioning? Intentional obscurity? Verbal stumblings of beginners at the bar? No. Every one is a real example of an experienced lawyer trying to get useful information. And the problem is not all in word order, either. Here are some of the words and phrases themselves that we work to death when simpler words (or no word at all) would be better:

previously	unusual	concede
indicated	context	all right
occasion	relate	now
observe	contact with	very well
vehicle	client	whether or not
prior	state whether	what, if anything
subsequent	I direct your attention to	in question
previous	is it correct that	in relation to
aware	a time came when	with respect to
occur	you are aware that	let me ask this
appear	surveillance	strike that
determine	stipulation	

234

This language is bad enough in itself, because the judge or jury has to make too great an effort to follow the questions and answers. The overly long questions unnaturally slow the rate of information, helping to put a flagging jury to sleep. But the harm does not stop there. Most witnesses adopt the pace of the questioner, compounding the rate at which the testimony develops. Worse, before long the witnesses start talking like the lawyers, subconsciously dominated (in word choice at least) by the lawyer who asks the question. And if that is not enough, the lawyers often get tangled in their own syntactical webs, asking the court reporter to strike an attempted question that defies diagramming even by Miss Grundy.

Convinced that we do it, the next question is why? It is a useful question, because it can help us understand some of the possible cures. In fact, understanding why can often be the cure.

One possible answer is the atmosphere of the courtroom itself. Formal, distant, forbidding, it seems to turn plain-speaking men and women into stiff parodies of lawyers as soon as they walk inside. It almost seems wrong to use everyday language in a court of law.

Law school may be another reason. Law teachers seem to enjoy the argot of obscurity and students who are anxious to become professionals pick it up. If they stumble in class they may actually be told that if they cannot answer a question they should at least ''make a sound like a lawyer.'' Stilted talk is actually a badge of our profession, and our notions of self-worth and identification may make us want the world to know we are lawyers.

That may not be saying very much. (At this point it would be embarrassing to say that the previous paragraph begs the question.) It only helps a little to know we ask questions like lawyers because we are lawyers and that is the way lawyers ask questions.

There is a historical reason that may be somewhat true. Scriveners are among our professional ancestors, and they were paid by the word. We, then, have inherited a professional habit that once made good economic sense.

There are some modern explanations that seem more realistic. One is the police witness whose testimony may actually influence our questions. Bent on sounding impartial, a policeman will not tell about chasing a car but will relate an incident in which he gave pursuit to a motor vehicle. He did not watch someone but rather kept a subject under surveillance. He will detain an alleged suspect and then take him into custody instead of stopping and arresting him.

Another explanation is that we try to avoid asking leading questions by using abstract language, interspersed with unnecessary "whethers" and "if anys"; a misdirected effort. Finally we use some crutch words and phrases to give us time to think of what to ask next, a practice that creates an instant habit of starting each question with, "Let me ask you this," and following every response with, "I see."

Is there a cure? They may hurt a little, but there are several. The first step is to read your transcripts with a critical eye and ear—not to achieve grammatical perfection, by any means. Effective oral communication follows a different set of rules than written work. Instead look for awkward words and phrases that get in the way of clear speech. Being aware of your own common verbal obstructions, you will cure many of them automatically. You will start to become simple, clear and direct.

In doing this you generally do not need to worry that you will be "talking down" to the judge or jury. There is nothing condescending about using direct and forceful language. Talking down is a product of assuming that your listener is unintelligent and signalling that idea with unnecessary explanations and patronizing remarks. It is not a result of plain language.

Even though you make an effort to be simple and direct, you will find that some bad habits persist; usually crutch words and phrases you use without being aware of them. Part of the cure for this is better preparation so you will not need verbal crutches. The other device is a simple and effective one which will work on your "ums" and "ers" as well as "let me ask you this" and "I see." It is from Dorothy Sarnoff's fine book unfortunately titled *Speech Can Change Your Life.* It is based on the realization that most speech patterns are subconscious. We simply do not think fast enough to consciously choose each word. Dorothy Sarnoff's idea is to write the word or phrase on several small cards, drawing a large red X through it. Put these around your home (and office, if you do not mind telling people why you have crossed out "prior to that occasion") where you are bound to see them every day. Your mind will automatically do the rest.

Finally, clear language is really worth the effort. It is one mark of the master trial lawyer.

236

CHAPTER 22

An Introduction to Direct Examination

Direct examination is the heart of most trials. Except for those criminal cases where the defendant calls no witnesses and does not take the stand himself—where cross-examination, objections and argument is all the defense lawyer does—direct examination is more important than cross-examination, the opening statement or closing argument. For unless the outlook is so dismal that the only hope in litigation is to create confusion, a coherent statement of the facts by the witnesses is essential to the jury's understanding and acceptance of your position.

But the obstacles to making the facts understandable are formidable. First, they must be developed through other people—the witnesses. Second, the question and answer method is a strained device for obtaining information in an orderly fashion. Third, the rules of evidence limit the form of questions, as well as their content. Fourth, objections break up the testimony, diverting the minds of the jury. Fifth, cross-examination chops the progression of witnesses, requiring quite an effort by the jury to piece things together. Certainly it is understandable, if not forgivable, that direct examination is often poorly done.

The rules governing direct examination are really quite simple to state, even if they are not so simple to follow. First, leading questions are usually not permitted. But that rule is not strictly applied. Leading is really only prohibited of a friendly witness being questioned on material matters which are in substantial dispute. Leading is perfectly proper on preliminary matters and is usually a good way to start the examination, since it helps the witness over the initial moments of anxiety in testifying. It is also permissible, in the court's discretion, when the witness has a temporary lapse of memory and is standard for the hostile witness, who technically should be hostile in fact not merely associated or identified with the opposition. Almost universally the opposing party in a civil action may be called as an adverse witness and examined with leading questions. Leading is also allowed, as a matter of discretion, to keep very young or very old witnesses on the subject.

Questions calling for a narrative answer are within the discretion of the trial court and, when the witness has been properly prepared, can be very effective. But not all trial judges permit them, and most will terminate the process if the response develops information which is impermissible under the exclusionary rules of evidence. In other words, a trial lawyer must know how to use questions and answers to develop testimony. You cannot count on setting your witness on automatic pilot with a narrative question and letting him fly alone.

Trick questions and multiple questions are objectionable, and often are only recognizable in context. Whether a question is unfair or is a multiple question depends entirely on what has gone before. Finally, repetitious questions, which merely serve to restate what the witness has already testified to, are impermissible as time wasters.

Organization of direct examination deserves more thought than it usually gets. It does not come automatically for most people because we tend to remember things in association with something else. Unbridled associational organization results in stories within stories until the original thread is completely lost. So, while associational organization may be an acceptable personal retrieval mechanism in our own minds, it is usually an inadequate and sometimes painful means of presenting information to others.

The trick, then, is to use some other systems of organization which will develop the testimony so that it is short, crisp and understandable. The most obvious method is to use chronological organization. Equally important, but often neglected, is the organization of logical interrelationship.

A good example of chronological organization is in the effective direct examination of an eyewitness to an assault or an automobile collision. After the usual preliminaries, the witness is directed to the time and place and questioned step by step concerning everything that happened.

But chronology is not the only method to use. Sometimes it can be disastrous. Assume the case of a doctor who is charged with medical malpractice for failing to identify a ruptured spleen when the plaintiff's decedent, following an automobile accident, came to the emergency room on a busy evening. The chronology may represent chaos. At the time the patient first came in, the doctor was called away to attend to the victim of a knifing and then returned to complete taking information for the medical history. Shortly thereafter, in the middle of the physical examination, a head injury victim from another automobile crash came in, who needed immediate attention until the neurological team arrived. Then after a cup of coffee and a check with the nurse about the knifing victim, the doctor returned to the plaintiff's decedent, who had been resting while a nurse monitored his temperature, pulse, respiration and blood pressure. The rest of the physical examination suggested the possibility of an internal injury, so a hematology report was ordered. While awaiting the results of the blood tests, the doctor saw several other patients and finally returned, deciding that it would be safe to let the decedent go home with some cautionary instructions.

Using the chronology gives the impression of confusion and disorganization; using logical organization might be much better advocacy. Asking the doctor to list the tests which should be conducted to rule out the possibility of a ruptured spleen and then asking whether each one had been performed would make the testimony far more understandable from the defendant's standpoint, provided he performed them all. On the other hand, if the doctor is called as an adverse witness by the plaintiff, and some tests were omitted, a combination of first the detailed chronology to create the mood of confusion and then logical progression to show the resulting omission might be more effective.

The pace and flow of direct examination is just as important as its content and organization. Tedium is the most obvious quality of most direct examinations. A boring direct examination has actually been suggested as a deliberate ploy to put the opposing counsel off guard so that some objectionable matter may be put to the jury. The difficulty with this proposal, beyond the ethical objection, is that the jury is just as likely to be asleep as the opponent.

Like most other good qualities in a well-conducted direct examination, an interesting pace is the product of careful preparation. First, you must prepare yourself, not only outlining what the wit-

239

ness has to say, but also organizing the examination of the witness, using logical or chronological organization or a combination of the two. Second, you must prepare the witness for the questions you are going to ask. Third, if you prepare an outline or a proof checklist for each witness who will testify, you may speed the presentation of your case. Such a checklist will make you feel a lot more comfortable letting the witness go after only five or ten minutes on direct examination. The truth is that a number of direct examinations are prolonged with desultory and repetitive questions because the lawyer is going over in his own mind whether he has covered everything a particular witness has to offer.

The checklist suggestion is not a proposal that the questions be written out. Writing out questions for direct examination sometimes makes the examiner a slave to the yellow pad, losing essential flexibility during the trial. But there are some questions, particularly hypothetical questions put to expert witnesses, which should be written out in advance of trial and put to the witness exactly as written.

Pace is also a product of the power of the examiner over the witness and his or her control over the courtroom. Witnesses usually adopt some of the speed in speaking or delay in responding that the questioner uses. With this potential control over the witness, the examiner makes a mistake if he does not use it to keep the pace of testimony up to the level necessary to maintain interest and comprehension.

Putting questions in plain language is not talking down to the witness or the jury. There is no requirement anywhere in the law of evidence or procedure that questions should be long, stilted or unnatural. "What, if anything, did you do next with respect to the operation and control of your motor vehicle?" is a pathetic example of a real lawyer at work. There is no reason why questions should sound like form book pleadings.

Even the most mundane case is filled with potential drama. Although it is possible to overdo the dramatic effect in a trial, it usually does not happen in direct examination, where good possibilities for making the case come alive are often neglected. A man who can no longer tie his shoes carries a greater impact than a plaintiff whose ability to bend at the waist has been impaired. The witness who describes a crash where one of the vehicles folded in half tells more to the jury than the witness who testifies that he observed a collision.

Suspense is another part of drama. People naturally want to find out what happened. By holding something back, their interest is maintained. Juries are no different. For example, in a bank robbery case, a teller might be questioned on direct examination concerning the precise chronology of what happened. The actual in-court identification of the defendant might be held until the very end of the examination. But to make it really count, the jury must know that it is coming, and so the groundwork must be laid throughout the direct examination to create the necessary anticipation. Five or ten minutes spent in planning the build-up and final climax when the witness points and says, "There he is, sitting over there," can make the difference between dull and fascinating testimony.

CHAPTER 23

More on Direct Examination

In one sense this discussion is meant for experienced litigators—lawyers who have tried enough cases to know that a good direct examination may not have as much flash as cross-examination, but is far more important. It is for people who are already familiar with the basic principles of direct examination.

Yet in another sense, this article is for beginners as well. Advanced techniques necessarily depend on fundamentals. Like good football, superior trial advocacy lies in the clean execution of a simple plan, and even the most sophisticated moves are extensions of basic skills.

The appropriate starting point is the most basic consideration—the content of the witness's testimony; and the goal is the most sophisticated quality of all—simplicity.

You already know that the information you will bring out from the witness will be shaped by your theory of the case—your analysis of the facts and the legal theory they support. See Chapter 5, *The Theory of the Case.*

You will ask the witness about the facts that advance your theory of the case and not about other matters. The most conspicuous fault of trial lawyers—even experienced ones—is the tendency to ask too many questions, to flood the record with trivia.

Good lawyers must be careful how to use detail. While generalities lack the power to spark the minds and emotions of the fact finders, too many details can make a trial turgid and leaden. A few of the right details can set the tone for an entire case, and used carefully, the intensity of detail can slow down or speed up an event for the jury.

In short, details are important, but of the morass of facts in the file, how do you decide which to pick?

Set the scene, establish the general background with a few quick strokes. Only a few details are necessary to give the picture some shape before the action starts. The real place for details is in the "action" part of the witness's testimony, not in the background.

Even then, use restraint. Choose only those details that matter. It is not enough that a point is technically relevant. It must be either legally essential or truly useful to your theory of the case.

One common complaint of jurors is that lawyers go over unimportant, non-disputed background information with every witness. Asking only about essential details will help you avoid this. Once the background information has been established, you do not need to bring it out again with each new witness. Everyone will appreciate it if subsequent examinations start something like this:

> Q: Now, Mr. Collins, other witnesses have already told us about the background negotiations between the buyer and the seller of the Jackson Street property, so I would like to start by asking you some questions about the meeting in July, when the contract was signed . . . .

One of the details worth more attention than it gets is the brief personal background of the witness. The judge and jury are entitled to know who is talking to them, and it is the custom in virtually every jurisdiction to permit a reasonable amount of background information about witnesses before they testify. Usually a witness is asked his age, address and employment. In addition, most judges will permit a question or two about the witness's family status. When the witness is a party, more background is allowed.

Do not treat these "routine" matters routinely. Many people are sensitive about their age, family status or whether they are employed. You should avoid, for example, asking married women whether they are "employed" or whether they are "just housewives." The restrictive assumptions that underlie such questions will annoy jurors as well as witnesses.

Asking whether the witness is "employed outside the home" may help but is not a complete answer. The best way to handle the problem of preliminaries is to know whether the witness has an outside job, is unemployed or feels sensitive about some other "routine" matter before the witness takes the stand, and frame your questions accordingly.

Matters such as these are really manifestations of good manners, and they are worth paying attention to because they make a difference.

In some parts of the country, for example, it is appropriate for a direct examination to begin like this:

> Q: Good morning, Ms. Alberson. I want to thank you for coming down to court this morning. You know why we are having this trial, don't you?
>
> A: I guess so.
>
> Q: We are concerned about an automobile crash that occurred on Route 751 last May. I am going to ask you some questions about that crash, but before I do, there are a few preliminary matters first . . . .

In other courts (especially in larger cities), even taking that much time to be pleasant will bring an instruction from the judge to "move it along." But no matter where you try cases, it should be permissible to say "thank you" to the witness before announcing to the judge, "I have no further questions, your honor." Consider how much more pleasant "thank you" is than a curt "your witness" or an even more curt (and cryptic) "pass the witness."

Good manners also suggest honest (and not contrived) concern for the comfort and feelings of the witness. Many lawyers seem to understand that some care is required when questioning about bodily functions, obscene language that must be repeated (which should be done only when it is truly essential), or matters that touch on sexual relationships or personal loss.

Generally speaking, the jury will be predisposed to believe whom they like, and disbelieve whom they dislike. The jury usually will like a witness if they see that you like the witness. Fortunately, you do not need to worry about how to tell the jury you like a witness. It will come to them through your body language and tone of voice. You cannot fake it, so do not try.

Understanding that how you feel about a witness will influence how the jury feels will help you decide which witnesses to call, how long to keep them on the stand, and whether to stress their testimony in final argument.

You can help a jury like a witness by showing interest in his personal life by asking a few short follow up questions about the witness's background:

Q: What do you do for a living, Mr. Pliester?

A: I am an English teacher at Riverside High School.

Q: Riverside High. Is that the one located on the East side of town near the new auditorium?

A: That's right.

Depending on the setting, you may even go just a bit (but not much) further:

Q: Tell me just one thing before we get started, Mr. Pliester—do the students still have to read all those Shakespeare plays in the tenth grade?

A: No, I'm afraid that the school board has spared them that.

Content is not all manners and preliminaries. One of the difficult questions you must answer in nearly every trial is whether to include information that is damaging to your case in direct examination. Should you try to "steal your opponent's thunder" by bringing out impeaching material before he can?

The current bias is in favor of bringing out harmful information rather than leaving it to the other side. Surely that is better than trying to conceal it and having your case seriously harmed when it is revealed by your opponent. When you bring it out yourself, you can deal with it in your own way, and remove as much of the sting as possible.

But, rather than automatically exposing information that hurts, there are a number of considerations to take into account. Who is the witness: someone closely identified with your case, a neutral observer, or an adverse witness? What is the harmful information: a prior inconsistent statement, some inconsistent conduct, or a prior conviction? Do you have a satisfactory answer for the damaging material? Does your opponent know about the damaging material or the response? If your opponent brings out the information on cross-examination, will it appear that you or the witness was trying to conceal something, or will it look as if your opponent was trying to "take a cheap shot" at you or the witness?

Obviously there is no "school answer" to questions such as these. Just remember that as a general rule it is a mistake to create a false impression, and if you are in doubt about what to do, err on the side of disclosure. "When in doubt, bring it out," sounds corny, but is good advice.

But how do you bring out the damaging information? When it is minor, simply have the witness testify to it without emphasizing it. When it is the prior record of convictions of a criminal defendant who elects to testify on his own behalf, it must be done fully and fairly. Any omission will probably appear to be deliberate, and if it looked like an omission was an honest failure it would be even worse—"Good grief, he's got so many convictions he can't remember them all."

Rule 609 of the Federal Rules of Evidence implicitly recognizes what many states expressly permit: A defendant who testifies and is impeached with prior convictions may make a brief "explanation" of the convictions. See Burleson, *Rule 609: Impeachment with Prior Convictions*, 2 LITIGATION No. 1 at 14 (Fall 1975). Wigmore called the practice of admitting such explanations a "harmless charity" to the witness. 4 Wigmore, *Evidence* § 1117(3) (Chadbourn rev. 1972). Wigmore's choice of words was apt. It is typically harmless and ineffective. There is an argument that if the witness has reformed—particularly if he has been employed since the conviction—that it is more impressive than denying guilt now or urging that there were mitigating circumstances.

Sometimes a witness has made a mistake of judgment that provides the cross-examiner with an opportunity for real impeachment. Then the challenge for the direct-examiner is to draw the poison from the situation before the cross-examiner strikes. Strangely enough, one good way to do this is to join in the attack. It involves three distinct steps:

First, confront the witness with the damaging material. Second, challenge the witness to explain what is seemingly inexplicable. Third, with your follow-up questions and your tone of voice, show that you accept the explanation.

If it sounds complicated, do not be concerned; it is not. It is a normal way to respond to the situation. (Naturally, you will not ask for explanations you do not personally accept, because if you cannot believe them, it is unrealistic to expect that a jury will.) See how simple and appropriate it is in practice:

> Q: Now then Sergeant Herr, would you tell us what you did with the revolver, People's Exhibit 5 for Identification, when you returned to the station house?
>
> A: I tagged it and then put it in my desk drawer.
>
> Q: I'm sorry, Sergeant, you *what*?
>
> A: I tagged it and then put it in my desk drawer.
>
> Q: Is that standard police procedure for dealing with evidence taken from the scene of the crime, to put it in your desk drawer?
>
> A: No, sir.

Q: But that's what you did?

A: Yes, sir.

Q: What was the proper procedure, Sergeant?

A: To tag it and turn it over to the evidence locker and obtain a receipt for it.

Q: Why didn't you follow the correct procedure?

A: There was a new man at the desk in charge of the evidence locker, and he was backed up about twenty minutes. As I was waiting to turn it over to him, my partner and I got an emergency call, so I put the gun in my desk drawer and locked the drawer, and I didn't take it out of the drawer until the next morning.

Q: Sergeant, do you know the reason for turning exhibits over to the evidence locker?

A: Sure, it's to keep the evidence safe, and to keep it from being tampered with.

Q: Does anyone else have a key to your desk drawer besides you, Sergeant?

A: No, sir. Just me.

Q: When you came back to your desk the next day, was the drawer locked or unlocked?

A: It was locked. I had to open it with my key.

Q: What did you find?

A: The gun—just as I had left it.

Q: Did it appear to have been tampered with or altered in any way from the night before?

A: No, sir. It was just as I left it.

Q: Thank you, Sergeant.

Once you learn the technique, you will find occasions to use it popping up all the time—not just in direct examination, but in redirect examination as well.

If you are convinced that simplicity is a guide to the content of direct examination, it should be easy to convince you that simplicity is also a mark of good organization.

A well organized direct examination is not put together simply by instinct. Consciously pick a system for how you want to present the information. Chronology will help the jury understand information that is dated or that progresses from one point to another. When there is an important sequence of events, taking them in order makes them simple to understand, while discussing them out of order generally creates chaos.

On the other hand, logical and physical relationships do not

247

need to be tied to a chronology. A location does not need to be described in the order of its creation (even though James Michener does that beautifully).

Sometimes the law requires that foundational facts be proved before you can show what you are really after. And generally it is a good idea to establish the background—whether it is a physical setting or some events that set the stage—before discussing the main points. In fact, failure to follow this pattern can sometimes cause trouble. If you leave out important validating facts until after establishing what they support, you run the risk of having the validating material look contrived.

Good organization not only helps to present the facts clearly, it can itself be a means of persuasion. What people hear first and last have a bearing on what they remember and believe.

Primacy is the effect of coming first. Between two equally plausible versions of an event, the one that is heard first is more likely to be accepted as true. The instinctive recognition of this advantage is one of the reasons we have given the party with the burden of proof the right to make the first opening statement.

Recency, on the other hand, describes the effect of what is heard last. When the listener later reflects on what was said, the last words are the most easily remembered, and have their special value for that reason.

Understanding primacy and recency can help to organize direct examination. Instead of proceeding along a stream of consciousness, go back to the theory of the case and ask, what part of this testimony will the jury have the most trouble accepting, or what part is most important to the case. Those are good candidates for the beginning or the end—or both—of your direct examination. They also suggest that the right place for damaging material that you decide to bring out yourself is probably tucked in the middle of the examination, rather than sticking out at the beginning or the end.

One of the most effective forms of persuasion is to lead the judge or jury into reaching the conclusions you want. People take pride in their ideas, and if their conclusions are a product of their own thought, then they are more likely to cling to them than if they are merely told what conclusions you want them to reach.

One way to do this is to stop just short of saying what you want the jury to accept. Innuendo can be powerful advocacy.

A variation of this is the tendency of people to complete familiar patterns that have been interrupted. To see this at work, try a little experiment with a friend—one old enough to remember cigarette ads on radio and television. Say "Winston tastes good . . ." and then stop to see if he answers, "like a cigarette should." Or, try "Out of sight . . ." and see if the response is "out of mind."

In the following situation, the lawyer used both of these techniques in organizing the most important direct examination in the case.

He represented a young mother who was seeking to regain custody of her child. The father had been given temporary custody when the mother was institutionalized for severe alcoholism. The mother said that she had been cured of her drinking problem, and, in the best interests of the child, would be the better guardian.

Her lawyer realized that people are reluctant to believe that a drinker has been cured, and that the mother would be in a far more persuasive position if the judge believed that the reason for her drinking no longer existed.

Simply telling the judge that the woman's husband drove her to drink by mistreating her would make it appear that the mother was a complainer, who wanted to blame someone else for her own shortcomings.

So instead of having the petitioner tell the judge why she had been a drinker, the lawyer organized the direct examination to lead to that conclusion. Furthermore, he repeatedly put the same pattern of simple questions for each event so that the judge would find himself answering them (like a good judge should) right along with the witness.

We join the hearing as the petitioner, Ms. Simmons, tells the judge that after a New Year's Eve party, her husband came home with lipstick all over his face, and his clothes were disheveled.

Q: Did he say anything about it?
A: Yes. He said that he had slept with another woman.
Q: How did you feel about yourself then?
A: I don't know . . . terrible . . . like just awful.
Q: What did you do?
A: I started drinking.

And then the next incident a few weeks later:

Q: When did he return?
A: Not until the next afternoon.
Q: Did he say anything about what he had done?
A: Yes, he said he had spent the night with two women, and that he was tired of sleeping with me.

Q: How did you feel about yourself then?
A: Like I wasn't a person any more.
Q: What did you do?
A: I drank.

There was the pattern, again and again: What did he do? How did you feel about yourself? What did you do? It was a series that ended with this:

Q: Ms. Simmons, how old were you when you got married?
A: I had just turned eighteen.
Q: And how old are you now?
A: Twenty-three.
Q: Did you have a drinking problem before you were married?
A: No. I never really had anything to drink before I was married.
Q: Do you have a drinking problem now that you are separated from your husband?
A: No. I've been going to A.A. meetings every week for over a year now, and I've stopped drinking entirely.
Q: Thank you, Ms. Simmons. No further questions, your honor.

After the organization of direct examination comes the kind of questions to ask. Heading the list is whether to use leading questions. They are ordinarily not permitted on the direct examination of friendly witnesses, but are permitted on cross-examination, on the direct examination of hostile witnesses, on preliminary matters, when witnesses have lapses, and to keep very young or very old witnesses on the track.

While the rules of evidence provide a good reason not to ask leading questions, there is a good tactical reason for avoiding them as well. Leading questions give the jury the impression that the lawyer is putting words in the witness's mouth, whether or not there is an objection. On the other hand, leading questions help put the witness at ease at the beginning of direct examination, and they speed up preliminary questions, wherever they arise.

While you will want to use leading questions on some occasions, should you ever ask a witness a narrative question and let him run with it? Questions that ask a witness to give a narrative are tempting, dangerous, unreliable—and useful.

They are tempting because the lure of putting the witness on "automatic pilot" to fly alone is undeniable. But they are dangerous for both the questioner and the opponent. By turning over everything to the witness, it becomes harder to keep track of the facts and to know whether all the topics have been covered properly. On the other hand, narratives are dangerous for the opponent because it is impossible to object to anything improper until the jury has already heard it. They are unreliable because you cannot count on being able to ask for a narrative. Since they are discretionary with the trial judge, if an objection to a request for a narrative is sustained, you will have to proceed with traditional questions and answers.

But narratives have their use, and if you have a good witness capable of narrating, it is worth trying. You will probably be more successful if you ask for a limited narration than if you just try to turn the witness loose.

One step down from the question calling for a narrative is the open-ended question. An open-ended question invites a full explanation:

Q: Would you describe that intersection, please?

A closed question, by contrast, just asks for a specific bit of information and no more:

Q: What time did you leave the house that night?

The right mixture of open-ended questions, closed questions, and narrative depends primarily on the kind of witness being examined. The witness who can make a good impression should be the center of attraction on direct examination, and is a candidate for questions that just gently shape his testimony. Less impressive witnesses, on the other hand, may need more control, and at some point it may be worth intruding on the scene by asking primarily closed questions to help an unimpressive witness avoid looking too bad on the witness stand. The point is simply this: how unobtrusive you will be on direct examination depends on the witness. The better the witness, the less you should interfere.

The form of questions can also emphasize important testimony. A little emphasis is a good thing, but avoid habitual or continual emphasis. Like the college freshman who underlined every word in his text books, when you emphasize everything in a direct examination, you emphasize nothing. That is why, for example, echoing a witness's answers is such a bad habit. It emphasizes every answer.

It does not take much trial experience to encounter a lawyer who tries to underscore favorable testimony by pretending he did not hear it and asking it to be repeated. That practice is a crime that tends to carry its own punishment. Pretending to have missed what you obviously heard undercuts your credibility with the jury—a heavy price to pay for highlighting what a witness says.

There are more legitimate ways to emphasize. The direct examiner is entitled to limit the questions in the way he wants. It is perfectly proper to incorporate a fact you want emphasized into your next question. Suppose, for example, that the witness tells you she was only five feet away from the defendant, and you would like to underscore that fact. See what can be done:

> Q: Now, Mrs. Walker, how far away was the defendant standing from you when you were under the light?
> A: No more than five feet, I would say.
> Q: As he was standing five feet away from you, did he say anything?
> A: Nothing that made any sense.
> Q: And as he was standing five feet away from you, Mrs. Walker, were you able to see his face?

The pause is a less controversial form of emphasis that can be used for any kind of verbal underlining from a simple highlighting to setting off the most dramatic point in a trial. The most important requirement for using a pause is to be comfortable doing it. So long as you look like you know what you are doing, you can pause for quite some time. But when you look embarrassed, someone else will occupy the silence just to protect you and themselves from your awkwardness.

By far the most sophisticated technique on direct examination is the short, clear question. While it looks easy, it is not, because it is contrary to nearly all of our legal training. It is the skill of making inquiries such as:

Where did he go?

What did he say then?

Who else was there?

When did they leave?

Why did you stop?

Tell us what happened.

Would you explain how it works?

Questions like that are understood by the jury. Even more importantly, they are understood by the witness, and will tend to keep him out of trouble, since he will not have to guess what you want.

When witnesses get flustered and start floundering around on direct examination, it is usually because of a poor question. But no matter how hard you try to keep it from happening, witnesses will occasionally get in trouble. Whatever the cause, when your witness is in trouble, it is up to you to get him out. Often the best way to do this is for you to take credit for the confusion:

Q: (As you interrupt the struggling witness) I'm sorry, Mr. Kaufman, I'm afraid I didn't put that question very well. What I would like to know is whether you ever answered Mr. Mollica's letter?

The atmosphere you create on direct examination is a study all itself. Your tone of voice, your pace, the use of demonstrative evidence and audiovisual aids all make a significant difference. Changing from the past to the present tense in putting your questions will make everyone unconsciously perk up:

Q: What did he do then?
A: He pushed me into the corner.
Q: All right, now you are in the corner. Tell us what is happening.

Then keep on asking questions in the present tense. The chances are that before long, the witness will start talking in the present tense as well. The effect is that the event comes alive without anyone (other than you) knowing why.

Some lawyers feel that asking questions that call for "no" answers creates a negative mood, while asking questions that result in "yes" answers gives a more positive feeling. Surely there is a difference in atmosphere created by the stern direction to "tell the judge and jury" and the pleasant request to "tell us" what happened.

The position you take in the courtroom—which should be a matter of careful thought, provided you have the option—will make a difference. Generally, on direct examination you should find a place to ask questions where the witness will be looking at the jury when he is looking at you; it is hard for witnesses to remember to turn towards the jury before giving each answer. On cross-examination, on the other hand, you want to take a position where the witness will have to look away from the jury to look at you and answer your questions.

Little demonstrations, such as having the witness step down from the stand and show how something is done, only take a minute or two, and provide a new starting point for the jury's attention span. Besides, there are some things that are simpler to show than they are to tell.

253

The final thing you need to know about direct examination is when it is over. If your organization is good and you are following a simple outline, then you will know when you have covered everything, and you will not have to stretch the examination out for another half hour. If you have planned it right, there will be nothing left but to stop and thank the witness.

CHAPTER 24

An Introduction to Cross-Examination

The beginning trial lawyer, about to conduct his first cross-examination, feels hemmed in by all the seemingly contradictory lore of the experienced practitioner: do not go over direct examination; do not fail to cross-examine; do not ask why; do not ask one question too many; do not ask any question you do not know the answer to; do not signal your attack; do (or do not) hop, skip and jump from one subject to the next; do not give the witness a chance to explain.

To the beginner, all these bits of folk wisdom may seem as consistent as ''out of sight—out of mind'' and ''absence makes the heart grow fonder.'' Small wonder that the lore also has it that the ability to cross-examine is one of those gifts which is either bestowed at birth or else gained in an unspeakable bargain with the powers of darkness.

The result is that too many lawyers are afraid of cross-examination. This fear helps keep some of them from trial practice altogether and strangely, may lead others to think that, with enough experience, a golden moment of inspiration will come, either during the opponent's direct examination or just as they rise to conduct their cross—the sort of expectation which makes twenty years of experience amount to one year of experience repeated twenty times. Still others, perhaps pursuing the dramatic dream of devastating a clever liar and causing justice to triumph, bullyrag and browbeat witnesses in such a fashion that they convince the jury that the witness really was telling the truth on direct.

The truth is that like other aspects of trial practice, cross-examination is difficult but not impossible. Careful preparation that takes into account the objectives of cross-examination and the available techniques is far more likely to bring solid results than the hoped-for moment of inspiration. This is not to suggest that good cross-examination is uninteresting or lacks spontaneity. Rather, in most cases, even the moments of highest drama should be worked out in advance.

The law governing cross-examination is the logical starting point, and for the most part, is quite simple. First is the right to do it at all. This right is so firmly entrenched in our law that a denial by the court of the right to cross-examination is usually reversible error, while the refusal of a witness to submit to cross-examination is typically justification for excluding the direct examination. See *McCormick on Evidence* 43-46 (2d ed. 1972).

Second is the question of the scope of cross-examination, which, in the majority of jurisdictions, is limited to the scope of direct. That principle is followed in Rule 611(b) of the Federal Rules of Evidence, which nevertheless gives the court discretion to permit questioning outside the scope of direct. In any event, the limitation on the scope of cross-examination does not prevent inquiring into bias or prejudice or using prior convictions or inconsistent statements to impeach a witness. Nor does it prevent exploring collateral matters to test his ability to observe or recollect. Moreover, as long as a line of questioning reasonably relates to what was testified to on direct examination, it is considered within the scope. Even the rule that prohibits "impeaching a witness with collateral matters" does not prohibit cross-examining on collateral issues, but rather prevents showing that the witness was wrong on these issues by introducing "extrinsic" evidence.

Third, the cross-examiner has the right to ask leading questions, an important advantage which is necessary to deal with adverse witnesses and which is complemented by the right of the questioner (and not the opposition) to object to non-responsive answers and have them stricken from the record.

There are, of course, other rules. Some of them are applicable to special situations such as the cross-examination of character witnesses. Most states still hold that it is improper to ask "did you know" that the defendant was arrested on three previous occasions, but permit the question "have you heard," on the theory that reputation is being tested, and that personal knowledge of the character witness is irrelevant. This distinction is rejected by

Rule 405(a) of the Federal Rules of Evidence, a change from the common law which is consistent with the additional provision of the Federal Rules permitting character evidence generally to be shown by opinion testimony.

Still other rules, which permit varying the terms of a hypothetical question or impeaching opinions with learned treatises, relate to the cross-examination of expert witnesses, a subject beyond the scope of this article.

Just as important to good cross-examination as a thorough understanding of the law is a firm idea of the objectives you have in mind when questioning the witness. Generally, they fall into two broad categories: minimizing or even destroying the effect of direct examination and developing independent evidence on your behalf. While these two categories seem pretty self-evident, the value of consciously taking them into account becomes clear when you consider the difficulties of achieving both in one cross-examination. Then you may be walking on eggs, both discrediting a witness in general and also asking the jury to believe a particular bit of information which is crucial to your case.

Starting with the goal of minimizing the effectiveness of direct examination, there are a number of ways to go about it. They include:

1. Impeaching the witness with an admission if he is a party, or with a prior inconsistent statement if he is not. While prior inconsistent statements of mere witnesses require confrontation of the witness, and admissions, being independently admissible, do not, admissions do serve most admirably to impeach.

2. Demonstrating the implausibility of the witness's testimony by having him admit facts which turn out to be inconsistent with his testimony.

3. Attacking the witness's ability to observe and recollect. Unless it is well prepared in advance, this classic means of cross-examination may get bogged down in a boring quibble about unessential details.

4. Showing bias for the opponent, prejudice against your client, or some basic aspect in the action. Surprisingly often, bias and prejudice are attacked in such a heavy-handed manner that the attack seriously backfires.

5. Attacking the witness for lack of truth and veracity. The most blatant of all attacks, this technique is the treasured tool of the prosecutor cross-examining the defendant

with a prior record who elects to testify on his own behalf. The rules of evidence permit its use on other witnesses as well, but discretion dictates care outside the criminal courtroom, where juries may resent exposing old incidents, particularly if they are not very probative of truthfulness.

Each of these methods of attacking a witness is susceptible to use in a number of different styles and techniques. With all of them the cross-examiner is aided by two reasonably consistent aspects of human nature. First, most people tell the truth—as they see it—most of the time. Even the most unprincipled people learn that economy of falsehood, the idea that a lie should be kept to the minimum dimensions possible, makes their position more manageable and hence seemingly more easily protected. Second, most witnesses are biased in favor of one side or the other in any lawsuit. It is natural to believe in the justice of the cause for which you are testifying. While the original perceptions of a transaction may or may not have been influenced by this sort of loyalty, recollection and relation to the jury usually are influenced by it because by the time of trial it is difficult for a witness not to have taken sides.

It is here that the cross-examiner's knowledge of the facts becomes indispensable. A defense counsel, for example, trying a simple personal injury case brought by a motorcyclist against the driver of the car he claims turned abruptly in front of him, is vastly aided in cross-examination by having visited the scene and learned as much as he could about motorcycle riding and defensive techniques. The ability to use this background material with a sense of what is important and what is not is indispensable. Once again, the hallmark of poor cross-examination is arguing over unessential details.

Part of the problem of the needless quarrel is the demeanor of the cross-examiner. Usually it is not a good idea to ask questions in an accusatorial manner. The jury has a lot of sympathy with the person in the witness box. The advantage of the lawyer in being able to ask questions and insist on answers to them is obvious to the jury. Unnecessary hostility is likely to backfire.

Yet there may be a time for a raised eyebrow, a series of rapid-fire questions or even righteous indignation. To some extent the jury gets its cue from counsel how to respond to testimony, and you should not neglect this role. The problem is to strike the proper balance without putting on a transparent act. One good way to approach this balance is to keep from being hostile with a witness, even one you *know* is lying, unless the jury can see you have a good reason for it.

But even with all of the appropriate law, a sense of the objectives sought and an appropriate style, no trial lawyer is ready to cross-examine without some knowledge of the various techniques which the profession has developed.

1. Impeaching with a written or oral prior inconsistent statement is one of the most effective techniques available. First, you must commit the witness thoroughly to the testimony to be impeached. Then, if you have a written statement made (or at least signed) by the witness, read it out loud to him and the jury. Finally, save impeachment with prior inconsistent statements for occasions where there are real inconsistencies about important matters.

2. Set questions which are prepared in advance can often be effective. In nearly every trial there is some situation that can be dramatized by a series of questions which you know can reasonably be answered only one way, so that you almost do not care how they are actually answered. Often this sort of questioning will take the form of a ''flanking attack'' where apparently innocent truisms and preliminary matters suddenly add up to a major inconsistency.

3. Like set questions, there are other techniques for establishing facts which turn out to be inconsistent with the testimony on direct. One of these deals with attacking estimates of speed. It is helpful to remember that multiplying miles per hour by one and one-half gives a very close approximation of feet per second. Thus 60 mph x $1\frac{1}{2}$ = 90 feet per second (the exact figure is 88 feet per second). Since most trial judges will take judicial notice of this relationship, and since most witnesses' estimates of time and distance vary widely from their estimates of speed, having the witness help you perform a little calculation on a blackboard can often convince the jury that none of his estimates are very valuable.

4. Occasionally it becomes important to attack a time or distance estimate itself. While it is usually necessary to ask the judge's permission to conduct in-court experiments, when you are testing the ability of the witness to estimate

time or distance, the custom in most courts is to permit it without obtaining any special leave. But this sort of ploy is dangerous, and you must be as ready to let the jury know that the estimate was accurate as if it had been faulty, which leads most careful counsel to ask for the estimates in an innocuous fashion before proceeding to demonstrate their inaccuracy.

5. Sometimes it is not possible to question a witness in advance of trial. Prosecutors in criminal cases operate under this handicap. Frequently they may have no idea what witnesses the defense may call. In some cases, especially where self-defense is an issue, the defendant can almost be counted on to testify on his own behalf. The usual defense practice is to call the defendant as the last witness. Because the sequestration of witnesses obviously cannot apply to the defendant, some prosecutors ask for leave to withhold cross-examination of all other witnesses, delaying their cross until after the defendant has testified. Their hope is to keep the defendant from changing his story to fit the details on which the other defense witnesses have not yet committed themselves. This device obviously requires the cooperation of the trial court and a somewhat quiescent defense lawyer. Moreover, separating cross-examination from direct examination, especially in a long trial, gives the defendant an opportunity to develop his case without serious interruption. On the other hand, there are prosecutors who claim substantial success with this technique.

6. A more marginal device is the ''I don't know'' cross-examination. In a well prepared civil case there are usually complete depositions of all witnesses. These often contain large numbers of questions to which the witness simply does not know the answer. The ''I don't know'' technique is to scour the deposition of the witness for every question which the witness does not know the answer to, and then ask that question on cross-examination. If he now knows the answer, he can be impeached with the deposition. Usually, however, he still does not know and gives that answer to a long string of questions. The net effect is that the witness has very little information of any importance to the action. Of course, if the technique is not carefully employed and is spotted by

the direct examiner, it can usually be put to rest with a very short and telling re-direct examination.

Of all the techniques, the most important and, sadly, the most usually neglected, is good organization. As is true with direct examination, organization is essential to short, crisp cross. But organizing of cross-examination is more difficult. In direct examination, the primary objective is to make the information understandable and interesting to the jury. That same objective is important in cross-examination, but in addition the cross-examiner must take into account at least the following matters:

1. Maximizing the effect of any concessions the witness may make.
2. Closing all possible escape hatches from a position which will turn out to be untenable.
3. Avoiding telegraphing the punch until it is delivered.
4. Placing related impeaching materials such as prior inconsistent statements next to the subjects to which they pertain.
5. Placing general impeaching materials, such as bias, character and impaired capacities, at the point where they will have the most effect.
6. Placing beneficial testimony at a point in the cross-examination where it will not be damaged by the attacks which are made on other testimony or on the witness in general.

Some of these points deserve explanation. Suppose a supermarket slip and fall case where a defense witness has just finished direct examination, testifying that she had warned the plaintiff to watch out for the spilled mayonnaise in the fourth aisle.

You have the following materials with which to work: The witness is the cousin of the manager of the store. The witness made a prior statement in which she said she had warned several customers of the spill, but was not sure she had told the plaintiff. Although the witness did not see the fall, she heard it and came to the assistance of the plaintiff. In her deposition, the witness said the plaintiff was still lying on the floor when she got to her, she had difficulty getting up and she was in a great deal of pain.

One way to organize this cross-examination might be as follows: Start with the fall and the severity of the pain. It is a strong point, and after attack, the witness will be less likely to give the cross-examiner anything. Next, the damaging direct examination must be dealt with. Here it is important to go over direct, perhaps with an air of disappointment, to close all routes of escape. Then the witness may be impeached with the prior inconsistent statement. At this point the witness will probably come up with some reason why her memory has gotten better or why she did not happen to think of this at the deposition. You may even want to reinforce the switch:

"But now, Mrs. Allen, that you have had a chance to reflect on it, you are *certain* you warned Mrs. Fischer of the spilled mayonnaise?" (It opens up the chance to explain the switch to the jury.)

"Yes."

"I see. Mrs. Allen, aren't you the cousin of Ronald Hunter, the manager of this supermarket?"

"Yes."

"I have no further questions."

This is not the only way to organize this cross-examination. Moreover, you may not always have that much material to work with. However, by using basic principles of organization, cross-examination is almost always more effective than when you simply take things as they come to mind.

There are exceptions, to be sure. Some lawyers claim the only way to catch the wily liar is to "hop, skip and jump" from one topic to another. But this approach is usually more confusing to the jury than to the witness. Arguably the "hop, skip and jump" theory is just an excuse for lack of preparation. And even the claimed successes of that method do not necessarily prove it works. Even a blind pig finds a chestnut from time to time.

Finally, while solid preparation is invaluable, it is a mistake to adhere doggedly to your plan no matter what happens. You must always be ready to vary or even abandon your attack to suit what happens on direct examination. Nevertheless, it is wise to have a checklist of what you want to accomplish on the cross-examination of each witness so that you do not overlook any essential points if the direct examination forces you to shift your approach.

CHAPTER 25

The Story Line in Cross-Examination

Never before have trial lawyers paid so much attention to the techniques of cross-examination. It is a well-directed effort. If you had been watching a giant gauge that could indicate the general quality of cross-examination in American courts, you would have seen it move—slowly but perceptibly—upward in the past ten years.

Much of this is due to the fine trial advocacy training programs offered during the last decade. Thousands of lawyers have had their cross-examinations of witnesses in hypothetical cases critiqued by experts in advocacy workshops and seminars across the country. It has had an effect.

For the most part, this effort has concentrated on only one aspect of cross-examination—the kind of questions to ask to keep the witness under control. Witness control is, for example, the central thrust of Irving Younger's Ten Commandments. See Younger, *A Letter in Which Cicero Lays Down the Ten Commandments of Cross-Examination*, LITIGATION, Vol. 3, No. 2, at 18 (Winter 1977). It is undoubtedly in asking this kind of question that we have, as a group, made progress.

But the unfortunate truth is that a lawyer can follow all of the commandments about how to ask questions and still conduct a poor cross-examination.

There is a reason for that. There is more to cross-examination than just the form of the questions.

And that is the purpose of this chapter. It does not deal with the form of questions. It is not concerned with the basic techniques of how to ask short, leading questions, how to keep from quarreling with the witness, or how to avoid asking one question too many. For a discussion of those topics, see Chapter 24, *An Introduction to Cross-Examination*, and Chapter 28, *Witness Control*. Instead, this discussion will address the next step: how to organize cross-examination.

It may seem a strange topic for those not used to thinking about it. They are the lawyers for whom cross-examination (and the practice of law) is a spontaneous affair. You can hear their questions now. *Organize* cross-examination? How? Why? What good would it do? Would it inhibit flexibility? Would it give away too much to the witness? What is the point of it?

The poetic answer to these challenges may be the best, so it comes first. There is a persistent American folk myth that a song that was popular years ago was really an inversion of a melody written by Handel. Not surprising. But if true, then the difference between the "Hallelujah Chorus" from *The Messiah* and "Yes, We Have No Bananas," is not their notes—but their organization.

If that is not enough, and if you do not intuitively appreciate how organization might help cross-examination, then consider these objectives: understandability, emphasis, persuasion, and even witness control are all aims of organizing cross-examination.

In fact, there is a definition of cross-examination that will make these points more clear and that you should remember as you go through this chapter: *Cross-examination is the art of honest innuendo.*

It is a definition worth remembering. It means that good cross-examination assembles what cannot be disputed, and inexorably leads the fact-finder to fill in the blanks with the right conclusions. It is a process founded in an organization that understands human psychology. If cross-examination can be likened to surgery, then the form of questions is the way the knife is held. But it is the organization of cross-examination that tells where to make the cut.

There is more to organization than mere order. Organization is necessarily a discussion of content—what is included and what is not—as well as its order. In other words, if organization is thought of in the broader sense, it includes the subjects for cross-examination as well as the order in which they should be covered.

With this in mind, there are some principles worth following in cross-examination. They are not commandments—or even rules. They are suggestions, and they will help.

264

Do not cross-examine in a vacuum

The test of good cross-examination is what it accomplishes in the case—not how it impresses bystanders. One of the problems with concentrating on technique is that it can lead the unsuspecting lawyer away from content—and his theory of the case. A beautiful incision in the wrong place is not good surgery. Cross-examination that does not advance the objective of the case is not good cross-examination.

It is the theory of the case, then, that provides the starting point for organizing cross-examination. If we once again take organization in the broader sense—content as well as order—the first question is not just what to include, but whether to cross-examine a witness at all.

The obvious answer is, do not cross-examine a witness unless it would help the case to do so. The only difficulty with that is knowing when it would help the case.

Understandably, it is a point about which thoughtful lawyers can disagree. There are some, for example, who are quick to say "no questions." And there are far more who ought to follow their example.

On the other hand, there are some lawyers who think that it is a rare witness who cannot be cross-examined to good effect. They maintain that it is usually wise to ask just a few questions of the witness who has not hurt you, just to show that properly limited, you have no objection to what he says.

An example is in order. The defendant is charged with murder and pleads self-defense. An assistant medical examiner testifies for the state that the victim died as the result of a gunshot wound. A careful cross-examiner might ask a few questions designed to show that the medical examiner has no way of knowing whether the man was shot in self-defense or whether he was an innocent victim.

But watch out. It is in just such "safe" areas that lawyers sometimes get greedy and try to take things too far. Too often the medical examiner does have an opinion about self-defense and is just waiting for a chance to give it.

The result is that while it is possible to get hurt either by failing to cross-examine or by asking questions you should not, far more lawyers are done in by asking questions than are ever damaged by silence.

Pick only a few main points

People have limited attention spans. It is said that television (with its interruptions for advertisements) has created 20-minute cycles in people's minds so they cannot absorb more than that at any one time. Whether that is literally true is not important. It emphasizes a good point: A short, coherent cross-examination will be more effective than a long, rambling one that makes as many (or more) good points.

Forget trifles

One of the perversities of language is that it usually takes longer to describe a minor point than a major one. Big ideas usually have their own familiar words. The little points are the ones that take an excessive amount of time and effort.

Understanding this should make it easier for you to cull out passing unconnected inconsistencies. If you are not convinced already, here is another reason. Minor points—like "The Shadow" on the old radio adventure series—have the power to cloud men's minds. Adding a trifle cuts everything else down to its size.

Sell only what you will buy

A common pitfall in cross-examination is making an attack you do not believe in, just because the rules permit it.

A trial is not an evidence examination. Objections should not be made just because the law permits them. Cross-examination is the same. Do not mount an attack you cannot honestly sponsor.

Some young lawyers are reluctant to accept this idea, because they struggled in law school to eventually come to the understanding that it is ethical to defend a person you think is guilty or represent a cause with which you do not agree.

Ethical it is and should be. Still, that does not mean you will represent your client well if you do not believe in his case. It is the lawyer who does not agree with his cause who is told by the jury at the end of the trial that he was undoubtedly the better advocate, but his opponent just happened to have the better facts. For a more complete discussion, see Chapter 7, *The Credibility of the Lawyer.*

Get friendly information before you start an attack

Most of the discussions of cross-examination in recent years have centered around destructive techniques. It is easy to understand why. They are difficult skills and unlike what is needed for direct examination.

But they are not always appropriate.

It is interesting that witnesses do not always neatly divide themselves into two groups—friendly and adverse. Often a witness has some helpful, friendly information to give but is hostile on other matters.

A little thought shows why you should ask for the helpful, friendly information first—even if it would otherwise belong someplace else in the examination. After war is declared and you attack the credibility of a witness, it is a mistake to think that he will testify with much warmth and detail.

Furthermore, you do not want to appear to be in the inconsistent position of sponsoring the witness as to some information and asking the jury to disbelieve him about something else. This makes it important to separate the two parts of such a cross-examination by a pause, a change in voice, and even your position in the courtroom.

Start strong

The beginning of any examination has special importance. The psychological principle of primacy explains why. What is heard first is more likely to be accepted as true than what comes later. So important is this principle that you may want to organize cross so the biggest issue will come first.

But there is more to take into account.

Often important questions cannot be asked without first laying a groundwork. Sometimes the preliminaries for the most important issue would get hopelessly tangled if they had to come at the very beginning.

For that reason you will sometimes choose a simpler point on which you can get a quick firm concession as your beginning.

Assume, for example, you are to cross-examine a doctor about the cause of death in a murder case. In his autopsy report he notes a condition that has nothing to do with the cause of death—but he makes a mistake in doing it. The autopsy report said that the aponeurosis—a group of tendon fibers—was ruptured at the base of the victim's brain.

Your medical dictionary and your own medical expert tell you this was a minor mistake. The reason is that the base of the brain is inside the skull, and the aponeurosis is on the outside. The chances are the doctor meant to say ''base of the skull'' and said ''base of the brain'' instead.

What to do about it? You decide that although it is an error, it is not really linked to anything else in the autopsy. There may be mistakes of observation and analysis, but this is probably an error of expression.

You might well choose to let it go as a trifle. On the other hand, you might decide to gently ''tweak'' the expert with it at the very start of cross:

> Q: Doctor, before we get started, I have a question. The expression muscle head is just a figure of speech, isn't it?
> A: What do you mean?
> Q: Well, there are no muscles inside the skull, are there?
> A: No, of course not.
> Q: The brain is inside the skull?
> A: Yes.
> Q: But any muscles associated with the head are on the outside of the skull, correct?
> A: Yes.
> Q: And the base of the brain, that's inside the skull, too?
> A: Yes.
> Q: And this aponeurosis thing—that's a tendon group, isn't it?
> A: Yes.
> Q: So it's on the outside of the head, too?
> A: Yes.
> Q: So when you said in your report on page 2, ''The aponeurosis was torn at the base of the brain,'' you probably just misspoke when you were dictating, or just missed a typographical error, or something like that, right?
> A: May I see that? I didn't say that, did I? (Examining the report) I can't understand what I meant by saying . . .
> Q: Don't worry about it, Doctor. We are going to come back to some other things you wrote in your report in just a few minutes, but first I want to ask you a little about how you conduct autopsies. You typically work with an assistant, don't you?

Notice a few points before we leave this case. The cross-examiner was careful not to try to make too much out of this. It was a ''tweak,'' not an assault. On the other hand, the expert was caught in an error, and everyone will be waiting for more. Even without anything else, there is a general air of suspicion about the autopsy report. Finally, two things were done that were especially effective. First, the cross-examiner minimized the error himself. The only thing the doctor could do by commenting on it was to make it seem worse. Second, by telling the doctor not to worry about it, the cross-examiner both cut off this discussion and impliedly suggested that even better things are coming.

Set the tone at the beginning

Change is difficult. If you want to assert witness control, the time to do it is at the start, not when the witness has taken over. The same is true of the general attitude you want the fact-finder to take concerning the witness. The time to set the tone is at the beginning. A good example comes from the cross-examination of a prestigious eastern psychiatrist testifying in a West Texas court about the severe emotional distress suffered by the plaintiff. The defense lawyer knew exactly what mood he wanted to create:

Q: You are a psychiatrist, is that right?
A: Yes, that is correct.
Q: Would you tell me one thing before we get started?
A: Yes.
Q: Is there *anything* you all agree on?

Use chronology carefully

Most people are accustomed to getting information in chronological order. It helps understanding because it implies a causal relationship between the unfolding events.

It is a great tool for direct examination.

It is also helpful for creating understanding on cross-examination.

The danger is that it can get the witness back on the same ground as direct examination. Direct examination may not be home cave for the witness, but it is at least familiar territory. The result is that unbridled chronological questions tend to give the witness too much freedom.

But because it is a natural system of organization, you must not interpret this caution about chronology as an instruction to abandon it. Within any given topic, it is probably the best way to proceed.

On the other hand, it should be avoided as an overall organizational scheme for an entire cross-examination.

Use logical relationships

It is the implication of cause and effect lurking in chronology that makes it so valuable for direct examination. A slightly different organizational system is often more effective for cross-examination. It is that of logical relationship.

Here is how it works. The appropriate facts are selected by the cross-examiner, and then put in the order that leads to the inference he wants.

If you observe that this is the process of "taking things out of context," you are right. It is taking things out of the context of direct examination and showing that the events do not necessarily add up to what was suggested on direct.

That is the system of logical relationship. It is at the heart of the definition of cross-examination given a little earlier. Cross-examination is the art of honest innuendo.

Enough abstraction. An example will make it clear. The plaintiff in a personal injury case, Martin Drewek, was injured when he lost control of his motorcycle and crashed into a tree.

Drewek claims he lost control because the defendant, Brewster Morris, threw a tree limb across the street in a deliberate attempt to cause the crash.

The defendant Morris took the stand, and freely admitted putting the tree limb in the street. It was, he said, so the city crew could pick it up with the trash the next morning. The limb did not stick out into the street more than a foot or two. Morris said putting out the tree limb was part of a general yard cleanup and had nothing to do with Drewek. The crash, he said, was because of Drewek's reckless driving.

Morris denied wishing the plaintiff any harm and instead told a compelling story about how the plaintiff was one of a gang of motorcyclists that invaded a nice residential neighborhood one Sunday morning and how Drewek returned that afternoon to roar up and down the street with his Nazi war helmet strapped on the back of his big bike. Morris said that at one point he tried to flag down Drewek to ask him to ride somewhere else, but Drewek answered his wave with an obscene gesture.

Now comes cross-examination. The plaintiff's counsel realizes that Brewster Morris would never admit that he had been trying to use the limb as a roadblock. So instead of asking him that directly, he keeps that idea in mind in arranging cross-examination.

270

Q: Mr. Morris, you were unhappy when motorcyclists came down your street, Shadow Bend Lane, that Sunday morning, weren't you?

A: Oh, I don't know. I guess you wouldn't call it unhappy.

Q: Well, you called the police, didn't you?

A: That was after they had been there about a half hour.

Q: You called the police?

A: Yes.

Q: And they did not come, did they?

A: No. Not in time, anyway. Those bikers left before the police arrived.

Q: Mr. Drewek came in the afternoon, didn't he?

A: Yes, he returned.

Q: You have the impression he was one of the people that had been there in the morning?

A: Yes.

Q: Mr. Drewek was alone that afternoon, wasn't he?

A: Yes.

Q: And you were unhappy he was there?

A: Well, I don't know if you would say unhappy.

Q: This time you didn't call the police, did you?

A: No.

Q: You tried to wave him down?

A: Yes.

Q: You were going to tell him to leave?

A: Well, yes.

Q: But he did not stop when you waved, did he?

A: No.

Q: You thought he made an obscene gesture?

A: He sure did.

Q: And kept on riding up and down your dead-end street?

A: Yes.

Q: Then you put the limb in the street, didn't you?

A: Yes. But it was only sticking out two or three feet.

Q: When you put the limb in the street, you knew Marty Drewek was still down at the dead end, didn't you?

A: I don't know.

Q: His motorcycle had not suddenly gotten quiet, had it?

A: No.

Q: You could hear it inside your house?

A: Yes.

Q: But you weren't in the house, were you?

271

A: No.

Q: You were in the yard, carrying a 15-to-20-foot tree limb to the street?

A: Yes.

Q: And when Marty Drewek came back from the dead end, he hit that tree limb, didn't he?

A: Well, yes. He skidded on the leaves.

Q: And the leaves he skidded on were leaves on the limb you put in the street?

A: Yes.

Q: And then you saw him fly through the air, didn't you?

A: I saw it, yes.

Q: He was not on his motorcycle then, was he?

A: No.

Q: He was wrapped around the tree across the street, wasn't he?

There it is. Inference? Certainly. Innuendo? To be sure; honestly assembled from the information that was in the case.

Use headlines

A good cross-examination will not cover every topic mentioned on direct. It should cover only a few. For this reason it is necessary to let your organization show—so the witness and the jury will know what subject is being discussed.

Probably the best way to do this is not the time-honored system of twisting a declarative sentence into a question: "I direct your attention to the evening of October 25, and ask what, if anything, you were doing on that occasion?"

Instead, Jim Jeans suggests that we simply announce the new topic—whether on direct or cross-examination—with a topic sentence, much like a headline. Jeans, *Trial Advocacy* 222 (1975). It works wonderfully: "Now I want to ask you about the evening of October 25. You were at the roller rink that night, weren't you?"

Besides doing a fine job of orienting the jury, headlines help in witness control. If the witness wants to get off the track, you can just remind him what the appropriate topic is that you have already announced. Because judges and witnesses instinctively understand that the cross-examiner has the right to ask questions in whatever order he wants, this technique often works better than telling the witness to just answer the question.

Link impeaching materials to what hurts

One of the most important organizational lessons is also one of the easiest. It is this: link general impeaching materials to the most damaging statements the witness made on direct examination.

A simple example will serve. You are cross-examining an eyewitness to a slip and fall incident in a supermarket in which your plaintiff was severely injured. On direct examination, the eyewitness, Mrs. Johnston, testified to three things. First, the plaintiff, Blattner, got up immediately after he fell and said he was all right. Second, Blattner admitted he had been looking at a produce display when he slipped on some spilled mayonnaise on the floor. Third, the manager announced over the loudspeaker that there was a spill, and asked everyone to avoid aisle three until it was cleaned up. Mrs. Johnston is certain Blattner heard the warning.

The one bit of impeachment you have is bias. The witness, Mrs. Johnston, is the cousin of the store manager.

If just the bias is brought out on cross-examination, it will not have much impact. That is where linking comes in. In analyzing what Mrs. Johnston said, you are certain that some of it does not hurt much. Since Blattner has substantial medical bills, it does not matter that he did not know how severely he was injured right after the fall. Mrs. Johnston can at least be forced to admit that Mr. Blattner was not trying to exaggerate any injury.

Blattner's looking at the produce display is probably an advantage, although the defendant obviously did not mean it that way. The plaintiff's point is that the defendant cannot complain if he was looking where the defendant wanted him to—at a display—instead of just looking at the floor.

But ignoring a warning may do serious damage to Mr. Blattner's case on liability. So that is what you choose to link to Mrs. Johnston's bias, and here is how your cross-examination goes:

> Q: Mrs. Johnston, I gather that from what you could see, Mr. Blattner was not particularly watching where he was going, but rather looking at a produce display when he slipped?
>
> A: Yes, that's correct.
>
> Q: So it would be fair to say that—as far as you could tell—he never saw that spilled mayonnaise before he fell?
>
> A: Yes, that's right.
>
> Q: And after he fell, he got right up, didn't he?
>
> A: He sure did. He jumped right up.

273

Q: Acted kind of embarrassed, is that it?

A: Well, I don't know.

Q: You would have been embarrassed, wouldn't you?

Opposing Counsel: Objection, irrelevant.

The Court: Sustained.

Q: Now, Mrs. Johnston, did I hear you right? Did I hear you say that the store manager made a warning about the spilled mayonnaise over the loudspeaker system?

A: Yes, he did.

Q: And you are certain that Mr. Blattner just ignored that warning and went on shopping anyway?

A: Yes. He must have. He certainly didn't look out for the spilled mayonnaise.

Q: You saw him fall?

A: Yes.

Q: *You* did nothing to warn him?

A: I, ah, no.

Q: And you are positive a warning went out over that loud-speaker?

A: Yes.

Q: Tell us, Mrs. Johnston, are you any relation to the manager of the store?

A: What does that have to do with it?

Q: You don't have any objection to answering that question, do you, Mrs. Johnston?

A: I, ah, no.

Q: Would you answer it, please?

A: He's my cousin.

Q: Ah, yes. Your honor, I have no further questions.

Now you are in position to see what organization can do. Because the cross-examiner put the bias question right next to the adverse testimony about the warning, the jury draws the inference—entirely justified—that there is a relationship between the two.

One other thing before we go to the next point. You should notice that it was essential to violate one of the "commandments" of cross-examination and go over at least a part of direct examination to make this cross-examination work.

Validate impeaching material before the attack

One of the organizational mistakes the beginning cross-examiner makes is to try to validate impeaching material after it has been used to attack the witness.

274

A good example is a written report that has a serious omission. The witness does not know why you are asking about the report if you go into how important the reports are and how professional the witness is to prepare them properly. He may suspect something is amiss and be a little cautious but does not dare attack his own report or make excuses for it until he knows what you are up to.

On the other hand, if you confront him with the inconsistency first and try to validate the report second, you will watch an otherwise good impeachment crumble before your very eyes.

The lesson is easy. Validate first, confront second. There is another way to put it that will also introduce the next point. In any cross-examination, the ''set-up'' must come first.

Have the witness lock himself in

One of the real joys of cross-examination is organizing your questions so that the witness locks himself in with his own self-protective efforts. It is an especially appropriate tool for the witness who thinks he knows where the cross-examiner is headed, and is not above stretching his testimony a bit to protect himself from what he thinks is coming.

Medical expert witnesses are a good example. Some of them fancy themselves lawyers, and enjoy sparring with cross-examiners.

Many of these know that (in some jurisdictions, at least) they cannot be impeached with a learned treatise unless they at least recognize it as authoritative. As a result, getting these witnesses to admit that anything is authoritative is almost impossible. It is one of the reasons that Rule 803 (18) of the Federal Rules of Evidence permits the testimony of other witnesses or even judicial notice as a means of recognizing that a learned treatise is authoritative.

But there is another approach that does not depend on the Federal Rules. Instead of asking the witness for a list of what is authoritative, give him a good reason for giving you a very complete list. One of the best ways to do this is to make a friendly suggestion that he is not keeping current. Here it is in a deposition of a medical expert:

Q: Well, Doctor, after all those years of education, you probably never have to look at another book again, is that right?

A: Well, now, I wouldn't say that.

275

Q: You don't have to read or study anything to keep current, do you?

A: As a matter of fact, medicine is such a complex field that it is changing every day.

Here the witness is heading off the charge.

Q: But there is no law that you have to study these things, is there?

A: Well, maybe there is no law, but it is what every careful practitioner does.

Q: Do you do it, Doctor?

A: Certainly.

Q: Like read books?

A: Yes.

Q: And articles?

A: Yes.

Q: Well, what kind of book would a person like you read to get the latest information in the field? Do they publish any books like that?

A: Yes. All the time.

Q: And have you read any of them?

A: Certainly.

Q: Would you be good enough to tell me the names of any books you have read or consulted in the past year, just to keep up in your field?

There it is. If he names a few books he would not have listed if he thought you were looking for impeachment material, he has his own greed to thank.

Keep the organization simple

One of the liabilities of a legal education is that it leads to some facility with long chains of reasoning, with each carefully stated premise leading to the next inference, inevitably resulting in a reasoned conclusion.

That is not the kind of organization to use in cross-examination. Sophisticated syllogisms will not do in the courtroom. Remember, each link in the logical chain is another opportunity for it to break.

Summarize

On direct examination the repetition of the same point would be ordinarily objectionable as "asked and answered." That is not always true on cross-examination. Considerable latitude is given cross-examiners to pursue points with some persistence.

Partly for this reason, and partly because the object of cross-examination is to clarify, the cross-examiner can do something the direct examiner ordinarily cannot:

Summarize.

Please understand. If, during the middle of cross-examination you turn to the judge and ask, "Your honor, may I summarize what has been developed so far?" the answer will be "No!"

Instead, approach it something like this:

Q: Let me see if I have this straight. You say you got out of the car?

A: Yes.

Q: And you saw no one?

A: That's right.

And you summarize by going over it again in the name of clarity. But be careful. Within reasonable limits it is appropriate. Just do not do it excessively, or you will be rebuffed by the judge.

Do not hop, skip, and jump

If you have thought about what has been said so far, you probably already agree that a hop, skip, and jump is not a good approach for cross-examination. The idea behind it is that it will lead an otherwise wily witness to inadvertently blurt out the truth because he is thrown off guard by the confusion of constantly shifting subjects.

It is true that hop, skip, and jump creates confusion. It descends on the courtroom in the following order: first, the judge (who may be having trouble staying awake in the afternoons anyway); second, the jury (which is learning the facts for the first time and working hard to stay with things); third, the opposing counsel; fourth, you; and finally the witness—because he was there and actually remembers what happened.

But that is not the main problem with a hop, skip, and jump. Its main problem is that it gives up the advantage of honest innuendo in an effort to get a witness to change something he said.

It is almost never worth it.

Use the story-line method to test your organization

One problem with a trial is that unless there is a successful appeal, it is tried only once. Unlike the theatre, if a trial is done well, opening night is also closing night.

277

That is more of a problem for cross-examination than anything else. Direct examination can be rehearsed with the real witnesses, and you can go over the opening statement and final argument in your office, in your car, or as you walk to lunch.

But not cross-examination.

To rehearse it requires that you teach someone else what the witness would say and then try to train them to act like the witness would in answering questions.

It is rarely done. When it is, usually the lawyer and witness concentrate on techniques of witness control rather than the niceties of organization.

Because organization is so important, that is a real mistake. This is why the story-line method is valuable. It is a simple way to test your organization.

Here is how to do it. First outline your cross-examination using the appropriate principles of organization. Do not write out your questions and answers. If you do that, you will stick yourself with a script that will be impossible to follow. Unless you read the questions, you will never ask them the same way twice. If you do read the questions—a serious error—the witness will still not answer them as you anticipated. Before long, you will have to abandon your questions, and be without any guide at all. But most important, writing out the questions will make you think about the form of questions when you should be thinking about organization. Do not write out questions. Make an outline.

Second, just go through your outline, telling the story you have arranged. Tell it to other people. See if it makes sense to them, if it leads to the inferences you want. If it does not, rearrange it until it does. The point is that the story-line will naturally bring you to the kind of organization we have been discussing.

Third, after you have the right story-line worked out, then you can go through cross-examination in question-and-answer form if you need practice in the techniques you can use.

There it is. The story-line method of preparation for cross-examination is one of the most effective techniques you can use.

Stay flexible

Organizing cross-examination does not mean that you will follow your plan no matter what happens at trial. You must be ready to abandon a line of attack, add a new line of inquiry, reorganize cross-examination or decide not to cross-examine at all, depending on what happens at trial.

Interestingly, the story-line method of cross-examination makes it easier to do that when you need to. The story-line provides a simple way to conceptualize the entire cross-examination. It gives you a total grasp of cross that is essential for reasoned flexibility.

End on a high point

While ending in the dignity of silent defeat is better than trailing off in a never-ending whimper, it is better still to end on a high point.

The only way to do that is to have it planned in advance; you cannot count on it coming to you like a thunderbolt as you struggle through an unprepared cross-examination. The only reliable procedure is to know what you plan to finish with even as you rise to start.

CHAPTER 26

Impeachment Through Prior Inconsistent Statements

Probably the single most effective means of attacking the testimony of an adverse witness is to show that he previously made statements in direct conflict with damaging testimony he has just given in the trial. Properly done, exposing a prior inconsistent statement can be an electrifying turning point in a trial. All too often, however, the attempt to discredit a witness who has changed his story fails. The witness will give a plausible explanation for an apparent inconsistency, and the change in testimony escapes the jury's attention or the jury may even be bored by what seems to be incessant quibbling over unimportant details.

There is often little excuse for such bad results. They can be avoided with a solid understanding of the rules of evidence relating to prior inconsistent statements, use of the proper technique, careful planning of cross-examination and good judgment concerning what should be used and how much emphasis it is worth.

First, a quick review of the appropriate evidentiary rules. While the requirement of relevancy is somewhat relaxed on cross-examination, so that the cross-examiner can test a witness's ability to observe and recollect, it is often said that you ''cannot impeach a witness on collateral matters.'' This traditional way of stating the rule is misleading because the rule does not mean a witness cannot be questioned about or even forced to admit making an error on a collateral issue. It simply means you cannot contradict a witness on a collateral matter with testimony from another witness. This rule applies to prior inconsistent statements. For that reason, attempting to prove that a witness made a prior inconsistent statement on a collateral matter by calling another witness is impermissible. It does not, however, prevent you from confronting the witness with the collateral inconsistency and using the witness himself to prove the prior statement.

Confrontation is essential. To introduce any prior inconsistent statement, whether it is written or oral, collateral or direct, the witness must first be confronted with particularity concerning the prior statement. In other words, the witness must have his attention directed to the time, place and circumstances under which the prior inconsistent statement was made and asked if he made it. Only if he denies making the statement and it is not collateral may it be proven by extrinsic evidence—evidence outside the cross-examination. If the inconsistent statement is in writing, the witness must be shown the instrument and given an opportunity to read it. These confrontation requirements are known as the rule in *Queen Caroline's Case*, 2 Brod. & Bing 284, 313, 129 Eng. Rep. 976 (1820), adopted uncritically by American courts mainly after it was already abrogated by Parliament in 1854. St. 17 & 18 Vict. c. I25, § 24.

The rule in *Queen Caroline's Case* has been modified by the Federal Rules of Evidence. Rule 613 dispenses with confrontation during cross-examination provided opposing counsel is informed, on request, concerning the statement, and requires only some opportunity for the witness to explain the inconsistency if it is to be proven by extrinsic evidence. Even then the trial court is given discretion to waive opportunity to explain if the "interests of justice otherwise require." Except for a few jurisdictions, the rule in *Queen Caroline's Case* continues to be law in most state courts. While *McCormick on Evidence* 57 (2d ed. 1972) asserts that its use in trials is "relatively infrequent," the same may probably be said for a good many rules of evidence. The truth is that many lawyers have let it spoil impeachments by giving the very sort of witness most in need of destruction with a prior inconsistent statement an opportunity to wriggle out of a tight spot.

An important limitation on the confrontation rule is that it applies only to non-party witnesses. Prior statements of adverse parties which amount to admissions can be offered without confrontation of any sort, and are admissible to prove the truth of their contents, not merely to impeach. It makes no difference, therefore, if the party becomes a witness and is questioned concerning the prior inconsistent statement—confrontation is not required. While some trial court judges are occasionally confused on the matter, this rule is almost universally recognized.

An attempt was made in drafting the new Federal Rules of Evidence to make prior inconsistent and consistent statements admissible generally—that is to prove the truth of the matters asserted, rather than simply to impeach or rehabilitate. However, Rule 801(d)1, as modified by Congress, makes no such broad change in the common law. Instead, such prior statements are only admissible when they were made under oath, subject to the penalties of perjury, and may now be the subject of cross-examination. This is similar to the common law former testimony exception to the hearsay rule, altered to dispense with the requirements of identity of parties and issues and the unavailability of the declarant when used as a prior inconsistent statement.

The challenge presented by cross-examining the non-party witness, then, is to employ a technique which complies with the rule in *Queen Caroline's Case*, but which minimizes the opportunity for a dishonest witness to invent a plausible excuse for his change in stories. The first step is the most difficult. The witness must be firmly committed to the version you wish to impeach. Well done, the witness has the impression he is besting you in an important matter. Each question goes a little further; each answer makes his version appear more solid and closes, through the witness's own insistence, another avenue of escape. Depending on the cross-examiner's manner, it may help to appear to be trying to hide disappointment at the damaging responses. The witness must be led down the path completely and must himself close every door without any sign from the cross-examiner that the witness is trapping himself. Most certainly the manner in which this is done requires thorough planning and a careful assessment of the witness.

The second step is the required confrontation. If this is done quickly and cleanly, following a solid commitment by the witness to the story to be impeached, the jurors will realize they are watching a witness who knows he has been caught. If he admits the inconsistent statement, you have won the point. If, on the other hand, he denies it, you are in a position to prove it by extrinsic evidence, the foundation having been completed.

Written prior inconsistent statements offer special problems because the witness must be given an opportunity to read the statement. One extremely valuable technique is to have the witness read the statement out loud before he can read it silently to himself and, during that time, concoct an explanation for the inconsistency. When the jury hears both stories out of the same mouth, the dramatic effect is far greater than if the statement is introduced later and read by counsel or another witness.

Be careful in letting the witness read the statement. Only have him read it if you are reasonably sure that he will not be able to squirm out of the uncomfortable position you are putting him in. Otherwise, you do all the reading.

One possible objection to having the witness read the statement is the suggestion in cases such as *Larkin v. Nassau Electric R. Co.*, 205 N.Y. 267, 98 N.E. 465 (1912), that it is improper to read a prior inconsistent statement to the jury before it is admitted in evidence. However, since it is proper—indeed mandatory—to confront the witness with the contents of an oral prior inconsistent statement, something which the jury hears and takes into account in assessing the demeanor and credibility of the witness, the same process should be available for use with written prior inconsistent statements. It permits the jury to evaluate the witness at the crucial time of confrontation, an opportunity which is lost if the witness merely reads it to himself.

Finally, impeachment with a prior inconsistent statement is a device which should be used with some discretion. Catching a witness on a minor slip can be a two-edged sword. While the jurors may infer that bad memory or deceitfulness on one matter indicates a more general pattern, they may also conclude that the witness was impeached with the only matters in which he was mistaken. They may well conclude that if bigger errors had been made they would have been exposed with even greater vigor. The moral is simple: Impeachment with a prior inconsistent statement is a good trial technique that is best saved for occasions when it will make a difference.

CHAPTER 27

Prior Statements

It happens every day. A witness is called to the stand. You know what he is going to say—you have his deposition, a statement he signed, or even a tape recording he made of everything he knows about the case.

The witness takes the oath, and then the puckish gods of litigation go to work.

The result? A change of emphasis. A forgotten detail. A small mistake. Something never said before. An entirely contradictory story. A total failure to recollect; temporary or permanent, feigned or real.

It is a problem that calls on the law of prior statements; rules and practices drawn from the nooks and crannies of evidence, procedure, local rules and customs. It is a body of law rich in theories and techniques ranging from gentle reminders to frontal attacks.

First, gentle reminders. Almost anything—including prior statements—can be used to refresh the recollection of a witness. It is the appropriate step when the witness has an honest failure to remember something. See *McCormick on Evidence*, pp. 14-19 (2d ed. 1972).

Since it is the testimony of the witness that will be evidence—and not the prior statement—it usually is not marked as an exhibit. On the other hand, courtesy suggests that you let your opponent see what you are using to refresh the witness's recollection. Certainly the opponent is entitled to it on demand, and under the rules or customs of some localities, the item used to refresh recollection is actually marked as an exhibit, but not offered in evidence except at the option of the opponent, who may try to use it to buttress an argument of fabrication.

Sometimes the theory of refreshing recollection is used to get a witness to correct testimony. It is, in fact, a favorite ploy in jurisdictions that forbid impeaching one's own witness—especially in those states having an exaggerated notion of what is impeachment. (Surely it is in the finest common-law tradition to stretch one concept to get around another.)

Suppose, for example, that instead of forgetting that a business meeting took place on October 12, the witness erroneously testifies that it was held on October 15. The difference is significant because October 15 is the date of another important event in the case.

Faced with this situation, many lawyers might simply ask, "Do you mean October 12, instead of October 15?" But there is some justification for the position that remembering wrongly is a failure of recollection. Here is how it might go:

Q: What day was it that you met with Mr. Vinson and Ms. Corrigan to discuss the paving contract?

A: Let's see, it was October 15.

Q: I sense that your memory is a little vague as to the exact date, Mr. Weaver. Perhaps it would help you recall if you looked at the office memorandum you made of that meeting?

The smooth, confident use of the office memorandum to correct the testimony lets the jury see that the information is coming from a reliable source—not just the partisan lawyer's own memory.

The only difficulty is that stretching the idea of refreshing recollection might bring an objection from the other side. It is an objection that should not cause any real difficulty except in those jurisdictions where (unlike Rule 607 of the Federal Rules of Evidence) one may not impeach his own witness. Then it must be made clear that the question was in no way an attack on the credibility of the witness—something that should be obvious from the start.

Of course, there are occasions when a witness virtually testifies from his statement. A store manager relating a list of stolen items, a policeman testifying to the license numbers, descriptions, skidmarks and positions of the cars at an accident scene, or a pathologist reviewing the results of an autopsy are all examples of witnesses whose frequent need for their memoranda justifies having it with them on the stand. See *McCormick on Evidence*, p. 19 (2d ed. 1972).

285

More troublesome for the litigator is his own witness who must be called, but who cannot be trusted to stick to what he has already said. It is the kind of witness careful trial lawyers learn how to identify and then approach with caution.

The reason is, even if one can impeach his own witness, that may not do much good. It is usually better to have a witness testify consistently with the prior statement in the first place than to try to use it for impeachment later on. Even if the prior statement is admissible to prove its truth, a single turncoat witness can irretrievably mar an entire trial.

The task is to hold the witness to his statement.

The trick is to let him know, from the very beginning, that you are going to do that.

The artistry lies in how it is done.

For example, you may not wish to have the witness give a deposition. The other side may feel the same way. Still, you suspect that the witness may vary from the statement you already have.

Knowing that some people have the strange idea that they are free to deviate from any statement not given under oath, you may feel it is worth upgrading the witness's original statement.

One way to do this is to have the witness go over the statement well in advance of trial. Then, while he is still committed to that statement, have him give it in a more formal setting. Call in a court reporter who will place the witness under oath. The statement is then taken down verbatim and signed by the witness.

Whether this formal statement will qualify for admission into evidence is not the point. Even though it is under oath, as an ex parte statement it may not be subject to the penalties of perjury. Then it would not be admissible for its truth even under Federal Rule 801(d)(1)(A).

But never mind. For the purpose of holding the witness to what he has said, the magic is in the oath, the court reporter, and the formally signed document—not the rules of evidence.

In going through this preparation it is important not to signal to the witness that you do not trust him, but to indicate that certain formalities are necessary to prepare for litigation.

Later, on the eve of the trial, it is time to go over the statement with the witness. Here, the mood is not ''are you sure you can still say this,'' but ''the trial is coming up, and I wanted you to have a chance to go over your sworn statement.''

Depending on how much of this preparation you have been able to do (and how effective you feel it has been), you may want to signal the witness that you will hold him to his statement even as he takes the stand. You would love to say, "This is your sworn statement. Stick to it and you will stay out of trouble." But however much you would like to say that, you will have to choose other words.

It may, in proper circumstances, be appropriate to show the iron fist, but it should be gloved. It can all be done with some pleasant preliminary questions:

Q: Mr. Schmidt, you understand that you are here to tell us what you know about the events you witnessed on February 21?

A: Yes.

Q: You and I have had a chance to talk about this before today, haven't we?

A: Yes.

Q: In fact (picking up the statement so the witness can see it, and holding it in view during the rest of the witness's testimony), you have already taken an oath and given a sworn statement concerning what you say on February 21, isn't that right?

A: Yes.

Q: And now, you understand, it is necessary for you to explain what you saw to the judge and jury, so they can make a proper decision in this case?

A: Yes.

If it is necessary, the reminder can be expanded. The witness can be asked whether he raised his hand and swore to tell the truth, just like he did a minute ago, whether the court reporter took down everything he said, and whether he then read and signed the final document.

The procedure may draw an objection. It may appear to your opponent that you are laying a foundation for impeaching your own witness before he has even testified. A more subtle objection is that you are trying to bolster the witness's testimony with the implication that he gave a prior consistent statement. Probably no response will be required for either objection. If an answer is needed, it should be enough to tell the judge at side bar quite frankly that you are concerned about controlling the witness and hope to avoid the necessity for impeachment.

Obviously it is not a technique for use at every trial, but is for those occasions when you do not trust your own witness.

Is it worth the trouble? It depends. Certainly it is more pleasant

287

doing this at the beginning of the testimony than it is frantically bailing out a sinking case later on.

Impeaching witnesses is entirely different from controlling them, correcting them or helping them remember. Deciding to impeach a witness is usually a major determination to declare hostilities; it spells an end to helpful information from the witness.

Even so, there is a gentle impeachment with a prior statement that may sound more like a helpful reminder to the witness than open warfare. It starts with a pleasant smile that gently turns to friendly puzzlement.

Here it is in a commercial case where the defendant wants to show he did not refuse to accept the plaintiff's deliveries, but required them to be made on time:

> Q: I was listening to what you said on direct examination, Mr. Wallace, and I thought I heard you say something you may not have intended. You were telling the plaintiff's lawyer about what you heard John Simpson—the defendant—say to the plaintiff on May 25, isn't that right?
>
> A: Yes, that's right.
>
> Q: As it happens, you told both the plaintiff's lawyer and me about what you heard on May 25 some time before this trial, didn't you?
>
> A: I guess so.
>
> Q: Well, you remember when your deposition was taken, don't you?
>
> A: Yes.
>
> Q: We were all gathered in the law offices of the plaintiff's lawyer?
>
> A: Yes.
>
> Q: And a court reporter was there. Remember that?
>
> A: Yes.
>
> Q: You took an oath, just like today?
>
> A: Yes.
>
> Q: Now, that was—let's see-about ten or eleven months ago, wasn't it?
>
> A: Yes, I think so.
>
> Q: In November of last year—just about six months after this meeting on May 25?
>
> A: Yes, that's right.
>
> Q: Things were pretty fresh in you mind then?

A: Yes, I would say so.

Q: One of the things I asked you about then was what John Simpson said to the plaintiff on May 25. Page 37, counsel. Do you remember that?

A: I guess so.

Q: And you told me—let me quote from what you said—'Mr. Simpson told the plaintiff that he would have to make all his shipments on time, or he would not be able to accept any more deliveries.' That's what you said, isn't it?

A: That's right.

Q: So I suppose that's what you meant when you told the plaintiff's lawyer that John Simpson refused to accept any more deliveries?

A: Yes, that's right.

Pay attention to the techniques; it is not merely a pleasant impeachment. First, the questioner carefully avoided repeating what was said on direct examination until he was ready to explain it away. There was no commitment to the testimony under attack.

Second, the witness was given an acceptable way out. He was not attacked. The implication was (not too strong, lest there be an untoward objection in the middle of this) that the plaintiff's lawyer led the witness into an inadvertent error.

Third, the deposition was set up as a formal affair the jury could compare with the testimony in court.

Fourth, the witness agreed that his deposition testimony was the product of an accurate memory—with the implication that the plaintiff's lawyer led the witness into an inadvertent error on direct examination.

Fifth, the examiner and the witness seem to be on a joint effort to make the testimony more accurate.

If you get results this good, rejoice. It means you have correctly read the temperament of the witness and chosen a technique to fit it. You have not impeached the witness, you have helped him correct his testimony. There is no need to worry about the admissibility of the prior statement. It has been adopted by the witness in open court and is now his testimony.

Certainly, not every use of a prior statement can be so friendly. There are times when the only choice is an outright confrontation with the witness.

Take the same case again. The difference is that this time the witness has made a strong statement on direct examination that cannot be explained away as inadvertence, and he shows every sign of being a partisan for the other side:

Q: As I understand your direct examination, Mr. Wallace, John Simpson—the defendant in this case—told the plaintiff at this May 25 meeting that he would refuse to accept any more deliveries from the plaintiff. Is that correct?

A: Yes, that's right.

Q: (Inviting the witness to attack an apparent weakness) I don't suppose you really paid that much attention to what John Simpson said at that meeting, is that right?

A: No, I wouldn't say that.

Q: (Deliberately violating an otherwise cardinal rule) Why do you say that? There wasn't any particular reason to remember what John Simpson said, was there?

A: Oh, yes. I remember it distinctly because Mr. Simpson was so positive.

Q: You don't mean that Mr. Simpson definitely said he wouldn't accept more deliveries from the plaintiff?

A: That's exactly what I mean.

Q: (With the tone of voice that says, 'Come on, give me a break—just make some small concession.') But Mr. Simpson held out *some* possibility for accepting more deliveries from the plaintiff, didn't he?

A: No. Not at all.

Q: It was a complete refusal to accept any more?

A: That's right.

Q: So that even if the plaintiff were to have made all his deliveries on time, Mr. Simpson told him he would not accept them, is that it?

A: That's what he said.

Q: (With a firmer tone) And you do not know what Mr. Simpson said to the plaintiff at any other time, because you were only at one meeting, is that correct?

A: That's right.

Q: But you do know what Mr. Simpson said on May 25, because you were there?

A: Yes.

Q: And paying close attention to what he said?

A: Yes.

Q: This is not the first time you have testified under oath about what happened on May 25, is it Mr. Wallace?

A: Yes it is . . . what do you mean?

Q: You remember when your deposition was taken, don't you?

A: Yes.

Q: *That was on November 12, nearly a year ago, wasn't it?*

A: I guess so.

Q: That was just six months after this meeting, when everything was still fresh in your mind?

A: Yes.

Q: And it took place in the offices of the plaintiff's lawyer?

A: Yes.

Q: The plaintiff's lawyer was there, just like today?

A: Yes.

Q: A court reporter was there, just like today?

A: Yes.

Q: You raised your right hand and swore to tell the truth, just like today?

A: Yes.

Q: And you did tell the truth, didn't you?

A: Yes.

Q: And when the lawyers asked you questions and you answered them, the court reporter wrote everything down, just like today, isn't that right?

A: I guess so.

Q: In fact, Mr. Wallace, you read over that deposition to make certain the court reporter made no mistake about what you had said, isn't that so?

A: I . . . yes.

Q: When you finished reading that deposition, you had no corrections to make, so you signed it, didn't you?

A: Yes.

Q: Now, Mr. Wallace (approaching the witness and pointing to a question and answer in the deposition), during that deposition, did I ask you this question—page 37, counsel—'Just what did Mr. Simpson say to the plaintiff?'

A: Yes.

Q: (Pointing to the answer in the deposition) What was your answer?

A: I said, 'Mr. Simpson told the plaintiff that he would have to make all his shipments on time, or he would not be able to accept any more deliveries.'

Q: Were you asked that question, and did you give that answer on November 12, last year?

A: Yes.

There are some things to notice about this impeachment in contrast to the other. First, the apparent bumbling on initial cross-examination was used to get the witness to overcommit himself. Like sharks, some partisan witnesses just cannot resist the smell of blood. The lawyer seems wounded, and the witness is only too happy to try to make it worse. Every invitation to back out is rejected, and the witness himself blocks each avenue of escape.

The first step, in other words, is to commit the witness irrevocably to the story to be impeached.

The second step is to dramatize the deposition. Juries do not know what depositions are, and running through the litany really heightens the impeachment. The question, "And you did tell the truth, didn't you?" is an important one. Of course the witness will say he did, and it makes it much harder for him to back out later. The questions show, by the way, the advantage of not waiving the reading and signing of the deposition.

The third step is confrontation, a common law requirement that is modified but not abandoned by Rule 613 of the Federal Rules of Evidence.

With a contradiction this strong, it is possible to have the witness read the contradictory statement himself. It is a technique dramatizing that the same person has told two different stories. The jury hears them both from the same mouth instead of hearing an accusation from the lawyer that the witness has been self-contradictory.

There is a danger in having the witness read the prior statement. If it is capable of shading through voice inflection so that its meaning gets lost, do not do it. (But if it is that ambiguous, perhaps you should not use it anyway.) There are some lawyers who choose never to let the witness read the impeaching material to the jury.

Finally, this impeachment ended with the magic words that are customary in many jurisdictions—"are those the questions you were asked and the answers you gave?" Interestingly, the way the two previous questions were phrased, the magic question could have been avoided, since it had been answered already.

After the magic words, it is the practice in some jurisdictions to offer into evidence the portion of the deposition that was read. Unless the deposition was originally taken for some other case, however, it is usually neither marked nor received as an exhibit.

292

Unfortunately, not all inconsistencies are as positive and direct as that in the examination of Mr. Wallace and his faulty recollection.

What about something that is stated for the first time at trial, but not mentioned in the prior statement? Is that an inconsistency? Here the law seems clear enough in theory, but is sometimes difficult to apply. There is an implied inconsistency if the former statement fails to mention a material fact that would have been natural to mention then, but is first stated at trial. The prior statement is admissible to impeach. *Esderts v. Chicago Rock Island & Pacific Co.*, 76 Ill. App. 210, 222 N.E.2d 117 (1966), *cert. denied*, 386 U.S. 993. See 3A Wigmore, *Evidence* § 1042 (Chadbourn rev. 1970), and *McCormick on Evidence* pp. 68-69 (2d ed. 1972).

The problem can get even worse.

What if the witness does not recall the events recorded in the prior statement, even after the attempt to refresh his recollection? Assume for the moment that the statement is not a deposition and cannot qualify as any exception to the hearsay rule.

Under the orthodox approach, the prior statement cannot be introduced after the attempt to refresh recollection has failed. The reason is that prior inconsistent statements are admissible only to impeach. With maddening consistency, it follows that if there is no testimony, there is nothing to impeach. *Taylor v. Baltimore and Ohio R.R.*, 344 F.2d 281 (2d Cir. 1965), *cert. denied*, 382 U.S. 831.

Is there no escape from this logic that puts litigators at the mercy of witnesses whose recollection may be conveniently hazy.

Before going to the very edge of evidence law, notice that the best answers—the simplest ones—are those that "fight the problem."

We assumed that the prior statement was *not* admissible as an exception to the hearsay rule. But the truth is, the statement will often qualify for a recognized hearsay exception, and if it does, your troubles are over.

To begin, if the witness is an opposing party, the statement is an admission. It must be authenticated, to be sure, but hearsay will not be a problem.

Second, the statement may be admissible as former testimony. Federal Rule 804(b)(1) admits:

> Testimony given as a witness at another hearing of the same or a different proceeding, or in a deposition taken in compliance with law in the course of the same or another

proceeding, if the party against whom the testimony is now offered, or, in a civil action or proceeding, a predecessor in interest, had an opportunity and similar motive to develop the testimony by direct, cross, or redirect examination.

The additional requirement that the witness be unavailable to testify is satisfied by his failure to recollect the events. Rule 804(a)(3).

Third, the prior statement may qualify as past recollection recorded. The required foundation is a writing, made at or near the event, by someone with firsthand knowledge, who has no present recollection, but who can testify that the writing was accurate when it was made.

There is no question that the statement is a writing by someone with firsthand knowledge, and the failure to recollect is the very purpose for wanting to use the statement. The difficulties lie in establishing that it was made at or near the event and that it was accurate when it was made.

Federal Rule 803(5) provides considerable help. It does not require that the statement be made at or near the event, but merely that it was "made or adopted by the witness when the matter was fresh in his memory . . . ." Interestingly, if the document qualifies as past recollection recorded under the Federal Rules of Evidence, it may be read into evidence but not received as an exhibit unless it is offered by an adverse party.

The Federal Rules' liberalization of past recollection recorded is significant, and it appears that even depositions prepared for some other trial are admissible under Rule 803(5). (The problem surely does not arise every day, but there could be circumstances in which a deposition prepared for another trial would not qualify for admissibility under Rule 804(b)(1), former testimony, or Rule 801(d)(1), prior statements of witnesses, yet arguably be admissible as past recollection recorded under Rule 803(5).)

The fourth hearsay exception that may provide an avenue of admissibility for a prior statement made by a witness who now cannot recall the events is the declaration against interest.

If the prior statement is against the pecuniary or proprietary interest of the witness, it may be admissible. Under the declaration against interest exception, there is no necessity that the statement be made at or near the event.

On the other hand, the common law requires the declarant to be unavailable before admitting declarations against interest. Once again, the Federal Rules give some help. Under Rule

804(a)—as well as the common law in some states—a declarant is "unavailable" if he refuses to testify or testifies to a lack of memory about the event.

Rule 804(b)(3) also expands declarations against interest to include statements that would expose the declarant to criminal liability. On the other hand, the rule provides that declarations against interest are not admissible to exonerate an accused in a criminal case unless "corroborating circumstances clearly indicate the trustworthiness of the statement."

One possibility that occurs to many lawyers comes from the Federal Rules' new "catch-all" exceptions to the hearsay rule. (Really, there is only one "catch-all" exception, because Rule 803(24) is identical to Rule 804(b)(5).) The principal difficulty with the "catch-all" exception is that pretrial notice is required to make the evidence admissible. Rule 803(24) will simply not work as a last minute theory of admissibility.

Of course there are other possibilities—most of them rare instances where the prior statement may pass muster as a business record, or public report—not the sort of thing to arise in the ordinary trial.

And that takes us back to the problem: The witness does not recall what happened. He has given a prior statement and it does not qualify as an ordinary exception to the hearsay rule. Is there anything else that can be done?

Maybe.

Wigmore thought about the problem and argued that when a witness claimed he could not recall what happened, courts should have discretion to admit the prior statement. 3A Wigmore, *Evidence* § 1043 (Chadbourn rev. 1970). His point was that the statement should be admissible to *impeach*, not to prove its truth, so he advised generally admitting the statement when it would be used to attack a witness called by the other side.

Some cases have gone further—but raise disquieting questions as well. As long ago as 1925, Judge Learned Hand discussed the issue of admitting prior inconsistent statements not just to impeach, but to prove their truth:

> The possibility that the jury may accept as the truth the earlier statements in preference to those made on the stand is indeed real, but we find no difficulty in it. If, from all that the jury see of the witness, they conclude that what he says now is not the truth, but what he said before, they are none the

less deciding from what they see and hear of that person and in court. There is no mythical necessity that the case must be decided only in accordance with the truth of words uttered under oath in court.

DiCarlo v. United States, 6 F.2d 364, 368 (2d Cir. 1925).

In a mail fraud case the Second Circuit more recently attacked the problem of the "forgetful" witness. A co-defendant, who pleaded guilty before the present defendant's trial, and who gave a complete statement both to the United States Attorney and the grand jury, became evasive on the witness stand. He finally asserted he could not remember essential details—after admitting that he did not want to "hurt nobody."

The trial court found that the witness's failure to recollect was feigned, and the Second Circuit agreed. They held that the grand-jury testimony was admissible, not only to impeach, but to prove its truth. Significantly, the court said the feigned lack of memory was an "implied affirmation" that the prior statement was true, *United States v. Insana*, 423 F.2d 1165 (2d Cir. 1970), *cert. denied*, 400 U.S. 841.

Four years later the Fourth Circuit faced a slightly different problem. Again a co-defendant gave an earlier statement. This time, however, it was just a statement made to the police and was not under oath or subject to the penalty of perjury. The witness— a brother of the defendants on trial—had already pleaded guilty and testified at the trial to his inability to recall.

Whether this failure to remember was honest or feigned is an interesting problem. The majority opinion gives the strong impression that the failure to remember was a false assertion. The dissent, on the other hand, emphasizes that the trial court found it was an honest lapse of memory. The majority held the prior statement was admissible to prove its truth. *United States v. Payne*, 492 F.2d 449 (4th Cir. 1974), *cert. denied*, 419 U.S. 876.

And now the disquieting problems that have caused so much difficulty-the right to effective cross-examination and confrontation of witnesses in criminal cases.

In *Pointer v. Texas*, 380 U.S. 400 (1965), the Supreme Court held that the right to confrontation applies to the states. Then, in *Bruton v. United States*, 391 U.S. 123 (1968), the Court held that the right to confrontation was violated by admitting a co-defendant's confession implicating Bruton when the co-defendant did not take the stand and could not be cross-examined by Bruton.

Those cases set the stage for *California v. Green*, 399 U.S. 149 (1970). Green was a man who was charged with selling marijuana to Melvin Porter, the state's sixteen year old star witness. Porter gave extensive testimony at the preliminary hearing, but at trial testified he was uncertain how he had obtained the marijuana because he was high on LSD at the time of the sale. So parts of Porter's preliminary hearing testimony were read by the prosecutor and admitted into evidence for their truth under 1235 of the California Evidence Code.

The California District Court of Appeal reversed the conviction, and the Supreme Court of California agreed, holding that the use of the prior statement denied the right to confrontation, even though Porter was cross-examined at the trial.

But in upholding the conviction the United States Supreme Court said that ''there is good reason to conclude that the Confrontation Clause is not violated by admitting a declarant's out-of-court statements, as long as the declarant is testifying as a witness and subject to full and effective cross-examination.''

The Supreme Court took some pains to point out that the right to confrontation is different from the right to cross-examination, a matter disputed in Kenneth W. Graham, *The Right of Confrontation and Rules of Evidence: Sir Walter Raleigh Rides Again*, 9 ALASKA L. J. 20 (1971). The historical basis for distinguishing between cross-examination and confrontation receives extensive treatment in Judge Widener's dissent in *United States v. Payne*, 492 F.2d 449, 455-465 (4th Cir. 1974).

So what does it all mean?

In civil cases, where the right to confrontation is not an issue, prior statements—even those never tested by cross-examination—may pass the test of constitutionality despite the witness's present testimony that he does not remember. The statements would not appear to be admissible under Federal Rule 801(d)(1), which admits prior statements made under oath, because it seems that the witness is not ''subject to cross-examination concerning the statement'' at the trial.

Strangely enough, the most effective argument for admitting such prior statements in civil actions comes from a criminal case, *United States v. Insana*, 423 F.2d 1165 (2d Cir. 1970). The court said that a dishonest lack of memory is an ''implied affirmation'' of the prior statement.

But criminal cases are different. The Fourth Circuit's position in *United States v. Payne*, 492 F.2d 449 (4th Cir. 1974), is a borderline one. The court seems to feel that the disappointed cross-examiner cannot complain when the witness's memory failure appears to be prompted by a desire to help the defendant. Remember that the ''forgetful'' witness was the defendant's brother. Surely, if the prosecution can show that the defendant somehow caused the lapse, then the case has been made for spoliation of evidence—a classical sort of admission.

On the other hand, lacking complicity by the defendant, should he be estopped to complain when the motivation of the witness seems to be to help the defendant? It may well be that the defendant would be better off with adverse testimony he can attack than with a transparent attempt to avoid testimony—especially when that is coupled with a damning prior statement. As the old saying has it, ''With friends like these, who needs enemies?''

The results of both *Payne* and *Insana* have an interesting effect. They discourage defendants from trying to convince adverse witnesses to keep quiet. Perhaps the most that can be said for both decisions is that the Second and Fourth Circuits have no intention of letting the Confrontation Clause become a tool for mocking justice, and if it seems on all the facts that the witness is ''forgetting'' at the defendant's behest, then the prior statement will be admissible.

Finally, the problem of cross-examination and confrontation is thoroughly discussed in Michael Graham's *The Confrontation Clause, the Hearsay Rule and the Forgetful Witness*, 56 TEX. L. REV. 151 (1978).

CHAPTER 28

Witness Control

They come in a variety of packages: fractious and argumentative, fairminded but stubborn, breezy and ebullient. But whether good-natured, hardheaded or combative, uncontrollable witnesses share a common feature.

They threaten to blow things apart.

For if their answers capture the imagination of the jury, it is not just the witness—the whole trial is out of control.

It can even happen when the witness is one of your own.

That is a good place to start.

Controllability is an attribute that is so important that most trial lawyers assess it on an instinctive level. It is part of the total package that makes a ''good witness.'' Because a potentially unruly witness can have a profound effect on the outcome of a case, he is always a good candidate for replacement if there is someone else who can be called to establish the same information.

In other words, the first rule of witness control—whether on a conscious or unconscious level—is to avoid calling the difficult witness in the first place.

The second rule—if the difficult witness must be called—is to keep direct and cross-examination to a minimum.

These are the dictates of prudence. Avoid a problem witness if possible, understanding that failure to call a witness whose testimony would ordinarily be expected to be favorable can sometimes be used to support the inference that the witness would have testified adversely. (See *McCormick on Evidence* at 656 (2d ed. 1972).)

But there are times when prudence must be cast aside, and the witness with the potential for becoming difficult to control must be called to testify. What then?

The cardinal principle is to start working on witness control during trial preparation. It is a good idea when preparing witnesses for trial to subject them to a rigorous cross-examination. Sometimes even the most friendly and loyal witnesses can be difficult to control; not only on direct examination, when you are asking the questions, but also on cross-examination, when your opportunity to correct anything is greatly diminished.

The difficulty is, some loyal and friendly witnesses will want to do battle with the cross-examiner. That desire is a prelude to disaster. You can minimize the danger of such witnesses getting out of hand by instructing all witnesses to wait for a full second or two before answering any question on cross-examination. The avowed purpose for this delay is to give you time to object to improper questions, but the pause will also tend to curb the argumentative witness's tendency to talk first and think later.

A second kind of friendly witness control problem relates more to the content of the witness's testimony than to his behavior on the stand. Some people, for example, tend to give wildly improbable estimates of speed, time and distances in automobile collision cases. It is not necessarily that their observations are faulty; rather it may be merely a difficulty in expressing recollections in abstract numbers. Such a witness may profit greatly from being questioned at the scene in pretrial preparation, giving him a chance to test for himself the accuracy of his estimates and the plausibility of his recollections.

The next sort of friendly witness control has perhaps been best developed by Theodore I. Koskoff. It is a principle that trial lawyers are just beginning to appreciate. Drawing on the work of Dr. Elizabeth F. Loftus at the University of Washington, Mr. Koskoff demonstrates the remarkable power of the examiner who chooses his words carefully. In *The Language of Persuasion*, 3 LITIGATION, No. 4, at 24 (Summer 1977), he shows that simply asking ''How *near* to the car were you?'' will bring a different, *nearer*, response than ''How far from the car were you?''

The point is that the way the question is put influences the answer. Beyond that, Koskoff observes, the way a question is put also influences the way the answer is perceived by the finder of fact.

Not every problem of friendly witness control is so refined. A good deal of energy must be spent just getting the witnesses on the subject and keeping them there.

One of the traditional ways to put the witness on the right subject is to torture a topic into an awkward question:

> Q: I direct your attention to the evening of Friday, February 13, and ask you what, if anything, unusual you were doing on that occasion?

There you have it: vintage trial lawyer cliché.

Of course, just because it is overworked and trite is no reason to get rid of it. While it is a tired sort of question to our ears, it is new to witnesses and juries.

So do not abandon this contrived question because it is shopworn—get rid of it because it is awkward and difficult to understand, and because there is a much better way to get the witness on the track and keep him there. It is a method suggested by James W. Jeans, *Trial Advocacy*, at 22 (West 1975). It is an idea of brilliant simplicity.

Do not torture a topic into a question. Instead, just state the topic as a simple declaration.

Instead of asking:

> Q: I direct your attention to the evening of Friday, February 13, and ask you what, if anything, unusual you were doing on that occasion?

Try this:

> Q: Now let's talk about the evening of Friday, February 13. Would you tell us, please, what you were doing that night?

The key to the system is the first sentence. It announces a new topic. It does not ask any question. Once you grasp how simply and effectively it works, you will find yourself using it to good effect all the time.

Here is what it does: It orients the judge and jury to the subject matter much better than the old twisted question method can. It orients the witness too—and helps keep him on the subject. It is a good way to start an examination and a good way to switch to new topics.

Finally, the topic sentence can be used for a friendly reminder:

> Q: I understand you are concerned about what happened Saturday morning, but before we talk about that, let's finish talking about Friday night.

There it is. Now let us talk about leading questions and friendly witnesses.

The traditional way of putting the rule is that it is permissible to lead on cross-examination, but not on direct.

301

That is not completely accurate. It is perfectly proper to lead a friendly witness—even on direct examination—on preliminary matters and other facts not seriously in dispute. J. Weinstein and M. Berger, *Weinstein's Evidence* ¶ 611[05] (1975). In the words of the Federal Rules of Evidence, leading questions are permitted on direct examination when they are "necessary to develop [the witness's] testimony." Rule 611 (c). It means that leading questions, especially when coupled with sensible topical sentences, perform an important function in keeping witnesses on the subject.

To be sure, friendly witnesses sometimes need control. But when someone talks about witness control, the picture that comes to mind is not the helpful person who needs to be kept on the subject.

Witness control suggests the argumentative fact witness who refuses to make the most reasonable concessions—the sharp-tongued young man or woman who keeps asking *you* questions, or the sparkling professional expert who takes every cross-examination question from you as a jumping-off point for a miniature lecture that entertains the jury and drives his point home.

More than that, witness control brings up the picture of the pitched battle of wits where the witness—with the emotional advantage we Americans give to the underdog—will win if you lose or win if you win too well.

How about that kind of witness control?

First, let the witness know that you know the facts. There are times when you would love (outside the presence of the jury) to say to a witness at the beginning of your cross-examination: "Look here. I have been to the scene of this accident, and I have studied it from every angle. I know what is there and what is not, so do not try anything funny." The trick is to send the same message to the witness, right in front of the jury, without seeming to be heavy-handed.

One way to do this is to refer to details which would only be remembered by someone who had actually been to the scene:

> *Q:* Officer Wilson, on direct examination you told us you were standing in front of Benson's Pawn Shop on the corner of 17th and Beloit at the time you heard the shots.
>
> *A:* Yes.
>
> *Q:* Now, could you tell us, which side of the pawnshop you were closest to—the east side, near Silver's Music Shop, or the west side, right next to Capitol Liquors?

It really does not matter whether the witness remembers the

302

name of the liquor store and music shop, since the point of the question was to tell him that the questioner knew what he was talking about.

There are times when this sort of subtlety is not the best approach. Suppose, for example, that you know that the distance between two buildings is only nineteen inches. The witness claims he squeezed himself in that space. You would like to use the measurement on your cross-examination. Two days from now, during your case in chief, you can easily prove an exact measurement of the space by asking one of your own witnesses, but you would much rather confront this witness now:

Q: Officer Wilson, I went to the corner of 17th and Beloit to see those buildings you hid between. They are pretty close together, aren't they?

A: They are close, but not so close that you can't get between them.

Q: As a matter of fact (as you let the witness see you are consulting a little notebook) they are only about nineteen inches apart, isn't that right?

A: I guess so.

Q: You are not suggesting they are any further apart than that?

A: No.

Q: Now I wonder, Officer Wilson, if you might help me with something here. Would you please help me move this blackboard so that it is nineteen inches from the wall?

A: All right.

Q: Would you hold this measure, so that I get it the right distance?

A: All right.

Q: Is that it?

A: That's nineteen inches.

Q: And that's the distance, now, between the south wall of the courtroom and the portable blackboard, right?

A: Right.

Q: The same distance between the pawnshop building and the liquor store?

A: Yes.

Q: Now, I wonder, Officer, if you would be kind enough to step through that space that is left between the blackboard and the south wall of the courtroom?

A: Okay.

Q: Thank you. Now, Officer Wilson, I wonder if you would mind doing it again, this time without turning sideways?

A: I, uh, can't make it.

Set aside for the time whether the cross-examiner really made any headway with his little demonstration, and concentrate instead on how effectively he set it up.

Having the witness testify that the buildings were only nineteen inches apart was essential to getting him to show he would only fit sideways between them. The witness, we assume, is smart, quick, argumentative and biased toward the other side.

The cross-examiner has shown that he is thoroughly acquainted with the scene, and the witness's temptation to argue the distance is contained.

Notice that the cross-examiner did not represent that he had measured the distance and that it was nineteen inches. That would be improper, unsworn testimony. On the other hand, cross-examiners are surely permitted to lead. They are, furthermore, entitled to visit the scene and let the witness know that fact.

Finally, if you employ this technique, be certain never to exaggerate any fact contained in any leading question you ask. Even without considering the ethical problems, any exaggeration is fraught with danger.

The most innocent overstatement, when exposed, can make the jury think you were deliberately trying to mislead them.

The power in letting the witness know you are certain of your facts lies in the implied ability to prove that the witness you are cross-examining is wrong. It is a device that works best when used in advance before the witness commits himself.

In the hypothetical measurement case, the signal came before the question about the distance between the buildings.

Compare the result with the attempt to contain the witness after he commits himself:

Q: How far apart would you say those two buildings are?

A: About three, to three and one-half feet apart, in that area.

Q: You think they are about three feet apart?

A: Yes.

Q: You are quite certain of that?

A: Yes. After all, I was able to walk in between the two buildings without any real difficulty. It was close, but I could do it.

Q: Well, if another witness testifies that those buildings are less than two feet apart, will he be lying?

Opposing Counsel: Objection, Your Honor.

The Court: Sustained.

> Q: All right, if another witness testifies that those buildings are less than two feet apart, will he be mistaken?
>
> A: I don't know what anybody else thinks. All I know is that they are about three feet apart. Maybe a little more.

Result? Disaster. And the effect of specific contradiction two days later will be slight.

Let us look at the "would the other witness be lying" routine first.

It is always an improper question. No witness can know whether another witness was lying. That is—old as it sounds—for the jury to decide. Lying requires guilty intent—an intent the witness on the stand could not possibly assess.

But even if the question were proper, it would still be ineffective. The threat implicit in the whole routine is "change your story, or I will call another witness." It is not a very terrifying idea.

Not that you should take the next step, which (sadly) you have probably tried or have seen someone else try:

> Q: So you say those buildings are three feet apart?
>
> A: Yes. About three to three and one-half feet apart. In that area.
>
> Q: You are quite certain of that?
>
> A: Yes.
>
> Q: Do you realize you are under oath?
>
> A: Yes.
>
> Q: And you still say they are three to three and one-half feet apart?
>
> A: Yes. That's my best estimate.

The cross-examiner is not in control; the witness is, and the questioner's blustering only serves to validate the reasonable-sounding answers that the witness is giving.

So what is the lesson? Use your knowledge of the facts to control the testimony of the witness *before* the answer—not after.

Signaling the witness that you know what you are talking about is just the first step toward controlling the hostile witness. The second step is just as important.

Ask short questions.

Actually that rule can be restated. Ask *only* short questions.

The rule is justified for several different reasons. First, short questions are less likely to be objectionable, since it is difficult for them to be multiple questions or to state assumptions that are not yet in evidence. They are, moreover, less likely to be objected to as confusing or misleading.

Second, short questions are less likely to confuse the jury. If they can follow you, they are more likely to pay attention during your cross-examination.

Third, if you make a mistake in framing a short question, you are more likely to be able to correct it yourself.

Important as those reasons are, they are insignificant in comparison with the fourth (and best) reason.

Short questions control the witness:

Q: You were standing in front of the Wade's Super Drugs?
A: Yes.
Q: You saw a man approach?
A: Yes.
Q: He was wearing a dark coat?
A: Yes.
Q: And carrying a package?
A: Yes.
Q: You were concerned when he asked you for a match?
A: Yes.
Q: You had heard it was a dangerous neighborhood at night?
A: Yes.

Short questions are usually (but not always) narrow in scope. It is interesting, because one would think that the narrowest question was the one with the most qualifiers in it, and that the question with the most qualifiers would be the longest question.

Not so.

Why?.

Because each qualifier is an additional invitation for an argument—another avenue of escape for the wily witness. The question with multiple qualifiers is the sort that is asked by lawyers who think that every question must stand on its own, outside of any context.

Fortunately, we are entitled to use context.

The narrow scope—giving the witness fewer avenues of escape—is not the only advantage of short questions. They also tend to be more memorable, and evasions are thus more obvious.

This means if a short question is not answered, then repeating it will make it clear that the witness is avoiding the question:

Q: Doctor, did you perform a spinal tap on Mr. Morris?

306

> *A:* Well, actually, the spinal tap is not always an advisable procedure.
>
> *Q:* Doctor, did you perform a spinal tap on Mr. Morris?
>
> *A:* Under the circumstances, there were other diagnostic measures that had a higher priority. One of these is the electroencephalogram which we administered at University Hospital.
>
> *Q:* Doctor, did you perform a spinal tap on Mr. Morris?

If the witness avoids answering again, the examiner is justified in asking in a friendly voice:

> *Q:* That's just a long way to say no, isn't it Doctor?

The technique of asking short questions is invaluable in witness control. Surprisingly, it is one that many lawyers who have been trying cases for years have not learned. If you need a final endorsement, here it is: It takes only a few minutes to learn, and it will literally revolutionize your ability to cross-examine.

The next rule is almost as important.

Use leading questions.

You will notice that the rule does not say, "Ask only leading questions." There may be times when that is hard to do. There will be occasions when you deliberately ask nonleading questions to provide a change of pace, or because you do not care how the witness answers the question. The leading question format, moreover, can get awkward or even tiresome. The question, "Doctor, did you perform a spinal tap on Mr, Morris?', controls the witness just as well as "You did not perform a spinal tap on Mr. Morris, did you?" or "Isn't it a fact that you never performed a spinal tap on Mr. Morris?"

There are some questions that are simply better off in a non-leading form. The time will come when it is more effective to say to the witness:

> *Q:* Tell the jury the name of the man you met that night,

than it would be to ask:

> *Q:* You saw John Hirsh that night, didn't you?

This does not mean the beginning lawyer should forget about leading questions on cross-examination.

On the contrary.

Most questions on cross-examination should be leading questions. Leading is an important right of the cross-examiner and crucial to effective witness control. But there are times to avoid it.

So far, witness control seems to be centered around the use of techniques that are simple enough for anyone to use, and that is true. Yet, you will encounter some experienced litigators who have the reputation of always being able to keep control over witnesses, and whose approach might surprise you:

"Forget about all those trial techniques. The real answer to witness control is strength of character."

There is something to this. If you believe that it would be out of place for a witness to volunteer extra information, avoid answering a question or argue with you, both the witness and the jurors will get that idea from your demeanor.

This is not an invitation to browbeat and bullyrag witnesses. On the contrary, using strength of character to control witnesses means employing the sort of civility that people find difficult to cut through with interruptions and arguments. It is not a product of being overbearing; it is the result of being quite obviously fair.

Yet not everyone has this kind of aura. It is in part the product of the one thing that cannot be rushed—time. So for those of us who have not yet reached the stage where people automatically do whatever we want, we must study the techniques of witness control.

These four methods—signaling the witness you know the facts, asking short questions, using leading questions and adopting an air of authority—are all helpful things to do.

There are also things not to do, including a few that are generally accepted techniques by some lawyers.

The first practice to avoid is one on which you will find almost universal agreement. Do not ask "why?" on cross-examination.

Why not?

Because asking why gives the witness a chance to explain. It surrenders control of the witness. It is astounding how often witnesses will have explanations for apparent inconsistencies that you are certain are beyond any redemption. Your temptation is to let the witness sweat just a little more, to let him dangle in front of the jury, so you ask why, only to learn there is an answer.

Most lawyers also agree that it is unwise to ask one question too many. The problem lies in knowing what *is* one question too many.

The infallible test is, you can always tell what is one question too many by the answer to the question.

A more useful test of what is one question too many is a predictor. Any time you hear yourself saying, "Well, if that is true, then how can you say . . . ?" you are asking one question too many. The magic words are "then how can you say?" If you hear yourself using those words—or some substitute for them—you are about to ask one question too many.

What should you do?

The answer is unequivocal.

Stop! Do not finish the question. Go on to another topic or sit down.

Why?

Because asking one question too many is like asking "why?" It gives the witness a chance to explain. It surrenders control.

There is less agreement on the next point.

You will recall the doctor who was being asked if he gave Mr. Morris a spinal tap. He did not answer with a direct response, but went into other matters:

Q: Doctor, did you perform a spinal tap on Mr. Morris?

A: Well, actually, the spinal tap is not always an advisable procedure.

At that point, the cross-examiner may be tempted to respond:

Q: Just answer yes or no, Doctor.

What could be wrong with that?

Plenty.

To begin, trying to confine a witness to yes or no is (in itself) perfectly proper. It is not the end that is faulty, it is the means. If an answer to a question is nonresponsive, then the lawyer who asked the question can have the response stricken. *See Hester v. Goldsbury*, 64 Ill. App. 2d 66, 212 N.E.2d 316 (1965).

Of course, if it would be unfair to confine the witness to a yes or no answer, then the judge has discretion to permit an explanation.

That means, unless it is an attempt unfairly to keep the witness from explaining his answer, it is perfectly all right to tell the witness, "just answer yes or no."

So why not do it?

First, telling the witness, "just answer yes or no" tends to create sympathy for the witness.

Second, your opponent may seize the opportunity to help make it appear that you are being unfair when you are not.

"Objection, Your Honor, the witness is entitled to explain his answer."

Third, using the techniques of witness control already developed, as well as those to come, will be more effective without making you look overbearing.

Another move that may tempt you is to ask the judge to control the witness. There are some judges who have tried enough cases to realize that occasionally trial lawyers need help. If a witness really needs to be instructed how to respond to questions, it is better coming from the judge—the neutral authority figure—than from you.

On the other hand, appealing to the judge for help is, by definition, having the judge and not you control the witness. The distinction is important. Because *you* should control the witness for the results it will bring, do not be too quick to ask the judge for help.

Of course, when it must be done, then do it. Surprisingly, some judges are as reluctant to be stern with a witness in front of the jury as the lawyers are. It is sometimes helpful, therefore, to approach the trial judge at sidebar and ask him to admonish the witness outside the presence of the jury rather than to ask for help in open court. With some judges, at least, you are more likely to get realistic assistance.

There is another timeworn phrase to avoid in cross-examination. It relates to witness control and surely has an effect on jury reaction. It is the standard announcement of the cross-examiner as he sees the end of the tunnel:

Q: I only have one more question, Mrs. Murdock . . . (and then goes on for another half hour).

It is unfair to the jury. They honestly believe there is just one more question. Of course, it does not fool the judge or the opposing counsel. They know the phrase for what it is, a meaningless promise.

What does it do to the witness? Keep him off balance? No, going on after the "last question" has been asked certainly does not control the witness. On the other hand, it gives the witness a bit of a breather to adjust to the additional subjects, since his expectations have been thwarted—along with the jury's.

It is silly to say "I only have one more question." It is almost never true. It does not help, and it can hurt. Do not do it.

The deep and abiding difficulty with all of these techniques—the things we should and should not do to control witnesses—is that they may work fine for the average sort of problem, but there are some instances when they are just not enough. Some witnesses require truly extraordinary methods to keep them in line, and it is evident that the standard methods are not enough for them.

One advanced technique for containing argumentative witnesses is called the "loopback" system. The principle is a simple one. When a witness gives an argumentative answer, the cross-examiner loops back three or four questions and repeats both the questions and answers to show the witness (and even more importantly, the jury) that the witness is capable of answering questions with a simple yes or no.

Here is how it works. Assume that the cross-examiner wants to show that an expert witness doctor did less than a complete job evaluating the injured plaintiff because the doctor failed to conduct a new, computerized, X-ray scan of the head (known as a computerized axial tomography, or CAT scan):

Q: As I understand it, then, Dr. Ward, you definitely suspected that Mr. Pincus had brain damage the first time he visited you professionally?

A: Yes, that is correct.

Q: Dr. Ward, are you familiar with a diagnostic technique called a computerized axial tomography, or 'CAT scan'?

A: Yes I am.

Q: Briefly, Dr. Ward, a 'CAT scan,' as it is called, is a picture created by a computer, based on a series of very narrow X-ray scans?

A: You could put it that way.

Q: And the result, Dr. Ward, is a sort of composite picture that is more detailed than you could otherwise expect to get from an ordinary X-ray?

A: Yes.

Q: In other words, this 'CAT scan' is a modern way of using both a computer and an X-ray machine to get a better, more detailed picture than you would otherwise obtain?

A: Yes.

Q: This is not what you would call an 'invasive technique' is it?

A: No.

Q: In other words, it is not necessary to cut the body open to do this test?

A: No.

Q: And other than having to sit still for the X-ray machine, it is not painful?

A: No.

Q: And aside from the accumulation of some extra X-rays, not particularly dangerous?

A: No.

Q: Then I suppose, Dr. Ward, you feel that a 'CAT scan' is often an effective diagnostic technique to determine whether someone has an abnormality in their brain?

A: Yes, it often is. Not always, but often.

Q: Thank you, Doctor. Now, these machines are not as rare as they used to be, are they, Doctor?

A: That's right.

Q: No longer necessary to travel across state to use one?

A: No.

Q: In fact, for the past two years, there has been at least one 'CAT scan' right here in town?

A: Yes.

Q: And now there are three, right here in town?

A: Yes.

Q: Well, Doctor, when Mr. Pincus came into your office thirteen months ago, and you suspected that he had brain injury, did you schedule him for one of these 'CAT scans'?

A: Well, it is a long and expensive diagnostic technique that is really not that valuable, and under the circumstances, I did not want to subject Mr. Pincus to what it involved.

(The witness starts to argue, so here comes the loopback.)

Q: Doctor, I'm sorry. A minute ago I asked if you suspected Mr. Pincus had brain damage on his first visit to you, and you said, 'yes.'

A: Yes.

Q: Then I asked you if you felt a 'CAT scan' could be an effective diagnostic technique to determine whether someone has an abnormality in their brain, and you said it was not always, but it could be an effective technique. Right?

A: Yes.

Q: Then I asked whether these machines were available in town, and you said they were, right?

A: Yes.

Q: Then I asked you whether you scheduled Mr. Pincus for one of these tests, and you said, 'Well, it is a long and expensive diagnostic technique that is really not that valuable.'

(Already the witness is taken aback just a little, since he is impressed with the 'recitation' of questions and answers. Actually, it is quite easy, since it involves only short-term memory. Try it.)

A: Yes.

312

Q: The answer to the question is, no, you did not schedule Mr. Pincus for a 'CAT scan'?

A: No, I did not.

Q: Thank you, Doctor.

If you doubt, on reading the printed page, whether the loopback system is effective, try reading this last transcript excerpt out loud, and see how quickly it goes.

And it does work.

Why?

Partly it is because it puts you back in command during the quick recitation, and if you recall the questions and answers accurately, the witness is literally forced to agree with what you say he said. Partly it is because the recitation looks a lot tougher than it is. But mainly it works because it points out to the witness and the jury just how out of line the last, argumentative answer is. It lets the jury see you have a good reason for showing the witness that he could have fairly answered your question with a yes or no answer.

One of the reasons the loopback system works so well is because it is flexible. That means looping back just three or four questions in a pleasant tone of voice will provide a measured amount of control for a response that is just a bit argumentative, while stopping more completely, going back a bit further, and adopting a more ''official'' tone can keep nearly any witness in line.

One of the things juries inherently sense about the rules of a trial is that a cross-examiner is entitled to take up topics in whatever order he likes. (It is, by the way, implicit in the usually misguided attempt to ''hop, skip and jump'' on cross-examination, an effort that usually confuses the judge, jury and counsel more than the witness.)

Because juries realize you can take up whatever permissible topic you like in your own order, they will naturally forgive you if you simply tell the witness that you will get to the point he would like to make in a short time.

That is the whole idea, right there. Because it works so well, especially when done in a pleasant tone of voice, it is too good a technique to entrust to a single sentence, so here it is in transcript form, based on Dr. Ward and Mr. Pincus:

Q: Well, Doctor, when Mr. Pincus came into your office thirteen months ago, and you suspected that he had a brain injury, did you schedule him for one of these 'CAT scans'?

A: Well, it is a long and expensive diagnostic technique that is really not that valuable, and under the circumstances, I did not want to subject Mr. Pincus to what it involved.

Q: (In an understanding tone) Doctor, I understand that one of your concerns is avoiding unnecessary expense for your patients, and we are going to get to the subject of what these tests would cost in just a minute. Right now, though, we are interested in knowing just what you did and did not do. All right?

A: Yes. (The answer is one you have literally forced by pleasantness.)

Q: And the answer to my question is no, you did not order a 'CAT scan' for Mr. Pincus, did you?

A: No, I did not.

Q: As it develops, you still have not had him take a 'CAT scan' have you?

A: No.

Q: Thank you, sir.

Now, then, having promised Dr. Ward to "get to" the topic of expenses, must you discuss that at some point?

No. You are to be forgiven once again if you forget to return to the subject. After all, there is redirect examination if your opponent feels the topic is worth the trouble.

Sometimes, no matter what you try, the witness persists in coming out with an argument in response to every question. What then?

Remember that juries are not as sensitive to these difficulties as you are. They will not see the witness's argumentativeness as soon as you do. They will not appreciate any attack you make on a witness unless they can see that you have a good reason for it.

Only when you are certain the jury understands that the witness is giving a hard time are you justified in saying something such as, ''Please, Doctor Ward, your lawyer, Lewis Morgan, is going to argue the case at the end of the trial.''

If you asked a group of careful lawyers to list the uses of prior statements at a trial, here is what you would probably get:

Refresh Recollection
Past Recollection Recorded
Admission (if made by a party)
Impeach with Prior Inconsistent Statement

It is a list of the principal *evidentiary* uses of prior statements. It, therefore, ignores one of the other primary uses of prior statements.

Witness control.

When your object is to contradict or impeach a witness, you do not confront him with the prior inconsistent statement until he is thoroughly committed to the story you want to attack. Only after he has himself closed all the avenues of escape is the trap sprung.

Witness control is another matter. When you want to use a prior statement to keep a witness within reasonable bounds, you will do everything you can to let the witness know you have his prior statement right in your hand.

You may even wish to remind the witness about the prior statement at the beginning of your direct or cross-examination.

Q: Mr. Reynolds, you understand that you are here to tell us what you know about the contract between Mr. Schmidt and Mr. Burgess?

A: Yes.

Q: This is not the first time you and I have had a chance to talk about this contract, is it (picking up the former statement so the witness and jury can see it)?

A: No.

Q: In fact, you came to my office just about a month or so after Mr. Schmidt and Mr. Burgess made that contract and told me about it, isn't that right?

A: Yes.

Q: And you gave a sworn statement concerning what you saw and heard?

A: Yes.

Q: And now, you understand, because of the rules of evidence, it is necessary for you to explain in person to the judge and jury just what you saw and heard?

A: Yes.

Interestingly, this introduction, which is designed to hold a dangerous witness to a prior statement, explains something that many witnesses are confused about. They do not understand that once they have given a statement, they may still have to appear in person. The overt message here is, "you understand that even though you have already testified, you must do it again." The covert message is, "I have your statement in my hand. You'd better not deviate from it, or you are in trouble."

With all the different means of witness control, it would seem that every major problem is covered. Yet there is a nagging sort of difficulty that comes up more often than it should. What should you do with the witness who asks you a question instead of answering yours?

There are two principal temptations, both of which are dangerous.

The first is to answer the question. That is the most natural response. It is, after all, what we do in normal human conversation. And unless we have some learned response other than normal conversation to cover a problem in witness examination, normal conversation is what we will use.

Do not answer the question.

Learn another response.

Why?

If you answer the witness's question, you surrender control. The examination will quickly degenerate into an argument—one that you may well lose. Even if you do not lose the argument, you will have an extremely difficult time recapturing the control necessary for an effective cross-examination.

The second temptation is to remind the witness of your respective roles. "Look, I'm the lawyer, you're the witness. I'll ask the questions, if you don't mind, and I would appreciate it if you would answer them."

You may appreciate it, but the jury may not appreciate how instantly overbearing you appear.

The danger, moreover, goes beyond merely looking as if you are taking unfair advantage. The danger is that you look as if you have not given a good reason for refusing to answer the witness's question. Later in the deliberation room, someone may say, "Remember when the doctor asked that lawyer—what's his name—the question? Boy, did that lawyer squirm. "Just answer the question,' he said." The response comes from another juror, "Well, you know why, don't you? Because he didn't have an answer." Could something like that happen?

Certainly.

It seems then, that a cross-examiner is on the horns of a dilemma when a witness fires a question back instead of an answer: he dares not answer the question for fear of losing witness control and he dares not fail to answer it for fear of the inference that he has no answer.

How delightful it would be if you could tell the witness you have an answer but are not going to say what it is. (Is there *any* chance a jury would accept that?)

This is it—an answer that works in a wide variety of occasions, with only minor variations:

Q: I am sorry, Dr. Ward, but the rules of evidence do not permit me to answer your question. If they did, I would be happy to explain just exactly what you should have done.

Consider the advantages: Control is maintained. The jury cannot possibly think you do not have an answer. You have given an excellent—because it is true—reason for not answering the question now.

Here is the best part. You have the entire remainder of the trial to think up the answer you will give during final argument.

CHAPTER 29

Rehabilitation

Evidence textbooks use the word too narrowly. They use rehabilitation to mean those specific antidotes that are permissible once a witness has been impeached or his credibility attacked with another witness. But trial lawyers have a broader understanding of the word. Rehabilitation addresses a common problem that continually pops up throughout trials: "Suddenly I am in a hole. How do I get out?"

It is not much comfort to reflect from inside the hole that the best answer is to avoid getting in it in the first place. But it is true. It is usually advisable to anticipate what the opposition is going to try to do to your witnesses—and do it yourself before the other side gets a chance. In other words, try to steal the thunder of the opposition; bring out the weak points in your case as soon as possible and in your own way rather than trying to explain them away later.

Avoiding the necessity for rehabilitation requires witness preparation for both direct and cross-examination. It means the kind of preparation that is not limited to pamphlets and general discussions but which actually goes through direct and cross-examination. As with Sir Robert Morton's cross-examination of Ronnie in Terrence Rattigan's play, *The Winslow Boy* (1946), the toughest cross-examination your witnesses face should come from you before the trial ever starts.

So that has been done; yet still there are holes for which the question is not will you get in, but how to get out. It is in answering this question that the textbook use of "rehabilitation" is too restrictive. The categories tend to suggest that there is a particular remedy for each situation. Rehabilitation should not be thought of as automatically using some predetermined tactic, procedural device or rule of evidence, but rather making an intelligent choice from a broad range of realistic alternatives. Put it another way if you like: Rehabilitating a witness is too narrow a concern. Instead, think of rehabilitating the case.

Start with direct examination. No matter how carefully witnesses are prepared, they will sometimes have lapses. It is an entirely human phenomenon. Consider the situation. The courtroom is a terrifying place. It has all the trappings of officialdom: flags, robed judge, formal language, a jury, a lonely witness stand, and a court reporter taking everything down verbatim. All a witness has to do is reflect for a moment on what is happening, and a brief hesitation turns a healthy mind to jelly. Suddenly, it is totally blank.

What to do?

There are at least four ways to deal with the problem. First is the leading question. While the popular notion is that leading is forbidden on direct examination, that is not entirely true. Leading is perfectly acceptable on preliminary matters and other points not in dispute. 3 Wigmore, *Evidence* § 775 (J. Chadbourn rev. 1970). In fact, it is often a good way to put the witness at ease at the beginning of direct examination, gradually working into non-leading questions:

> *Q:* Your name is Michael Roberts?
> *A:* Yes.
> *Q:* And you live at 4619 South Ravenel here in Charleston, is that correct?
> *A:* Yes.
> *Q:* Are you married, Mr. Roberts?
> *A:* Yes.
> *Q:* Would you tell us your wife's name, please, sir?
> *A:* Margaret.
> *Q:* Do you and your wife have any children, Mr. Roberts?
> *A:* Yes, three boys. John is twelve, Douglas is ten and Allen is six.

That kind of progression makes testifying more comfortable for witnesses and helps prevent them from "freezing" on the stand.

But still it happens, and leading may help. In the discretion of the trial court, the direct examiner may lead very young or very old witnesses, hostile witnesses and those whose memory has become exhausted. Wigmore, *Evidence* § 770 (J. Chadbourn rev. 1970).

Probably the best way to approach it is openly, rather than by just jumping in with a late question: "Your honor, the witness seems to have some difficulty remembering this event, and I think it will save us all time if I am permitted to ask a few leading questions."

> Q: Mr. Roberts, in July 1977, some real estate agents did come over to your house to discuss this sale, didn't they?
>
> A: Yes, that's right.
>
> Q: Was Mr. Ephross one of them?
>
> A: Yes, that's right. Now I understand. There was a Mr. Ephross and his partner. Sanders, I think it was, Emil Sanders.

Sometimes leading is not enough, is not permitted, or will not do. So there is a second device, present recollection refreshed. Once again, the idea is to jog the memory of the witness who has a temporary lapse. Ordinarily a writing made by the witness at an earlier time is used, but in most courts there is no requirement that the thing used to spark the recall of the witness be written by him or even be a writing. *McCormick on Evidence* p.16 at n. 54 (2d ed. 1972). The thing used to refresh recollection is not evidence to prove its contents, but can be inspected by the opponent and even be shown to the jury if the opponent wishes. 3 Wigmore, *Evidence* §§ 758-765 (J. Chadbourn rev. 1970).

But what happens if the witness's memory is not revived? All is not necessarily lost. The third device for dealing with witness lapses is past recollection recorded. There are five elements in the foundation for this exception to the hearsay rule: a writing, made at or near the event (while it was still fresh in the witness's memory), by someone with firsthand knowledge, who has no present recollection, but who can vouch for its accuracy. 3 Wigmore, *Evidence* §§ 734-757 (J. Chadbourn rev. 1970).

It is important to notice that before such a writing can be introduced into evidence, it should first be used in an effort to refresh the witness's recollection.

The fourth remedy for a witness lapse should be reserved for when the situation appears to be in extremis. Consider the following:

The trial is a criminal case in federal court. We will call the judge Harold McIntire. A witness, Mrs. Helene Schwartz, is called to the stand:

Q: Would you state your name for the record, please?

A: [A glassy stare and a wooden tone of voice] . . . Judge McIntire.

Q: I'm sorry. Perhaps you did not understand me. I have asked for *your* name, please?

A: . . . Judge McIntire.

Q: Pardon me, ma'am, but that is Judge McIntire over there, sitting on the bench. I have asked you for your name?

A: . . . Judge McIntire.

Now the lawyer is ready for the fourth remedy.

Q: Your honor, may we have a brief recess, please?

Witness lapses are just the start of what can go wrong on direct examination. Take the problem of the outburst from your own witness in the middle of trial. Should it ever happen? Certainly not. Does it ever happen? Unfortunately, yes. Will it hurt your case? Almost always. Should you do anything about it? Of course.

How you respond depends on the situation. If there is a general rule, it is that sympathy for the outburst is better than hostility, and that you (not the judge or the other side) should be the first to respond.

The problem is worth an example. The case is a civil action against a construction company that built a house for the plaintiff under contract. The foundation proved seriously defective within a year after the plaintiff took occupancy, and huge cracks developed in the walls of the house. The plaintiff, Jonas Hogan, is on direct examination:

Q: After you first noticed the crack in the basement wall, did you contact anyone at the Bladen Construction Company?

A: Well, I called those shysters, but they . . .

Q: [Interrupting] Mr. Hogan, please. I'm certain that everyone can sympathize with someone whose dream house suddenly starts falling apart, but I'm going to have to ask you just to refer to the Bladen Construction Company by name, and not to tell us how you feel about them, because the rules of evidence do not permit that. Do you understand that?

A: Yes, I'm sorry.

The perfect response? Hardly, but not bad in an emergency. It was short and reasoned, and its sympathy helped take the sting out of the witness's hostility. Certainly it is better than what hap-

321

pened recently in Cleveland when a lawyer put his hand over the mouth of his client to stifle an outburst. Taking the initiative is important, because it helps soften the response from the bench and the opposition as well.

One reason direct examination is difficult is because of objections, which necessarily interrupt the witness's testimony. Once again, prevention is important. One good general rule is to make sure that none of the questions asked are objectionable. In support of this, it is wise to have short (one-page) memoranda in support of questions you think may draw objections.

While these steps may help, they will not prevent all objections, particularly because some lawyers are willing to risk a possible jury reaction that they are trying to hide something with repeated objections in return for breaking up the pace and flow of an effective direct examination.

Since you cannot count on the trial judge to be strong enough to keep your opposition within bounds, you must be ready to smooth out a direct examination that has been chopped up with needless objections.

Exasperation with the other side is not the answer. Instead, try a reasonable amount of recapitulation as an introduction to the next question. We return to the Construction Company case for an example:

> Q: Mr. Hogan, you had just testified that the day you returned from your vacation, you went down into the basement and saw a crack in the wall you had never seen before. The question I put to you then was, 'Did you contact anyone at the Bladen Construction Company about this crack?'
>
> A: Yes, I did.
>
> Q: Would you tell us about it, please.

The art of recapitulation is a subtle one. Certainly it is appropriate to help the witness understand the context for the next question. That will also help the jury maintain a sense of continuity. Taken too far, it will draw another objection. If permission is asked for recapitulation, it may be denied. If you seek to ask the last question or two again, the "asked and answered" objection is almost certain. But a ten- or fifteen-second recapitulation which ends with the question that has not yet been answered can actually strengthen direct examination. It may even convince your opponent that you cannot be thrown off your stride by specious objections.

322

Unfortunately, not all objections from the other side will be ruled in your favor. Often it is not clear from either the objection or the ruling just what was the reason for the objection or the judge's response. Once again, there are some options. The first is suggested by Judge Philip W. Tone's article, *Invoking and Applying Rules of Evidence*, LITIGATION, Vol. 2, No. 1, p. 11, 40 (1975).

> If the reason for the trial court's ruling on any evidence point is not apparent from the context, which includes the ground for the objection stated by counsel, the lawyer against whom the ruling is made is entitled to a statement by the court of the reason for the ruling. It is error for the judge to refuse to give a reason and if prejudice results from the refusal—as it would if the basis for the ruling would show that there was some problem which could be cured—the error is a ground for reversal.

Regrettably, not all trial judges follow this rule. There is, therefore, another move that can be made before asking the judge to justify his ruling—which is how he is likely to take your request, no matter how delicately put. If the opposition just says "objection," and the judge only says "sustained," you should assume that the objection was as to the *form* of the question and simply rephrase it or lay a specific foundation for firsthand knowledge. No matter what your opposition or the judge had in mind, this procedure is remarkably effective:

Q: What did the defendant say when he got out of his car?
DEFENSE COUNSEL: Objection.
THE COURT: Sustained.

Q: Were you able to hear whether the defendant said anything when he got out of his car?
A: Yes.
Q: Would you tell us what that was, please?
A: He said, 'I'm sorry, it's all my fault.'

If the objection is reasserted before the answer (and a surprising number of times it is not), counsel is then in position to respond: "I am sorry, your honor. I had thought the first objection was to the form of my question. We are offering the statement of the defendant as an admission in this case, your honor."

If that does not work and the second objection is sustained without explanation, it is then more comfortable to respond, "If I may inquire as to the basis for counsel's objection, your honor, perhaps I can cure whatever problem he sees."

323

Notice that the inquiry was prompted by the other side's obscurity in objecting, not the judge's uninformative ruling.

But reason does not always triumph over the powers of darkness. Suppose in this case the objection to the defendant's statement is excluded as hearsay. There is still an opportunity for an offer of proof, or as it is called in some jurisdictions, a "proffer," or "bill of exceptions."

Whatever its name, there is usually more than one way to do it. In a few states there are older cases that suggest that an offer of proof must be made by examining the witness under oath, outside the presence of the jury. *Chicago City Ry. Co. v. Carroll*, 206 Ill. 318, 68 N.E. 1087 (1903); *Eschbach v. Hurtt*, 47 Md. 61 (1877). Where the offer is long or its impact would be blunted by a mere summary, actually examining the witness can be the most effective way to make an offer of proof. Usually, however, that formalism is not necessary. Instead, the court reporter can be called to the bench, and the offering counsel can read a short statement into the record, or, in the judge's discretion, it can be offered when the jury is in recess.

Besides completing the record, there is an advantage to the offer of proof that is sometimes overlooked. Making a full statement of the excluded evidence can often impress the trial judge that it is indeed relevant and admissible, especially since the offer itself is an implicit preparation for an appeal.

One of the standard parts of preparing a witness for cross-examination is the instruction to pause just a second or two after each question is asked, to give counsel an opportunity to object if there is something improper about the question. This is valuable advice, since not only does it minimize the possibility of waived objections, it also is likely to give the witness a chance to think about his answer, and cut down the chances for getting rattled on cross-examination.

It is important to assure witnesses that you will protect them from misleading, argumentative or multiple questions during cross-examination. It is a promise on which you should deliver unless it is quite clear that the witness does a better job of protecting himself than you could do for him. Often, however, the witnesses who think they can protect themselves are just the sort who are likely to get into an argument with the cross-examiner, which will probably wind up to your detriment.

The lesson is that most witnesses need protection if your adversary uses that kind of tactic.

In making such protective objections, do it in a way that is easily understandable by both judge and jury. While most judges will not let you make a speech when you object, you usually will have four or five seconds—do not count on having a longer—to say, "Objection, your honor, counsel is making an argument, not asking a question," or "Objection, your honor, counsel has asked three questions before the witness has had a chance to even answer the first."

All this seems easy enough. What good is it when the other side is embarrassing your witness with a devastating cross-examination.

It is probably good advice to resist the temptation to object just for the purpose of throwing the other side off its stride. First, specious objections, while unlikely to be the subject of a grievance committee proceeding, have a very doubtful claim to ethical behavior. Second, they are often transparent to the judge and the jury and may well backfire. Third, if your opponent knows how to pick up the thread again, they may not do any good, anyway.

But notice: That does not mean you should waive a perfectly good objection when the other side has got your witness on the run. At issue is not your motive, but rather the legal basis for the objection. So if asserting a perfectly proper objection has the side effect of letting things cool off on the witness stand, there is nothing wrong with it.

Probably the most effective impeaching technique is the proper use of a prior inconsistent statement. Is there anything that can be done about that?

Fortunately, there is. Two things can be done immediately, while some other tactics must wait for redirect examination.

The first step is to insist that the cross-examiner follow the rule in *Queen Caroline's Case*, 2 Brod. & Bing 284, 313, 129 Eng. Rep. 976 (1820). Under this rule, before evidence of a prior inconsistent statement can be introduced, the witness must be confronted with particularity concerning the prior statement. This means the witness must have his attention directed to the time, place and circumstances under which the prior inconsistent statement was made and asked if he made it. If it is a written statement, he must have an opportunity to read it. Rule 613 of the Federal Rules of Evidence modifies the confrontation requirement, but does not eliminate it. Under Rule 613, the statement need not be shown to the witness at the time he is questioned about it; but it still must be shown to counsel on demand, and the witness must ordinarily be given a chance to "explain or deny" the statement before it is introduced into evidence.

Confrontation is a valuable right. Sometimes there is a rational explanation for an apparent inconsistency. Other times, of course, there is not. A common situation shows why it is important for you to examine the document that is going to be used to impeach. The opposition has taken something out of context. What seems damning when viewed in part is explained elsewhere in the document.

The important thing is that the "rule of completeness" will let you put the explanatory context into evidence immediately without having to wait for redirect examination. The proposition is well put in Rule 106 of the Federal Rules of Evidence. "When a writing or recorded statement or part thereof is introduced by a party, an adverse party may require him at that time to introduce any other part or any other writing or recorded statement which ought in fairness to be considered contemporaneously with it."

In other words, the rule in *Queen Caroline's Case* and the "rule of completeness" provide two immediate antidotes to the sting of impeachment with a prior inconsistent statement.

Because prior inconsistent statements can be so powerful, there is yet another remedy, prior consistent statements.

Some jurisdictions take a simple approach, and if there is impeachment with a prior inconsistent statement, then a prior consistent statement may be shown. Other jurisdictions require a more complete foundation. In virtually every state, however, if impeachment with a prior inconsistent statement is accomplished by or can be interpreted as a charge of recent fabrication, then prior statements that were made before the motive for falsification arose are admissible. See *McCormick on Evidence* 106 (2d ed. 1972).

Sometimes a witness is the target of an entirely baseless attack. In some jurisdictions, for example, it is permissible to cross-examine witnesses concerning prior bad acts that did not result in a conviction, as a means of attacking credibility. *People v. Sorge*, 301 N.Y. 198, 93 N.E.2d 637 (1950); Rule 608(b), Federal Rules of Evidence. When credibility is the only relevance of this line of questioning, the cross-examiner must "take the witness's answer." In other words, cross-examination concerning the prior bad acts is permitted, but independent proof of those acts is not, even if the witness denies them.

It is usually said that the cross-examiner must have a reasonable basis for asking the question. But what if he does not? First, the trial court can inquire about the basis for asking the question, and stop the line of questioning if it appears that there is not a sufficient basis for it. Second, the cross-examiner may even be called to the stand and asked for the basis for his cross-examination. *United States v. Pugliese*, 153 F.2d 497 (2d Cir, 1945). That is strong medicine, indeed. Since it is an invitation for the cross-examiner to justify himself, caution suggests it not be used except in the clearest of cases.

Of course, in a proper case, the results can be devastating. It illustrates the fundamental tactical point that any time you can prove that your client was the object of a baseless attack, you are better off than if the attack had never been made. For a delightful example of this situation, see the account of the fictional Ephraim Tutt in Arthur Train's *Yankee Lawyer: The Autobiography of Ephraim Tutt*, pp. 364-369 (1943).

One technique in cross-examination that can be particularly effective is called the "laundry list." The purpose of the laundry list is to give dramatic effect to an important concession (which could be elicited in one or two questions) by asking a whole list of questions. Here is how it works. Suppose the defendant in a pedestrian run-down case testifies on direct examination that she turned left onto a street—call it Euclid Avenue—and did not see the plaintiff—a 72-year-old man—until just before her car struck him. Of course, this was presented as sympathetically as possible on direct examination.

Now the cross-examiner wants to emphasize this evidence.

Q: Mrs. Morgan, when you reached the corner of 25th Street and Euclid, you were planning to turn left, isn't that correct?

A: Yes.

Q: Before you made your left turn, you said you looked both ways to make sure the intersection was clear, isn't that right?

A: Yes.

Q: Now, Mrs. Morgan, when you checked to make sure the intersection was clear, did you see Mr. Wagner on the sidewalk or in the street?

A: No.

Q: Then you started into the intersection of 25th and Euclid, didn't you?

A: Yes.

Q: And when you started into that intersection did you see Mr. Wagner on the sidewalk or in the street then?

A: No.

Q: Then after you had gotten about half way across the intersection, you started to turn to the left, didn't you?

A: Yes.

Q: When you started turning left onto Euclid Avenue, did you then see Mr. Wagner on the sidewalk or in the street?

A: No.

Q: And you completed your turn onto Euclid, didn't you?

A: Yes.

Q: And started heading south on Euclid Avenue?

A: Yes.

Q: Mrs. Morgan, when your car started heading south on Euclid, did you see Mr. Wagner on the sidewalk or in the street then?

A: No.

Q: In fact, Mrs. Morgan, you didn't see Mr. Wagner until your car was only four or five feet away from him, isn't that so?

A: Yes.

There it is. The question is whether anything can be done about this line of cross-examination.

There is an objection that can be made. The time to do it is when it is clear the laundry list is being used. The problem is whether to make it at all.

''Objection, your honor. These questions are all repetitive theatrics. Mrs. Morgan has already testified she did not see the plaintiff until he walked right in front of her car.''

And now you see the problem with deciding whether to use this objection. Its advantage is the jury can see what your opponent is up to, however the judge rules on the objection. Its disadvantage is that you must concede exactly what your opponent is trying to drive home. On the other hand, it is a concession you get to do in your own way. So do you make the objection? The answer is, it all depends.

Cross-examination is not necessarily the most effective way to impeach a witness. As Aron Steuer pointed out in *Max D. Steuer, Trial Lawyer*, at p. 38 (Random House, 1950), it is often more profitable to lay a foundation on cross-examination and follow that with contradictory material later in the trial, thus depriving the witness of an opportunity on redirect to explain away what he said.

In the same way, redirect examination is not necessarily the most effective way to rehabilitate a witness who has been impeached on cross-examination.

Suppose the case of a man who suffered a spinal injury as the result of a fall from a defective scaffold. One of the plaintiff's witnesses is a neurologist who testified to the extent of the injury to the spinal cord.

On cross-examination the defense counsel raised a smoke screen. He forced the neurologist to admit that several of the plaintiff's symptoms were like those associated with lead poisoning. The neurologist protested that lead poisoning has nothing to do with the plaintiff's condition. The defense counsel countered.

Q: So you apparently think. Would you tell this judge and jury just what laboratory tests you have ordered which could rule out lead poisoning?

A: Well, uh, actually, I did not conduct any.

Q: And you did not order any either?

A: No.

Q: I have no further questions of this . . . witness.

Certainly you could deal with this on redirect examination. On the other hand, there is an alternative which may be more effective. Suppose you are confident that the defendant's own expert witness in the case—who will dispute the extent of the plaintiff's injuries—nevertheless will freely concede that the plaintiff does not suffer from lead poisoning. Furthermore, it already seems that your expert has protested too much.

Under these circumstances it might well be more effective to have the defendant's doctor testify on cross-examination that testing for lead poisoning would be a waste of time and money.

Properly done, the jury can feel that defense counsel almost cheated them, even though he was just trying to show that the plaintiff's expert was less than completely thorough.

Obviously, one has to be careful. If the original attack was more than a smoke screen, or if the defense expert cannot be relied on to help out, redirect examination of the plaintiff's expert and perhaps some other corroborating witness may be necessary.

This device can be used in other circumstances as well. The thrust of an attack on the character of a witness is that he is not worthy of belief because of something in his past. When witnesses who have been attacked with character and reputation evidence are corroborated with other, less impeachable evidence, the jury may conclude that the original attack was a "cheap shot," and resent the embarrassment to which the witness was subjected.

It is not always wise, however, to avoid redirect examination or to save rehabilitation for later. Implicit in the policy behind the rule of completeness is the recognition that prompt rehabilitation—everything else being equal (which it never is)—is better than delayed rehabilitation. The general rule is, if something is misleading, straighten it out now, while it is still fresh in the jury's mind. The same reason for the rule of completeness is the justification for redirect examination.

If cross-examination was effective, and if redirect examination will help, then conduct a redirect. Otherwise, do not bother. Vying for the last word from a witness—especially when it is a meaningless quibble—annoys both judges and juries.

Can you lead on redirect examination? That is an interesting problem. In many jurisdictions there is an unspoken rule that permits leading on redirect. In other states, it is not permitted. The CALIFORNIA EVIDENCE CODE § 767 (a) (1966), expressly forbids leading on redirect examination; Rule 611(c) of the Federal Rules of Evidence is silent on the matter.

According to one theory, when a cross-examiner asks questions on "new matters" not relating to the scope of direct examination, the witness becomes his own and leading is forbidden on these new subjects. 3A Wigmore, *Evidence* §§ 914 and 915 (J. Chadbourn rev. 1970). It would seem to follow from this interesting line of reasoning that leading would be permitted on redirect, at least for the matters first brought out on cross-examination.

Leading can be helpful in rehabilitation after a damaging cross-examination. Whether it can be done effectively probably depends more on the attitudes of the trial judge and opposing counsel than whether doctrine theoretically applies. The lesson is made in Mathew, *Forensic Fables by O* 267-68 (1961). In the story of "The Beginner Who Thought He Would Do It Himself," the beginner tried to imitate the successful redirect examination leading of a Big Pot, and learned the moral, "*Wait till You're a Big Pot.*"

An important rule in cross-examination is to avoid asking "one question too many." The corollary of that rule is that the redirect examiner should ask that question whenever it will help. There is even an introduction to the question which is only a little argumentative:

"Mr. Walker apparently does not want to ask you this question, so I will. Why is it you are certain the man you saw was not John McMillan?"

Listening to cross-examination is essential not only for deciding what to cover on redirect examination, but also to determine if anything beyond redirect is required. Often a cross-examiner will open a door to evidence that would not otherwise be admissible. See McCormick's classic article, *The Procedure of Admitting and Excluding Evidence,* 31 TEX. L. REV. 128 (1952), reprinted in SELECTED WRITING ON THE LAW OF EVIDENCE AND TRIAL, at p. 137 (W. Fryer, ed., 1957). Especially valuable is Section VII, ''Fighting Fire with Fire: Inadmissible Evidence as Opening the Door.''

Ordinarily redirect examination should be planned well before trial. Then only minor modifications of your plan need be made to meet the cross-examination that was actually conducted.

Redirect examination should be shorter than anyone expects, and should end with a handful of questions—no more—that epitomize the testimony of the witness.

Take the following case as an example. It is a child custody dispute in which the mother, Mrs. Williams, is trying to retain custody of the six-year-old daughter, Karen. Mr. Williams claims his ex-wife has a serious drinking problem which makes her unfit. On direct examination of the wife, she freely admitted that she drank in excess while she and her husband lived together. She also testified that she was continually rejected and sexually belittled by her husband. The direct examination did not link the two subjects.

Cross-examination dwelt at length on her drinking.

Redirect consisted of only the following questions:

Q: Mrs. Williams, did you have a drinking problem before you were married?

A: No.

Q: When did you start to have a drinking problem, Mrs. Williams?

A: After we had been married about four years.

Q: During the time you and your husband were together, did you ever reject any of his sexual advances?

A: No.

Q: Did you ever make fun of him or belittle his manhood in any way?

A: No, never.

Q: Mrs. Williams, how long have you and Mr. Williams been apart now?

A: A little over one year.

Q: Do you have a drinking problem now?

A: No.

Q: No further questions, your honor.

The point of this redirect examination was not to refute what had been brought out on cross-examination, but rather to reinforce the respondent's theory of the case—that her drinking was the *result* of the way her husband had treated her, not the other way around. It was rehabilitating the case, not the witness.

This concise redirect examination also draws on another principle. Bring the fact-finders up to the conclusion you want them to reach, and then let them draw the conclusion themselves. Lloyd Paul Stryker put it this way:

> No point is ever better made than when not directly made at all but is so presented that the jury itself makes it. Men pride themselves on their own discoveries, and so a point which the jury are allowed to think their own ingenuity has discovered can put the advocate in a position where the jury begin to regard him as not only their spokesman but their colleague.

L. Stryker, *The Art of Advocacy,* at p. 125 (1954).

Finally, not every problem has a remedy. Wisdom lies in knowing when to leave something alone, and courage resides in not letting your anguish show. There are times when the only thing to do is to resort to the anesthetic used in Revolutionary War amputations: When it starts to hurt, bite the bullet.

PART VI

Expert Witnesses

CHAPTER 30

Expert Witnesses and the Federal Rules

A casual reading of the rules pertaining to the examination of expert witnesses gives the impression that not much is changed by the new Federal Rules of Evidence, an impression which is wrong. Nearly everything is affected by Article 7 (Opinions and Expert Testimony) and some exceptions to the hearsay rule found in Article 8. Most of the departures from familiar practice were thoughtful measures which were proposed by the drafters and were unaltered in the long legislative process. They owe their deceptively simple appearance to the style with which they were written and to the rather complex set of common law rules concerning experts which must be thoroughly understood to follow what the Federal Rules accomplish. But not every change was advertent nor was every problem solved, with the result that some serious questions remain, including the applicability of some rules in diversity cases.

The easiest way to appreciate the scope of the changes made by the Federal Rules is to see how they will actually work in comparison with the customary method of examining witnesses, particularly medical experts. The problem is a simple one, with only a few twists to get as much out of it as possible.

A diversity action is brought in federal court for personal injuries to the plaintiff, Mr. Rockwell, who claims that he received a severe head injury as the result of the defendant's negligence. Shortly after the incident Mr. Rockwell consulted his family physician, Dr. Lombard, complaining of headaches and dizziness. Suspecting possible brain damage, Dr. Lombard referred the plaintiff to a specialist in neurology, Dr. Braun, sending him a review of Mr. Rockwell's worsening condition and the treatment thus far. Dr. Braun conducted a thorough neurological examination and also ordered an electroencephalogram, which was performed at a local hospital by a Dr. Willis who sent his findings back to Dr. Braun.

Being careful to cover all possibilities, particularly in view of the helpful but inconclusive electroencephalogram report, Dr. Braun referred Mr. Rockwell to a psychiatrist to rule out the possibility that the symptoms were psychological in origin, a distinct possibility in a number of apparent neurological disorders. The psychiatrist, Dr. Schulman, spent a number of hours with Mr. Rockwell and wrote Dr. Braun a complete psychiatric report, indicating that the plaintiff had essentially no psychiatric problems.

Armed with this information, Dr. Braun proceeded with his course of treatment which, unfortunately, was only partially successful. He was prepared to testify that Mr. Rockwell has indeed a serious brain injury that is difficult to treat. To add weight to the plaintiff's case, a nationally recognized expert, Dr. Brill, was consulted. He reviewed the case and would support Dr. Braun's conclusions in every respect.

But now, on the eve of trial, complications arise. Dr. Braun, the treating expert, dies, and Mr. Rockwell's new personal physician, while certainly competent, is a most unimpressive witness who is reluctant to testify. So, tactically, his role in the trial must be minimized, if not eliminated. Can Dr. Brill, the impressive expert, be called to supply the testimony that the late Dr. Braun might have given? In this sort of situation, the common law rules governing expert witnesses present a confusing maze, and while the case may be tried, it will be long and difficult, particularly against determined opposition.

The first problem is that Dr. Brill is not a treating doctor. Almost everything he knows is hearsay for which he cannot prove the necessary foundations to establish whatever exceptions to the hearsay rule might be available. In addition, because he does not base his opinions on firsthand information, he will not be able to give his actual opinions. And because the usual role is that every essential fact in a hypothetical question must already be in evidence—or promised to be connected up later—the entire medical history will have to be proven by the testimony of the various other doctors, if they are available, or by hospital or business records, which may be extremely difficult because they contain not only factual data but also opinions and diagnoses.

Assuming these hurdles have been successfully overcome, Dr. Brill may be called to testify. After the plaintiff establishes his expertise (and resists the defendant's offer to stipulate to it), Dr. Brill is asked to assume a long list of facts. Finally he is asked with the familiar words, "Now, then, Dr. Brill, assuming all these facts to be true, would you have an opinion, based on a reasonable degree of medical probability (or certainty in some states) as to the nature of such a condition?" Then he responds, "Yes, I do." Then plaintiff asks, "What is that opinion?" At last Dr. Brill can testify—not about Mr. Rockwell himself but rather about some hypothetical person like him.

The difference between the necessary preliminary proof and ultimate questioning of Dr. Brill under the common law approach and what might be done under the new Federal Rules is startling. Not that it would necessarily be tactically sound to conduct the examination in this way, but here is how it might be done:

All of the preliminary medical proof may be omitted. After establishing that Dr. Brill is an appropriate expert, he may be simply asked, "Dr. Brill, are you familiar with Mr. Rockwell's medical history?" His answer is, "Yes, I am." Then he is asked, "Would you explain to the judge and jury, Dr. Brill, what condition he is suffering from?" "Certainly," he responds, and, without magic words or special form, he gives his opinion of Rockwell's injuries, their cause and the outlook for the future.

Rule 701 opens Article 7 with a simplification of the rule against opinions, and, instead of attempting to list the various opinions which lay witnesses are permitted to give, states that lay opinions are admissible if they are "rationally based on the perception of the witness and . . . helpful to a clear understanding of his testimony. . . ." Rule 702 (Testimony by Experts) performs a similar simplifying task for the recognition of experts, adopting Dean Wigmore's suggestion that the test ought to be whether this witness can help a jury on this subject. J. Wigmore, *Evidence* § 1923, Vol. 7 at p. 21 (3d ed. 1940). Rule 704 abolishes the irksome ultimate issue rule, which was a silly attempt by the common law to protect the province of the jury.

These rules, simple and straightforward, are the type one would expect. While they make the conduct of litigation easier, they were easily predictable progressions from the common law. Even Rule 706, which codifies the court's right to call its own expert witnesses and which raises a few troublesome questions, takes no giant steps.

Rather it is Rules 703 and 705, tucked in the middle of these unsurprising provisions, taken together with a short phrase in Rule 702 and a few exceptions to the hearsay rule found in Article 8, which offer such a complete alteration of the practice which was developed by the common law.

Rule 702 (Testimony by Experts) provides that an expert witness may testify ''in the form of an opinion or otherwise.'' At first reading, this provision seems to track the common law rule completely. Close examination, however, raises an interesting question which is not entirely resolved by the legislative history or the Advisory Committee's notes. The problem is whether this language changes the usual practice of asking an expert witness whether he has an opinion to a reasonable degree of scientific certainty or probability.

The Advisory Committee's note is only somewhat helpful:

> Most of the literature assumes that experts testify only in the form of opinions. The assumption is logically unfounded. The rule accordingly recognizes that an expert on the stand may give a dissertation or exposition of scientific or other principles relevant to the case, leaving the trier of fact to apply them to the facts.

It would seem logical that, if opinions are not the required form for testimony, when they are used no particular style need be followed in eliciting them. The difficulty is obvious. The common law developed a rather rigid method for obtaining expert testimony.

In some jurisdictions, for example, the question, ''Doctor, do you have an opinion to a reasonable degree of medical probability as to the nature of this condition?'' is considered to be foundational. That is, it must be answered in the affirmative before the opinion itself is admissible. If the reason for this requirement is a fear that juries are not capable of drawing inferences from opinions, Rule 702 as explained by the Advisory Committee logically alters that requirement, and the preliminary question need not be asked. That result follows because the rule was specifically drafted with the view that juries are capable of drawing their own inferences from expert testimony.

In a number of other jurisdictions, the traditional preliminary question, while it might in practice be put to experts in a variety of settings, is only required when the opinion is establishing causation in personal injury actions. See Musslewhite, *Medical Causation Testimony in Texas*, 23 Sw. L.J. 622 (1969). Applying Rule 702 in these states would allow questioning the expert in any reasonable form without the usual magic words, but the degree of certainty or probability would still have to be established by the preliminary question or in some other manner, such as the totality of the expert's testimony. Such a requirement is imposed because the preliminary question is used in these states to insure that there is a sufficiency of the evidence to establish causation.

These considerations do not mean that litigators should use the liberality of Rule 702 to justify careless examination of experts. Judges are accustomed to hearing questions phrased in traditional ways. But it does free the careful lawyer from the procrustean bed of a stylized litany which conveys little meaning to the jury. Under Rule 702 the expert can be examined in any way that makes sense and that ultimately satisfies whatever rule that applies to the sufficiency of the evidence. So in the hypothetical Rockwell case, it was not necessary to ask Dr. Brill whether he had an opinion to a reasonable degree of medical certainty before asking his opinion. If that degree of certainty was not reasonably implicit as Dr. Brill developed his opinion for the jury, he could even be asked after the main body of his testimony how firmly he held the opinion. The result is a simpler, more comprehensible flow of expert testimony.

Rule 703 states:

> The facts or data in the particular case upon which an expert bases an opinion or inference may be those perceived by or made known to him at or before the hearing. If of a type reasonably relied upon by experts in the particular field in forming opinions or inferences upon the subject, the facts or data need not be admissible in evidence.

This rule starts with a recognition of current practice. If an expert is a fact witness, as well as one interpreting those facts, there is no change. Examination is only as complicated as the subject matter, since the traditional rules of evidence impose no hurdles other than the possible requirement of a foundation question relating to the certainty of the opinion. Having an expert listen to the testimony in the case to form an opinion is also permitted. Although the notes of the Advisory Committee give it no special emphasis, the rule seems to liberalize that proce-

dure, since the rule does not contain the restriction some jurisdictions impose that the evidence on which the expert relies
must be substantially undisputed. This limitation is actually one
of formality. Since an expert responding to a hypothetical question gets his information from the question, it has always been
possible for an expert to attend the trial and form his opinion
based on what he learns there, whether or not the testimony is in
dispute. But when the information on which he relies is not in
dispute, many jurisdictions have permitted a shortening of the
hypothetical question. Instead of reciting the entire basis for the
opinion in the hypothetical question, the expert could merely be
asked to assume that the testimony he heard was true. Rule 703
permits this practice even though the evidence is in dispute, a
provision which matches a major change made by Rule 705.

Rule 703 makes another change which writers have been urging for years. The facts or data which an expert relies on in forming his opinion need not be admissible in evidence if they are of a
type reasonably relied upon in the field. The Advisory Committee's argument for this provision seems attractive. Many experts,
particularly doctors, make life and death decisions on information which is not admissible in evidence. If they carry out their
professional responsibilities in that manner, why should they not
be able to testify to the opinions they reach on the basis of such
information, so long as it is reasonably reliable?

The logic of the common law in opposition to this position was
a tightly closed syllogism. If an expert opinion was based on hearsay information, relating the opinion to the jury would be giving
them hearsay in disguise. Since hearsay is considered unreliable
unless it falls within one of the exceptions to the hearsay rule, the
opinion was obviously fatally tainted.

In recent years, however, this rigid approach has been relaxed
in many states, and most experts were permitted to base their
opinions in part on information which was not admissible so long
as it was the simple, mechanical type of hearsay, such as the
results of a urinalysis or blood grouping, and those findings were
not the central issue in the case. In other words, courts came to
recognize that a doctor or other expert could still be a fact witness
even though he did not personally perform all of the typical laboratory tests upon which he relied in reaching his opinion.

But Rule 703 goes much further. It has become virtually like a
major exception to the hearsay rule. It is no longer necessary to
prove independently the opinions and diagnoses of other experts

upon which the opinion being introduced rests. Since all of the information that Dr. Brill, the non-treating expert witness in the Rockwell case, used was certainly reasonably reliable in the field of medicine, it would not be necessary to prove it independently—or at all.

Rule 703, then, is a rule which, when properly understood, should ease and simplify complex trials. The central expert or the one who is the most effective witness and who is in position to give the essential opinion for a favorable finding can be called as the only expert witness. In the Rockwell case, Dr. Lombard (the general practitioner), Dr. Willis (who conducted the EEG), Dr. Schulman (the psychiatrist), and Mr. Rockwell's new physician may all be eliminated. Moreover, Dr. Braun's death no longer creates difficult problems of proof. While it would probably be helpful to have his findings and records admitted, they need not even qualify as business records for Dr. Brill, the testifying expert, to take them into account. In short, the case can be tried with one expert instead of four. The number of witnesses actually called will now depend on the importance of the issue to the trial and the economic value of the case rather than on rigid evidentiary rules.

One question which this discussion implicitly raises is whether the language of Rule 703, which permits opinions to be based on reasonably reliable facts or data, includes opinions, since evidence law usually distinguishes between facts and opinions. The Advisory Committee notes which say that facts or data includes opinions ought to settle the issue.

A final point on Rule 703 is who determines what is reasonably reliable in the field, the witness and the jury or the judge? The language of the rule suggests that the norms of the field of expertise control. On the other hand, the Advisory Committee notes suggest that "reasonably reliable" is a standard to be applied by the judge: "The language would not warrant admitting in evidence the opinion of an 'accidentologist' as to the point of impact in an automobile collision based on statements of bystanders, since this requirement is not satisfied."

But this hypothetical problem hardly puts the issue to rest. What about a policeman gathering information from bystanders from which he forms an opinion as to the speed of a moving vehicle, assuming his competence in the field? Would his apparent disinterest make his evaluation of bystanders' accounts any more reliable? Certainly policemen sometimes have to make life and death decisions on the information they gather from bystanders.

The drafters relied on that rationale in dealing with medical doctors and their exchange of information and opinions.

If the example of the policeman does not seem close to the borderline, what about the emergency room doctor who acts on information from an ambulance driver? Such information would seem to be exactly the type the drafters contemplated as being within the rule. But what happens if the doctor's information comes from a policeman, or better yet, a bystander?

The point is that what is reasonably reliable for emergency measures is probably the best information the expert can get at the time, a standard which has scant relationship to what is reliable for making a deliberate decision on contested facts in a subsequent trial. So while the desire of the drafters to free expert opinions from rigid common law restrictions is understandable, they chose a seductively simple appearing rule which may prove hard to administer. Moreover, it can provide a special set of problems because of what happens in Rule 705.

Logically, Rule 703 gives a hint of what is to come in Rule 705. Hypothetical questions are no longer required even for non-treating doctors or other experts who have no firsthand knowledge of the facts on which their opinions are based. This result fits with the provision of Rule 703 that the basis for an opinion need not be admissible in evidence. It would hardly make sense to permit that and then require that the expert assume the truth of those inadmissible facts, much less other facts already in the case.

It is interesting that Rule 705 eliminates the requirement for hypothetical questions without mentioning them. Instead, the rule rather cryptically provides:

> The expert may testify in terms of opinion or inference and give his reasons therefor without prior disclosure of the underlying facts or data, unless the court requires otherwise. The expert may in any event be required to disclose the underlying facts or data on cross-examination.

Thus the casual reader must remember that the hypothetical question was a means for requiring that the bases for an opinion be stated in advance of the receipt of the opinion itself when the expert was merely interpreting data and was not also a fact witness to the basis of his opinion.

Obviously, Rule 705 does more than merely do away with the requirement for hypothetical questions. It also permits the direct examiner to omit having the fact witness-expert recite the information on which his opinion is based even when a hypothetical question was not required at common law. Rule 705 is a major change from familiar practice. While it does not abolish hypothetical questions, it makes them optional for the examining counsel, unless the trial court affirmatively requires that they be used.

Most litigators are aware that the hypothetical question has been under sustained attack by some evidence scholars for years. Following Wigmore's lead, they have argued that the hypothetical question is misleading to the jury and admits an opinion into evidence which might be far different from what the expert would say if he were to give his actual opinion on the facts as he knows them. And, one suspects, some writers have never been happy about a device which offers such a beautiful opportunity to make a succinct summary of the party's case in the middle of the trial.

For this very reason it is possible that Rule 705 will not get the attention it deserves. The chances are that some good trial lawyers who have developed the art of using hypothetical questions will simply ignore this rule which makes them unnecessary. Such an approach would probably be a mistake.

The common law requirement for an expert opinion was that every major basis for the opinion had to be testified to in advance of receiving the opinion. That requirement applied whether or not the hypothetical question was required. Certainly in the usual case, an expert opinion is far more persuasive if the jury can see that the expert has a good reason for entertaining it. So it makes sense to keep this part of the hypothetical question practice.

On the other hand, the strict requirement of the common law made hypothetical questions too long, even though trial courts were not always strict about enforcing the rule that every major basis of the opinion come in advance. Thus, the real advantage of Rule 705 is that it permits a streamlining of hypothetical questions. Now they do not need to be as stiff and stylized as before. And so long as they are not unfair or misleading, there is no reason why an examiner cannot be far more selective than previously in choosing the contents of the hypothetical questions he puts to a testifying expert.

It should be stressed that Rule 705 presents some problems. It makes it far more possible for the jury to hear an opinion which ultimately turns out to be inadmissible because it is based neither on admissible evidence nor on ''reasonably reliable'' information, as permitted under Rule 703. One effect of the common law rule was to screen expert opinions in advance of their receipt.

Now, because of the procedure permitted under Rules 703 and 705, that screening process can be delayed until cross-examination. Such a result is not necessarily bad. After all, it is the method used for almost all other evidence except confessions and other exceptional matters, unless the opposing counsel takes some active steps in advance.

The lesson for the careful litigator, particularly defense counsel in personal injury cases, is to keep on his toes. Rules 703 and 705 do not "de-escalate discovery." They make it even more important. Furthermore, a number of cautious lawyers will probably make it a custom to ask for a voir dire examination of expert witnesses, perhaps outside the presence of the jury, because of the impossible task of "unringing the bell" with an instruction to disregard previous testimony. The other way to deal with the problem is for the trial court simply to insist on the use of hypothetical questions and the recitation of the bases for an opinion by fact witness-experts. Such a procedure, however, would merely undo the change permitted by Rule 705 and return to the long and confusing common law procedure.

Some provisions of the hearsay rules in Article 8 directly affect expert testimony. Under the common law, a statement of present bodily condition—no matter to whom it was made—is an exception to the hearsay rule. Rule 803(3) follows that doctrine without change. Closely associated with this familiar rule is the additional hearsay exception that admits statements of past bodily condition—medical history—which were made to a doctor consulted for the purpose of treatment. Federal Rule 803(4) follows this exception as well. But once again, a close reading of the rule and the Advisory Committee notes suggests that it goes much further, although such a result was not entirely understood by the drafters of the rules.

Under Rule 803(4) relevant medical histories are an exception to the hearsay rule if they are "made for the purposes of medical diagnosis or treatment." The most obvious effect of this language is to free this hearsay exception from the requirement that the statement be made directly to a treating doctor. As the Advisory Committee notes point out, the statement may be made to "hospital attendants, ambulance drivers, or even members of the family." Thus the test for admissibility under the new rule is merely the purpose for which the statement was made rather than to whom it was said. The Advisory Committee suggests that the reason for the rule which the common law evolved that a person seeking medical treatment is likely to tell the truth because he wants to be cured—applies equally to statements of previous bodily condition which are not made directly to a doctor. All this seems to make perfectly good sense and is an entirely expected reform.

But there is an additional effect of this language. The rule says the statement may be made for the purpose of "medical diagnosis *or* treatment." (Emphasis added.) Does this mean that a medical history given to a non-treating doctor who is consulted for the purpose of diagnosis and *testimony*, rather than diagnosis and treatment, is also admissible under this exception to the hearsay rule? It does.

While it is perhaps unwarranted to read too much into a simple "or" without other evidence of the intention to make such a major change, the Advisory Committee notes help considerably.

> Conventional doctrine has excluded from the hearsay exception, as not within its guarantee of truthfulness, statements to a physician consulted only for the purpose of enabling him to testify. . . . The . . . rule rejects the limitation. This position is consistent with the provision of Rule 703 that the facts on which expert testimony is based need not be admissible in evidence if of a kind ordinarily relied upon by experts in the field.

The first point is clear enough. The non-treating doctor limitation on the medical history rule is abandoned. But the second statement makes little sense. Since under Rule 703 an opinion may be admitted even though the bases are not, that rule creates little need to make a medical history to a non-treating doctor admissible. Instead, it seems far more rational to defend this change on the basis of simplicity. Why make a distinction to exclude testimony which is not likely to be misleading to jurors, since they can see how motive in giving a medical history can affect its reliability?

Even more puzzling is the interpretation of the language by Dean Mason Ladd, one of the drafters, in his recent book, Ladd & Carlson, *Cases and Materials on Evidence* (1972). Discussing the identical language, he said at page 952: "Proposed Federal Rule 803(4) goes no further than the Model Code or Uniform Rules and limits statements given by a patient for diagnostic *and* treatment purposes." (Emphasis added.) Dean Ladd's interpretation seems unwarranted. While it could be argued that diagnosis should be construed to mean evaluation for the purpose of seeking treatment, the Advisory Committee notes are in disagreement. Moreover, the House Committee on the Judiciary assumed that statements made to non-treating physicians would be admissible under the rule: "After giving particular attention to the question of physical examination made solely to enable a physician to testify, the Committee approved Rule 803(4) as submitted to Congress."

The effect of this rule on the Rockwell case is impressive. If Dr. Brill merely examines Mr. Rockwell and listens to his medical history, he will be permitted to testify to what Mr. Rockwell tells him, so long as it is medically germane. In other words, Rule 803(4) will help the non-treating doctor be a far more effective witness. It will also encourage actual examination of a party by the testifying doctor, since if Dr. Brill merely got Mr. Rockwell's medical history from other doctors and medical files, he would be able to base his opinion on that information but could not testify to it since it would be double hearsay, only one part of which would be cured by a hearsay exception.

The business records exception, Rule 803(6), puts to rest a persistent problem with hospital records. While many early business records statutes were limited to "acts or events," the new rule admits records of "acts, events, conditions, opinions, or diagnoses." This overrules a substantial line of cases which excluded opinions in hospital records.

One of the most effective ways to impeach an expert witness is to confront him with a learned treatise which contradicts his opinion. So long as the language is understandable to the jury, the importance which average individuals attach to the printed word, particularly in books, makes this basis of impeachment a very powerful device.

But the common law practice has some difficulties. One of them is the minor annoyance that the treatise is not admissible for the purpose of proving the truth of the matter asserted, but only to impeach, requiring a limiting instruction of little meaning which can serve to break the spell created by a dramatic impeachment.

More troublesome is the requirement that the expert must have relied on the treatise in forming his opinion or at least acknowledge that it is authoritative in the field. This requirement has always meant that a wily and well-prepared expert witness is difficult to impeach with writings in his field. Rule 803(18) solves this very neatly. It makes learned treatises admissible in evidence as an exception to the hearsay rule. So long as some expert witness in the field establishes the treatise as a reliable authority, it can be used to impeach any expert during the course of the trial. If there is no other expert to validate the treatise, the court can even take judicial notice of its prominence and reliability.

CHAPTER 31

Qualifying Experts

It seemed inconsistent.

The young lawyer was attending a trial advocacy workshop—one of the summer programs that teaches basic skills. When they got to expert witnesses, everyone agreed it was important to do a thorough job qualifying the expert for the benefit of the jury. As one faculty member put it, "By the time you are done qualifying the witness, he will not simply speak the truth, he will *be* the truth." That sounded like advocacy of a high order, and the young lawyer spent a lot of time that evening preparing to qualify the expert witness who was to testify the next morning.

But the next morning, only two lawyers in the entire class got to ask any questions at all about the expert's qualifications. That part of the exercise was over in five or ten minutes. The rest of the time was spent on the substance of the witness's direct and cross-examination. The faculty critiquers all agreed that qualifications were important for the jury, but were too boring to do during class.

That did not sound like advocacy of a high order to the young lawyer. But he was a little reassured when a lecturer on expert witnesses said that qualifications were so important that if your opponent offered to stipulate to them, you should refuse the stipulation. Instead, the lecturer said you should say, "Your honor, as I understand it, Mr. Johnston intends to call his own expert to the stand. If the jury is to decide which to believe, they need to hear both witnesses' qualifications." One of the older lawyers in the class suggested asking, "Your honor, is counsel stipulating that all of Dr. Williams's testimony will be true? In that event, I will be happy to accept his stipulation.''

That night made things even more confusing. The workshop put on an expert witness demonstration. The direct examiner did a complete job qualifying the witness. The young lawyer noticed that most of the 175 lawyers in the audience paid almost no attention until the witness got into the substance of his testimony. That is when the young lawyer decided that he would go beyond the traditional learning about qualifying experts.

The starting point is the law itself. While some states say there are additional requirements, the Federal Rules of Evidence state the law of most jurisdictions: ''If scientific, technical, or other specialized knowledge will assist the trier of fact to understand the evidence or to determine a fact in issue, a witness qualified as an expert by knowledge, skill, experience, training, or education, may testify thereto in the form of an opinion or otherwise.'' FED. R. EVID. 702.

More simply, the question is whether a witness with specialized knowledge or skill can help the jury. An expert is an explainer.

When we qualify experts, we are introducing evidence that is directed at both the judge and the jury. The judicial questions are whether this is a proper subject for explanation and whether this witness is qualified to serve as an explainer. The jury question is whether his background is good enough to make his testimony persuasive. For now we are not concerned with the judicial questions—what kinds of experts judges will recognize, or how well qualified they must be to meet the minimum. Instead, we are concerned with the jury question—how to qualify an expert persuasively.

There is, unfortunately, a ''standard'' way to do it. The usual approach is to put the expert on the stand and push the automatic pilot button like this: ''Doctor, would you tell the ladies and gentlemen of the jury about your professional background, please?'' The witness (who has been properly rehearsed) gives a summary of his entire professional career. After 15 to 20 minutes of uninterrupted background, the lawyer asks a few wrap-up questions and is ready to move into the substance of the witness's testimony.

What could be wrong with that?

First, when the witness testifies with no questions from the lawyer, there is the danger that the jury will think he is not interested. That is not a problem when an eyewitness is testifying to an exciting event. Then the lawyer should fade into the woodwork and let the witness occupy center stage. But it is different with expert qualifications. It is like the cocktail party host who instructs a guest to tell a fascinating story, and then announces he is going out to the kitchen because he has heard it before. The signal is devastating.

Second, it is awkward for an expert to talk about himself in the terms that lawyers want during the qualifications. As Doctor John Burke, a Cleveland economist who has testified in more than 400 cases, put it, ''Frankly, I find it embarrassing.''

This is material that you want the jury to be interested in. The only way they will care is for you to care. As Federal District Judge Herbert J. Stern of New Jersey puts it, ''Lawyers get lazy and let the witnesses do it themselves. If witness qualifications are going to be done with zest, they *must* be done with questions and answers.''

The question and answer approach also tends to overcome the witness's embarrassment. Modesty is not a fault of many experts who testify frequently, but if it can seem that the lawyer has to work just a little to get the witness to admit to his awards and accomplishments, it will not hurt with most American juries.

That is more important than you might think. Some juries actively resent experts who parade their qualifications too flagrantly. As Professor Arthur D. Austin reported, ''Many jurors are not well educated (especially in the matters tried in complex litigation) and have a built-in antagonism toward a witness who is led through a self-serving description of degrees and honors. Some jurors have complained bitterly of having their noses rubbed in credentials.'' A. Austin, *Second Trials*, 10 LITIGATION No. 2, at 34, 36 (Winter 1984).

Part of the problem of jury reaction hinges on what kind of expert is involved. For our purposes three basic categories will do: First is the ''hands-on'' expert who designed the bridge, repaired the broken weld, or treated the sick patient. Second is the paid consultant—the expert of high standing who works in the field, and who knows about this case because he was hired to testify. Third is the professional witness, whose principle work is not in the field, but on the witness stand.

You probably recall that the law of evidence distinguishes between experts who explain facts they observed themselves and experts who explain facts that come from other witnesses. That distinction is the justification for the hypothetical question. But do not worry about that now. That is a problem for another time. Our present concern is how the expert will be received, and these categories help us look at some ideas about experts:

- The witness with the highest qualifications is not necessarily the one who convinces the judge or jury. The "hands-on" expert may command serious respect. A machinist or designer who knows how things actually work may be more impressive than a laboratory theoretician.

- The paid consultant is not necessarily dismissed as a hired gun—but there is always that danger. The analogy that a witness is like a jukebox, and will play any tune you want if you drop in a quarter and push the right button, can be devastating if the evidence supports it.

- Professional witnesses are not necessarily disregarded. If a jury likes a particular professional witness—and they may—it may actually be an advantage. Cleveland economist John Burke is sometimes asked on cross-examination if he is a professional expert. With a twinkle in his eye, and a touch of Irish brogue, he responds, "Certainly! This is no job for an amateur." The jury laughs, and they are on his side, not the cross-examiner's.

- Experience on the witness stand is not necessarily an advantage. Some experts get more arrogant every time they are in court. Others—like good teachers—learn how to get their ideas across effectively so that the jury may actually enjoy their testimony.

- Experience on the witness stand is not necessarily a disadvantage. Generally, the more a questioned documents expert testifies, the better. That is what they are supposed to do. On the other hand, if the witness is someone who always explains what other people do—and never does it himself—then be careful. A doctor who spends all his time in court is suspicious.

The point is, there is no magic rule as to which expert is better. Rather you must think about what kind of expert you have and how you are going to introduce him to the jury. As with other introductions, the worst thing you can do is pretend he is something he is not.

That raises an important point. You must read your witness's resume of professional experience. Chances are he will call it a *curriculum vitae* a term both of you should avoid unless you have (may the gods of litigation forfend such an event) a jury of academicians.

Do not stop with the resume. Read everything your witness has published on the subject of his testimony. You should assume that your opponent will do that, too.

There is a reason for this. Witnesses who are anxious to impress juries sometimes pad their resumes with the most amazing irrelevancies. A pamphlet that your witness wrote and calls a book in his resume is not even a pamphlet in the hands of a good cross-examiner—it is an embarrassment. The lesson is, *edit the resume.*

But if the real problem is that expert qualifications tend to bore or offend juries, or even do both, then something more is needed besides being careful who you pick as a witness and avoiding exaggeration about his past accomplishments.

One of the happy by-products of the Federal Rules of Evidence is they have spurred some lawyers into trying new methods even in areas in which the law remains unchanged. Apparently that has happened with expert witnesses. The Federal Rules make important changes in the examination of experts, but not in qualifying them to testify.

So it is that some trial lawyers have been experimenting with methods that make qualifying experts quicker, more interesting, and less likely to annoy juries. Here they are:

- The quick preview
- The tailored qualification
- The strategic placement

Each deserves a short explanation. We start with the quick preview. If you are in the middle of trial, the jury may have only a rough idea of why you are calling a particular witness. Think how much more gracious a trial would be if you could turn to the jury as your next witness was stepping forward and say (as if you were introducing him to some interested friends), "A few days ago I told you I would be calling the orthopedic surgeon who examined the plaintiff. He is going to tell us about what the doctor in the emergency room might have done in this case. Before he tells you about that, I would like to give you some idea of his background. As it happens, he is head of a special project at the Cleveland Clinic that is doing some research in this area."

That would be gracious, but so highly improper that the judge would not wait for your opponent to object. He would either invite you for a little discussion about the rules of evidence, or simply hold you in contempt.

So instead of starting that way, most lawyers just put the doctor on the witness stand and push the automatic pilot button.

But you do not have to do that. You can use the principle of the quick preview and get the witness to do what the law would not let you do yourself:

Q: Doctor, could I ask you to briefly introduce yourself to the jury.

A: Certainly. I am Patrick Sweeney, and I am a medical doctor here in town.

Q: Doctor, do you practice in any particular branch or specialized field of medicine?

A: Yes, I am a neurologist. I specialize in the brain and the nervous system.

Q: Doctor, before we go any further, did you—in your work as a neurologist—examine Mrs. Dorothy Marshall?

A: Yes, I did.

Q: Have you been able to make a professional determination about Mrs. Marshall's condition?

A: Yes, I have.

Q: Before I ask you about your evaluation of Mrs. Marshall, Doctor, we first need to talk for a few minutes about your professional training in this area.

Now you see the point of the brief preview. It permits a pleasant introduction that gives a hint of what is coming. But it stops short of giving the jury the witness's opinion. That is saved for after the qualifications. But now the jury knows (or is reminded) why this witness is here. The qualifications that follow are more interesting because the jury knows why they matter.

On to the second idea, tailored qualifications. Now that the jury knows roughly what the witness is going to talk about, how much of his qualifications must he testify to? The dreary tradition is to leave out nothing that might possibly impress someone—and you already know the net effect: boredom and annoyance.

Why not tailor the qualifications to suit the situation? Instead of unloading the witness's entire professional career on a captive jury to prove one point, we can limit the qualifications to what is relevant. It is a good point to continue questioning Doctor Sweeney:

Q: Before you give us your opinion, Doctor, would you tell us what in your professional background qualifies you to give this jury your opinion about that problem?

A: Certainly.

You will notice that the question has just a hint of challenge in it. That has some interesting effects. It focuses the witness and the jury on the right point, and it also tends to validate you as an individual who is interested in finding reliable information for the jury. Just do not overdue it and alienate the witness.

In addition, limiting the qualifications to what is pertinent makes them sound much less like the witness is beating his personal drum than if he went through his entire professional resume.

Chances are you have already thought of the next step. Experts usually testify to more than one opinion. Instead of having all the qualifications come at the beginning of the testimony, try linking them to the important opinions throughout the testimony of the witness. As Federal District Judge Ralph B. Guy, Jr., of the Eastern District of Michigan observes, ''The most effective way to qualify a witness is not to do it all at once, at the beginning of his testimony. Instead, work it into his testimony as it becomes relevant to the points he is making.''

Each one of these ideas makes good sense. When all three are used together, the difference between this combination and traditional expert testimony is striking.

''Grand,'' you say, ''but what about this resume you had me edit? What am I supposed to do with it?''

Try introducing it into evidence—not as duplication of the witness's qualifications, but rather as supplementary material the jury can look at if they want. It is a nice way to tell them there is more and that you have just covered the major points.

Here is where the evidence scholars revolt. An expert's resume is hearsay. How can you introduce it in evidence?

The traditional hearsay exceptions do not offer much help. It cannot be past recollection recorded. The writing was probably not made at or near the events it lists, and even if it was, the witness can recall the contents. The policy in favor of live testimony (the very thing we want to avoid) keeps the writing out.

Nor can it be a business record. Although a resume is undoubtedly made in the ordinary course of business and it is surely relevant to business, it is made with a view toward litigation, especially if the lawyer edits it.

What about that new catchall exception to the hearsay rule, FED. R. EVID. 803(24)? The basic idea is that hearsay that has the equivalent guarantee of trustworthiness of other traditional exceptions (whatever that might be) can be admitted even if there is not a specific exception that covers the situation. There are only three conditions to satisfy, but one of them presents a real problem. Under Rule 803(24)(B), the statement must be ''more probative than any other evidence which the proponent can procure through reasonable efforts.'' In other words, non-standard hearsay is admissible only when you really need it. You do not really need it here because the witness could simply testify to his qualifications—exactly what you are trying to avoid. So how can the resume be admitted? The answer is not in doctrine, but convenience. Many thoughtful, scholarly judges routinely admit experts' resumes in evidence. Some are surprised if there are objections. Some judges even require the resumes to be admitted in pretrial orders in an effort to minimize the time spent on qualifications.

But other judges disagree. They reason that the hearsay rule does not have enough flexibility to permit the introduction of resumes, or that admitting resumes in evidence would give them undue weight. (That is an interesting objection. The point of offering it as an exhibit is to let the jury look at it if they want instead of thrusting it on everyone's attention.)

So the resume you have gone over may make it in evidence, or it may not. What do you do if the judge admits it?

If you are Phil Corboy in Chicago, you might have 15 copies of the resume—one for each of the jurors, one for the judge, one for the opposing counsel, and one for the court reporter. That way they can all look at it at once. But if you are his partner, Tom Demetrio, you might not introduce it at all on the theory that you would rather have the jury looking at your expert than at a piece of paper. But whatever you do, you have the flexibility to make the introduction of your expert fit the situation.

CHAPTER 32

Direct Examination of Expert Witnesses

The appearance of an expert witness in a trial should be the signal for a time of clarity and reason, when the expert, who in legal theory has been called to help the jurors understand complex evidence, will explain the significance of what they have already heard. Every now and then, one would expect an expert to provide a moment of sparkling interest and, not too rarely, even a bit of high drama.

Experienced trial observers know better. Expert testimony usually means a hopelessly turgid assemblage of words and phrases which have little meaning to men and women of ordinary understanding. To add to this difficulty, the questions put to experts are often so prolix and convoluted that even the expert does not understand them.

The natural order of things does not require these murky interludes. Expert testimony can be lucid and absorbing. Properly presented, it can be the high point of a trial, impelling the jury or judge to a favorable verdict.

The starting point in presenting effective expert testimony is an understanding of the law relating to experts and opinions: a strange mixture of insupportable reasoning and solid practicality that only the common-law system of evidence could produce. Today, when many jurisdictions are considering adopting the Federal Rules of Evidence, but most have not yet actually done so, the careful litigator must be thoroughly at home with both the federal and the traditional common law rules to present expert testimony effectively.

First, the law generally insists that testimony be given in the language of perception. Witnesses are expected to relate what they saw, heard or did. Interpretation of what this means is left to the jury. Of course, there are exceptions, and lay witnesses are permitted to testify to a number of opinions, including those concerning weights, measures, speed, time, distance, sobriety, sanity and other common matters where an opinion is the only useful form of testimony anyone could expect, or where it is an acceptable short-hand rendition of more basic observations which can be adequately tested on cross-examination.

But the rule against opinions does not apply to expert witnesses. They are called for the very purpose of interpreting data. They are permitted to do this whether or not they have any first-hand factual information about which to testify in the trial. In other words, an expert witness is an explainer, whether he explains his own observations or someone else's.

There is, however, an important distinction between the witness who explains facts and one who explains the testimony of others. When the expert is explaining his own observations (for example, a treating doctor who testifies about his diagnosis), he is a fact witness who is permitted to give his opinion on his observations in a straightforward fashion. The non-fact expert, on the other hand—the one who explains the meaning of other witnesses' testimony—is not permitted to give his actual opinion, but rather must answer hypothetical questions, a strained device concocted to prevent an expert's giving the impression, even inadvertently, that he believes the facts on which his opinion is based.

Actually, instead of being a point of distinction between fact and non-fact expert witnesses, the hypothetical question was originally intended to put the two on an equal footing. The early common-law rule, which still obtains in most jurisdictions that have not adopted the Federal Rules of Evidence, requires that *any* expert state the bases for his opinion before giving the opinion itself. For the fact-witness expert, the process is simple enough: first testify to the observations and then explain what they mean. To impose the same requirement on the expert who merely interpreted, a compensatory mechanism was required. That is the hypothetical question, which is designed to set forth what is being explained without the witness saying whether he believes that the bases for his opinion actually occurred.

But the requirement that the bases for an opinion be fully stated in advance was not followed closely in every jurisdiction. Some states left it to the cross-examiner to determine what the opinion rested on, while others continued the rule in a more strict fashion. Of course, it is impossible to state *all* of the bases, either before or after the opinion itself. Accordingly, even in the stricter jurisdictions, it is usually only necessary to state the principal bases in advance.

One difficulty this creates when dealing with non-fact experts is the order in which witnesses are called to the stand. The hypothetical question requires the expert to assume facts to be true. Since it was thought that the jury might believe something was testified to because it was recited in a hypothetical question, it is typically required that all of the facts assumed in the hypothetical question be established by independent evidence before the question is asked. Thus it is objectionable for a hypothetical question to "assume facts not in evidence." Fortunately, this rule is tempered with the discretion of the trial court to allow the question anyway, if the proponent promises to prove the missing elements by "connecting up later."

But still, the hypothetical question, awkward and misleading, continued to give trouble. So the common law came up with at least three ways to avoid it in typical situations. The first was to allow the expert to listen to the evidence during the trial, and assume it to be true in blanket fashion without bothering to recapitulate it. This method is permissible if the evidence on which the expert relies is not in substantial dispute. It works well enough if you can find an expert willing to sit through an entire trial. The second method was to create hearsay exceptions, especially for doctors who were consulted for the purpose of treatment, which allow the expert who is a partial non-fact witness to be treated as if he were a completely fact-witness expert. In other words, a doctor whose opinion was based partially on hearsay information given to him as the medical history of a patient who consulted him for treatment is permitted to testify to his actual opinion and need not, for that reason, be examined hypothetically. In fact, in many jurisdictions, the "treating doctor" exception to the hearsay rule is not really a hearsay exception at all, since the medical history is not admissible to prove the truth of what was told the doctor, but rather to "explain" his opinion. The third device used to make non-fact experts like fact experts was simply to ignore some hearsay problems, particularly when the expert was relying on the results of standardized tests only peripheral to the opinion, even when those results were pure hearsay.

Understanding this shows how much common law the drafters of the Federal Rules of Evidence were able to change (including abolishing the requirement for hypothetical questions without even mentioning them by name) when they provided that "the expert may testify in terms of opinion or inference and give his reasons therefor without prior disclosure of the underlying facts or data, unless the court requires otherwise. The expert may in any event be required to disclose the underlying facts or data on cross-examination." Rule 705, Federal Rules of Evidence. In fact, the bases of the opinion need not even be admissible in evidence if they are of a type "reasonably relied upon by experts in the particular field in forming opinions or inferences. . . ." Rule 703, Federal Rules of Evidence. Fortunately, the Federal Rules have also done away with the irksome requirement that the expert's opinion could not embrace the ultimate issue of fact in the case.

The opinion rule, with its exceptions and its progeny in the list of hearsay exceptions, is only the starting point for the direct examination of expert witnesses. There is an additional group of customs, procedures and rules that have grown up around expert testimony with which the litigator must be familiar.

The first thing to do when you call an expert to the stand is establish two things: one, that this is a problem on which expert testimony can help the jury, and two, that this witness is qualified to do that. J. Wigmore, *Evidence* § 1923, Vol. 7 at p. 21 (3d Ed. 1940). In some states additional points are claimed to be necessary parts of the foundation, such as showing that the witness actually used his skill and training in forming his opinion on a particular issue, *Deaver v. Hickox*, 81 Ill. App. 2d 79, 224 N.E.2d 468 (1967). This, however, is essentially redundant of the requirement that this is a problem on which expert testimony can help the jury.

In the usual situation, only the second point—the qualification of the particular witness—receives any attention. Medicine, ballistics, fingerprinting, handwriting identification, physics, engineering and many other fields are so well established that their value is self-evident. On the other hand, some jurisdictions, although they recognize that economics is a legitimate field of expertise, refuse to permit economists to testify to the damages in wrongful death cases, saying in essence that it will not help the jury on this issue. Accidentology, on the other hand, is not always recognized as a legitimate field. Accordingly, in dealing with a new area of expertise, such as suicidology, you must be careful not only to pick an expert with impeccable qualifications, but also to lay a good foundation on the value of the field itself.

One of the games the beginning litigator must learn to play is called expert qualifications stipulation. When you call an impressively qualified witness to testify on a contested issue, your opponent may offer to stipulate to his expertise, a gracious sounding gesture often accompanied by a comment that he is doing this to save the jury's time. Typically, the opponent has his own expert—perhaps not so well qualified, whom he will call to rebut yours. One response is to inquire whether your opponent is offering to stipulate that everything your witness will say is correct, in which case you are happy to accept; but if he is planning to disagree and the jury must choose which expert is correct, then it should know your witness's background to help it in this task.

After the witness has been qualified, it is the custom in many jurisdictions to ask for a ruling that he be recognized as an expert and permitted to testify to his opinions. In absence of an objection, this is technically unnecessary. It is, however, a good practice, since it gives the impression of the judicial seal of approval to the testimony that will follow.

Before such a ruling is given, the opposition should have the opportunity to conduct a voir dire examination of the witness on his qualifications. It is a dangerous thing to do, however, unless there is a decent opportunity to destroy a prima facie foundation that he is qualified. Should the trial judge decide that this preliminary cross-examination ''goes to the weight and not the admissibility'' of the expert's testimony, the jury is not likely to understand the ruling. They may well feel your attack, even though it was nearly devastating, was ruled invalid by the judge. While some lawyers feel that two cross-examinations are better than one, it is probably wiser to save for the real cross-examination any attack that would not keep the witness from testifying.

After the witness has been recognized as an expert, the next step is to establish the reasons for the opinion that is to come. Even though the bases are no longer required under the Federal Rules of Evidence and the law of some states, an unsupported opinion, even from a highly qualified witness, does not carry as much weight with either a judge or a jury as does one that on its face is the product of careful consideration.

With a non-fact expert, the hypothetical question should be worked out in advance, and not be the product of momentary inspiration. It is easy, in the heat of battle, to leave out an essential element of a hypothetical question, and it is embarrassing, on completing the question, to hear that the witness does *not* have an opinion based on the facts you have just recited. Indeed, it is a good practice to reduce the hypothetical question to writing, and provide the witness with a copy in advance of trial. You can also give a copy to the judge and your opponent just as you read the question to the witness. This practice actually reduces the possibility of having the hypothetical question interrupted with a spurious objection, since it shows your confidence in the unobjectionability of the question at the same time that it divides your opponent's attention between the written word and what you are saying at the moment. It will also make the reporter grateful if you give a copy to him.

After the bases for the opinion have been established, either by the witness's reciting what he observed or through the hypothetical question, the next step is to ask the witness whether he has an opinion to a reasonable degree of certainty or probability. In fact, it is the usual practice to make this a particular kind of probability or certainty, such as medical or scientific probability. Thus the question put to a ballistics expert might be: "Based on what you have told us, Mr. Lawry, do you have opinion, to a reasonable degree of scientific probability, as to what gun the bullet marked Prosecution Exhibit 14 was fired from?"

The proper answer to that question is "Yes," the witness has an opinion. Only then should the question be asked: "What is your opinion?" Then comes the answer, "This bullet was fired from the pistol marked Prosecution Exhibit 6."

The law varies from state to state whether the opinion must be held to a reasonable degree of certainty or merely a probability. In some jurisdictions it is only required to establish causation between the defendant's acts and the plaintiff's injuries in tort cases; in other states it is considered an essential part of the foundation for any expert opinion.

There is a good argument that this "magic question" need not be asked at all under the Federal Rules of Evidence, since Rule 702 permits an expert to testify "in the form of an opinion or otherwise," and the Advisory Committee's Note specifically states that "it seems wise to recognize that opinions are not indispensable and to encourage the use of expert testimony in non-opinion form when counsel believes the trier can itself draw the requisite inference." Thus, if the "magic question" on certainty or probability is a mere custom of form in your jurisdiction, its omission is justified under the Federal Rules. But if the question is required in your state to establish a sufficiency of the evidence, then the necessary certainty or probability must be established somehow. The "magic question" is one good way to do it. There is also a good argument that it is improper under any rules to require an opinion to be held to a greater certainty than the burden of proof would otherwise demand.

The central thrust of Article 7 of the Federal Rules of Evidence is to streamline expert testimony so that it is more understandable to the fact-finder. But the most important thing that can be done by a good trial lawyer is not found in any rules of evidence or procedure. It is in the rules of good communication. Experts are accustomed to talking in the argot of their profession. Even under ordinary circumstances, their language takes serious effort for a layman to follow. In a trial, the situation becomes even worse; first, because the witness stand is a frightening place, causing many experts to retreat to the safety of carefully phrased obscurity. Thus will a usually affable doctor testify about "contusion, abrasions, lacerations and severe eccymosis" instead of "bruises, scrapes, tears, and black and blue marks."

This is unforgivable—not for the witness, but for the examining lawyer. Good preparation means not only that the witness knows what is going to be asked, but also that the phrasing of the answers, including the choice of words, has been gone over carefully in advance. If the witness delights in arcane terminology, you should consider calling some other expert. Usually, however, you will be able to explain the challenge to the witness in ways that make him want to communicate clearly to laymen without condescending. One reinforcing remark to make to such a witness is that the expert who really understands his field can explain almost any point to an intelligent twelve-year-old. In fact, Karl Menninger of the Menninger Clinic reputedly insisted that all of his residents present cases in plain language, absolutely forbidding the use of technical jargon. It may not be true, but it is a great story that may help your witness testify in an effective manner.

Once on the witness stand, all of your pre-trial warnings may evaporate in the stress of the courtroom's formality. Then it is up to you to remind your witness in a friendly manner, "Now, Doctor, I am not a specialist in this field, so I am going to ask you, whenever you use a medical term, to explain what it means, all right? And if you use some term during your testimony which I do not understand, I hope you will forgive me if I interrupt and ask you to tell us what it means, is that fair enough?''

Finally, make your direct examination brief and well organized. By making an outline of your direct examination, you will be able to go through it quickly and cleanly, avoiding the outrageously prolix repetitiveness which is the keynote of the lawyer who keeps on asking questions just to make certain he has covered everything. While it would be a mistake to read all the questions to the witness, it is a good idea to work out the exact wording of the important ones in advance, making the direct examination of your expert witness a high point in the trial.

CHAPTER 33

Cross-Examining Expert Witnesses

Put it in perspective, right at the start. The average expert witness knows as much about his or her field as you know about law.

That means a lot of different things. It means, for example, that the knowledge and ability of nearly any expert is uneven. It means that the typical doctor knows no more about hepatitis, pyloric stenosis or coronary arrhythmia than the average lawyer knows about promissory estoppel, *renvoi*, or the doctrine of worthier title. It means that a lawyer, intent on doing it, can learn enough about the flash point of waxes to cross-examine an electrical engineer who specified wax-paper condensers in a color television set designed to operate at just five degrees lower than the burning point of wax. It also means that the witness—unless he has had previous courtroom experience—is going to be scared.

The law concerning the cross-examination of expert witnesses is an addition to, not a substitution for, the other rules of evidence. Experts can be impeached, contradicted and attacked just like any other witness. To be sure, the opinion rule lets experts interpret facts, whether or not they have any first-hand information. But the status of being an explainer is no shield if the expert has made a prior inconsistent statement, is guilty of bias or prejudice or even has a prior conviction.

In fact, one of the favorite attacks on expert testimony is to ask about the fee the witness expects to be paid at the end of the trial. It often is overdone, but in a proper case, virtually invites a devastating summation:

Now, you heard Dr. Foster, who treated Mrs. Coleman, tell you her condition is going to continue for the rest of her life. The twenty-five hundred dollar doctor—the man who just looked at her medical files—doesn't think so. He thinks she is going to get better.

The rule is important enough that denying the cross-examiner the right to ask about fees can be a reversible error, *State v. Clarkson*, 58 N.M. 56, 265 P. 2d 670 (1954).

The other most popular way to impeach expert witnesses is with learned treatises. That can be difficult in jurisdictions that still treat impeachment with expert writings as an offshoot of prior inconsistent statements. In most states the expert must have relied on the treatise in forming his opinion, or at least regard it as authoritative. All it takes is some well-coached skepticism to make the treatise inadmissible.

That does not mean it cannot be used. A lawyer has to get information for cross-examination somewhere, so many states permit reading passages from books or articles to the expert and asking if he agrees with what they say, so long as the source is not revealed to the jury. See *Pacific Employers Indemnity Co. v. Garcia*, 440 S.W.2d 335 (Tex. Civ. App. 1969).

That can be awkward. One of the refreshing changes made by the Federal Rules of Evidence, Rule 803(18), deals with the use of learned treatises. First, the rule makes these writings an exception to the hearsay rule, so the trial is not cluttered with a meaningless limiting instruction. Second, the rule permits learned treatises to be authenticated not only by the witness who is being impeached, but also by other experts or even the judge, who can take judicial notice that the work is considered authoritative in the field.

Impeaching with learned treatises still bears some resemblance to prior inconsistent statements. Even under the Federal Rules, the witness must be confronted with the writing on cross-examination before it is admissible.

That is really the best way to do it, too. As with prior inconsistent statements, first commit the witness to testimony you want to impeach. Have the witness repeat it. Let him become more positive as you seemingly retreat in confused misunderstanding. Then after the witness has closed the door to every exit, have him read it out loud to the jury so they can hear the two opposing opinions, one right after the other, out of the same mouth.

Like impeachment with prior inconsistent statements, it can be dramatically effective. Like impeachment with prior inconsistent statements, it should be saved for something that counts. And be careful; there are some additional concerns.

The first is that, because the field is likely to be one in which the lawyer's knowledge is narrow—even though it may be intense within its limited bounds—there is a greater danger of taking something out of context that can be explained away, leaving the cross-examiner with an attack that is exposed as being invalid. That can undercut an entire case.

The second problem is somewhat like the first. Often there are legitimate differences of opinions in the field, and the cross-examiner may unwittingly set up the other side for a redirect examination that explains the "theoretical errors" to which you have fallen prey. That response can be forestalled if the cross-examiner emphasizes there are two schools of thought, rather than leaving the point to the other side for rebuttal.

The Federal Rules of Evidence, in addition to easing the use of learned treatises, have created some problems in cross-examining experts.

The common law requires an expert to give the basis for his opinion in advance of the opinion itself. If the expert is interpreting facts or data he personally observed, he first testifies to these facts and then gives the opinion based on those facts. On the other hand, if the expert is not basing his opinion on first-hand information, but rather on facts or data developed by others, things are a little more complex.

Before a "non-fact" expert gives his opinion, the factual basis must first be introduced into evidence through other means—such as records, documents or the testimony of other witnesses. Then the non-fact expert is asked to assume those facts are true in a hypothetical question. While it is technically objectionable for a hypothetical question to "assume facts not in evidence," most judges will permit the practice if the questioner promises the court he will "connect up later" by subsequently introducing evidence of the missing facts. Furthermore, many jurisdictions permit a short-cut hypothetical question based on the testimony of others, if he hears it and it is essentially free from dispute. That way the non-fact expert can be asked to assume the testimony of the other witnesses is true and give his opinion on it.

Either way it is done—through a hypothetical question or the witness testifying to the facts himself—the common law required the bases to come before the opinion.

The beneficiary of this rule is the opposing party, who can test the admissibility of the opinion in advance.

All that is reversed by the Federal Rules of Evidence. Under Rule 705, "The expert may testify in terms of opinion or inference and give his reasons therefor without prior disclosure of the underlying facts or data, unless the court requires otherwise. The expert may in any event be required to disclose the underlying facts or data on cross-examination."

The common-law rule screened opinions before they were admitted; the Federal Rules save that screening for cross-examination, after the opinion is already in evidence, unless the judge affirmatively requires that the underlying data be given first.

This can cause problems. Under Rule 703, the facts or data on which the expert relies do not need to be admissible if they are of the sort "reasonably relied upon by experts in the particular field in forming opinions or inferences upon the subject. . . ."

Rules 703 and 705 create two distinct difficulties for the cross-examiner. First, an expert who is interpreting data that is *not* reliable under Rule 703 may testify to his opinion, and its inadmissibility may not be discovered until cross-examination. Second, the expert may be relying on information that is inadmissible even though reliable under Rule 703. If asked on cross-examination for the bases of his opinion, the expert would be required to testify to information otherwise inadmissible—and very possibly damaging to the cross-examiner's case.

Neither is a very comfortable situation, but what can be done about it?

The answer lies in careful pretrial discovery. Under the Federal Rules, interrogatories and even depositions of expert witnesses are more important than ever. The time to find out about the admissibility of the expert's opinion is before it is given, rather than relying on the dubious assistance of a motion to strike and an instruction to disregard what turns out to be inadmissible.

Advance information about the bases of an opinion gives the opponent an opportunity to deal with it before the witness testifies. The first is the classical method of testing any foundation in advance, the voir dire examination of the witness. The second protective device is to ask the trial court to require that the bases for the opinion be established in advance—retreating to the pre-rule practice.

Since hypothetical questions are not popular with many trial court judges, the best way to ask for them is to tell the court you have a good-faith basis for making the request: The opinion is going to turn out to be inadmissible, something you can only know from thorough discovery.

Now comes the homily on preparation, which is going to be mercifully brief. It can be squeezed down into three words: read, consult and scout. Well, maybe a little explanation is necessary. Read as much of the leading literature as you can on the subject. But do not go at it randomly. Consult your own expert for information and for additional reading. After you have gotten into the literature, follow some of your own leads as well. Finally, scout the expert you are going to cross-examine. Find out about his experience as a witness, how he is regarded in the field and what kind of person he is.

Do as much preparation as possible before submitting interrogatories or taking the deposition of the expert you are going to cross-examine. If the expert is deposed, resist the temptation to show off anything you have learned unless you are reasonably certain the deposition will be used in lieu of testimony. Then it must be treated more like testimony itself.

Now you are ready to start organizing your cross-examination.

One of the first decisions to make in organizing your cross is to decide what your general approach will be.

Much of that depends on what you learned when you scouted the witness. Assume that the witness is not only well qualified, but has years of experience as an expert witness. He may have tried more cases than you. Furthermore, suppose this witness has the reputation of being pleasant, outgoing and good at explaining things and actually enjoys jousting with cross-examiners. Like some other experts, this one has the ability to figure out where the lawyer is going on cross-examination and loves to explain why a question is misleading.

The problem is how to control a witness like this on cross-examination.

One technique is called the bargain. It takes effort, but it can work surprisingly well. To be effective, it must be done at the very beginning of cross-examination. It goes like this:

Q: Dr. Lewis, my name is Bill Maxwell, and I represent the defendant in this case, Mrs. Carol Nicholson. You and I have met before, haven't we, Doctor, when your deposition was taken?

A: Yes, that's right, at Mr. Porter's office.

370

> Q: Now, Dr. Lewis, I noticed during your direct examination how you tried to cooperate with the plaintiff's lawyer, Mr. Porter, in answering questions, and I wondered if I might have the same cooperation?
>
> A: I'll try.
>
> Q: Now you know, Dr, Lewis, as the lawyer for Mrs. Nicholson, and as an officer of the court, it is my job to ask you some questions about your testimony. You understand that, don't you?
>
> A: Yes.
>
> Q: I am going to try to ask you questions that will call for a yes or no answer.
>
> A: What if I can't answer yes or no?
>
> Q: Well, Doctor, as I was saying, I am going to try to ask you questions that call for a yes or no answer. If you *can* answer them yes or no, would you be willing to do that?
>
> A: Yes.
>
> Q: But if I should ask a question what you cannot answer yes or no, then please tell me you cannot answer the question, and I will try to rephrase it so you can, or I will go on to another question. Is that fair enough?
>
> A: Yes, I guess so.
>
> Q: So then, Doctor, the answers you will give will be either yes, no, or I'm sorry, Mr. Maxwell, but I can't answer that question. Can we agree on that?
>
> A: Yes.
>
> Q: Fine, thank you, Doctor. Now, then . . .?

This looks like a lot to go through to gain control over the witness, and it is. The elements of this "bargain" are worth your study, since if you attempt it and leave out an important part, it will not work. Instead you will look unfair, as if you are trying to hold the witness to a yes or no answer when that sort of response would be misleading.

Before we go any further, please notice that there is nothing improper about exercising this amount of control over a witness on cross-examination. So long as the questions you ask actually call for a yes or no answer, there is nothing wrong with insisting on that kind of response. Moreover, the trial court ought to support you in this effort but it may not. That is the beauty of the bargain; you can reinforce it yourself:

> Q: As I understand it, Dr. Lewis, a spinal tap is one of the diagnostic techniques commonly used by doctors to help

> determine the nature of possible brain injury, is that correct?
>
> *A:* Yes.
>
> *Q:* Nevertheless, Doctor, you did not perform a spinal tap on Mr. Osmond, the plaintiff in this case, did you?
>
> *A:* I didn't need to.
>
> *Q:* Dr. Lewis, do you remember our agreement?
>
> *A:* Yes.
>
> *Q:* And you agreed you would answer either yes or no, or 'I'm sorry, Mr. Remington, but I cannot answer that question yes or no.' Isn't that correct?
>
> *A:* Yes.
>
> *Q:* Thank you, Doctor, so tell us, please, whether or not you performed a spinal tap on the plaintiff in this case?
>
> *A:* No, I did not.

This is the time to reinforce the bargain—before the witness explains why he did not use this test, and it is perfectly fair. There is nothing misleading about the answer to the question. To be sure, you may be creating an inference that the doctor neglected a valuable diagnostic test. That does not mean he is entitled to "explain his answer" at that point. Why he did not do a spinal tap is something that can be explained on redirect examination.

Not all trial judges—particularly those with limited trial experience before rising to the bench—understand the distinction between fair and unfair questions that call for yes or no answers. The direct examiner has the advantage of preparing the witness for trial and going over all the questions in advance. The direct examiner does not need the unfair advantage of being able to coach the witness to make non-responsive additions to the information which is sought on cross-examination. The principle prohibiting such interjections on cross-examination is solidly established in every jurisdiction. It is the rule that lets the lawyer asking the questions object to an answer because it is non-responsive.

That the non-responsive rule is designed to protect the cross-examiner is shown by the fact it is an objection available only to the lawyer asking the questions and not the opposition. All that a non-responsive answer does for the lawyer who did not ask the question is permit a delayed objection on some other ground, such as hearsay or relevance. See *McCormick on Evidence* 113 (2d ed. 1972); P. Tone, *Invoking and Applying Rules of Evidence*, Litiga-tion Vol. 2, No. 1, p. 11, 12 (1975).

As a final point on controlling a witness on cross-examination, once you strike a bargain like this with a witness, you must live up to your half as well. Every question you ask must be fairly susceptible to being answered yes or no. Furthermore, you must not let down your guard. Once you start letting a witness volunteer additional information, it is extremely difficult to regain the control you have lost.

Strict control over an expert witness is not always desirable. There are times, for example, when a cross-examiner needs the expert witness to explain something to the jury. On other occasions, tight control may only serve to mask the witness's argumentativeness, which may be your strongest point. Then you may prefer to "egg him on" into taking a partisan stance by testifying to propositions that are more effectively impeached by learned treatises or by contradiction from a more plausible expert.

Fortunately, many expert witnesses are more reasonable and require a different approach. One method that can be successful with such witnesses is to have them concede that their field, unlike, say, mathematics, is not a precise science. It is one in which reasonable people can differ, and other experts—as well trained as the witness on the stand—might well come to a contrary conclusion. That is the sort of wedge which, when well developed, can undercut the witness's entire testimony on direct examination.

There are some specific techniques that may apply to all sorts of experts, irrespective of the general approach taken by the cross-examiner.

The first of these techniques is emphasizing that the expert has no first-hand knowledge when he is a non-fact expert. It is too valuable a point to throw away with just one or two questions. Instead, it should be developed in a whole series:

> Q: Dr. Lewis, if a man whom you had never met called you on the telephone and described a series of symptoms, you would not feel very comfortable prescribing a course of treatment for acute gall bladder attack, would you?
> A: No.
> Q: In other words, Dr. Lewis, we can agree that in the field of medicine, there usually is no substitute for actually examining a patient when it comes to making a diagnosis. Isn't that correct?
> A: Yes, most of the time.
> Q: And Doctor, you are not telling this judge and this jury

you were actually in the emergency room of St. Michael's Hospital when Ronald Morgan was brought in, are you?

A: No, I was not.

Q: In fact, you did not examine him that night at all, did you?

A: No.

Q: And you were not with Dr. Deerfield when he visited Ron Morgan the next morning, were you?

A: No.

Q: And when Ron Morgan left the hospital, you did not examine him then, either, did you?

A: No.

Q: The fact is, Doctor, you have never examined Ronald Morgan, have you?

A: No.

Q: And everything you have told this judge and jury about your expert opinion—that's all based on reading the file, isn't it?

A: Yes.

Q: And not based on any examination done by you?

A: No.

One of the techniques for cross-examining an expert witness has a slightly misleading name. It is called varying the hypothetical question. When a non-fact expert is cross-examined, the term is accurate enough. The cross-examiner is entitled to vary the terms of the hypothetical questions that were asked on direct examination to test which of the bases for the opinion the witness considers essential.

As a simple example, a strength of materials expert may have testified that a particular choice of steel girder was inadequate for a fifty-foot truss bridge with a load capacity of 50,000 pounds. But what if the load limit of the bridge were 35,000 pounds, would those girders be adequate then? That sort of question varies the hypothetical that was asked on direct examination.

The reason the term is misleading is that the technique is permissible whether or not the expert was asked a hypothetical question; indeed, whether or not the witness is a fact or non-fact expert. It is a proper means for cross-examining any expert witness.

It is no secret that there are experts who earn their living by testifying. When a ballistics expert, questioned document specialist, or some other individual whose field is necessarily connected with litigation testifies, extensive courtroom experience does not have much impeachment value. On the other hand, when an expert works in a field that does not require testifying, then repeated courtroom appearances can be worth exposing on cross-examination.

Finally, most expert witnesses who testify frequently enjoy showing off a little to the jury. Some of these experts delight in putting the simplest ideas into nearly incomprehensible jargon. If the direct examiner did not have the sense to make the witness translate these terms into ordinary English, then the cross-examiner has been handed a wonderful opportunity to expose pretension.

Exposing overstatement is a means of impeachment that can be used for ideas as well as just language, as in the following example adapted from John A. Burgess's audio tape, *Debunking the Expert*, Cassette No. 106A, The Association of Trial Lawyers of America:

> Q: Now, Officer Dixon, this breathalizer which you have described to the jury, it is an electrical device, isn't it?
> A: Well, actually it works on mechanical principles.
> Q: You have to plug it into the wall to make it work, don't you?
> A: Yes.
> Q: Essentially then, it is an electrical machine—an appliance—like a washing machine or a toaster, except it is more complex; isn't that correct?
> A: Yes.
> Q: And you say, if I understand your testimony, it is relatively foolproof?
> A: Yes, if properly run, it is foolproof.
> Q: In other words, it never malfunctions if it has not been abused; is that correct, Officer Dixon?
> A: Yes.
> Q: Like a toaster?

Finally, an admonition. Do not quibble with the witness. It is a vice to which lawyers are prone anyway. Some lawyers seem to reach their peak of petty argumentativeness when they cross-examine experts, and are drawn into a battle with the expert on his own ground. Your field is the courtroom; hold on to your advantage.

PART VII

Tactics

CHAPTER 34

Traps

It was years ago, and Hanley was not in Chicago, his old stomping grounds. He was in a state court in Salem, Massachusetts, representing the defense in a products liability case. He had the good sense to have local counsel at his side, both to introduce him to the court and to help him negotiate his way through the pitfalls of local practice.

At the end of the plaintiff's case he stood up and made what he thought was a pro forma motion: "Your honor, the defense moves to dismiss the plaintiff's case."

Imagine his shock then, when the local counsel said to Hanley as he sat down, "My God, Hanley, you certainly have nerves of iron."

"What do you mean?"

"You made that motion like it was just some perfunctory matter."

"It was. I simply moved to dismiss the plaintiff's case."

"Don't you know," asked local counsel, "the effect of that motion? You have just waived your right to put on your entire defense. After that motion, either the judge rules in your favor, or you are stuck arguing this case with none of your evidence. The only issue on appeal could be whether it was proper to deny your motion."

The puckish gods of litigation smiled, and the judge granted Hanley's motion—but the lesson stuck. There are traps out there, and the way to avoid falling in is to know about them.

Right at the start there is the academic's favorite problem—the proper definition. What is meant by a trap? An obscure technicality? A rule that is necessarily unfair? Some procedure that is out-of-step with the general American common law? The difficulty with any of those is that what is obscure to one lawyer is common knowledge to another, and what seems unfair in one setting may be highly appropriate somewhere else. There is nothing wrong with the rule that nearly caught Hanley—as long as you know what it is.

So we will not worry about an exact definition of what is a trap, a snare, or a pitfall. For our purposes, any rule of evidence or procedure that has unexpected consequences will qualify—and there are plenty of them. Here are the favorite traps from a number of different trial lawyers across the country. They share a common quality: if you do not watch out, they can catch you.

① Start with FED. R. CIV. P. 50. It follows the usual rule about directed verdicts: moving for a directed verdict does not waive the right to put on evidence if the motion is denied.

In fact, <u>a motion for a directed verdict is *required* if you later want to make a motion for a judgment notwithstanding the verdict</u>. In other words, if the jury returns a verdict against you, a motion for judgment notwithstanding the verdict is only proper if you first moved for a directed verdict. And not just any motion for a directed verdict will do. It must come "at the close of all the evidence." Rule 50(b). Do you have it? No motion for a directed verdict at the right time, no motion for a judgment notwithstanding the verdict later. It is a simple doctrine of waiver, right?

Not so fast, you say. What is the relationship between these two motions? Why should the failure to make one waive the other?

The reason is conceptual and historical. If you make a motion for a directed verdict, you are saying, "Judge, this case is so clear that you should not even let it go to the jury." And if you make a motion for a judgment notwithstanding the verdict, you are saying, "Judge, this case is so clear that you should not have let it go to the jury." Because the ideas behind the two are closely related, the law concluded that a waiver of the first motion was a waiver of the second.

But wait a minute. What about how things really work? Everyone knows that judges do not like to grant directed verdicts. They are likely to wait and see what the jury will do, so they will not have to take responsibility for a decision that the jury might make for them. Typically, judges reserve ruling on motions for directed verdicts—and then give serious thought to the problem for the first time afterward, when they consider the motion for a judgment notwithstanding the verdict.

The result is that <u>most of the time there is no real meaning to the motion for a directed verdict.</u> The words are spoken, but no one expects anyone to do anything about them. But come time for a judgment notwithstanding the verdict, and then the motion for directed verdict takes on a magic air. Like eye of newt and wing of bat, the words had to have been added at just the right time to make the potion work.

Is there any practical justification for the rule other than an over-active doctrine of waiver?

Just maybe. If moving for a directed verdict and stating the grounds for it would have alerted the opponent that some part of his proof was inadvertently missing—and if the judge would have permitted the opponent to reopen the case and offer that proof—then there is the possibility of "detrimental reliance" by your opponent in your failing to make a motion for a directed verdict.

But that is pretty theoretical. It assumes that the motion is treated seriously when it is made, which it seldom is. Instead, it is treated seriously later, when the other motion is made. So think of it this way: it is a trap, and if you want to preserve your motion for a judgment notwithstanding the verdict, do not forget to move for a directed verdict at the close of all the evidence.

② In every state the statutes of limitations can get tricky. That is why careful lawyers make it a habit to check on limitations almost before they do anything else. Technical enough already, statutes of limitations get even tougher when they are mixed with the notice requirements found in many states. Notice requirements are like extra statutes of limitations in some situations. For example, you may have a year to bring an action for negligence. But if the action is against a municipality or a utility—and if a statute requires written notice to the potential defendant within 90 days of the injury, the case may be over before it comes in your office—or even worse, the day after.

Lesson? Make a chart of the statutes of limitations that includes any special notice requirements.

Even with a chart, time limitations can be complex. Consider this case from Florida. It is an action for personal injuries. The jury awarded the plaintiff a sizable verdict. The defendant moved for a new trial, and to everyone's surprise, the trial judge granted the motion.

Rather than simply appeal the order granting a new trial (which he could have done), the plaintiff thought he could talk the trial judge into reinstating the verdict. So the plaintiff petitioned the court for a rehearing on the order to grant a new trial. The idea was that the court might reconsider its ruling and let the verdict stand.

There is a feeling of deference in what the plaintiff did—give the judge the opportunity to correct his own mistake before running to the appellate court.

In due course, the court denied the rehearing. And the price of deference seemed too high when it developed that the time for appealing the order granting the new trial *had run* while the judge was considering the motion for a rehearing. In other words, the right to appeal was lost by waiting for the trial court to correct its mistake. *Cf. DePadro v. Moore,* 215 So.2d 27 (Fla. Dist. Ct. App. 1968). Luckily for the plaintiff in this case, he also won the second time it was tried.

Lesson? Read the rules literally, and do not assume that your motion will toll the time to file, respond, or appeal.

③ If everyone thinks that something is a rule, then it might as well be the law, even if it is not. But what about a rule that only some of the lawyers believe in?

Douglas Connah reports that in Maryland, one local bugaboo that older lawyers watch out for is a ''rule'' followed by a few of the judges. The ''rule'' says you are not entitled to a directed verdict at the end of the plaintiff's case if you have introduced any documents during the cross-examination of the plaintiff's witnesses. The idea is that introducing evidence for consideration by the trier of fact waives the directed verdict.

The results of this ''rule'' are fascinating. The lawyers who follow it actually go ahead and use their own documents during the cross-examination of the plaintiff's witnesses, but they do not formally offer them into evidence until the start of their own case-in-chief. You can spot the believers in the ''rule'' by their first words for the defense: ''Your honor, I offer into evidence defendant's exhibits already marked one through one hundred twenty for identification.''

④ There are probably more snares in evidence than in procedure. Sometimes they are caused by ''simplifications'' in the law. Take learned treatises as an example. FED. R. EVID. 803(18) makes them an exception to the hearsay rule. No longer are learned treatises admissible just to impeach, and no longer are cumbersome limiting instructions required. Furthermore, learned treatises can be authenticated by the testimony of the witness who is being examined with them, by some other expert, or even by judicial notice. To keep deliberations uncluttered, the books and pamphlets are not admissible as exhibits but may be read into evidence.

The rule seems to invite a simplified procedure: just mark the text, lay the proper foundation, and have the witness read from the book. No need to make a formal offer, right?

Wrong, says *Maggapinto v. Reichman*, 481 F. Supp. 547, 550 (E.D.Pa. 1979). You must make a formal offer of the treatise even though it is not an exhibit. If the offer is not made, then it does not become substantive evidence. What does that mean? It cannot be used for its truth.

Ⓒ The Federal Rules of Evidence also simplified the law of prior inconsistent statements. It used to be that prior inconsistencies were admissible only to impeach witnesses, not to prove the truth of the statement (a difficult distinction for both laymen and lawyers to follow). And it used to be that the rule in *Queen Caroline's Case*, 2 Br. & B. 284, 129 Eng. Rep. 976 (1820), was followed in nearly all states. That rule required confrontation with the prior statement before any outside proof of the prior statement was admitted in evidence. Both of those rules were changed by the Federal Rules of Evidence.

Here is the "simple" result: There are now two classes of prior inconsistent statements. The first is found in the definition of hearsay. Prior inconsistent statements *are admissible for their truth* if:

1. the declarant testifies at the trial or hearing
2. the declarant is subject to cross-examination about the statement
3. the statement is "inconsistent with his testimony," and
4. the statement "was given under oath subject to the penalty of perjury at a trial, hearing, or other proceeding, or in a deposition." FED. R. EVID. 801(d) (1) (A).

In effect, some prior inconsistent statements are admissible as exceptions to the hearsay rule. So where are the traps?

Snare number one: You will not find prior inconsistencies listed as an exception to the hearsay rule, or in the rules on witnesses and impeachment. Where will you find them? Right where they do not belong, in the definition of what is *not* hearsay.

Snare number two: If you read all the Federal Rules of Evidence, you might be tempted to believe that only prior inconsistent statements that qualify under Rule 801 (d)(l)(A) are admissible. Why might you think so? Because nowhere else in the rules is there any definition of a prior inconsistent statement that is admissible for any purpose. But if you thought there were no other admissible prior inconsistent statements, you would be wrong. Rule 801 only defines the prior inconsistent statements that are admissible for their truth. Other prior inconsistent statements are still admissible but are not mentioned by the rules. Without saying so, the Federal Rules made two classes of prior inconsistent statements—some admissible for their truth and some admissible just to impeach.

Snare number three: Rule 613 says you need not confront a witness with the prior statement before cross-examining him about it. It is a simplification, remember? But what too many lawyers forget is that the rule does not abolish the requirement of confrontation—it just delays it. It is no longer necessary to confront the witness with the prior statement just to ask questions about it. On the other hand, extrinsic evidence of the prior inconsistent statement—evidence outside of the examination of the witness—such as the statement itself, or some other witness's testimony about it—is *not* admissible unless "the witness is afforded an opportunity to explain or deny" the statement.

So is it a trap or not? It depends on your point of view. On the one hand, the Federal Rules of Evidence have not simplified this area very effectively. It is more like a maze than a straight line. On the other hand it is not so hard, once you realize that there are two kinds of prior inconsistencies and that confrontation is still required. Do not forget about confrontation, or Rule 613 will be a very real trap.

ⓒ Some of the most dangerous pitfalls come from being guilty of full trial preparation.

Assume a simple situation. You have a case involving a questioned document. One of your key witnesses, Joanna Squires, is personally familiar with the handwriting of the dead man said to have written the document. While Miss Squires is not an expert, you think her testimony will be impressive because of her impartiality. In fact, you plan to call her to the stand before your handwriting expert testifies.

Now you are getting ready for trial. Your natural tendency is to spend some time preparing Miss Squires, checking her ability to identify the signatures on some known and questioned exemplars. It is not a good plan.

If you read FED. R. EVID. 901(b), you will see why: non-expert opinions about the genuineness of handwriting are only admissible if they are ''based on familiarity not acquired for purposes of the litigation.'' Your pretrial preparation of this witness will have to be careful, indeed. Otherwise you will prepare the witness until the evidence is inadmissible.

It can get even more dangerous. Refresh a witness's recollection in preparation for a deposition or trial with an otherwise privileged document, and the privilege may be lost. *See Prucha v. M & N Modern Hydraulic Press Co.*, 76 F.R.D. 207 (W.D. Wisc. 1977).

Well, if woodshedding the witness has pitfalls, at least it is safe to take a deposition, correct?

As Professor Edward J. Imwinkelried of Washington University Law School in St. Louis points out, maybe not. In some states merely taking the deposition of a witness who would otherwise be disqualified under the Dead Man's statute is a waiver of the incompetency of the witness. *Fulmer v. Rider*, 635 S.W.2d 875 (Tex. App. 1982). It is the sort of mistake that could alter an entire case—admitting otherwise incompetent evidence and changing the outcome. As Imwinkelried says, it could even amount to malpractice.

⑦ Be careful with blanket claims of work product privilege. If you claim a work product privilege to a document, you may make it inadmissible. How?

Easy. If you claim that the document was prepared for litigation, you have just made it inadmissible as a business record under the rule of *Palmer v. Hoffman*, 318 U.S. 109 (1943), which holds that business records that are prepared with a view toward litigation are inadmissible. Even so, they might still qualify as past recollection recorded. The trouble is that under FED. R. EVID. 803(5), past recollection recorded may be read into evidence, but may not be received as an exhibit unless offered by the opponent.

⑧ Some of the most interesting traps are entirely local, and like all law they are subject to quick change. In Texas, for example, it once was required to take formal exception to the judge's ruling to preserve error in a criminal case, but not in civil cases. That inconsistency is gone, but Texas has made up for its loss. The Federal Rules of Evidence have been largely adopted by the Supreme Court of Texas for civil actions, but the old common law still applies to criminal cases. Only the legislature can change the criminal evidence rules, and it has not done that yet.

Pat Hazel of the University of Texas Law School reports that

Texas has a special rule for preserving error. It is necessary to have an adverse ruling from the judge in response to an evidence objection. According to Hazel, you must keep escalating your demand until the judge turns you down:

"Objection, Your Honor."

"Sustained." (The error went away.)

"Request a limiting instruction, Your Honor."

"Granted." (It went away again.)

"Move for a mistrial, Your Honor."

"Denied." (Error was finally preserved.)

Arkansas has its own twist on this progression. Suppose the prosecutor commits a serious error, such as commenting on the failure of your defendant to testify. You object and ask for a mistrial. Instead of granting the mistrial, the judge simply tells the jury to disregard the comment. According to William R. Wilson of Little Rock, you must renew your request for a mistrial, or it is waived. See *Howe v. Freeland,* 237 Ark. 705, 375 S.W.2d 666 (1964).

As Professor Michael H. Graham at the University of Illinois College of Law points out, there is a different trick to preserving error in criminal cases in Illinois. A clear objection on the record is not enough. There must also be a posttrial motion calling particular attention to the error. *See People v. Edwards,* 74 Ill.2d 1, 383 N.E.2d 944 (1978).

Ⓠ Perhaps the most troublesome traps of all come from a doctrine called "opening the door." The idea behind it is an elemental sense of justice. At the start it does not even involve retaliation, just filling in the details. FED. R. EVID. 106, as the "rule of completeness," lets the opponent to evidence overcome the selectivity of the other side and require the opponent to offer the rest of the document or statement in evidence (or any other document or statement) that "ought in fairness to be considered contemporaneously with it." In other words, offering part of something may open the door to the rest.

Opening the door just sounds like basic fairness. How could it be a trap?

Take a simple case suggested by Irving Younger. The witness on the stand is the plaintiff in the case. He gave a statement to an insurance investigator in which he admitted running a red light. So on cross-examination you confront him with the statement (which you did not have to do, since he is a party, but it was the most effective way to use it).

You have opened the door to the plaintiff's redirect examination. The witness says, "The insurance claims agent told me if I signed that paper I would receive a check in settlement of my claim within a week."

If you are not ready to call that situation a trap, then how about this case from Professor Paul Giannelli at Case Western Reserve University? (Before we start, there is a rule of evidence you need to know. When hearsay is admitted under the Federal Rules of Evidence, Rule 806—as a sort of special door opening rule— permits the opponent to attack the declarant's credibility. Now you are ready.)

You represent the defendant in a criminal case. We will call him Mark Huggins. Huggins is charged with burglary, and his defense is an alibi. He claims he was at his girlfriend's house when the robbery took place. Unfortunately, Huggins had some serious on-the-job training, so he has two prior convictions for burglary in the past three years.

There are other problems as well. Shortly after he was arrested, Huggins confessed. But in a stroke of good luck, you convinced the trial judge that there was a defect in the warning he was given by the police, so the confession is inadmissible.

But the confession is another reason to keep Huggins off the witness stand. Under *Harris v. New York,* 401 U.S. 222 (1971), a confession that is inadmissible because of a bad Miranda warning may still be admissible to impeach. If the defendant testifies and says something inconsistent with what he said in the "inadmissible" confession, then he can be impeached with it on the witness stand. The limiting instruction to the jury that they are not to consider it for its truth is likely to escape them.

With all of that, it is not difficult for you to recommend that Huggins not take the stand, especially because his girlfriend, Emily Richards, will testify to Mark's alibi.

You call Miss Richards to the stand, and she tells about Huggins's being with her while the prosecution claimed he was committing the burglary. Then, at the end of her testimony, she adds—all on her own—"Besides, I know he is not guilty because he told me he did not do it."

The prosecutor does not object, and in fact does not even cross-examine Emily Richards. He has another plan in mind. He has some evidence to offer in rebuttal, and manages to wait until the defense rests its case. That is when he rises and asks to approach the bench.

"Your honor, at this time the prosecution offers the record of prior convictions of the defendant as well as the confession he gave to the police on September 23."

"But your honor," you reply, "this is outrageous. The defendant has not testified. He has not even taken the stand."

"He does not have to," replies the prosecutor. "The defense offered the defendant's hearsay denial into evidence through the testimony of Miss Richards. Under Rule 806, your honor, the people are entitled to attack the declarant's credibility "by any evidence that would be admissible for those purposes if declarant had testified as a witness.' "

A trap.

Is there any way out? Perhaps. The hearsay statement was not requested—it was volunteered. Even though the defendant is legally responsible for the statement, and could have objected to it, the retaliation seems excessive. So you keep your fingers crossed as you respond, "Your honor, this evidence may be proper under Rule 806, but it is still excluded by Rule 403. The prejudicial effect simply outweighs the probative value."

Will it win? Good question.

Perhaps the most bizarre opening-the-door rule comes from Maryland. If you ask your opponent to show you a document during trial and you inspect it—for whatever reason—your opponent is automatically entitled to offer it in evidence. It is one of those oddities that Marylanders are actually a little proud of, and they trace it back to *United States Fidelity & Guaranty v. Continental Baking Co.*, 172 Md. 24, 32, 190 A. 768 (1937).

But it is nothing like the opening statement rule. The opening statement rule is shocking partly because of its results and partly because it debunks a great American myth. We are so used to lawyers and judges repeating the cliche that "opening statements are not evidence," that we begin to believe it. But it is not entirely true. An opening statement is not evidence for the party who makes it, but it can be evidence when it is offered against him.

Why? Because lawyers are agents who are authorized to speak for their clients. So facts recited in an opening statement may operate as an admission and dispense with the need for the opponent to offer any proof of what was said. See *McLhinney v. Landsdell Corp.*, 254 Md. 7, 254 A.2d 177 (1969). And when it is clear from your opening statement that you do not have a case, even assuming that you proved everything you said you would, some states permit it to be the basis for a directed verdict against you. J. Jeans, *Trial Advocacy* § 8.17 (1975).

The lesson? Be careful to state a case or a defense.

You have noticed, I hope, that all these traps work with virtually no interference from your opponent. They are not set by the other side. They are already there in the law, waiting for you. The only thing they need to make them go off is an unsuspecting lawyer.

CHAPTER 35

Dealing with Dirty Tricks

Whom the Gods would destroy they first make mad.

Longfellow

Anger is a short madness.

Horace

The spectrum of dirty tricks is wide indeed. This chapter deals with dirty tricks not because they should be emulated but because they all too often must be answered.

It is difficult to talk about appropriate responses without first setting the scene. We will go into the tricks themselves, content with the thought that most lawyers are honorable folks and that *Trial Notebook* cannot be entirely responsible for the morality of the trial bar.

There is no real agreement about the borderline between what is fair and what is not. Some litigators feel it is even a questionable practice to ask a witness whether he has discussed his testimony with anyone before trial or to ask an expert how much he is being paid for his testimony. Other attorneys seem to build entire practices (not very impressive, to be sure) around questions like this, and careful litigators routinely prepare all their witnesses for this kind of assault.

It is interesting how far the prepared ripostes have been developed.

Q: Have you discussed your testimony with anyone before coming here to testify?

A: Certainly. I talked about it with Lawyer Brooks.

Q: Oh yes? What did she tell you to say?
A: She told me to tell the truth.
Q: Was she afraid you would not tell the truth?
A: No, she said you might try to trick me into telling something other than the truth.

But this kind of banter is not what is ordinarily meant by dirty tricks. Real dirty tricks run the gamut from personal attacks all the way to the actual destruction of evidence.

Sometimes it is the little personal attack that is most difficult to deal with. Your opponent, for example, deliberately sets up two or three huge catalog cases on his table so it is impossible for you to see anyone on the jury without standing up. It is just a minor thing, but what do you do about it?

First, understand that no one "school answer" automatically solves any of these problems. There are principles, to be sure. There are also genuine opportunities to come out ahead or behind in a quick exchange with your opponent.

Second, you should develop a warning signal that automatically goes off whenever you start to get angry. All it needs to say is that you are becoming angry and it is probably because your opponent did something to get that result. That knowledge alone is enough to bring back your self-control.

Third, if your opponent did something to annoy you, you are probably the only one who noticed it. The jury is concentrating on the evidence. The judge is concerned with the testimony or the preparation of instructions. If you suddenly respond in annoyance to something, everyone but your opponent is likely to wonder why.

That means if you suddenly get angry, the judge and jury may think that you are needlessly peevish and irascible unless they can see you have a good reason for getting annoyed.

This does not mean there is no place in the courtroom for firmness, justifiable indignation, or even outrage at manifest unfairness. But these will not be emotions that will take control of you. They will be felt only because you allow them to be felt.

This suggests two conclusions: never lose your temper unless it is on purpose; and never show annoyance unless the jury can see you have a good reason for it—and you have no other good option available.

Usually there is a better choice. In the multiple briefcase example, it would be a lot better to get up with a warm smile and say, "John, I know you didn't mean to do it, but I can't see what's happening with these three briefcases here, and I am supposed to be one of the lawyers in the case. I wonder (as you take two of them off the table) if we might be able to move a few of them."

The problem is a little different for a new woman trial lawyer when she is pitted against a middle-aged male troglodyte who insists on calling her "sweetie," "darling," or "honey" throughout the trial. The opportunities for effective responses are almost without limit so long as you remember not to lose your temper.

There are times when the situation calls for something more than just good humor and bonhomie. Take, for example, the praise that lawyers sometimes heap on their opponents, each vying for the image of David who will be forced to use his slingshot against some Goliath. Mostly this sort of chatter is best handled by ignoring it.

But suppose a prosecutor uses this sort of praise to drop a bit of poison in the well during jury selection:

> Many of you have undoubtedly heard of the defendant's attorney, Mr. Robert Fowler. Mr. Fowler has gained a nationwide reputation defending criminals in a number of famous cases.
>
> Now you understand that under our system, you can hire whoever you like as a lawyer. Does everyone realize that it would be improper to hold it against the defendant in this case just because he has hired a nationally famous lawyer like Mr. Fowler?

The lawyer we are now calling Robert Fowler realized that the tactic needed to be exposed without any real sign of anger. The opportunity came when it was his turn on jury voir dire. He said with a twinkle in his eye:

> You realize that you must give both the *state* and the defendant a fair trial. I take it that none of you will hold it against the state that they have tried to influence your decision by talking about the lawyer that the defendant has hired to represent him.

So far we have been dealing with tactics directed against the lawyer. The next level of tricks is designed to distract the attention of the fact finder—almost always the jury—away from the evidence so as to make the opponent's case less effective.

Virtually everyone has heard of the Amazing Cigar Ash That Refused to Fall, an artifice often attributed to Clarence Darrow.

The story is that a nearly invisible wire is inserted into a cigar so that when the cigar is smoked everyone's attention will be focused on the ash, which magically does not fall. Not surprisingly, while nearly everyone has heard of this trick, almost no one claims to have seen it performed. However, there is a report from Dallas, Texas, that the cigar trick was recently played in an administrative hearing in which smoking was permitted. The famous near-invisible wire in the cigar was nothing more than a straightened paper clip.

Meanwhile, in Cleveland, older practitioners still talk about a local trial lawyer who reportedly took an immense bite of chewing tobacco and did not spit for over half an hour, a tale that will not impress you unless you have ever tried to chew tobacco.

Equally famous is the way Melvin Belli once handled an exhibit in a case in which the plaintiff lost a leg. At the first trial, Belli got a large verdict and the trial court granted a new trial on the grounds that it was excessive. Here is the way Belli describes the second trial:

We went to trial again. This time, however, I was glad I had a second chance. I came to court with more than a silver-tongued argument. I brought an exhibit. Along with my briefcase and my law books, I carried an L-shaped package wrapped in cheap yellow paper and tied with soft white string. The judge and the opposing attorney, John Moran, stared at it and wondered where they had seen that sort of paper before. It was butcher's paper.

Moran and the judge knew I was capable of doing almost anything in court. After the *Bryant* case, I had seen the value of good exhibits, and bringing a part of a skeleton or someone's brain preserved in alcohol into a courtroom wasn't beyond me. They continued to look at this package with more than ordinary curiosity. I didn't open it, but I did have occasion to move it from place to place on the top of the counsel table. On the second day of trial, I brought the package into court once more and ignored it. On the third day, I knew that the package was drawing more attention. I could see the jurors sizing up my client dressed in demure gingham, her one good leg in a black stocking, and then shifting their gaze to the L-shaped package and whispering among themselves.

John Moran gave the argument I had expected he would make. With one of these wonderful new artificial limbs, my client could do almost anything she could before: drive cars; play with her kids; swim; dance with her husband, a naval commander; make love. Then I moved to the package.

I took my time. I plucked at the knots in the string. I might have snipped the string with the scissors offered by the bailiff. I was strong enough to simply break the string. But I carefully undid each knot, then slowly peeled off the butcher paper, crumpled it and let it fall to the floor, Underneath, another layer of the same paper. I took a half-minute to loosen that. When I had milked the moment for all it was worth, I turned to the jury and with a sudden, almost violent move, I held what I had aloft.

The defense attorney started to cry out his objection, then fell silent. I was holding up Katherine's artificial limb, with all its lacings, glistening metal joints, suction cups, and new plastic shaft.

M. Belli (with R. Kaiser), *Melvin Belli: My Life on Trial* 107-108 (1976).

It is an instructive story because it shows the kind of tactic that can usually be put to rest in just a few moments by approaching the bench and making an appropriate objection. In fact, one wonders if the defense counsel allowed the entire business on purpose, expecting that the plaintiff's actual leg, pickled in formaldehyde, was in the paper and would automatically result in a reversal if it were displayed to the jury.

More troublesome is the apparent clumsiness of your opponent. Is he scraping his chair deliberately or is it an accident? What about passing notes and whispering from counsel to client or associate counsel?

Whether deliberate or not, interruptions *must* be dealt with promptly and effectively. Jurors have enough trouble understanding and remembering evidence when there are no obstacles.

Understanding that you must do something, what will it be? Knowing that anger is the response your opponent is hoping for, try something else, such as "Your honor, I wonder if we might have just a moment or two for Mr. Wallace to put his papers together before we go on."

In fact, one of the most delightful Baltimore stories involves such a response to a practitioner who suffers from "selective hearing," a malady that requires that favorable testimony be repeated. One opponent, a defense lawyer, bore up under this transparent device for several days without complaint. Finally it was his turn, and he put his client, a most impressive witness, on the stand. At one point the witness's testimony was devastating to the plaintiff's case.

It was then that the defense lawyer said to his client, "Now you have been here for the past three days, and you know that Mr. Johnson has a hearing problem, so would you please repeat your answer to the last question?"

Sometimes it is better to let the judge handle things. A good example comes from a New York lawyer we will call "Begging Your Pardon Maguire." When Maguire rises to object, it is not because he has an objection in mind. Rather it is because he feels his client is being cross-examined too effectively. Invariably the objection starts out like this:

> Begging your pardon, your honor, but I have an objection. The basis of my objection, your honor, if it pleases the court, and begging the court's pardon, your honor, is founded in the laws of the State of New York, in the Constitution and Statutes of the United States, and in the Common law. And the thrust of my objection, begging your pardon, your honor, is in the rule against the use of hearsay evidence . . . .

You have already noticed the effect of this preamble. In the time it took to state it, the harried witness's pulse rate fell from 150 a minute back to 72, his blood pressure dropped to 120/70 and his respiration rate returned to 16 times per minute.

What does it take to deal with such a lawyer? A good judge who will ask him to approach the bench and take matters in hand. Unfortunately, the number of such judges is decreasing. Judges seem more inclined to make absolute rules forbidding the use of "speaking objections." It is simply unnecessary to force every lawyer to approach the bench for each objection just to control the handful who abuse the right to object.

There is a legend that Baltimore has a lawyer whose technique is not as obvious as that used by "Begging Your Pardon Maguire."

The Baltimore lawyer wears "Woolworth Reading Glasses"— the sort that magnify but do not have any correction for nearsightedness, farsightedness, or astigmatism. Instead, they simply magnify everything a little bit. Their advantage in trial is threefold: they look like prescription glasses, they cost only a few dollars a pair, and when things start going wrong during trial, they fall on the floor.

At that point, the lawyer says, "Pardon me, your honor," and screwing up his face in a strained squint, gets on his hands and knees and feels around the floor for his glasses.

According to the legend, once when representing a defendant in a criminal case who made the mistake of testifying on his own behalf (and thereby subjecting himself to a withering cross-examination), the glasses fell on the floor in the middle of the cross-examination and the lawyer actually stepped on them during the search.

This is the kind of story that stimulates fantasies about how to respond. My own favorite imaginary response depends on knowing about the trick in advance and coming prepared with an attache case filled with Woolworth Reading Glasses. (Honest reflection, however, suggests using the advance knowledge to support an appropriate motion in limine before trial.)

Distracting tactics can get even worse. In one recent case, a young litigator was questioning a businessman about a loan agreement to show that the terms were bargained for and freely agreed upon between the parties.

During the examination, which was having its desired effect, the opponent pulled a giant magnifying glass out of his briefcase, and started waving it around the courtroom, suggesting fly-specks, fine print, and technicalities.

The young lawyer first noticed that this was going on when the judge started to laugh during the cross-examination. What should the young lawyer have done?

It is an important question, because under the pressure of trial, you are likely to respond not by instinct, but rather in accordance with learned responses that you have thought of as being appropriate to similar situations. To put it another way, there are no geniuses in the courtroom, there are only drudges in the office—and part of the drudgery is thinking about problems like this before they arise.

Consider another example. The place is a courtroom in Dallas. The case is a personal injury action. As occasionally happens in such cases, the defendant hired a private investigator who took moving pictures of the plaintiff engaged in athletic activities thoroughly inconsistent with the injuries he claimed at trial.

Usually such pictures are about the same quality as good home movies. You do not want them to appear *too* professional. This time, however, when the movies were shown to the jury, the picture was jumping around so badly that no one could make out what was happening on the screen. The defense lawyer and cameraman were at a loss until the lawyer saw that the plaintiff's lawyer was sitting next to the projection table, jiggling it up and down with his leg. The cure involved moving the plaintiff's lawyer and starting the pictures over from the beginning.

So far we have considered tactics directed toward the lawyer or designed to divert attention from legitimate evidence. The next level is when lawyers try to get improper evidence before the court or try to influence the judge or jury unfairly.

A simple example of this next step lies in a wrongful death action in a jurisdiction in which remarriage is not admissible on the issue of damages. Mrs. Paula Grieves is the widow of the late Harold Grieves, and has kept that name despite her remarriage to G. Sperling Megabucks. "Forgetful" of the name situation, defense counsel starts out his cross-examination:

> *Q:* Now then Mrs. Megabucks, I am just going to ask a few questions.
>
> *A:* I'm sorry, my name is Paula Grieves.
>
> *Q:* Oh, pardon me—didn't you just recently marry Mr. G. Sperling Megabucks?

Any objection obviously comes too late, so the situation is one for advance preparation and a motion in limine, requesting an order that the defense counsel not reveal the inadmissible information.

The order does not technically make the remarriage any more inadmissible. On the other hand, it is one thing to violate an abstract law and quite another to contravene a specific ruling of the very judge trying the case.

The motion in limine is also just the thing for controlling lawyers who like to flash pictures and other exhibits to the jury before they are admitted in evidence.

But not every problem can be anticipated before trial. Being a trial lawyer means being a professional at being alert.

Dealing with dirty tricks requires more than just good tactical sense. It helps to know the law. An illustration of this comes from Arthur Train's novel, *Yankee Lawyer: The Autobiography of Ephraim Tutt* 364–69 (Simon & Schuster, 1943).

Ephraim Tutt was defending a man charged with carrying a concealed weapon, and decided to put him on the stand to deny his guilt, even though he had a minor prior conviction:

The prosecutor was my ancient enemy Francis Patrick O'Brien, and the fact that I was for the defense made him more than ever zealous for a conviction. Having proved that Mooney was an ex-convict, he asked:

'Now, how many times have you been convicted of crimes in other states?'

'Never!' cried Mooney indignantly, 'and you can't prove it, either!'

'Well, maybe I can't prove it,' admitted O'Brien, 'but,' he added insinuatingly, 'I can inquire how many times you have committed burglaries—say, in New Jersey.'

Mooney, his face white, turned to the judge.

'Your honor,' he protested, 'has this man got the right—'

'Answer the question,' admonished Judge Babcock. 'This is proper cross-examination.'

'Well?' sneered the prosecutor.

'I never committed any burglary!'

'No burglaries? What kind of crimes, then, have you committed?'

'None!' declared Mooney defiantly.

And then O'Brien pulled the dirtiest trick in court that has ever come to my attention. He took a copy of Inspector Byrnes' *Professional Criminals of America* and, holding it so the jury could plainly see the title, opened it and ran his finger down a page as if reading what he had found there.

'Did you not, on September 6, 1927,' he demanded, 'in company with Red Birch, alias the Roach, Toni Sevelli, otherwise known as Toni the Greaser, and Dynamite Tom Meeghan, crack the safe of the American Railway Express at Rahway, New Jersey, and get away with six thousand dollars?'

Mooney leaped to his feet.

'It's a lie!' he shouted. 'I never knew any such people. I never was in Rahway in my life!'

'So YOU say!' taunted O'Brien. 'But don't you know that both the Roach and the Greaser swore you were there?'

Ephraim Tutt extricated his client from that one by using the kind of legal *deus ex machina* that made Arthur Train famous. He forced the prosecutor onto the witness stand to establish a complete chain of custody for the weapon that was offered into evidence. Then, once on the witness stand, he asked the prosecutor whether he really had been reading from Byrnes' *Professional Criminals of America* when he was questioning Mooney. The prosecutor's ultimate admission that he had not been reading from the book resulted in a directed verdict for the defendant.

What would have happened if the prosecutor had not blundered so he was forced to testify in the case? While in many jurisdictions you may cross-examine by asking about prior bad acts even though there has been no conviction, Rule 608(b), Federal Rules of Evidence, there must be a reasonable basis for asking the questions. Furthermore, it is permissible to put counsel on the witness stand to show that he did not have a reasonable basis for asking a particular line of questions. *United States v. Pugliese*, 153 F.2d 497 (2d Cir. 1945).

Putting your opposing counsel on the witness stand is drastic medicine indeed—particularly because any opponent unprincipled enough to conduct a deliberately dishonest cross-examination is likely to be difficult to cross-examine himself.

Consider the tactical judgment facing the plaintiff's counsel in a recent wrongful death case in Texas. The plaintiff was an attractive woman in her late thirties—Mrs. Caulfield. During the trial a handsome young man came up to Mrs. Caulfield as she was seated at counsel table, leaned over and whispered something in her ear.

The implication was clear—Mrs. Caulfield had a boyfriend waiting to share the proceeds of the wrongful death case.

Mrs. Caulfield's lawyer saw this happen, and asked her who the young man was. She did not know. She had no boyfriend, and had not even dated since her husband's death.

The problem was what to do about the situation. Put the defense lawyer on the stand? Put Mrs. Caulfield back on the stand? Would she look as if she was protesting too much?

The ultimate choice was brilliant in its simplicity. The handsome young man was himself put on the stand:

Q: Who do you work for?
A: The defendant.
Q: Do you have any information about the crash that gave rise to this case?
A: No.
Q: You leaned over and spoke to Mrs. Caulfield earlier today, didn't you?
A: Yes.
Q: Do you know Mrs. Caulfield socially?

399

A: No.

Q: Have you ever seen her or talked to her before today?

A: No.

Q: Was she pointed out to you?

A: Yes.

Q: No further questions.

There was no cross-examination.

One would hope that this kind of tactic is rare. Unfortunately, one East Coast lawyer even publicly advocated the "Caulfield" technique during final argument, so that the attorney for the other side would not know it had happened until it was too late.

That is one reason why careful lawyers who prefer to be alone at the trial table make it a point to have a friend, associate, paralegal, or secretary in the audience for the express purpose of watching the trial in case the lawyer misses something.

Not everything is designed for the jury. Back in the Southwest, an able young trial lawyer was representing a number of utilities before a judge who was not always sensitive to ethical rules. The young lawyer came back from lunch a bit early to find an entirely empty courtroom. Sensing something wrong, he walked back to the judge's chambers. Looking in the open door, he saw the judge and the opposing counsel poring over a pile of lawbooks.

It was the epitome of an ex parte communication. The problem was what to do about it: get a witness, make an accusation, put it on the record, notify the grievance committee of the bar association, or what?

First the young lawyer let them know he was there with a friendly, "Hello, I'm back, what's happening?"

It was the judge who replied. He said, "Oh, Bill here is trying to help me figure out how I can get a salary increase."

The young lawyer's response was immediate, "Well, for goodness' sakes, let me help," which is just what he did.

Why not something more drastic? The young lawyer knew that the evidence would not really support a formal charge. It would only serve to unite the judge and his opponent even more. As it was, the situation forced the judge to be more evenhanded throughout the rest of the trial. As the young lawyer later said, "I wanted to win that case."

Return to the East Coast for another jury trial. The defendant is charged in a serious personal injury case with having made a defective oxygen regulator that failed during use in a hospital.

400

The plaintiff called an expert to the stand to explain how the oxygen regulator failed. The expert was more effective in communicating his ideas than he was careful in formulating them. He captivated the jury with his judgment that the regulator was defective because the manufacturer failed to put a filter in the oxygen line. Indeed, there was no fitting or other provision in the gas line for an ordinary wire mesh filter to be inserted.

When the defendants heard the plaintiff's theory, they were overjoyed. Unknown to the plaintiffs, the oxygen line *did* have a filter—a better one than a bulging wire mesh inserted into a fitting. Instead, this filter was made of sintered metal (a kind of filter like those sometimes used in the gas lines of cars, formed by heating and pressing metal powder or slivers together without actually melting the powder or slivers).

The casual observer would not see the sintered metal filter because all that appeared was a thin metal collar at the end of the oxygen line. The rest—the part that did the filtering-fit inside the oxygen line itself.

When the plaintiff's expert missed this, the defendants got ready to pounce. They did not show their hand on cross-examination. Instead, they thoroughly committed the plaintiff's expert to his erroneous theory. He reinspected the very oxygen line in question on the witness stand and did not see the telltale metal collar.

But apparently the defendants were not careful enough. Somehow they had let their elation show, and during the start of a recess, the plaintiff's counsel and the expert huddled together around their exhibit in front of the defense counsel and the jury as they filed out.

When the trial was back in session, the defense lawyer was devastated to find that while the rest of the plaintiff's exhibit was intact, the sintered metal filter was gone—missing from the oxygen hose altogether.

Frantically he looked around the room, and then remembered where the plaintiff's lawyer and expert had been standing when they huddled around the hose. There on the floor was a patch of powdered metal, the remains of where that filter had been crushed underfoot.

The bailiff was enlisted as a witness, and swept the metal powder into an envelope that was marked and impounded with the other exhibits. The next day an expert from a nationally recognized testing bureau identified the metal powder as coming from a crushed piece of sintered metal.

When the plaintiff's expert was put back on the stand as an adverse witness, his choice was clear: admit removing the filter or face a perjury charge.

Under the advice of his own separate lawyer, the expert admitted having pulled the filter out of the oxygen line to see what it was, and then "accidently" stepping on it when it fell to the floor.

The jury was furious. They were rightly convinced that evidence had been destroyed under their very noses, and their verdict for the defendant took only minutes to reach. Once the filter had been destroyed, it became the only issue in the case.

Removing and crushing the filter was a craven, cowardly thing to do. It was unethical and illegal; yet it may not necessarily have meant that the plaintiff's entire case was without merit—even though the jury interpreted it that way.

If you discover that your opponent has set a trap for you, take heart. There is a quotation from the Bible that can be helpful in final argument:

He that diggeth a pit shall fall into it. . . .

ECCLESIASTES 10:8

There is apparently no prohibition against helping him fall in.

CHAPTER 36

Ploys

It was while the plaintiff's lawyer was in the middle of his opening statement that the lawyer for the defense noticed he had a pitcher of ice water at his counsel table and the plaintiff did not. It gave him a moment of satisfaction, and he thought he should send a thank-you note to Mr. Franklin, the paralegal who took care of trial logistics for the large firm in which he had just become a partner. Status, thought the lawyer for the defense as he poured himself a glass of water, does have some rewards.

He did not realize it was the thoughtfulness of the plaintiff's lawyer (who was even then talking to the jury) that had made sure a fresh pitcher of water—with ice and glasses—would be at the defense table every morning and afternoon throughout the entire trial. That way the defendant could drink whenever he wanted, and the jury (who had not realized they were thirsty until they saw someone else drink) would be sure to resent it.

A dirty trick?

Not really. It does not rise (or sink) to that level. Neither trick nor trap, it is something else. It is a ploy. And it is interesting how some lawyers, who have lots of other things to do in preparing their cases, will take the time to run their favorite ploys whenever they can. The ploys seldom (if ever) win cases. But they can have an effect. They can disconcert, annoy, interrupt, or convey a message. And the point of this chapter is not to explain how to do these things—you already know. Instead it is to alert you to what some lawyers do, so you can be on guard.

Like the water pitcher, some ploys can be run in every case.

There are lawyers who make it a point to touch their clients at some time during the trial—in an unambiguous and socially acceptable way—so the jury will get the impression that the lawyer finds this client honest and decent. Not surprisingly, it is a favorite of some criminal defense lawyers, who fear that if they look as if they are shunning them, they will be silently confessing that their clients really are triple ax murderers.

Some defense lawyers take this one step further. They reason that few things convey acceptance more effectively than sharing food. You cannot have lunch together in front of the jury, but some lawyers make it a point to pass Life Savers—an acceptable sort of eating in public—to their clients in the middle of trial.

Similarly, there are prosecutors who are not content with simply having an eyewitness or a victim point out the defendant to the jury. Instead, hoping it will cause revulsion for the witness and shame for the defendant, they say, ''So there can be no mistake, will you please step down from the witness stand with the court's permission and put your hand on the man who held the knife to your throat.''

And there are other sorts of planned body language. Some lawyers tell their clients, when they consult them at the end of jury *voir dire*, to nod in agreement as the two of them finish talking. That way the jury gets the impression that the client approves of them as the lawyer turns and says to the judge, ''The defense finds the panel acceptable, Your Honor.''

If forging bonds of identification underlies some ploys, breaking those bonds is the point of others. Where there are multiple defendants in civil or criminal cases, it is interesting to watch which of them have been instructed to wear bow ties and sit off in a corner, looking bewildered—as if they did not belong in court with the rest.

Other ploys come close to standard trial techniques. Mousetrapping, as Tom McNamara of Grand Rapids, Michigan, says, is as old as trials themselves. The mousetrap is usually baited by apparent fear of a subject on direct examination and snaps shut on cross. Properly done, the cross-examiner does not even know he was trapped—just that he got stung.

An example will show how it works:

The witness is the pathologist in a murder trial and says the victim died from cerebral edema—swelling of the brain—that was caused by a savage beating on the head from the defendant. Now edema of the brain can also be caused by alcohol, and the laboratory reports showed the victim's blood alcohol was high enough to cause genuine concern.

What was the pathologist's explanation for why alcohol did not cause (or at least contribute to) the victim's death? No reason came out on direct examination. Alcohol was not even discussed, much less set up and then knocked down. So the defense lawyer waded into cross-examination, holding his pet theory high. That is when he learned that this swelling of the brain was associated with an actual tear in the brain tissue that could not have been caused by alcohol.

There are some things that seem like ploys that are better thought of as ways to explain what might be troublesome. Take, for example, what happens when the judge stops your opening statement and says it is argument. You must, for the time, accept the rebuke. But the skirmish does not need to end in defeat. When you finally get to your point in summation, you can introduce it by saying, "You remember that this is something Judge Watson said I should talk about in final argument."

More commonly, you will hear lawyers actually thank judges for adverse rulings. Sometimes their idea is that they will create the false impression that the judge ruled in their favor. The trouble is, the jury probably understands that the ruling is adverse and may wonder whether the lawyer was smart enough to realize that. Worse, some judges will get angry and respond, "Counsel, you do not need to thank me for my rulings. I try to base them on the law and not personal favor." This should not deter you, however, from thanking the judge for an actual favor, such as granting you a few minutes to find an exhibit or declaring a recess so you can make an urgent call.

There are other ploys that raise ethical questions. Some lawyers brag that when they have minority jurors, they like to have a paralegal, secretary, or some assistant from that minority group come and have a discussion with them during the middle of the trial. It may be ignored or it may be seen as contrived—but it may not. And whatever the effect, it is a deliberate effort to try to influence those jurors by bias in a way that is totally unrelated to the proof.

Then there are ploys that are really dirty tricks. Take the tactics of the prosecutor in an East Coast city a number of years ago who was trying a capital case in a state that used the electric chair. He knew the defendant had a violent temper and wanted to expose it to the jury. So every time he walked near the defendant, he hummed out a soft little *bzzzt*, like the sound of an electric charge going through wires.

And it worked. Right in the middle of the trial, the defendant lost his temper, jumped to his feet, and attacked the prosecutor. The defense lawyer had never thought to object to the prosecutor's conduct until it was too late.

Even more obviously improper was the defense lawyer who purported to produce a prosecution witness's criminal record and then let the paper from a computer printout unfold all the way to the floor. On inspection, the "record" turned out to be the draft of a contract from the lawyer's office. That move cost the lawyer a trip to respond to an inquiry from the state bar's grievance committee.

We are more used to thinking that ploys are little moves, like publishing exhibits at the end of your direct examination, so your opponent will have to choose whether to let the jury look at them or have his cross-examination distracted by demonstrative evidence. And some lawyers make it a point to leave exhibits up on easels after they are finished with an examination, hoping the other side will not notice it, and the exhibit will continue to distract the jury.

If you start thinking critically about these tactical moves, you may conclude that many of them are simply not worth the candle. Often they do not work, and the cost in credibility with the judge or jury may be enormous. On the other hand, there are some ploys that are just one-time affairs and are definitely worth the trouble. Here are three:

The Crayons

The public defender had a difficult case. His teenage client had participated with some other young men in committing a vicious attack on an old man. All of the defendants were being tried as adults.

The defense was insanity, complicated by low intelligence. So this lawyer made sure that his defendant was provided with a coloring book and a box of crayons. Throughout the entire trial, he sat off to the side, coloring in his book. Lest you think it sounds contrived, realize that it could only be effective if it accurately reflected the defendant's mental state.

The Necktie

It was the kind of condemnation case that used to be more common in rural communities. The railroad needed land to run a set of tracks to another city and was given the power of eminent domain to get it. The farmers whose land was taken felt they paid a disproportionate price for progress, while the railroad was certain all farmers were bandits, asking for ten times the value of what they lost.

Representing a farmer in that situation was tough if you did not have a rural jury; railroad lawyers often convinced city juries that they had not taken much land. One plaintiff's lawyer stood up in rebuttal and said, "The railroad has told you they have really not done anything to hurt this farm. They just took a small strip out of the middle and even built a crossing so the farmer could get from one side of his farm to the other. So they claim they really didn't do any harm. Here is what they did . . ."

And then he took a scissors out of his briefcase, pulled his necktie away from his shirt, and cut it in half.

The Telephone

It was only a few months ago, in Kentucky, and it is already a small legend. The defense lawyer stood up and started his opening statement:

"Folks, I am really just a country lawyer and don't know much about this antitrust business the government is talking about. But these two people over here know all about it. They're specialists in antitrust. They work for the United States Government, for the Department of Justice Antitrust Division—they are the folks who shut down the telephone company."

407

CHAPTER 37

The Stock Phrases

But always he lacked the essential tool without which the workman can never attain true mastery: he did not know the names of any of the parts he was building, and without the name he was artistically incomplete. It was not by accident that doctors and lawyers and butchers invented specific but secret names for the things they did; to possess the' name was to know the secret. With correct names one entered into a new world of proficiency, became the member of an arcane brotherhood, a sharer of mysteries, and in the end a performer of merit. Without the names one remained a bumbler or, in the case of boat-building, a mere house carpenter.

James A. Michener
CHESAPEAKE

Lawyers are great at emulation. Our first instinct when confronted with a new problem is to seek the solace of precedent, find a form book and dutifully follow the working and style of some unknown draftsmen. Well might we ask, ''Upon what meat did these first formulators feed that they have grown so great?'' But we don't. We follow the path first broken and over the years that path through continuing affirmation of use becomes a rut that directs our travel without the need for thought as to direction or destination. We become experts at mimicking mediocrity.

James W. Jeans
TRIAL ADVOCACY

And there you have it—the continuous struggle between an oral tradition of high professionalism and the senseless repetition of meaningless jargon. The purpose of this chapter is to examine some of the standard phrases we have come to use in trying cases.

They are remarkably consistent from one side of the country to the other, with only a few terms that are truly local among them. They are, for the most part, neglected in our formal system of legal education. These are usually not the words and phrases we learned in law school courses. But yet they are the language of our profession, and if you stand outside any courtroom in the United States, you will hear them every day.

They have burrowed their way into every part of the trial. They are found in what we say to the jury, how we talk to the court, the way we conduct direct and cross-examination.

Talking to the Jury

Nothing I say is evidence.

In the short time afforded for opening statements, a good advocate wants to do at least three things:

1. Explain the case, so the judge and jury will know what it is all about.
2. Without engaging in outright argument, predispose the jury to look at the evidence from his point of view.
3. Start to build his own credibility with the fact-finder.

Anything that does not advance one of these goals is a candidate for exclusion from a good opening, and anything that actually detracts should definitely go unless there is a good reason for keeping it. Consider the traditional remark, "Nothing I say is evidence." Why would anyone say that or even go further: "What you hear in the opening statement, ladies and gentlemen, is not evidence, but rather lawyers' talk, designed to tell you what we expect the evidence will be"?

On the surface is a careful concern that the advocate should not be guilty of even unintentionally misleading the jury. But the comment is a standard instruction from the judge in many states, and the lawyer typically does not even need to say it.

About the only good the statement will do is give some protection from your opponent's attack, should he say, "That was a grand opening statement, ladies and gentlemen. There was only one problem with it. Not a word of it was evidence."

Whatever protection your "evidence disclaimer" affords, however, is bought at a high cost. Using the disclaimer does sly damage to your credibility; in it you tell the fact-finder to ignore what you say, and you denigrate lawyers—already beleaguered—in the process.

Rather than undercut your case in the name of protection, it is

409

usually more effective to approach the problem positively. <u>There is no need to say "what I say is not evidence." Simply explain as the opening statement starts that this is what the proof will be or what the evidence will show.</u>

One more word. In a five- or ten-minute opening statement it is not necessary to say "the evidence will show" more than once or twice (unless responding to an objection that what you had been saying was argument). If you want to say it again, consider ending your opening by turning to the judge and saying, "That will be the defendant's proof, your honor."

What I say is not the law. You will be instructed on the law by His Honor.

Like "nothing I say is evidence," "what I say is not the law" carries an unfortunately negative message. Besides protecting against the opposition, some lawyers use the "law disclaimer" in their final arguments to protect against the spontaneous interruption of a jealous judge. Once again, it is unnecessary to be negative.

It is, by the way, a good idea to refer to the court's charge during final argument. <u>Many lawyers think that picking key words and phrases from the instructions will cause the jurors to remember the argument when they hear the court's charge.</u> Whether this effect really works is not the most important question. Referring to the instructions at least helps orient the jury and points them to what you feel is important.

But for whatever reason you do it, referring to the charge does not require running down what you have to say. Rendering unto Caesar what is Caesar's does not require self-immolation.

We are here today.

A formal substitute for "this is a case about . . . ," this is a favorite introduction for appellate advocates and many trial lawyers as well. Its only real danger is that it is also the first part of a folk saying, and if you start with "we are here today," one of your listeners is likely to say to himself, "and gone tomorrow," even as you speak.

This is what we lawyers call an opening statement.

Other people call it that too, and this unhappy phrase is needlessly condescending. It is often (but not always) joined with the evidence disclaimer.

If you take out the "we lawyers call," it no longer talks down to the jury so much, and has a greater claim to being harmless. On the other hand, if the judge has already told the jury that you are about to make an opening statement, or if you are speaking to an experienced panel, it only gets in the way. Better to get on with what the case is about than to take too much time explaining what you are doing.

My client.

This phrase has two messages, each as bad as the other. The first is that you cannot remember his name (which is why we use the phrase in the first place). The second is that you are getting paid for speaking on his behalf—after all that is what clients are, people who pay the bill.

Do not talk about your "client," use his real name. If you need to talk about your relationship, say, "I am here for," "I represent," or "I am here on behalf of Mr. Abney."

It must be remembered that.

One of a group of three. The others are "it must be noted that," and "it must not be forgotten that . . . ."

They are nearly worthless phrases that lawyers learned to use in writing examinations. They look like intensifiers, but are really used as connecting words when the writer can think of no logical relationship between what has gone before and what will come next.

Their use in speaking is much the same as in writing. Say something else instead.

I would submit; we would contend; we would argue.

Another unintended byproduct of legal education. These phrases share two vices: first they are conditional. The tentativeness that pervades some lawyers' speech is a carryover from law school. Students pick it up from teachers, who talk about what they *would* do, because they are not doing it. The practice of law does not require that we continue to speak as if we were solving hypothetical problems.

Second, the phrases use words like "submit" (too fancy), "argue" (undercuts credibility—"what I am saying is not true, it is an argument") and "contend" (both too fancy and hurts credibility).

If I should misstate the evidence, follow your own recollection and not mine.

A standard in final argument.

From what has been said so far, this looks like the wrong thing to say, correct? Maybe not.

411

The phrase is part of a whole routine. Misstating the evidence is damaging. If the jury catches it and thinks it is intentional, they will treat it as a serious admission by conduct. It may well win or lose the case. On the other hand, if they think the misstatement is unintentional, it will merely shake their general confidence in the lawyer who said it.

Lawyers who know this want to make sure the jury understands that any misstatement is not intended, and not held against their client. For this reason, the phrase is usually joined with something like, "If I say anything that differs from your recollection of the evidence, please hold it against me, and not against Mr. Porter."

Recognizing that there can be a value in this line of argument, the job of the thoughtful lawyer (if he decides to use it) is to say it in a way that does not undermine his whole presentation.

This is the plaintiff's one day in court.

This is designed to impress on jurors that their verdict should not be tentative. It is an appeal—especially in personal injury cases—to give the whole award now, because the plaintiff cannot come back later if the jury does not award enough today.

Some plaintiffs' lawyers think the quaint "day in court" gets in the way of effective communication, and instead say something like "this is the plaintiff's one chance to get justice." However it is approached, it is an article of faith in the plaintiffs' bar that this line of argument is valuable, and images such as "do not give the plaintiff half a cup of justice" and "your verdict will be written with a pencil that cannot be erased" have become traditional.

This is my one chance to talk to you about the evidence.

A defense favorite in the final argument of both civil and criminal cases.

The psychological value of primacy (what is heard first tends to be more readily accepted as true) and recency (what is heard last tends to be more easily remembered) gives a great advantage to the plaintiff in civil cases and the prosecution in criminal cases. This phrase is part of an attempt to defuse some of that advantage. It is often used as part of an entire routine that concludes by urging the jury to argue the case on behalf of the defense:

> After I sit down, Mr. Montgomery is going to get another chance to talk to you. He will have an opportunity to say things that I will not be allowed—because of the rules of procedure—to answer. But you know that there would be an

answer. So I want you to do me a favor, please. Listen closely to what he says, and think, in your own minds, how I would have responded if I had the chance.

Can anyone doubt that . . .?

Certainly they can, and if you invite them to, they will. Now is the time to discuss rhetorical questions for just a moment.

Many lawyers condemn rhetorical questions. They invite devastating responses from your opponent, your listeners, or both.

On the other hand, there are some who know how to use rhetorical questions effectively. What is their secret?

Rhetorical questions are a marvelous introduction to factual material or opinions and conclusions that are beyond dispute. When they are used to introduce more arguable matters, they are dangerous.

The value of rhetorical questions is that they invite (and get) listener involvement. But if you cannot develop the sense when they are proper and when they are not, it is better to leave them alone.

Etiquette

May it please the court.

Judges and jurors alike expect lawyers to defer to the court, and this traditional phrase is universally understood as doing just that. If your feelings for the particular judge keep you from putting your heart in it, think about the court as an institution rather than an individual judge. In fact, if it suits you, think about saying just once during a trial, "May it please this honorable court."

None of this is a suggestion that you be obsequious in dealing with the court. One of the most annoying traits that some lawyers have is the habit of overdoing it. They lard everything they say with constant repetitions of "may it please the court." Generally speaking, there are only a few times when you must say "may it please the court:" at the start of jury selection, at the beginning of the opening statement and at the start of final argument. Other times address the court as "your honor."

In open court, the term "judge" used in direct address to the bench sounds flippant, but is proper in referring to the judge when speaking to the jury ("later, his honor, Judge Johnson will instruct you on the law").

413

"The court" is a useful term, especially in addressing an appellate panel. "Your honor" is fine in the singular, but does not take the plural form very comfortably. "Your honors" just does not sound right to some ears, and saying "the court" instead will usually solve the problem.

Plaintiff is ready, your honor.

The beginner is likely to forget to stand when asked if he or she is "ready." If it is not the custom to do so in your jurisdiction, start doing it anyway. As your opponent fumbles to his feet, you will have already gained an edge.

When the court asks if counsel are "ready," it is almost like the question in the traditional marriage ceremony, whether anyone knows any reason why these two should not be joined in holy matrimony. Giving the wrong answer is likely to be upsetting. So if you have an objection to going ahead with the trial, be sure to put it on the record *before* getting to the point when the question is asked in open court, at which time your "no" will be an affirmation of what has already been established.

There are a few lawyers who like to experiment with the announcement that they are "ready."

A leading criminal defense lawyer in San Francisco once announced, "The defendant is prepared to prove her innocence, your honor." Academics will notice that the statement assumed the burden of proving innocence. The lawyer who said it, however, pointed out that the remark was unlikely to have any effect on the jury's understanding of who had the burden of proof, but that the real message was, "Look out, folks, we have a genuine defense in this case." The difficulty with remarks like these is the possible reaction of the judge if he thinks you are taking advantage of the situation.

May we approach the bench, your honor?

This is the right way to say it. The problem is to keep from doing it unless truly necessary. Jurors rightly understand that you are talking about things you do not want them to hear, and they resent it. If you can, have these discussions when the jury is out, especially before they come in or after they leave for the day.

May I approach the witness, your honor?

Unfortunately, this phrase is increasingly required as more judges get the idea they should control lawyers' movements in their courts.

Strong judges, especially those who have had actual trial experience before going on the bench, are not so likely to impose strict rules about where you must stand. Rather they trust in their own ability to keep things in control, should any lawyer attempt to abuse his right to move throughout the court.

The point is to know how the particular judge feels about approaching the witness, and act accordingly.

Objection, your honor.

One of these is the right way to do it: "Objection," "I object," or "Objection, your honor." Rising authoritatively when you say it will increase the chances of being sustained.

Avoid verbal dances such as "I think I am going to object" (let us know when you decide), "I would like to object" (very well, if that would make you happy), or "I must object" (certainly not; you can waive any objection you like). It is even worse to start giving the grounds without making any objection, as, "I think that's probably hearsay."

When objecting, remember to address your remarks to the bench. Good courtroom etiquette requires that the judge be asked for a ruling, rather than a challenge hurled directly at the other side.

Objecting requires flexibility. If there is an instant "sustained," the objector should be ready to stop. On the other hand, a general objection that is overruled does not preserve error on the record. So if the judge overrules the objection, or invites or permits you to give a reason for your objection, you must be ready to state specific grounds. If the judge rules in your favor even as you speak, you must be ready to stop instantly, lest you talk him into changing his mind and ruling against you.

May we examine the witness on voir dire?

Voir dire is an interesting term. It is known to most lawyers as the examination of potential jurors. The same words are used to describe a preliminary examination of a witness. Why?

The reason lies in the oath that jurors were given in which they promised to answer questions truthfully concerning their qualifications. The same oath was given to witnesses. Hence the term "voir dire," which means in old French "to speak the truth," is used for both procedures.

This creates some confusion. In those states where the voir dire of a witness is not a common practice, making the request may draw a judicial blank. Then it is better to do a loose translation of the term yourself, and ask the judge if you can "ask the witness a few questions in aid of an objection."

415

No further questions.

This is the phrase to which lawyers give all kinds of different emphasis in an effort to communicate something dramatic to the fact-finder.

The British and Canadians are likely to say "you may examine" or "you may inquire" to show they have finished asking questions. "Your witness" is commonly heard in most states, and the somewhat less elegant "pass the witness" (as if he were on a butter plate) is usually understood. But "witness with you" is unlikely to be grasped by lawyers outside of Baltimore.

Good communication techniques suggest you choose a phrase the jury is likely to understand. Whatever you do, say *something*. Occasionally a lawyer will try for an outstanding effect by simply stopping cross-examination at a high point, walking back to counsel table, and sitting down, without saying another word. His moment of high drama is punctured by the judge who asks, "Mr. Wendell, have you finished your cross-examination?"

"I have, your honor," Wendell responds.

"Well, then, state that you have no further questions."

"I have no further questions, your honor."

Lawyers and judges are just too literal for little games like the silent walk back to the table.

The plaintiff rests.

Courtesy commands that you tell the court and your opponent when you have finished your case.

Unless there is an unusual local rule, you probably do not have to reserve the right to call rebuttal witnesses. In fact, rebuttal and reopening typically lie in the discretion of the trial judge. Rebuttal is technically reserved for information you did not anticipate, or evidence that was inadmissible until the defendant "opened the door." A judge may refuse to permit rebuttal when the evidence will be cumulative testimony on a point you have already addressed, or which you were aware was part of your opponent's case before you rested your case.

This means that if you "hedge" when you rest your case, you may actually hurt your later request to call rebuttal witnesses.

Magic Words

Doctor, do you have an opinion to a reasonable degree of medical certainty (or probability) as to the cause of Doris Morseby's condition?

416

Why do we do this? It is surely one of the most awkward phrases in all trial advocacy, yet it is heard in virtually every jurisdiction.

In the right setting, many lawyers will confess that they ask this question because everyone else does. But there are better reasons.

Some states require a reasonable degree of certainty (or, in more recent years, probability) as a foundational requirement for any expert opinion. See 'Note,' *Expert Opinions*, 18 BROOKLYN L. REV. 224, 240–41 (1952). Other states require that the causation of personal injuries be established "to a reasonable degree of medical probability." See Musslewhite, *Medical Causation in Texas*, 23 Sw. L.J. 622 (1969).

The Federal Rules of Evidence, Rule 702, permit experts to testify "in the form of an opinion or otherwise." But because the "magic words" still perform a protective function concerning the burden of proof—and judges are accustomed to hearing them—most lawyers still use them, even in federal court.

Fair and accurate.

This is the proper foundation for pictures, maps, and charts that are offered as demonstrative evidence. It is obviously not the proper foundation for exhibits such as sketches and drawings that are not done to scale, but are used only to help the witness. Then ask whether this is a "sufficiently accurate drawing of the human skull to help illustrate your testimony."

I ask the reporter to mark this as an exhibit for identification.

Handling exhibits properly means knowing all the incantations and when to use them. For example, it is technically improper to say anything about the exhibit in the request to have it marked, and you should leave it up to the reporter to determine what number or letter to use unless he makes a mistake.

After the exhibit is marked, show it to your opponent so he cannot complain that you are trying to sneak something past him.

The next step is as important as the first: "I show you what has been marked as Defense Exhibit C for Identification and ask if you can say what it is."

Then, after laying the proper foundation, say, "I offer what has been marked as Defense Exhibit C for Identification into Evidence," simultaneously with handing it to the judge. Finally, when the exhibit is admitted, remember to make a formal request that you be permitted to publish it to the jury.

417

Are you the same Myron Podboy who was found guilty of arson on February 5, 1979?

In some jurisdictions it does not matter how you inquire on cross-examination concerning prior convictions, provided they are generally admissible, and you do not seek to ask about aggravating details. In other states, however, this question (or something very close to it) is the only question that may be asked. Some states permit the question only when you have a certified copy of the conviction report in your possession at the time you are cross-examining.

The point is you should know whether your state has any special requirements.

Were those questions asked, and were those the answers you gave at the taking of your deposition on November 23, 1981?

This is the usual whimper that comes at the end of an impeachment with a prior inconsistent statement contained in a deposition.

If this is the first time that the witness is asked whether this is what he said at the deposition—especially if there was a waiver of the reading and signing of the deposition—then there is some logical claim for asking this question.

But must it be done so poorly? No. In fact, the best way is to do the impeachment so that the last thing the jury hears is the contradictory prior statement. You can do that by getting the information about the deposition before confronting the witness with its contents.

Would it refresh your recollection if you were to examine your notes on the subject?

Our custom is to permit each other to "refresh" the recollection of our witnesses rather freely. But in the right situation, it is important to know the difference between refreshing recollection—which is supposed to be just "jogging" the memory—and past recollection recorded—which is an exception to the hearsay rule. For past recollection recorded, there must be:
1. A writing
2. made at or near the event
3. by someone with firsthand knowledge
4. who has no present recollection of the event
5. but who can give a voucher of correctness concerning the accuracy of the writing.

Rule 803 (5) of the Federal Rules of Evidence recognizes past recollection recorded as an exception to the hearsay rule. The writing does not need to be made "at or near the event" under the Federal Rule—just when the information was still fresh in the witness's memory.

Strike that.

Some people claim that you can spot lawyers at cocktail parties because they are the ones who say "strike that" if they make a slip of the tongue.

Interestingly, when you say "strike that," nothing is stricken, but the court reporter just writes "strike that." Once you realize that, you are more likely to drop "strike that" in favor of something more human, such as "I did not put that very well, let me start over.

Examining Witnesses

State your name for the record.

(*We* do not care what it is, but the court reporter is required to write it down.)

Directing your attention to the evening of October 15, 1980.

Why not simply say, "I am going to ask you about the evening of October 15," and then start asking questions.

Did you have occasion to?

There is a notion that if we say something awkwardly, it is not leading. Awkwardness is not the test for leading. A leading question is one that suggests the answer. One could argue (but it would offer some embarrassment) that if a question is incomprehensible, then it cannot be leading.

What next, it anything, happened?

("Nothing happened after that. I have been in a state of suspended animation ever since.")

"If anything" does not make a question nonleading, it only makes it longer.

Did anything unusual happen?

("Yes. A giant bird dropped out of the sky and carried off my new car.")

Did a time come when?

Another ineffective effort to be nonleading.

Would you indicate for the benefit of the jury?

"Indicate" is a poor substitute for "show," and there is no

need to act as if the jury is at fault for not knowing something already. Think how much more pleasant it is to just ask ''would you show us, please, what you did?''

Let me ask you this question.

The real meaning of this phrase is, ''I am trying to think what in the world to ask next.'' It can come across with such aplomb, however, that nonlawyers have picked it up, and even network interviewers use it now and then. Its difficulty is that it is essentially a crutch. While crutches have their uses, you are probably better off without them.

Let the record reflect.

This is the usual way to introduce your interpretation of something that happened during the trial, such as a gesture or motion. Ostensibly, it is to make the record more complete. Often it is used just as a form of emphasis.

Interestingly, some judges think that you do not have the right to have the record show something, but that technically you should ask, ''may the record show . . .?''

Isn't it a fact that . . .?

An intensifier used on cross-examination. As with other intensifiers, it usually has the opposite of the desired effect. Do you doubt me? Call in your secretary and try a series of cross-examination questions. Go through the list twice, one time with the added luggage, ''Isn't it a fact that'' hooked on each question, and the other without. See for yourself which is more effective.

You are lying, aren't you?
''No.''

How much are you being paid for your testimony?
''I'm not being paid for my testimony, I'm being paid for my time.''

Have you talked to anyone about your testimony in this case?
''Certainly.''

Do you realize you are under oath?
''Yes.''

Do you know the penalty for perjury?
''No, do you?''

The frustrated barrister in England does not do much better when he says. ''I put it to you that your entire testimony is a fabric of lies.''

420

If another witness said . . . would he be lying?

Besides being argumentative, this question calls on one witness to speculate on the mental state of another when he could not even hear or see him. It is improper, and besides, it does not work very well. Ask something else.

Is your memory one of those, like fine wine, that actually improves with age?

This is still thought to be respectable cross-examination by many trial lawyers—even if it is argumentative. Be careful if—as recently happened at a hearing in Cleveland—the witness answers, ''Yes . . . well, I guess so, in a way. This was such an important event, and since you started this lawsuit, I've had to give this whole thing a lot of thought.

I only have one or two more questions.

Like ''the check is in the mail,'' this qualifies as one of the all-time great lies. The trouble is, for the first half hour it is said, the jury thought the lawyer meant it. Probably the best way to handle this is to avoid saying it in the first place.

CHAPTER 38

The Right Word

The difference between the right word and the almost right word is the difference between lightning and the lightning bug.

—Mark Twain

It is not easy. One reason is that it is contrary to our law school training. It was in law school that we learned to say things such as "It would be our contention that the defendant had not engaged in conduct giving rise to liability for professional malpractice"— with the astonishing notion that we were saying something persuasive.

Going to law school entails learning to talk like a lawyer. Trying cases involves learning to talk like a person once again. Picking the right word goes even further. It means becoming sensitive to how different terms affect people.

It is the sort of advocacy that leads plaintiffs' lawyers to avoid talking about "accidents" and choose "crash," "collision," or "smash-up" instead. It is what brings defense lawyers to talk about a "child darting out into traffic" rather than a person being "run down by a truck." It is a plaintiff's counsel talking about "a young woman who was killed when she tried to cross the street," while the opposition will characterize the facts as "jaywalking."

Picking the right word may mean a prosecutor asks the defendant about "doing drugs," or "snorting cocaine" (using subculture terms to add to his disgust), or the defense counsel asks an immunity witness about the "deal" he made with the prosecutor to stay out of jail. Picking the right word may be a plaintiff's law-

422

yer talking about "carelessness" so that his burden of proof does not seem overwhelming to a jury—and in the same case a defense lawyer asking the jury to find the defendant "not guilty" of any wrongdoing to create the opposite impression.

On the one hand, you should not expect too much from well-chosen words. The right words are no substitute for the right facts, and vigorous language will not make a case where there was none. Indeed, if "the right word" is an exaggeration, it will hurt, not help.

On the other hand, do not underestimate the power of language. As Job said, "How forcible are right words!" Job 6:25. The words we choose help shape the thoughts of our judges and juries. It should be no surprise that they make a difference, yet proving that they do can be difficult. Rare is the case when a jury tells a lawyer they found a particular argument compelling. A few years ago Henry Rothblatt tried a case in Maryland and kept calling the defendant by his first name, Bobby. Consider what it meant when the foreman said, "We find Bobby not guilty."

Sometimes a carefully chosen phrase can solve a difficult problem. An example is the dilemma that defendants often find themselves in. The plaintiff's case has a problem with liability, so the decision might well go either way. Liability will be the main topic in final argument, but what about damages? Can defense counsel talk about damages without weakening the defense on liability?

Typically the transition between topics is approached something like this: "Now ladies and gentlemen, I expect that you will really not need to discuss the amount of damages the plaintiff has because what happened is simply not Harold Herman's fault. But if for some reason you should decide that Harold is to blame, then there are some additional things I want you to think about."

A number of good defense lawyers feel this transition weakens the liability argument. Instead of conceding that the jury might find liability against your client, they suggest you blame the plaintiff for your having to talk about damages. "Because nothing Harold Herman did caused this accident, the plaintiff's injuries are not really an issue in this case. Yet because this is something that his lawyer has talked about, I must touch on it, too, for just a moment."

Plaintiffs face a different problem. How can they talk about money damages for the loss of a life without looking crass? Here is one approach: "One thing must surely occur to you. No amount of money could ever bring back Jay Benson. Why should there be money damages for the loss of his life? The answer is that it is the only way the law has to try to redress what one person does to another. If that is troublesome to you, think what a terrible system it would be if there was *nothing* the law could do for the loss of Jay Benson.''

One of the difficulties that defendants have in criminal cases is the underlying emotional credit the jury gives to the prosecution since it is the state (or even worse the United States) against just one person. Keith Roberts of Wheaton, Illinois has some questions to put to a defendant who takes the stand, which tend to take the government out of the case:

> Q: Mike, do you understand the nature of the charges this man has made against you?
>
> A: I guess so. He says I took his wallet.
>
> Q: Mike, did you do that? Did you take his wallet?
>
> A: I sure did not.
>
> Q: O.K., Mike, I'd like to ask you a few questions about Dec. 3, the day Mr. Wilson says his wallet was taken . . . .

This is also a convenient way to put the defendant's denial of guilt at the beginning of his direct examination, where it will probably do the most good.

If you are sensitive to how words sound, you have probably noticed that ''testimony'' has an authoritative ring to it. Some careful lawyers think that ''testify'' and ''testimony'' carry too much approval when questioning the opponent's witnesses or talking about them in final argument. They say ''testimony'' is what *your* witnesses told the court, while other words like ''said,'' ''stated,'' ''asserted'' or ''claimed'' describe what the opponent's witnesses did.

Just as there are the right words for some situations, there are some words to avoid because of the problems they create. ''I'' is a prime example. Not only will it convey a sense of egotism that will undercut your credibility, ''I'' often leads lawyers to state inadvertently their personal belief in the justice of their client's cause, which is forbidden by the American Bar Association Code of Professional Responsibility, DR 7-106 (1971).

''My client'' should be avoided; every time it is spoken the jury can hear your cashbox ring. Better to say you are the lawyer for Steve Rheel than to say he is your client; better still just to call him by name.

Stay away from ''again'' in direct or cross-examination. It is an invitation for your opponent to object that the question has already been asked and answered.

"Lying" is a powerful word, which is just its trouble. Juries are often reluctant to believe that a witness was deliberately false in his testimony. If you charge a witness with lying, there is a real danger that the jury will think it must conclude that the witness *was* lying for them to find in your favor. The point is that you should not lightly make the charge of lying. Usually there is a better way to accomplish your objective.

The most common words heard in jury selection—"fair and impartial"—are probably the ones that ought to be most avoided when trying to develop a challenge for cause.

Why?

Find the most biased and unfair person you know and ask him whether he can be fair and impartial. You already know what the result will be. Usually only very thoughtful and careful people are concerned enough about their ability to be fair and impartial to say they might have trouble.

The problem with the phrase is not that it lacks elegance or persuasive power. On the contrary. Rather, asking a juror whether he or she can be fair and impartial is almost certain to be answered "yes," killing any hope you may have to challenge the juror for cause.

An interesting study conducted in Durham, North Carolina confirms what careful litigators have long suspected: that intensifiers—words like "very," "definitely" and "surely"—have the opposite of their intended effect. Instead of making language stronger, their frequent use is part of a "powerless" speech style that is not convincing to juries. See Conley, O'Barr and Lind, *The Power of Language: Presentational Style in the Courtroom*, 1978 DUKE L.J. 1375.

Some words are right as much for how they sound as for what they say. Onomatopoeia (which is the *proper* term, but may not be the "right word" for words that imitate natural sounds) is valuable. Slam, clang, jingle and wheeze make an impression because they sound like what they represent. They are part of what Ted Koskoff of Bridgeport, Connecticut calls "impact phrases," words that create vivid pictures in the mind. "A wound that is oozing pus," for example, is more memorable to a jury than "a lesion that is suppurating."

Sometimes a word can convey an emotional message before you even know what it means. Suppose, for example, that you want to show a woman who was allegedly beaten to death actually died from alcohol poisoning (which usually causes death by

425

depressing respiration). The "victim" was a middle-aged woman who had only one lung, and it was damaged by emphysema. You learned this by reading the autopsy report which said that there were "bleb formations" on the one remaining lung.

Before you even look up "blebs," you are certain that they do not sound very good. You can imagine your cross-examination of the pathologist including a number of questions about blebs:

Q: Doctor, your report mentions 'bleb formations' on this woman's one remaining lung, doesn't it?

A: Yes.

Q: That is not a normal, healthy condition, is it?

A: Not exactly.

Q: Not unless emphysema is normal and healthy?

A: That's right.

Q: These blebs were probably caused by a lifetime habit of smoking cigarettes?

A: They may have been.

Q: That is the usual cause?

A: Yes.

Q: Doctor, were you able to tell how many blebs she had?

A: I don't recall. They were like blisters covering the lung.

Q: And you have no idea whether the lung that had been removed had blebs on it?

A: No.

Q: At any rate, Doctor, can we agree that a 39-year-old woman with only one lung—and that lung had enough blebs on it for you to mention in your autopsy report— had less respiratory capacity than when she had two normal, healthy lungs?

A: Yes, certainly.

If you do not overdramatize things, impact words can grow to become impact phrases and even themes for the case. The late Moe Levine spoke of damages in a wrongful death case as being the "grey, grim, grisly audit of death."

Here are some more impact phrases. But before you read them, one caution: Consider them one at a time. Listing them on a page concentrates emotions from several trials. They are not intended to be joined together.

"Carole Wageman does not need your sympathy. She has pillows of sympathy. What she needs is justice."

"Pain is a window into hell. Men have prayed for death to bring an end to constant pain."

426

"They became two pieces of charcoal. Their faces were gone, the upper part of their bodies were gone, their arms were gone, their legs were gone. They became nothing other than pieces of human charcoal."

These examples are based on arguments presented in Lawrence J. Smith's fine book, *Art of Advocacy: Summation,* pp. CA 1–73 (Matthew Bender, 1978).

Occasionally a phrase takes special meaning because of the actions that surround it. In a recent case in Cleveland, Craig Spangenberg was representing a plaintiff who was dying of leukemia. While the plaintiff was present for part of the trial, he was sent out during the direct and cross-examination of his own expert medical witness. At one point during the direct examination, Spangenberg walked over to behind the plaintiff's empty chair, put his hands on the back of the chair, and asked, "Tell us, Doctor, how much time does this man have?"

Good words—the right words—are not persuasive in a vacuum. They grow out of your knowledge of the values of the community—local, regional and national. A problem, for example, in trying medical malpractice cases is the kind of public response a plaintiff is likely to get to the word "malpractice." Many jurors will think that a malpractice suit is a baseless charge against an upstanding doctor.

One way to solve the problem is to try to educate the jury about malpractice. Another approach is to do what John Burgess of San Francisco recently did—avoid the word "malpractice" altogether and use other words instead. "That man (pointing to the doctor) had become entitled to use the term, 'doctor,' which has come to mean "trust' in our society, But by his actions, he has made that word mean not 'trust,' but 'unreliable.' "

Understanding the values of the community leads to making arguments such as the jury being the "conscience of the community, who will have to decide whether they will approve of the way this car was manufactured or whether they are going to send a message to Detroit that will be understood."

A special form of argument is the analogy, one of the most powerful forms of persuasion. One analogy that is currently used urges the jury to award all the damages the plaintiff has asked for. The jury is told to give the plaintiff a "full cup of justice, not half a cup of justice and half a cup of injustice." Or, as it is sometimes put, "75 percent of justice is 25 percent injustice."

Many plaintiffs' lawyers have felt it was worthwhile impress-

427

ing the jury that their assessment of damages was not subject to later revision, that this was the plaintiff's "one day in court." Here is an argument that makes the point even stronger:

> The pencil with which I have been making notes has an eraser on it. The pencil with which His Honor has been taking notes during the trial also, in essence, has an eraser on it. If one of the lawyers makes a mistake, and says something he shouldn't, there is a legal procedure to correct that error. If his Honor's charge to you is incorrect on the law, there is a legal procedure to correct that error. But as to your findings of fact, and award for damages, there is no way to correct an error. There is no eraser on your pencil. It writes with indelible ink and stays forever.

Lawrence J. Smith, *Art of Advocacy: Summation* p. CA 15 (1-C.03) (Matthew Bender, 1978).

One of the most famous analogies was used by Moe Levine about a man who had lost both arms. (As it is repeated by trial lawyers today, it sounds like it was argument off the record, but never mind that now.)

> When you had the lunch that the county provides jurors, I know it did not seem like anything special. But it was in one way. You were able to eat normally, like you always do. I wish you could have gone to lunch with me and Allen Bronstein. Allen had to put his face down on the plate and eat like a dog.

Sometimes using the right word means picking a term for the very reason that it is used by the law: it will be in the judge's charge to the jury. There is a value to this beyond making the charge more understandable. The judge is a respected authority figure. When she or he uses some of the same words you have been using, it seems that your argument is receiving implicit judicial approval.

During the trial you should be alert to everything that the witnesses and your opponent say, because sometimes a word that is spoken for the first time in court can become the theme for the entire case. An example is a woman on the witness stand who describes the defendant's Chevrolet Corvette as it sped down the road as a "white streak"—a description which will take on capital letters and become "The White Streak" in final argument.

Sometimes your opponent supplies the words. In the *Karen*

Silkwood Trial, 2 TRIAL DIPLOMACY J., No. 3, at 8 (Fall, 1979), Gerry Spence tells how his opponents insisted that 40 pounds of missing plutonium were not ''missing''—they were ''unaccounted for.'' It was a euphemism that invited devastating repetition by Spence.

Do not count on the right word popping up at trial, however. Most of the happy words and phrases that seem particularly powerful are the product of long thought and careful preparation. When Al Julien of New York was trying a medical malpractice case a number of years ago, his questions were not chance formulations; they were carefully worked out in advance. One of Julien's problems was the ''conspiracy of silence.'' He wanted the jury to understand how difficult it was to get expert testimony. That is why—when he cross-examined the defendant doctor— one of his questions was, ''Did you discuss your opinion with other members of the *medical fraternity?''*

By now you should be convinced that you can do what these other people have been doing. The answer is that you can, particularly if you have the right materials. At a minimum, your personal library should include *Bartlett's Familiar Quotations* (15th ed., E.M. Beck, ed. 1980) and *Roget's International Thesaurus* (4th ed., R. Chapman, rev. 1977). J.I. Rodale, *The Synonym Finder* (L. Urdang, rev. 1978) is quicker to use than *Roget's* and deserves consideration, too. To be sure, there are many other good source books including dictionaries and encyclopedias, but their selection is a matter of personal preference. Furthermore, most large libraries have reference departments that can help find sources or quotations.

You can use these materials to start your own file of favorite quotations where you can tuck gems like ''Anger is a weed; hate is the tree'' (St. Augustine) and ''Some people will believe anything if you whisper it to them'' (Mark Twain).

Then there is the Bible. It is worth having both the Revised Standard and King James Versions. While you are at it, get editions that have good concordances, which are indexes to words in the text. Then, if you have never done it, take the time to read the books of Job, Proverbs and Ecclesiastes.

You may think this is a call to become a ''bible-quoting backwoods lawyer.'' Not really. Even if you see yourself becoming that kind of advocate, the chances are you have decided to wait another twenty or thirty years so you can do it with the senior dignity of a Senator Sam Ervin.

But consider. There is nothing in any rule of court that requires footnotes or citations to what you say in opening statement or final argument. You are entitled to quote whatever you like without telling where you got it, if that would make you feel uncomfortable. How you use what you find is up to you. Here are a few examples to give you an idea of what is there:

For to him that is joined to all the living there is hope: for a living dog is better than a dead lion.
Ecclesiastes 9:4

A good wife, who can find? She is far more precious than jewels.
Proverbs 31:10

Who so diggeth a pit shall fall therein: and he that rolleth a stone, it will return upon him.
Proverbs 26:27

Wrath is cruel, and anger is outrageous; but who is able to stand before envy?
Proverbs 27:4

For everything there is a season, and a time for every matter under heaven . . . .
Ecclesiastes 3:1

Finally, start looking for the right word early in your preparation of the case. As Mark Twain said, ''It takes three weeks to write a good ad lib speech.''

CHAPTER 39

Breaking the Spell

It does not happen very often, but when it does, everyone knows it.

That is the way it was in Cleveland, Ohio, the last time Jim Jeans and Mike Schmidt locked horns in an argument. It was only a hypothetical case about a motorcyclist who was turned into a paraplegic when an irascible property owner used a fallen tree limb as a road block that the motorcyclist did not see until it was too late. But James W. Jeans, Sr., from Kansas City, Missouri, and C. L. Mike Schmidt, from Dallas, Texas, had argued against each other before, and both of them wanted to win. The case became very real.

The crowd—more than 100 trial lawyers gathered for a training program on opening statements and final arguments—knew they were watching something special.

It was a demonstration final argument, with the 100 lawyers serving as the jury, and Jim Jeans wove a magic spell for the plaintiff—the motorcyclist—that you could virtually touch and feel. If you had seen it, you might have been tempted to say the feeling was so intense you could cut it with a knife. But that would be wrong, because there was no way the spell could have been broken that easily.

The spell certainly could not have been woven quite the same way by anyone else. Jeans started with liability, and his approach was disarming. He left off all the customary boilerplate about thanking the jurors for their kind patience and trying to impress them with their ability to right a wrong. But he did not start off talking about the facts, either. Instead, he used an analogy to explain how unnatural—how indefensible—the defendant's behavior had been.

Jim Jeans actually started the final argument in a paraplegic case by talking about a television show he had once seen years ago—an installment of *Animal Kingdom* devoted to the mating habits of the bull walrus.

And it was spellbinding. Jeans explained how the walruses would select a leader of the pack not by actual combat, but just by communication. Rival bull walruses would shake their heads at each other, woof, snort, and make menacing gestures, but never actually attack each other.

From an introduction that started out seeming irrelevant to motorcycles, fancy neighborhoods, and a young man who was now dead from the waist down, it was only a minute or so before the jury saw that the defendant—a landowner belligerently protecting his own turf—did not even come up to the standard of civilization of a wild male animal actually in heat. And Jeans went on. The defendant was not content just to make menacing gestures. He had been an executive and was used to doing something to *execute* what he wanted . . . .

There was magic in the air, and the hundred lawyers knew it.

So did Mike Schmidt, who had to stand up for the defendant and answer Jeans's argument.

Schmidt thanked the court and without saying a word to the jury walked from his table over to the blackboard. He turned his back to the jury and the plaintiff's table and bent over, seeming to do some calculations in very small writing at the bottom of the board.

It certainly violated everyone's notion of what Schmidt *ought* to be doing—ingratiating himself with the jury, trying to beat back the spell that was still gripping everyone in the room. But if Schmidt knew that, he gave no sign. He was concentrating on a few tiny marks he was making at the bottom of the blackboard—his backside toward the plaintiff's table and the jury. He did not say a word for the longest time, and everyone started to think that for once Schmidt was stumped and did not know what to do. He stayed that way for more than a minute and a half.

Still bent over, he turned his head to his right and gave Jeans a sidelong glance. In a stage whisper that sounded like a school kid at the blackboard in La Mesa, Texas, asking a classmate for the right answer, he asked Jeans, "Whut kind of walrus you say that was?"

"Bull," said Jeans.

Schmidt straightened up and wrote the word as he spoke, in giant letters across the top of the board: "That's right, *BULL.* Now let's talk about the *EVIDENCE* in this case."

He had broken the spell.

If you talk to experienced trial lawyers about moments like this, they will say it is impossible to teach anyone how to do what Schmidt did. They say that breaking the spell (just like weaving it in the first place) is art.

Maybe.

But if you keep talking to those experienced trial lawyers, you will find there are some ideas worth knowing if you ever try to break the spell in the courtroom.

Real Spells Are Rare

Sad, but not one trial in ten—probably not one trial in 100—has a real moment of magic that will require your attention. And it is a mistake to use potent medicine when it is not needed. Jo Ann Harris of New York has a direct way to put it: "Do not dignify schlock."

There is a corollary to this rule that is worth remembering: Do not rise to the bait. If the attack seems too easy, if the situation is too inviting, look out. It may all be for the purpose of drawing you out.

Do Not Kick Over the Chair

If the spell is real, you will feel impelled to do something. Do not rush. Bide your time. Some ignoble impulse to drop a book, kick over a chair, crumple a note, or step on your glasses may suddenly come over you. Resist. You will be exposed (directly, indirectly, or by your own actions), and the cost will be far greater than if you had done nothing.

This rule is especially important, because there are so few real spells. Any number of them pop themselves. Mike Tigar of the University of Texas tells about a gunrunning case that was tried in Judge Charles Brieant's federal courtroom in New York a number of years ago. The defendant's final argument was that the prosecution simply had a "paper case." The defense lawyer was trying to weave a spell. He would pick up document after document, holding each one aloft, while shouting the rhetorical question, "What does this prove?" Finally, to nail it down, he picked up a whole handful and shouted, "What do they *all* prove?"

433

Juror Number Five answered the defense lawyer's question out loud: "Illegal dealing in guns." (Judge Brieant denied the defendant's motion for a mistrial on the grounds that if you do not want an answer, you should not ask the question.)

Break the Spell or Walk Away from It

There is another way to put this rule: "If you can't beat them, don't join them."

Nothing strengthens a case more than a failed attack. And failed attacks are everywhere. You will sometimes hear lawyers lamely imploring juries not to "vote for eloquence." Others will insist that it is a good idea to ask a few questions on cross-examination when there is no possibility of gain "just to let the jury know I'm still in the case."

If you can really break the spell, then do it. But if not, you are better off leaving it alone. You have already heard this rule in still other forms: "That's his issue, not mine," or "She is better off fighting the battle on her ground, not his."

Do Not Be Sarcastic

The saying in India is that sarcasm is the last weapon of the defeated wit. That is true enough so that sarcasm—real venom-laden sarcasm—is seldom the answer to any problem in a trial. That is especially true when your opponent has cast a successful spell.

But if this is true, why is sarcasm so popular with some lawyers? Because they are insecure. They think they have to say *something* and cannot think of anything else.

Use the Evidence or Common Experience

Sometimes, like Schmidt, you will find the perfect pin to pop the opponent's bubble. It may even occur to you before trial. A good example comes from a west Texas trial lawyer who had to cross-examine an impressive psychiatrist who had captivated the jury with his dramatic evaluation of the plaintiff's psychological injuries. And the cross-examiner had decided not to dignify the testimony with the assumption that any of it was based on real science. Here is how cross-examination started:

> Q: Pardon me, but would you tell me one thing before we get started here?
> A: Yes?
> Q: You are a psychiatrist, right?
> A: That's correct.

434

Q: Tell me, do you all agree on *anything?*

But suppose you do not have a pin like that, ready to pop the opponent's bubble. What do you do then?

There are two points to which you can always turn: the evidence and common sense (and for the sake of your case, I hope they support each other even though they are different). One introductory technique to remember is the pause. It is easiest to use in opening statements and final arguments, although it can be made to work while examining witnesses if you are careful. Certainly in argument you can pause as long as you like if you look like you know what you are doing. And it serves as an excellent way to introduce a new topic. If you think about it, half of Schmidt's technique in dealing with Jeans's argument was an extensive pause. (Just remember, you do not need to bend over to do it.)

Turn the Analogy Around

Few arguments are as powerful as an apt analogy. On the other hand, few rebuttals are as effective as an analogy turned around against the party who first used it. And if you work at it hard enough, almost any analogy can be turned around. Whether it is worth doing depends on you and your case.

Make Your Response Fit the Situation

This point (obvious enough in itself) is too often forgotten. The reason is that lawyers sometimes believe in what is called the "school answer"—the notion that there is a right answer to a problem that can be used in any setting.

That is not so. Your response to a gripping opening statement for the plaintiff in a personal injury case will be different from your reply to a stunning attack on the key expert in an antitrust case.

But you can take the point even further. Fitting the situation exactly is what eventually leads to what some trial lawyers say is the art that cannot be taught. John Burgess from San Francisco has an example from when he used to practice in Vermont.

It was in Orleans County, Vermont, more than 20 years ago. Ex-Governor Lee Emerson was trying a land condemnation case against a young Vermont lawyer, and each had his own expert on land values. The young lawyer had the most certified appraiser possible. He was a genuine expert, dripping with diplomas, certificates, and degrees. And the young lawyer understandably made the most of this, since Emerson's expert was just a self-taught storekeeper who was a part-time realtor, with the minimum licensing necessary to let him sell real estate at night and on the weekends.

In final argument, the young lawyer played on the difference between the two experts. He dwelt on the storekeeper's lack of formal education and his failure to attend supplemental classes. He made it clear that the storekeeper was (to the extent he was educated at all in the field) entirely self-taught. And all this was contrasted with *his* expert's outstanding qualifications.

When Emerson stood up in rebuttal, he needed something that fit the situation. He paused and took out his watch. He looked at the jury and then at the young lawyer and said, ''Well, you finally convinced me. We should never have elected Abe Lincoln president.'' Then Emerson sat down without another word.

Perhaps you think that others can do this, but you cannot. Defeatism is not the way to win any trial. On the other hand, you have to know the range of what fits you and your style. Indeed, there is one more rule that transcends all the others. It requires no further explanation, so here it is:

If It Isn't You, Don't Try It.

CHAPTER 40

The Blackboard

The young lawyer felt outclassed and outgunned at every turn.

They had first, second, and third chairs.

He was alone.

They had three-piece pin-striped suits.

He had his old dark blue suit, just coat and pants.

They had a row of black leather catalog cases, embossed with the firm name in gold, bulging with papers and books.

He carried his notes in a simple attaché case.

When it came to exhibits and demonstrative aids, they were dazzling. They had charts, summaries, pictures, computer reenactments—every modern communication technique.

He had only one thing to help him—a piece of chalk. But he knew how to use it.

And because of that weapon, he won two major conflicts: the battle for understanding and the war of credibility. As you might imagine, they dictated the outcome of the case.

It started with his opening statement. It was a products liability case, and the young lawyer was defending a small manufacturer whose conveyor belt had become the focus of attack from both an injured plaintiff and the other defendant, a soft-drink bottler. The conveyor belt was installed in the soft-drink bottling plant and had broken a bottle just when the plaintiff was visiting the plant. Flying glass had struck her in her right eye and blinded it.

It was the young lawyer's job to show that the bottle broke because the bottler misused the conveyor belt and that the woman was injured because she had not worn the protective glasses they gave her when she was touring the bottling plant.

"This is a case," he said in opening, "about three things: Risks, Rules, and Responsibilities." And as he talked, he wrote those three words on the blackboard, looking for all the world like an earnest schoolteacher. "There are risks—unavoidable risks—in everything that has ever been made. So there are rules, rules that are designed to minimize those risks and protect people from harm. Then there are responsibilities. One is the responsibility of people who are in control of machinery to use it properly. Another is the responsibility that comes when people do not follow the rules that are designed for their own protection."

Then he started talking about the facts in the case, while those three words, "Risks, Rules, and Responsibilities" stayed on the blackboard, tying his entire opening statement together, underscoring his theme as he spoke. . . .

There was a time, says James W. Jeans of Kansas City, Missouri, when courtrooms did not have blackboards, and lawyers were expected to do everything with the spoken word or ordinary exhibits. Today, courtrooms without chalkboards are rare, and many have shadow boxes for X-rays and special magnetic boards with little cars and trucks for automobile cases.

And there are all kinds of things a lawyer can take to the courtroom—slides, movies, audiotapes, videotapes, computers, overhead projectors, photographic enlargements, professionally prepared medical illustrations, charts, graphs, and summaries of records.

But this chapter is not about all those other things. It is about the blackboard.

Why the blackboard?

Think for a moment about symbols. As Craig Spangenberg of Cleveland, Ohio, said at a seminar nearly ten years ago, "What am I when I have a piece of chalk in my hand? I am a teacher. I am the one who taught the basic truths in grade school. I am someone you can trust. I am one of the most credible sources of information in our culture."

That is only one of the advantages of the blackboard. The blackboard is a communication device for small groups. There is nothing mysterious about it. It has no "high tech" odor that suggests the presentation is slick or canned. It is definitively temporary. When you are done, you can erase what you have written, and if you make a mistake, you can correct it as you go. Because people have been trained to read the blackboard (some even to copy laboriously from it), it commands the jury's attention.

But it has a host of drawbacks, too.

Blackboards are difficult to read from a distance. Unless they are washed, the chalk dust clings to the board, making it more gray each time it is erased. Some people seem incapable of holding chalk at the proper angle, so that every time they write on the board, it squeaks. Others are allergic to chalk dust or at least find it irritates their hands. Portable blackboards seem to have been made either so large that they take two people to move or so flimsy that you need to steady the board with one hand while you write with the other. Permanently mounted boards, on the other hand, are usually so far from the jury that it is hard for all of the jurors to see. It is not comfortable to write small with chalk, and in the hands of many, chalk seems to break into pieces too small to use. Because of your experiences in school, you expect there will always be chalk in the tray at the bottom of the board. But in court, it is usually not there unless you bring it. And if you find a piece of chalk in court, it will be so small it will run out before you have finished writing.

But before you dismiss the blackboard as perverse, archaic, and awkward, think back to the young lawyer giving his opening statement. Picture that opening statement delivered with posterboard and marking pen or with an overhead projector. Does either image carry the same sense of open credibility as the lawyer with chalk in hand?

Is there anything other than the symbol of teacher that makes it worth the trouble to write as you talk?

Yes, and it relates (appropriately enough) to how we learn. When we get ideas and information by either sight or sound alone, they are not understood or recalled nearly so well as when we both see and hear them at the same time.

Very well, you say, I can write a few words on the board during opening statement and final argument. And I might have a well-rehearsed expert draw a diagram on the board. What else is there that cannot be done better by some more modern technique?

Direct and cross-examination.

Take a simple example. You represent a doctor who is charged with medical malpractice. The patient, a middle-aged man named Mr. Quigley, was brought into the emergency room on Saturday night after an automobile accident. He was examined by your defendant, Dr. Herman, who decided to let him go home. Later that night the man died of a ruptured spleen—a common abdominal injury in automobile accidents.

The spleen is a dangerous organ, in some respects. Because it is so vascular, it bleeds rapidly when injured, and it is not easily repaired. If it is ruptured, the proper treatment is removal, and the prospects for complete recovery and a normal life are excellent. But if it is not removed, a ruptured spleen usually results in death due to internal bleeding—just what happened here.

Because of that, emergency-room physicians are careful to check trauma victims for injured spleens.

Now you have to explain why your Dr. Herman sent the patient home instead of diagnosing and treating him—and you need a good reason, indeed.

It is your theory that Dr. Herman performed all the proper tests but that because of an unusual condition that caused a delayed rupture of the spleen, the results of those tests were all negative. No one, you say, would have been able to diagnose a ruptured spleen when Mr. Quigley was in the hospital.

You conduct your direct examination of Dr. Herman with him on the witness stand and you at the blackboard:

Q: Doctor, are there any tests that can be used to determine whether someone has a ruptured spleen? [You write 'Tests' on the upper left-hand corner of the board.]

A: Yes, actually there are four major tests that should be run on anyone who is suspected of having an injury to the spleen.

Q: Could you tell us what they are?

A: The first is called rebound sensitivity. It is a special type of abdominal palpation.

Q: Pardon me, Doctor, that's quite a mouthful. Do you mind if we just call that 'rebound'?

A: That's fine, [And you write 'Rebound' under 'Tests' on the board.]

Q: How does it work?

A: Actually it is quite simple . . .

By the time you are through with this segment of the direct examination, you have a simple list on the board. It looks like this:

Tests

Rebound
Red Blood Cells
White Blood Cells
X ray

440

Everyone, by the way, has the impression that the doctor has been teaching a fascinating class in emergency-room diagnosis. But it does not stop there.

> Q: [You write 'Conducted' in the upper middle of the board, and 'Results' in the upper right-hand corner, and you continue.] Doctor, the first test you mentioned was the rebound test. Did you conduct this test on Mr. Quigley when he was in the emergency room on May 12?
>
> A: Yes, I did. [You write 'Yes' in the proper column under 'Conducted' on the board.] And because he was a little obese, I did it four or five times, just to make sure I got the right results.
>
> Q: What was the result, Doctor?
>
> A: Negative. [You write 'Negative' in the 'Results' column.]

By the time you finish going through the list a second time, here is what the board looks like:

Tests	Conducted	Results
Rebound	Yes	Negative
Red Blood Cell	Yes	Negative
White Blood Cell	Yes	Negative
X ray	Yes	Negative

You continue:

> Q: Doctor, on the basis of these tests and these results, what was your diagnosis of Mr. Quigley when he came into the emergency room?

Even before the witness answers, the jury has come up with the right answer on their own. The witness confirms what they have already decided. Because of the blackboard, you have engaged the jury's minds so they are more active participants in the trial. And because the jurors form their own ideas, they will hold onto them more strongly than if your witness had simply told them what he had done.

(Do not, by the way, think your work would be finished in this case. Dr. Herman still has to explain how Quigley could have had a delayed rupture of the spleen and why Quigley was negligent for ignoring the symptoms when they arose. But we will fry other fish and leave the good doctor in court.)

A few comments on blackboard technique:

Notice how simple it was. Simplicity is the product of practice in the office before presentation in the courtroom.

441

It was short. Resist the temptation to print more than a few words at a time.

Print, do not write.

Do it yourself. With this sort of examination, the witness must be truly accomplished to talk and write at the same time; typically both speech and writing suffer.

Drawings are different. Impromptu artistic chalk work is usually a disaster. Unless the drawing is extraordinarily simple, you are better off having the drawing prepared in advance on paper and introduced as an exhibit.

When you think about it, the blackboard direct examination is suitable for lots of different fact witnesses. The board helps you organize information and make it understandable. It helps keep you and the witness on track and is a visible outline for the jury. Usually the easiest technique is to make a short list—no more than five or six items—of one or two words each. If you need to do more, make another list or make your list shorter.

The blackboard direct is especially useful with experts. One good way is to have two columns. The first is for the facts, and the second is for their interpretations.

Take the direct examination of Chief Fire Marshal Olsen in the National Institute for Trial Advocacy case, *Flinders v. Mismo Insurance Company.* It is an action on a fire insurance policy, and the defendant insurance company claims that the Flinders Aluminum Fabrication plant burned to the ground as the result of arson. Chief Olsen testifies that his investigation shows the fire was deliberately set.

> *Q:* Chief Olsen, I would like you to take us with you on your investigation of the Flinders fire. I would appreciate it if you could tell us what you—as an expert on fires—saw. And then tell us what those things mean. [You write your headings, 'Saw' and 'Means,' on the board.] Did you notice anything in particular as you first approached the fire?
>
> *A:* As a matter of fact, I did. When we were about a block away from the fire, I could see that the flames leaping from the top of the building had a deep reddish brown color to them. [You know you should write 'Reddish Brown Flames' under 'Saw.']
>
> *Q:* What did those reddish brown flames mean to you as a fire investigator?

By the time you are done, here is what you have on the blackboard:

Saw	Means
Reddish Brown Flames	Chemical Fire
Horizontal Development	Good Ventilation
Water Made Flames Bright	Accelerant Was Used
Acid Found in Ashes	Acid Used as Accelerant

Look at what is on the board. Even if you know almost nothing about the case, it would lead you to think of arson, which is just what it is supposed to do.

The key to using the board is in characterizing the witness's answers effectively and asking follow-up questions that make it all clear to the jury.

And now something extra. As the board takes on meaning by itself, you might worry that the witness's testimony will not make sense without it. But the opposite is true. If you start using the blackboard, you will find that your examinations will improve even if the jury were not permitted to see the board.

Why?

Writing on the board is a simple mechanical process that forces you to organize the examination so it is understandable.

One more bit of blackboard technique before we leave direct examination. I hope you know you should erase the board before you say "no further questions." There may be some lawyers obtuse enough to leave what has been written on the board, but I do not know who or where they are. Chances are your opponent will think of something creative to do with what you have left, and you will not enjoy it.

The point? Erase it, even if you have to use your handkerchief.

Now, what about blackboard cross-examinations?

You already know that you must be more careful on cross-examination than you are on direct about how you ask questions. The need for increased care extends to the blackboard, too.

The simplest way to use the board with a fact witness on cross-examination is to write down a list of single words that represent the points you make as you cross-examine. Do not make the list too long—five or six words is usually about right.

Here is where you must be particularly careful. After you get that list of five or six points, you may feel you are on a roll. You may be emboldened, looking at your list, to read your points back to the witness in one mighty recapitulation that confronts him with his inconsistency.

443

Watch out. If you do this recapitulation, chances are you will be asking the classic one question too many.

As you may have guessed, one of the best uses of the blackboard cross-examination is confronting an expert witness with a learned treatise. A few words of caution:

First, do not let the witness do any of the work. He is not there to help you. So you, not he, will write on the board. And you, not he, will read from the book.

Second, understand that the expert will probably have an explanation he will want to give in response to some of the points you will write on the board. This means you will have to exercise extraordinary witness control if your examination is to be effective.

Third, expert writings encourage some lawyers to push points too far. Your purpose should not be to try to humiliate the witness but to undercut his direct examination.

Now turn to final arguments. Here is where lawyers are more accustomed to using the blackboard. Some plaintiffs' lawyers, for example, use the board to calculate damages. If you do that, just be careful to work out your math on paper in advance. A few defense lawyers like to write down key facts, while some prosecutors list the element offense or try to untangle criminal conspiracies with circles and arrows.

The unfortunate thing is, most lawyers are not creative or effective in using the blackboard on final argument, and the potential is almost unlimited.

- It can be your outline, listing the four or five main points you are going to talk about. If you do it right, that list can become a substitute for your notes, and you can check off the points as you go.
- It can state your theme once more. The chances are you could probably write the young lawyer's three words from his opening statement in the conveyor-belt case, which gives you an idea of the impact that technique can have.
- It can add up to your conclusion. One of the most effective methods of persuasion in all of advocacy is to give the fact-finder the information in the proper order so it adds up to the conclusion you want. Like Dr. Herman's list of tests and results, it impels the jury to reach the conclusion before you do. The blackboard gives you an opportunity to do that visually and orally at the same time.

By now, chances are you have some questions about the law and using the blackboard.

What about opening statements?

The purpose of opening is for the lawyer to explain what the case is all about—to tell the jury what the proof will be. So long as it is not improper argument, there is no objection to writing any part of the opening (or even the entire thing) on the blackboard, other than the discretion of the judge to control, in a broad sense, what goes on in the courtroom. Indeed, many courts regularly let lawyers use demonstrative evidence in their opening statements, so the blackboard should be no problem. In most courts, an objection to using the blackboard during opening statement (and especially during final argument) would not pass what is called the giggle test of legal plausibility.

But blackboard direct and cross-examinations are different from opening statements. Is there any chance the court might rule this is improper testimony by the lawyer?

A court might think it is testimony by the lawyer, but that would not make it so. If you look back at the examples, everything the lawyer writes down comes from the witness or an admissible exhibit, such as the learned treatise. This is not the lawyer testifying; it is the witness.

If it is not improper testimony, is it improper emphasis by the lawyer, amounting to comment by counsel or even argument in the middle of trial?

Just selecting which question to ask is emphasis of a sort. So are organization, voice inflection, pace of questions, volume, body position, and facial expression. But using the blackboard is different than repeating selected words out loud. The board is used to organize. The principal effect is to aid understanding. And if aiding understanding is wrong, then we have a sorry set of rules, indeed. Besides, to the extent that there is anything persuasive about what the lawyer writes, it is a technique the other side is free to use as well.

But how can you mark the blackboard as an exhibit?

By taking a picture—usually a Polaroid—and offering it as the exhibit in substitution for the blackboard. But before you do that, think for a moment. Is what is on the board entitled to be an exhibit? Do you want to make it a permanent part of the record? If the answers are yes, then go ahead. Otherwise, erase the board.

But what if my judge will not let me use the board anyway?

If you feel it would help you be an effective advocate to use the board, then make your record when the judge refuses to let you do it.

Fortunately, there is an increasing number of judges who realize that demonstrative aids help jury understanding. That is what the blackboard examination does. And increased jury understanding means better verdicts. As the Honorable Patrick E. Higginbotham of the United States Court of Appeals for the Fifth Circuit said at the Section of Litigation meeting in Dallas, Texas, in October 1985, ''If the jurors can hear it, they should be able to see it.''

CHAPTER 41

An Introduction to Proving Damages

Most lawyers have at one time or another dreamed of breaking the bank with a huge verdict. And because money damages are sought in the great majority of civil actions, the problems attendant to proving damages (and refuting that evidence on behalf of the defendant) is an important subject to litigators.

Establishing the basis for damages, like other areas of trial practice, is not so much a matter of arcane art or gifted oratory as it is of applying basic principles and solid preparation. And while damages are easiest to discuss with respect to personal injury cases, the underlying principles are applicable, for the most part, in all sorts of litigation. Unfortunately, the superficial reaction of some lawyers to commercial litigation is that damages are so commonly liquidated that they are not worthy of serious thought. The truth is that many commercial cases have doubtful or subjective elements of damage that may be recovered, and most commercial litigators could improve their clients' verdicts by giving damages the sort of imaginative attention it has received from the personal injury bar.

The first step to take in proving damages is to determine what the case is worth should it go to trial. This can only be done by researching all the permissible items of recovery—something that varies considerably from one jurisdiction to another: knowing what sorts of verdicts have been rendered in similar cases, evaluating the strengths and weaknesses of the facts and the witnesses, and, especially in the case of young lawyers, seeking the advice of more experienced litigators. Similarly, one of the benefits of local counsel consulted when trying a case in an unaccustomed forum is in evaluating what such cases are worth in the locality.

It is difficult to be too careful in setting a value on the case. On the one hand, making a demand that is too low is a breach of the duty you owe your client and, moreover, a sign of weakness the other side may exploit even further. On the other hand, an outrageously high demand not only bespeaks the sort of sloppy practice where the secretary drafts all the pleadings and the lawyer says, "Oh, let's ask for $100,000," without much thought, but also may actually damage the case.

For despite careful disclaimers to the client, an overly high *ad damnum* clause may create unreasonable expectations that will hamper settlement should the client hold out for more than the case is worth. Second, an exorbitant demand in the pleadings may well convince the jury that the plaintiff is being "piggy" and it may punish him with extremely low damages or even a finding of no liability. Third, an excessive demand detracts from your credibility in the bargaining process of settlement discussions. It is nearly always a stronger position from which to argue if the other side fears that you might actually receive a verdict for your demand. Finally, making a realistic demand is more likely to result in a settlement or verdict that will make the client happy—a corollary of the first proposition—since measured by the demand, the degree of success is likely to be higher.

Understanding that you should ask for neither too little nor too much (and there is often room for disagreement about what a case is really worth) how much should you ask for? The principles are simple to state but more difficult to apply. You should ask for no more than you can plausibly justify to the jury, and it should be about twice what you really expect to receive. Certainly the reason for the first principle is evident. But what about the second? Doubling what you actually expect to receive is important because of the natural tendency on the part of juries to compromise in their verdicts. The starting point in many jury discussions is what jurors see as the halfway point in the case. Asking for twice what you expect helps them start where you want. The difficulty is in harmonizing these apparently conflicting positions, which is accomplished by making the evidence and argument a believable justification for the amount you have demanded.

There is a contrary school of thought. In it, the idea is that you should ask for exactly what you want and prove every penny of it so solidly that the jury will give an award for everything you ask. There are those who have achieved real success with this method, and it appeals to one's sense of justice and candor. However, the tendency for juries to compromise is so strong that you ought seriously to consider demanding more than what you expect to receive, but not so much that the jury is offended.

In determining the value of any case you may also pay attention to what the jury will look at as a matter of common sense, irrespective of what the letter of the law may justify. For example, in representing a young, attractive, childless widow in a wrongful death case, you should not reasonably expect to receive all you might theoretically be entitled to, even if in your jurisdiction the defendant is not permitted to prove or argue the possibility of remarriage. The jury is likely to give such a person enough to "get started again," rather than endow her for life with a high income.

The second step is to plan in advance how you will prove every element of damages. In any action where the amount is going to be in dispute, the entire case should be prepared with a view toward proving what you want to recover.

A primary effort in this planning process should be gathering and creating effective demonstrative evidence. Charts, enlarged photographs, movies, video tapes, slides, celluloid overlays, models, skeletons—all manner of real and demonstrative evidence should be considered. The uncomfortable fact is that despite all that has been written about demonstrative evidence, too many lawyers neglect it utterly in favor of mere words—transitory sounds which lack force and vigor and are soon forgotten. Moreover, even among those lawyers who often take good advantage of demonstrative evidence, there is a tendency to use it for liability and to overlook it for damages.

The challenge to the litigator is to be imaginative and creative in fashioning new ways to impress the jury (or judge, for that matter) with the severity of damages. Take the case of a quadraplegic plaintiff injured in a motorcycle accident. While the jurors can see for themselves how he is in the courtroom, they literally have no conception of what his average day is like. Rather than have him detail his difficulties with the simplest problems of just living—which at some point runs the risk of creating the impression that he is complaining—consider hiring a professional photographer to make a videotape showing his mother helping him into his wheelchair, brushing his teeth for him, washing his hands and face, feeding him, combing his hair and exercising his useless

449

limbs so that they will not stiffen into immobility—tasks that must be performed every day.

This challenge to the effective use of demonstrative evidence is far greater in commercial litigation, and for that reason, or because some lawyers may mistakenly believe that demonstrative evidence is *infra dignatatem* for corporate litigators, is often neglected. Take the simple case of a broken contract to supply scarce materials in a rising market, causing a substantial dislocation for six months. Certainly, everything can be proved by testimony and documents. But it is an excellent opportunity for making a large calendar listing the lost profits caused by a temporary shutdown, the additional cost for obtaining materials elsewhere and the expenses incidental to searching for the substitute performance, together with whatever other damages might be recoverable.

Whenever you use demonstrative evidence to help prove damages, there are some guidelines worth following: First is simplicity. While charts and lists must be accurate, clear and simple exhibits are always preferable to ones that are needlessly complex. Make them easy to follow and understand. Second is size. Make exhibits bigger than life whenever you can. Photographic enlargements are almost always permitted, and they invariably create a strong impression. Third, take the effort to make the exhibits visually attractive. Fourth, choose exhibits that will maximize the dramatic impact of the damages in your case. Even the dullest seeming bit of litigation can be made to come to life.

Finally, in complex cases to be tried before a jury, consider making a booklet for each juror containing copies of all the important documents that must be referred to (whether or not they relate to damages).

Just as important as demonstrative evidence to proving damages is the skillful arrangement of testimony, which also must be a part of pretrial planning. To assist in this, some personal injury lawyers provide their clients with forms to fill out that show how their injuries affect them throughout an entire day. The advantage of this practice is to alert a careful litigator to details he might otherwise overlook. Obviously this form would not, except under unusual circumstances, be admissible in evidence, but is rather a preparatory aid.

However, there are documents the client can make that may be admissible in evidence. One example is a record of losses as they occur, like a record of time lost from work in a personal injury case or daily expenses incurred by a business in commercial litigation. While the latter may be objectionable as a business record because it was created with a view toward litigation, compare *Palmer v. Hoffman*, 318 U.S. 109 (1943), that rule is not a limitation on the admissibility of documents offered as past recollection recorded, which requires a record made at or near the event, by someone with first-hand knowledge who has no present recollection of the facts, and who can vouch for the accuracy of the document. See *McCormick on Evidence* (2d ed. 1972) pp. 712–16. While documents that qualify as past recollection recorded are considered exhibits in many jurisdictions and are permitted to go to the jury room, under the Federal Rules of Evidence (Rule 803 (5), they may be read into evidence but *not* received as exhibits unless they are offered by the adverse party.

One of the forms of proof litigators must consider in establishing damages is the use of expert witnesses. The most familiar example is the medical expert in personal injury actions who testifies to the nature and extent of injuries (and also establishes the causation of the plaintiff's condition). In recent years the use of expert economists has gained favor among some lawyers in trying wrongful death cases—a practice that has created some real controversy. Some courts have held, owing to the speculative nature of the bases for their opinions and the great weight that a jury might accord their testimony, that economists' opinions on damages should not be permitted in wrongful death cases. Even in jurisdictions where the practice is allowed, there is no unanimity among plaintiffs' lawyers whether it is desirable to use an economist. Some litigators have claimed good results with economists as expert witnesses, while others feel their testimony carries risks that outweigh their advantages, since skillful cross-examination can expose the weaknesses of the assumptions on which the opinions are based.

Finally, in preparing your case on damages for trial, you should consider including a summary of the damages and a proof checklist on damages as part of the file. A damages summary is especially useful in settlement discussions as well as being a trial aid, and if you follow the open file system of settlement negotiations, where you let your adversary see everything except impeaching materials, the summary can show the strength of your case as well as let your opponent know you are really ready for trial.

The third step in proving damages is what you actually do at trial. Once again, there are some basic rules worth following:

First, the jury should be selected with damages in mind. This does not mean that you should discuss the amount you expect to recover during the voir dire examination but that you should try to select jurors who are likely to be well disposed to award the damages you seek.

Craig Spangenberg, in his superb videotaped lecture on Summation, Association of Trial Lawyers of America Trial Advocacy Tape No. 172 from the 1972 National College of Advocacy, suggests that in our culture paying one's just debts is a far more powerful sentiment than sympathy and that jurors who have an A-1 credit rating from paying their bills before the first of the month often make the best plaintiff's jurors.

Second, the groundwork for damages must be carefully laid in the opening statement. It is generally agreed that the plaintiff should *not* mention the amount of damages sought in the opening statement of a personal injury or wrongful death case. The reason is that the specific amount of money, whatever it is, will seem terribly high until the jurors can see the justification for it.

This means that the emphasis in the opening statement should be on liability, while in the closing argument it should be on damages, after the jury has seen the reasons for a substantial award. This principle is so important that it is a good idea to get a ruling from the trial court in advance of the opening statement whether the defendant will be permitted to discuss the amount of damages should the plaintiff not mention any particular sum. In this way a plaintiff can keep the defendant from taking advantage of the tactical decision to wait on the damage issue.

None of this, however, means that you should not deal with the injuries or the loss that gives rise to the damages in the opening statement. You *should* do so. The fact of serious loss is an essential ingredient to any discussion of liability and must not be omitted from the opening statement.

Third, the logistics of the typical trial usually prevent a clear separation between liability and damages in your case in chief. But to the extent practicable, you should start with liability before moving to damages, a principle that should be reflected in the order in which you call your witnesses as well as in the direct examination of each witness.

Fourth, final argument, an immense topic in itself, is where you must bring all the elements of your case on damages into a coherent whole. One of the real concerns is what you will be permitted to argue. It is, for example, improper in most jurisdictions to ask the jurors to put themselves in the shoes of the plaintiff, such as asking them if they would be willing to sell their right arm today for $200,000.

One of the problems for plaintiffs in wrongful death cases is avoiding the appearance of being crassly commercial in demanding money for what is truly irreplaceable, a human life. Probably the best way to deal with this is to bring it out in the open, explaining to the jury the limitations on any human system of justice, and how unforgivable it would be to award *nothing* for the life of a person.

Finally, summation is a good time to use the blackboard in discussing damages, and to bring out all of your demonstrative evidence once again, remembering at the end of the case to ask the court to send your exhibits into the jury room so they may be used in the deliberations.

CHAPTER 42

Getting Along with Judges

It was a shock. The young lawyer had been ready enough for his opponent, the witness, the jury, and the trappings of musty formality. It was the judge who caught him unaware. He realized as he walked back to his office—deliberately avoiding the downtown bus that all the lawyers ride—that of all the difficult moments in law school, nothing compared with being humiliated in front of one of your first clients.

The young lawyer is not alone. While most lawyers and judges enjoy a relationship of mutual respect and even cordiality, there are times when the ties between them are strained. Even the heartiest friendships between lawyers and judges can be touched by moments of suspicion, distrust, hostility, and fear.

There are all sorts of reasons, he thought, for this uneasy relationship.

Most people think of the judge as the smartest and wisest lawyer in the courtroom, chosen for abilities that put him or her above other lawyers.

But lawyers have a different view of judges. They are aware of the lure of power—known as ''black-robe fever''—that draws some to the bench, while others are attracted by the formalities and perquisites (like bodyguards and drivers).

When lawyers turn into judges, their old loyalties, biases, and prejudices do not all disappear. They may mellow, but cats and lawyers are slow to change their stripes, so those stripes do not just go away. While judges want to do justice, their view of what that means is shaded by their past.

Selecting judges (either by appointment or election) is a difficult process. Even lawyers are often at a loss to know how to vote in elections, and the populace usually knows even less who is likely to have the proper judicial temperament.

Moreover, our feedback systems are primitive. Judges are rarely evaluated impartially on a case-by-case basis. Only a few bar associations across the country conduct evaluations of judges by lawyers. When they do, judges usually fight the evaluations as vigorously as some teachers fight evaluations by students, using arguments that are remarkably similar. Popular judges, they say, are not necessarily the best judges, and the ones who are voting do not know the proper criteria to use.

Because judges are overworked and underpaid, many of our best lawyers avoid the bench, and economics sometimes drive more able judges back into practice.

It gets worse. Lawyers think that some judges do not trust or do not understand the adversary process. They try to decide who should win the case by factors that lie outside the presentation of evidence and applicable law, then try to shape the trial toward that end.

Lawyers think that judges are, in effect, members of a new club who have forgotten what it is like to be in the old one. While Chief Justice Burger has helped the cause of trial advocacy training by focusing attention on our need for it, his charges of incompetence on the part of trial lawyers—a proud and independent group— have served to drive another wedge between the bench and the trial bar.

It should be no surprise that judges have a different view. When lawyers first become judges, most of them want to continue their old friendships to the extent they can. But something happens. Old friends are somewhat stiff—as if uncertain of the meaning of the new position. On the other hand, those who would not even speak to them before they went on the bench are suddenly patting them on the back and laughing at their jokes. When the new judge goes out for a few beers on Friday after a hard week and suddenly finds that his old companions are now counting his drinks, alienation sets in.

Suddenly judges understand that they are the constant object of advocacy and feel very much alone.

It is an accurate feeling. They are caught in a crush for efficiency by pressures from the chief administrative judge and an overwhelming caseload. The docket problems of the lawyers who come before them seem to wind up causing delays and wasted time in *their* courtroom. They have insufficient secretarial help. Many type their own professional correspondence when it is not directly related to their cases. Those most in need of law clerks often have none, while appellate courts with time to be contemplative seem to have plenty.

Trial judges are hemmed in by lawyers who shade facts and the law on the one hand and overly technical appellate courts on the other. They are sorely distressed when an apparently good claim or defense is mangled by the incompetence or indifference of someone who will get his fee no matter what the outcome.

They feel they are there to do justice—a haunting, elusive goal that seems inconsistent with being a mere umpire presiding over a game, who simply calls balls and strikes as they go by.

It is a situation that is helped somewhat by the judicial colleges that train trial judges. They have helped raise the competence of trial judges in the fields of evidence and procedure.

But there are some unfortunate by-products. Emboldened by some of the more outspoken "students," some judges return to their benches with overly strict rules that interfere with good advocacy.

In one outrageous example, a federal district judge in Ohio had a complex set of rules 23 pages long. Lawyers appearing in the court were required to follow them, but were forbidden to copy them except by hand; mechanical reproduction was prohibited. The rules required the lawyers to remain behind the podium except with the permission of the bench, forbade "speaking objections," ordered all briefcases off counsel table, and even undertook to prohibit the use of "voice inflection" when reading depositions.

It is the sort of thing calculated to make lawyers indignant. Many feel that it is wrong to chain attorneys to the podium. Certainly some lawyers can make witnesses feel uneasy on cross-examination when the lawyers invade their territory. But it can be handled in better ways. It is a sign of real weakness—an inability to sort out very different situations—that leads judges to make a blanket rule for a problem that occurs in one case out of a hundred.

Some lawyers think that such rules are not directed to the witness's comfort at all. Instead they think they are deliberately designed to control lawyers. If you can make someone stand in the corner, it is less likely he will talk back when he is there.

456

There is an even darker view of restrictive rules of court. They reflect a mistrust of the adversary system. Some judges forget that all of the law is a framework for advocacy, and that it is their job to make it work. Some of the judiciary do not believe in advocacy, but rather in an inquisitorial system. They seek to emasculate the system we have by interfering with the work of lawyers.

The surprising thing is that the system works at all. The truth is that most judges and lawyers are friendly, cooperative, and productive. They recognize that there is a genuine need for the bench to be in charge of the system, and are happy when it works. But the instances in which things do not mesh are common enough for thoughtful lawyers and judges to work at it.

The starting point in this effort is courtroom etiquette. There are some rules for lawyers to follow:

- Rise when the judge and jury enter or leave the courtroom. Make sure your client stands, too.
- Stand when speaking to the judge in open court. Normally you will not need to stand in chambers.
- Call the judge "your honor" in open court. "Judge" can sound flippant, but is the right term to use when referring to the judge when talking to the jury ("Judge McMonagle will instruct you on the meaning of that phrase").
- Rise when making or meeting objections.
- Direct objections and other remarks to the bench—not to your opponent.
- Do not give visible signs of anger or scorn at the judge's ruling. If you disagree with the ruling, make your record, not an enemy.
- Do not thank the judge for a ruling. Some lawyers think it fools the jury into thinking a ruling was not adverse. But it will annoy some judges, who may respond that they do not make their rulings on the basis of favoritism, but in accordance with the law. On the other hand, if you ask for a discretionary favor, such as a short recess, then it is entirely proper to thank the judge when the request is granted.
- Stand when you question the witness (unless you are in one of those jurisdictions that follows the strange rule requiring you to remain at counsel table unless you have the judge's permission to rise).
- Ask that the record reflect what you want rather than

457

simply announce it. Some judges are happier if counsel say "*May* the record reflect" rather than "*Let* the record reflect" what it is you want in the record. The difference is harmless, and is certainly worth adopting if it will keep the judge content.

- If you are in a courtroom that regulates movement of counsel (an increasingly popular and unnecessary rule of court), request permission to approach the witness.
- Do not lean on the bench at sidebar conferences. It does not bother all judges, but it really annoys some.

The central thrust behind most of these rules is respect for the court. It may be that you do not actually respect the person who occupies the bench. That is unfortunate. Make an effort not to show that feeling. It cannot help you be more persuasive with the judge. If there is a jury, your attitude may offend them. If you cannot respect the actual judge, you can show your deference and respect for the position.

Etiquette is just the beginning. If you are to be an effective advocate, you should earn the court's respect. Could there be any objection to that? Alan M. Dershowitz warns that it is possible for what he calls "Integrity Lawyers" to buy their good reputation at the expense of how they represent their clients. A. Dershowitz, *The Best Defense* 404, 405 (Random House 1982).

Surely there are some trial lawyers like that—but not many. We tend to be an independent lot who are willing to make real sacrifices to represent our clients. Dershowitz's suggestion that integrity is inconsistent with good advocacy is misleading at best.

The truth is that integrity is an integral part of the kind of credibility required for effective advocacy. That credibility rests on a reputation that is earned by going beyond mere etiquette.

1. Be prepared, prompt, and respectful.
2. Know the rules of evidence and procedure.
3. Know and follow the local rules of practice.
4. Do not make frivolous arguments. They cut good arguments down to their size.
5. Be scrupulously honest in any factual or legal representation. If you find you have made a mistake, correct it.
6. If you is being legally inventive—arguing for an extension of a rule beyond its present bounds—say so. The difference between legal ingenuity and untrustworthiness lies in letting the judge know your interpretation is novel.

7. If you promise you will do something, do it.

8. Do not threaten a judge with an appeal—just do it.

If you looked at that list carefully, you saw you were advised to know and follow the local rules of court. That is actually part of a larger process called scouting the judge. When trying a case before a judge who is new to you, find out what you can about him in advance so as to avoid awkward moments during trial. Some courts are easier to scout than others. Judge Warren Wolfson of the Circuit Court of Cook County in Chicago, for example, hands out a sheet that explains 11 basic ground rules he likes lawyers to follow in his court.

If you are trying a case in another town than where you normally practice, even more is required. If it is nearby, local counsel may not be necessary. On the other hand, if it is in another state—or even if merely some distance from home—hiring local counsel is an excellent idea.

Do not stop there.

There is another technique for learning additional information. Do not just scout the judge, try to get a reading on the whole community. It is a process that Bob Pryor of Knoxville, Tennessee, calls "taking the local temperature." And in a small town, one of the best places to do that is in the barber shop that is closest to the courthouse square. It was on just such a trip in south central Tennessee, for example, that Pryor learned that the otherwise friendly looking little town where he was to try a case claimed to be the founding place of the Ku Klux Klan—he read it on a historical plaque on the barber shop wall.

There are still more things to think about. Instead of being matters of courtroom etiquette or earning the judge's respect, these are better described as ideas for getting along with the judge:

- Avoid persistent or deliberate violations of any ruling.
- Do not continue arguing after the judge has made his ruling final. Know when to stop, and make an offer of proof instead of keeping up the argument.
- Use running objections whenever possible.
- Be forbearing and courteous with opposing counsel. Judges hate squabbles.
- Never withhold anything honestly discoverable to force your opponent to get a formal ruling. Judges dislike delay for its own sake.
- Do it the judge's way if you can. When the judge gives you a clue to what words he expects in a foundation,

make them the words you use. If you think something else is required, put that in, to be sure. But do not insist on your terminology just for its own sake.

- Do not take adverse rulings personally. Treating an adverse ruling as a personal affront is likely to make the judge into the enemy you think he is.

- Help the judge save face. Many judges will stick to a ruling they know is wrong rather than admit the mistake in front of the jury. If you are convinced the judge made an error that you care about, approach sidebar. Explain why you think the ruling you want is correct. Be willing to accept responsibility for the initial error—such as admitting that you did not argue the point properly the first time—so that the judge has a comfortable way to retreat.

- The adversary system applies to the lawyers, not the judge. Do not start a war with the judge—you are not likely to win. It is summed up in the title of a speech given by then Judge Stephen North of Nashville at a recent College of Advocacy at the University of Tennessee, ''The Judge May Be Right or the Judge May Be Wrong, But the Judge Is Always the Judge.''

If you remember the advice about earning the respect of the court (which includes the willingness to take on the judge when he is wrong), you already understand that the suggestions for getting along with the judge are not recommendations for unmitigated appeasement. That is important to keep in mind when dealing with judges who go beyond the acceptable limits for bias, prejudice, and irascibility.

There are such judges. Every bench of any size has its share. They can be obnoxious, overbearing bullies or subtly biased enemies who will do sly damage at every turn. In those jurisdictions that permit a challenge to the initial judge assignment without cause or hearing, they are the judges who always have plenty of room on their dockets. Generally speaking, that is the best way to handle them.

Sometimes there is simply no escape. Then the problem is how to beard the lion in his den. But there is one more stopping point before we get that far.

There is a trait that even some of the better judges exhibit. It is not necessarily done out of malice, but the harm can be just as real as if it were intentional. It is the old fire-horse syndrome.

Some judges think they are still counsel in the case, and when the bell rings, instead of racing to the fire, they examine the witness.

Please do not misunderstand. Asking a witness questions is undoubtedly within the powers of the common-law judge. There are times when it is highly appropriate, as when an inexperienced lawyer fails to lay a proper foundation and the judge can quickly set it to rest by asking one or two questions.

That is not the problem. The problem lies with the judge who interferes with the proper conduct of the case, or who attempts to influence the outcome with a protracted examination of a witness. There is a difference between clearing up an unintended ambiguity and conducting a major examination.

What to do then?

Jim Jeans tells of a St. Louis lawyer who once said to the court, ''Judge, I don't mind your trying the case, but for God's sake, don't lose it.'' J. Jeans, *Trial Advocacy* 136 (West Pub. Co. 1975). If you suspect that might cause an adverse reaction from the bench, consider. It is the very line that got Paul Newman into trouble when he rebuked the judge for his cross-examination of the expert witness in the movie ''The Verdict.''

There are occasions when lawyers are truly ingenious in dealing with such problems. One instance comes from Akron, Ohio. Bernard Rosen was trying a case in front of a judge who—despite his other fine qualities—was unable to resist questioning each witness at length.

Rosen was at a loss how to deal with the judge until he hit on a plan. The case was a personal injury action, and one of the principal witnesses was an expert who testified to the plaintiff's condition. The witness did such a fine job that Rosen had nearly decided not to call his second expert when he suddenly thought what he would do.

He called his back-up witness to the stand and asked all the preliminary questions to have him qualified as an expert. But he asked him no questions concerning his expert opinion. Instead he turned to the bench and said, ''Your witness, your honor.''

If only it were that easy with the irascible judge.

It is not.

There are times when you must stand up to injustice, and even risk contempt to do it. It is rare, but it happens.

Some suggestions for how to do that are easier to state than they are to follow. The first is to keep from losing your temper. If you or your client is being treated unfairly, losing your temper can take away the only opportunity you have to deal with it. A judge intent on forcing the outcome of a case has a whole panoply of tools with which to work. If you lose your temper, it is not hard for it to appear that whatever was done by the court was an appropriate response to your conduct.

Understanding that danger—and knowing that the court may be trying (consciously or unconsciously) to make you lose your temper—is one of the best protections you can have. Once you know someone wants you to get angry, it is much easier to stay calm.

Second, make the record. Do it calmly and politely, but firmly. Do it outside of the presence of the jury. "Your honor, I have respectfully asked for this hearing outside of the presence of the jury so that I can protest—on the record—the conduct of the bench during my direct examination of the defendant. The actions of the court in making faces, scowling, grunting, moaning, covering its face, and throwing its pencil down at a key moment of that examination signalled to the jury that the court does not believe the testimony of the witness.

"We object to this conduct, your honor, and respectfully move for a mistrial."

Fine, you say, but suppose that the court does not let you make an offer of proof.

Then do it by affidavit. Offer it as part of the record in the case. That is a procedure, by the way, that is specifically recognized by rule in some jurisdictions. It has its origins in the common-law practice called a "bystanders' bill of exceptions." The theory was that when a judge wrongly prevented an attorney from proving up a bill of exceptions—what today we call "making the record"—then what was improperly excluded could be made part of the record on appeal, provided it was attested to by the proper number of unbiased "bystanders."

Most lawyers agree that you should also try to get it across to the jury that you were treated unfairly. If the jury understands, the judge's tactics may well backfire. On the other hand, it may be easier said than done, especially since you are operating from within the boundaries of responsible professionalism to expose what lies outside the lines. One solace is that juries tend to be acutely aware of what they think is unfair, even though their initial threshold of pain to the judge's interference is higher than yours.

There are two final points. They are both made by an incident that took place in Vermont a few years ago.

A man from Barre, Vermont, was charged with homicide. The case against him was largely circumstantial, and the defense counsel thought there was some chance for an acquittal, especially since he was successful in having the venue changed to St. Johnsbury, about 60 miles away.

The judge was not an understanding sort. He was given to acerbic remarks at the expense of counsel and witnesses, and he had his own agenda. The trial started toward the end of the week, and because the judge had other plans for the start of the next week, ordered that the trial continue on Saturday morning, starting at 8:30 A.M.

The prosecutor, who was from Barre, went home on Friday night, while the defense counsel (who came all the way from Montpelier) spent the night in St. Johnsbury, where the case was being tried.

That night it snowed. Not just a few inches, but what qualified as a blizzard.

The judge, all of the local people, and the defense counsel made it to court by 8:30 A.M. But the prosecutor was not there. The next thing on the agenda was the cross-examination of a prosecution witness, and by 8:35 a.m., the judge was getting impatient.

He told the defense counsel to proceed with cross-examination. The defense lawyer, understanding about the snow, suggested it would be better to wait until the prosecutor arrived. But the judge would have none of it.

"Counsel," the judge said in front of the jury, "if you want to cross-examine the police officer, do so now. Otherwise you will waive your cross-examination."

The defense counsel, thinking discretion the better part of valor, protested no more, and began his cross-examination. It lasted about half an hour, and went quite well. There were no objections from the prosecution table, and this time the judge held his tongue.

Then, just as the cross-examination was finishing, the prosecutor walked into the courtroom, looking somewhat embarrassed for being late. The judge did not even see him enter—but the defense lawyer and the jury did.

The prosecutor sized up the situation, and instead of making any objection, simply sat down. In a minute or two, when cross-examination finished, the prosecutor said, "No redirect, your honor."

The judge went on with the trial as if nothing had happened.

When it came time for final argument, here is what the prosecutor said:

"The time has come for us to talk about the testimony of the police officer." And he went over what was said on direct examination. "Then there was cross-examination of the officer. But I was not here. Because of the intervention of an Act of God—the blizzard—I was unable to be here for the cross-examination, so I did not know what questions to ask on redirect.

"But you know that if I had been here, there would have been a redirect examination. And because you heard that cross-examination and you are familiar with the rest of the evidence in this case, you know what those questions would have been.

"When you retire to deliberate, I want you to ask those questions. And I am confident that the same Power that saw fit to keep me from asking those questions will help lead you to the proper answers."

When he heard this line of argument, the defense lawyer knew instantly what the outcome of the trial would be—and he learned two other lessons as well: First, the right response to unfairness is not always to protest; and second, the beneficiary of bias must do the most to keep it from happening.

CHAPTER 43

Keeping the Client Happy

Losing his first client hurt more than anything else so far in his legal career. It was much worse than simply losing a case. After all, he thought, cases are usually won and lost before they ever come into the office.

But this was different. This was *his* client—a small electronic manufacturing company for which he had tried several cases, all with excellent results. It was one of the first clients he had brought to the firm. Now he was shocked—hurt was the right word—to learn they had taken their business to another firm.

As he mused defensively about the situation, he thought it could not possibly be because of the quality of his legal work. It was superb. It was, in fact, ironic that when he first brought the client to the firm he knew much less about their work, his work, and the practice of law.

And, as far as he went, he was right. He was a fine lawyer. What he had failed to learn was how to keep the client happy.

It is an important group of skills for all lawyers, especially for litigators. Because some of their work is done in public, too many clients think that the courtroom is the only place where trial lawyers are truly on the job.

Keeping the client happy is an integral part of practicing law. And when clients are unhappy—as they often are—it usually means that the lawyer has not taken care to educate them and keep them up to date on what he is doing.

There are lots of reasons why it is a difficult job. The logistical problems of keeping a trial docket from crashing in on a lawyer get worse every year. The game of unlimited discovery seems to have gotten out of hand. The drive for efficiency makes the practice of law a bubbling cauldron of tension. All of that when the rest of the world is becoming increasingly impersonal, making it even more difficult to fight the tide.

But despite the difficulties, there are some lawyers who seem always to be held in high esteem by their clients. Here are some of their secrets for keeping the client happy.

Time. Donald Beskind of Durham, North Carolina, says that the single most important thing he does to keep his clients happy is to keep his case load at a reasonable level. That is the only way he can give each case the time it deserves. It sometimes means turning down cases he would like to take. But it is worth it.

Tired lawyers are not efficient lawyers. Even if you know all the little moves to keep clients happy, you will not have time to do them if your case load is so big that you are constantly practicing crisis intervention.

Activities. Bar association projects, speeches, law review articles, and civic and charitable activities are important. Good lawyers do their share. But the general rule in the office should be that the client comes first.

Interest in the Client. For Charles H. Smith of Dallas, Texas, the key to keeping clients content is interest—your interest in your client and his work. If your client is just another person engaged in just another money-making activity, the chances are you will not keep him very long. But lawyers who are interested in their clients and their businesses are likely to develop the kind of understanding that will make them valuable advisors and effective advocates.

Be Glad When They Call. Interest in the client translates into some attitudes that might not otherwise occur to you. Normally, you should be genuinely glad to talk to your client. To be sure, the vicissitudes of matrimonial (and some other) practices force some lawyers to have unlisted home telephones so they can have a few hours to themselves. But most lawyers should be glad when the client is on the telephone.

You may not agree with that. After all, clients usually call either to tell you about some new problem or because they have not heard from you in a long time, and they want to find out what is happening with their case. The chances are that not much has happened, and you have little to report. But the worst mistake would be to avoid returning the client's call. Justified or not, it would create the suspicion that you are not concerned about the case, that you are leaving too many things undone. Certainly, it is better to anticipate the client's concern and call him before he gets restive and calls you. On the other hand, a call from the client is still an opportunity to show what a good lawyer you are.

If you are one of those who has learned to hate the tyranny of the telephone, this may come as a surprising suggestion. But the lesson is profound: Do not let your dislike of the instrument and the power it gives other people over you make you less than gracious to your clients. It is misdirected ire that will cost you in ways you may never know. Instead, learn to manage the telephone.

Return Calls Promptly. Some law offices are proud that they have a 48-hour rule or a 24-hour rule. They return all telephone calls in one or two days. Actually, a same-day rule is just as easy and is more impressive. Here is how it works:

Return all telephone calls the same day that they are received unless they come later than, say, 4:00 P.M. Follow this rule invariably, even if it simply means having your secretary return the call to say that he or she tried to get in touch with you and will have you call back as soon as possible. The secretary call-back is the key to the plan. On the average, it only takes them a few minutes each day, and it makes the client feel important.

While you are at it, make sure your secretary's telephone manners are pleasant as well as professional. Some secretaries who revere their employers actually do them serious damage by protecting them too obviously or by trying too hard to sound impressive.

Call the Client. If you are really in control, you will call the client more than he will call you. Do not be afraid to ask for extra information, even at odd hours. Suppose, for example, you are working late one Wednesday evening, getting a brief ready to file. You realize some additional information might help. Go ahead and call your client at home. Tell him you are working on his case doing legal research and you need to know some additional information. Make the call at night or on the weekend even if it could wait until the next business day. Do you have any idea how favorably impressed the client is likely to be?

Be Accessible. Returning telephone calls is part of a larger policy. Be accessible to your clients, and give them prompt service. Strangely enough, there are always some lawyers who do not understand this principle. One otherwise brilliant lawyer in a large Midwestern city was known to his former partners as The Artful

Dodger because he was so adroit at avoiding clients. Once when a client (for whom he was unprepared) paid a surprise visit, The Dodger put on dark glasses and walked down eight floors rather than risk riding the elevator and being seen. There he was, 56 years old, a name partner in the firm and a respected leader of the trial bar—and it made sense to him to take the back stairs.

The Initial Explanation. The American public is not well-informed about our legal system and what they can expect from it. People have only vague notions about what lawyers do. Unconsciously comparing us with doctors, they can appreciate what they see, but have no idea of the amount of care and study a contested case may take. They assume that case preparation is like medical diagnosis: The lawyer already knows all the law, that is why he went to law school. After that, it must simply be a matter of understanding the facts and applying them to the rules to determine the outcome.

Knowing how people think might make you conclude that you have to give a miniature civics course to each new client. Not so. It would not be worth your time and effort. You would have too much to do. But there are things you should tell them for their benefit and yours:

1. What you agree to do.
2. The fee arrangement—put it in writing.
3. What result they can realistically expect. The world is not perfect, and neither is our legal system. There are limits on what lawyers can accomplish, just as there are limits on what doctors can do.
4. What it will probably cost. Some lawyers prefer to err slightly on the high side. That way, if there are any surprises when the bill comes, they will be pleasant ones.
5. How long it will probably take.

Explain as You Go. Just because you do not overload the client with too much information at the start does not mean your work as an educator is over. There are things that need explaining as you go along. Some of them will come up naturally during preparation for depositions or other appearances. Others, such as offers of settlement may take a lot of explanation—or very little—depending on the client. All clients need some guidance during settlement negotiations, and the biggest mistake is to fail to communicate an offer to the client. For plaintiffs, probably the two worst clients to work with in settlement negotiations are those who think their case is worth far more than it is and those who think it is worth far less. For defendants, on the other hand, the two worst clients tend to be those who want to stand on principle in the case where it does not apply, and conversely, those who do not have the stomach for a fight.

Send the Client a Copy of Everything. Send a copy of every paper, every pleading, every letter—everything—that deals with the case. The exception is the business client who tells you he prefers to have a memorandum or a report. But for other clients, send them everything.

You ask why. F. Wallace Pope, of Clearwater, Florida, has the answer. He says the average American probably sees a lawyer just once or twice in his lifetime, probably around age 40. If, when he dies 40 years later, you would open his personal safe, you would find all the papers his lawyer gave him, neatly tied in a bundle. He never knew what they were, but he felt that they were important, so he saved them. The truth is, he did not know what else to do with them.

Pope's theory is that we deal in a service, and you cannot touch a service. Sending the client all the papers (whether or not you explain what they mean) will communicate the important message that you are doing something for him, and taking the time and care to do it right.

Put on a Show. Some clients are in court all the time and need to be educated at regular intervals. One way to do this is with the opinion letter that brings them up to date. Douglas D. Connah, of Baltimore, Maryland, has another way. He represents publishers and broadcasters. Once a year he puts on a program for these clients in his office, bringing them up to date on subjects such as First Amendment rights, invasion of privacy, and recent developments in defamation. It is something extra he does without charge. It makes his work easier, and it keeps the clients happy.

Clients are often in trouble. Businessmen may be on the brink of ruin. Criminal defendants may be about to go to jail, civil defendants may be looking at unthinkably large verdicts, and plaintiffs may be in the middle of a personal tragedy. Jack Liber of Cleveland, Ohio, says that clients need:

advisers,
counsellors,
confidantes,
interested listeners, and
social workers.

That means that doing your best to win the case may well not be enough. You have to be alert to dealing with their other needs, or helping find someone who can. When it comes to letting the client know that you care, Liber says there is an attitude that you should always have: Make your client think his case is the most important case you have in your office—because to him, it is.

Winning is not Essential. It flies in the face of the contemporary wisdom that, ''Winning is not the most important thing—it is the only thing.'' But while clients naturally want to prevail, the evidence is that effort may be as, or even more, important than results. Clients rankle at the thought that a lawyer can get 25 percent of a settlement for simply picking up the telephone. On the other hand, losing does not hurt so much if the client knows that his lawyer made a serious effort and his case was fully and fairly tried.

Starting with the assumption that you are already making that kind of effort, the point is to let the client know what you are doing. One of the ways to do that is to think ahead, and share your thinking with your client. An example is in order.

Suppose in a commercial case you run into a serious snag. There are problems with your client's records, and you are troubled because you are now going to have to rely on uncorroborated testimony of a doubtful witness to prove an essential point. Discovery has not gone far enough for your opponent to know your difficulty. Now is when to share your concern with your client, telling him you have been looking ahead at his case and suggest you and he ought to sit down together and think about settlement once more. Because of what you know—and are confident your opponent has not yet realized—reopening settlement talks may be worthwhile.

It is, after all, not the best news you could give your client. On the other hand, it represents the kind of concern he will appreciate.

Keep the Client Out of Jail. Successful criminal defense lawyers like to win cases as much as any other lawyers do. But the percentage of cases that even the finest criminal defense lawyers win tends to be lower than the record of good civil lawyers.

If acquittals are difficult, what can a lawyer do for his client? As Gerald Gold of Cleveland, Ohio, says, keep him out of jail.

Winning the case is the best—and hardest—way to do that, so there are other ways to remember: pretrial and post-trial bail, helping the defendant get or keep a job so that a jail sentence is less likely, shock probation, and work release.

470

Give the Client Something to Do. Robert Pryor of Knoxville, Tennessee, says clients call when they wonder what is happening. Despite all your efforts, the answer often is, "not much." But if you give them something to do, then the chances are they will not call you until they have finished. Because they owe you something, they are not going to call until they get it done.

So what does he give them to do?

Pryor is a plaintiff's lawyer, and often has his clients write "books" about their injuries, or even the life of a family member who was killed. As he told the parents of a high school student who had been killed in a car crash, it is something they might even enjoy doing.

The purpose of the book—a series of essays on topics Pryor assigns—is primarily to educate him about the person and the case. He usually asks them to write it on a spiral notebook, and does not have it transcribed unless the handwriting is particularly difficult to read. He tells them that he does not care about neatness or spelling, he just wants to understand what happened. He gives them a list of the "chapters" he wants: Alan at School, Alan on the Football Team, Alan and the Boy Scouts, Alan and his Friends, Alan and his Plans.

The book idea is related to the diary that some lawyers have their clients keep. A diary is important because it helps plaintiffs remember details. That the plaintiff's back was in pain during the spring and summer is not nearly so poignant as Momma missing Jody's high-school graduation because her back was hurting so much. So the diary—another task that plaintiff's lawyers sometimes give their clients—is the instruction to make an entry *every day* about their condition, and what they can and cannot do because of their injury.

Itemize Bills. Good billing practices may not make your clients love you, but bad billing will make them hate you. Few things are more annoying than a statement that simply says: "Legal Services—$23,750.00."

You should be able to hear the reaction even now. "$23,000—that's outrageous. What in the world did that lawyer do to justify $23,000? Good grief, that's more than two brand new cars! Dora, get that shyster on the phone. I'm going to give him a piece of my mind." All this from a businessman you have just snatched from a half-million dollar disaster of his own making.

The chance of this happening is reduced if you explain the five basic points at the start of every new case. Remember what they are? Here they are again, so you will not have to go back and look for them:

1. What you agree to do.
2. The fee arrangement—put it in writing.
3. What result they can realistically expect.
4. What it will probably cost.
5. How long it will probably take.

But even if you explain this in every new case, you can still get in trouble. Here are some additional steps that will help:

Avoid surprises. Report on unexpected problems and costs as they arise, not months later.

Be specific. The bill should list in detail everything you did for the client. If you think this will turn billing time into a dreary ordeal, you are right if you wait until billing time to remember what you did. The time to itemize in detail is when you fill out your time slips. After that, it is just a matter for the billing clerk. When you fill out your time slips, be specific. Do not simply put down, "legal research, 5.2 hours." Instead, write something like "research on the admissibility of Federal Aviation Regulations and Manufacturer's Information Manual to show defendant's negligence."

Billing for Telephone Calls. A lot of work is done on the telephone, and it is only fair to bill for it. The trouble is, in many other callings, people cannot or will not bill for telephone calls. So tell clients that you bill for telephone calls. Some lawyers even prefer to bill for *conferences* whether they take place in person or over the telephone.

The Letter of Report. The itemized bill gives a lot of information, but it does not interpret it. That is what the letter of report can do. It is something you should include with every new bill. The letter need not be long to be helpful. It might go something like this:

Dear Mr. Johnson:

I am reporting on the work we did on your case this last month. As the bill shows, most of our time was spent in depositions, all of which went quite well. We also needed to do some legal research on whether the Federal aviation regulations and the airplane manufacturer's information manual can be offered in evidence and read to the jury during the course of the trial.

Because of the favorable impression our witnesses made

during the depositions, I think the defendants will probably increase their offer of settlement. I will let you know as soon as I hear anything.

> Very truly yours,
> Clarence Bryan

If you think about it, you will realize that most of these techniques can be used by other lawyers besides litigators. There are some things that are just for trial lawyers.

Pleadings. Be careful in drafting pleadings not to create unjustified expectations. In jurisdictions that still require a specific dollar demand in the damages clause, it is customary to ask for an amount far greater than you would ever expect to receive. It is usually a good idea to give the pleadings to the client, but it is a bad idea to create unrealistic expectations. So be careful to explain that the pleadings do not represent what would be a good result in your case.

A number of jurisdictions no longer require a specific dollar demand in the pleadings. If yours does not, you can see why it may be a good idea simply to say make your demand ''in excess of the jurisdictional amount'' of the court.

Prepare Witnesses and Clients for Testifying. One of the good effects of proper trial preparation is that some of it lets your client see how much you are doing on his behalf. Witness preparation is one of those activities. Inviting your client to other depositions in the case can be another. While sometimes there are good reasons for not having your client present at the depositions of other witnesses, letting him watch is an opportunity to see you at work. Because in modern litigation the deposition sometimes *is* the trial, it may be his only opportunity.

There are other benefits to having the client present at depositions. One is the effect of confrontation. In a business fraud case, for example, the plaintiff who has made wild accusations may tone down considerably if he has to look the person he is accusing in the eye as he gives his deposition. Another is education. A headstrong, uncompromising client may see the strength of the opponent's case and take a more reasonable approach toward settlement.

Always Appear Loyal. Of course you are going to *be* loyal, but you must appear loyal as well. A shocking number of clients do not understand the friendly (or at least friendly appearing) relationships between lawyers. They do not know why you do not

473

hate the opposing lawyer as much as they hate the opposing party. So they are suspicious when the lawyers go off and talk between themselves. They are afraid that their case is being sold out, perhaps for some private payment. They are even likely to be suspicious when the lawyers from both sides are called into the judge's chambers.

Not every client will worry about these situations, but enough will for you to do something about it. First, explain that lawyers often engage in friendly banter just like other adversaries do, and it is an unconscious effort that helps keep the process civilized. Second, never walk away from your client to engage in a secret talk with the lawyer from the other side. If you see someone else in the courthouse with whom you need to speak in confidence, ask yourself whether a whispered conference is worth the risk of creating a suspicious client, or whether you can simply tell the person you will call him later—something you can do in front of everyone. Third, if the judge asks the lawyers to come into chambers, ask that the clients be permitted to come, too.

Do Not Charge Corruption. Some disappointed lawyers intimate that adverse rulings are the result of friendship or collusion between the judge and the opposing lawyer, or sometimes even a bribe.

Of course, if you think this is truly the case, then you should do something about it—not just use it to excuse your performance at trial. In addition to being a poor way of dealing with a bad result, the casual suggestion of dishonesty does a lot of damage to the judicial system and to you as well. Your client will think that you are either willing to sit by while an injustice is being done, or that you are unfairly blaming someone else for your own shortcomings.

No matter what you do, there will be some clients who will not love you. That is all right. As Bill Cosby said, ''I do not know the way to succeed, but the way to fail is to try to please everyone.''

Many of the techniques for keeping the client happy will also help if the client later turns on you and charges you with malpractice. But that may not be enough. You must remember to protect yourself as well. How to do that is a subject for *Trial Notebook* all in itself. For now, just remember two additional techniques: put all important advice to the client in writing, and write memoranda to the file whenever they might help. If you cannot keep your client happy, at least you can stay out of trouble.

474

PART VIII

Final Argument

CHAPTER 44

The Law of Final Argument

It is easy to state the basic rules of final argument:
- You may not misstate the evidence or the law.
- You may not argue facts off the record.
- You may not state your personal belief in the justice of your cause.
- You may not personally vouch for the credibility of any witness.
- You may not appeal to passion or prejudice.
- You may not urge an irrelevant use of evidence.

There they are, elegant in their simplicity. And as blackletter principles, they are easy enough to follow in the security of an office chair. It is only in the heat of argument that they offer any difficulty. Then what seem simple propositions may suddenly look like snares in which a single misstep can bring an objection, a reprimand from the bench, a pointed instruction to the jury, a mistrial, or just a shrug of judicial indifference.

But before talking about snares, the place to start is with the right to argument and the normal procedural rules.

You would expect that there is a right to argument in an adversary system—and there is. But there are limitations. Just as the power to tax is the power to destroy, so is the power to limit the time of argument ultimately the power to take it away. Consequently, while trial judges have great latitude in setting the time for argument, they are subject to review for abuse of discretion. The general notion is that enough time must be given so each side can fully and fairly present its case. *Pirrung v. T. & N.O.R. Co.*, 350 S.W.2d 50 (Tex. Civ. App. 1961).

Talking about the right to argument necessarily raises the question of what *is* argument. It is a perfect example of lawyerly reasoning to say the right to argument is the right to do whatever argument is—but no more than that.

Consider these examples:

First, is reading law from a book—to a jury—proper final argument? The cases are in disarray. Some suggest it is necessarily an invasion of the judge's province to instruct the jury on the rules to follow in deciding the case. They recognize that it is fine for the lawyer to talk about the judge's instructions, and to discuss them as they apply to facts. But they draw the line on actually reading from cases. *Wallace v. Pere Marquette Fiberglass Boat Co.*, 2 Mich. App. 605, 141 N.W.2d 383 (1966).

There is another approach. Judicial decisions are not pure law. They often contain social comment and folk wisdom of the sort that is appropriate in an argument on the facts. While a judge can properly forbid a lawyer to urge that the jury disregard the court's instructions, not every quotation from a case is a frontal attack on the power of the judge. The consequence is that some courts permit reading from a decision if the purpose is to aid a factual argument.

As a result, there are some quotations that have become favorites, such as Justice Douglas' remark in *Wilkerson v. McCarthy*, 336 U.S. 53, 68 (1949), that "The Federal Employers Liability Act was designed to put on the railroad industry some of the cost for the legs, eyes, arms, and lives which it consumed in its operations."

Because of the danger of being misunderstood—and risking an unnecessary adverse ruling that would never be reversed on appeal—it is a good idea to tell the trial judge you are planning to read a quotation from a case to the jury. Explain you will use it for its literary value and factual persuasion rather than to argue what the law ought to be.

Second, what about reading part of the transcript to the jury? It is proper in nearly every state. As Thomas Singer pointed out in *Testimony as Demonstrative Evidence,* 3 LITIGATION, No. 4, at 19 (Summer 1977), a partial transcript containing important testimony can be used as an exhibit during final argument. The technique is to get the right page of the transcript prepared—complete with the reporter's jurat—and then use a photographic enlargement to show the jury key testimony from the case it has just heard.

Third, most jurisdictions permit counsel to use diagrams, charts, or blackboard drawings during argument—even if they were never introduced into evidence. The idea is that spoken communication is not the only kind, and no one is misled into thinking that a lawyer's blackboard presentation is evidence. On the other hand, if your opponent uses a chart or diagram in a way that leads a jury to think that it is evidence, an objection is in order.

The next question is the order of final argument. In virtually every state it is said that the party with the burden of proof "has the right to open and close." The only disagreement (you have guessed rightly) is in what that means.

In most states "open and close" applies to every part of the trial. It means the party with the burden of proof makes the first opening statement, offers the first evidence, makes the first argument, and has rebuttal at the end of the case.

It means something else in New York and Massachusetts. There the right to open means making the first opening statement, and the right to close means giving the last final argument. From this, they conclude that the other party—usually the defendant—gives the second opening statement *and the first final argument.*

It troubles lawyers from other states when they hear about the New York and Massachusetts interpretation of the rubric, "the right to open and close." They wonder how the defendant can fashion an argument designed to respond to one that has not yet been made. They puzzle over how a plaintiff can give up the starting position that seems logically to go with the burden of putting everything in order.

But like the bumblebees who are unaware that their wing loading is too great under the rules of aerodynamics to permit successful flight, New York and Massachusetts lawyers seem to do just fine.

There are advantages to going first and last. The psychological notion of primacy is that what is heard first has a special claim to acceptance. The effect of recency—what is heard last—is that it is more easily remembered than other things that were said. To be both remembered and believed is valuable, indeed.

Small wonder that defendants sometimes mold their cases (if they can) so they are what our legal ancestors called "confessions and avoidances." If you admit the opponent's case, but assert some reason why the normal result does not apply to you, that is a confession and avoidance. The term is not magic in itself, but what accompanies it sometimes is. If the only burden of proof is on you, then you should have the right to "open and close" whether you are nominally a plaintiff or a defendant. The exception is in criminal cases, in which the government always has the burden of proof.

No matter how valuable you feel it is to go first, it should not surprise you that there are lawyers who deliberately try to avoid it. It is the waiver ploy—and here is how it is supposed to work:

If you argue second instead of first, then you will have the chance to answer your opponent—but he cannot respond to you. If you are the plaintiff and want to keep the defendant from answering your arguments, then you merely waive the initial final argument. The defendant will have to go first (and have the disadvantage of having to deal with the surprise as well) and you can save all of your argument for "rebuttal."

If you expect that this sort of game can cause problems, you are right.

First, it takes an acquiescent judge. Rebuttal is supposed to be just that, and many judges will not let you sandbag your opponent. They do this by exercising their power to limit the time of rebuttal to just a few minutes.

Second, the plan can go awry. Suppose you waive the first final argument. Then assume your opponent waives his argument as well. Now you rise to deliver your "rebuttal," and your opponent objects.

The right ruling is that the court can deny you any further argument. Since your opponent waived argument, there is nothing for you to rebut. *Santure v. Detroit Trust Co.*, 275 Mich. 661, 267 N.W. 583 (1936). The court has discretion to permit the plaintiff to remove himself from his own trap, but then should let the defendant answer the plaintiff's argument. *Fire Ass'n of Philadelphia v. Farmers' Gin Co.*, 39 Okla. 162, 134 P.443 (1913).

Objections to improper argument, like objections to evidence, must be made promptly or they are waived. *Thomson v. Boles*, 123 F.2d 487 (8th Cir. 1941), *cert. denied*, 315 U.S. 804 (1942). While there are a few cases that do not require a timely objection if the argument was grossly improper, it is not a good idea to rely on an appellate court taking that view of your case.

A "prompt objection" usually means interrupting opposing counsel's argument—which some lawyers fear the jury might hold against them. On this point *London Guarantee & Accident Co.*

v. Woelfle, 83 F.2d 325 (8th Cir. 1936), said the objection had to be made either at the time of the remark or at the close of argument, a rule that at least permits civility.

One last point in this introduction. What lawyers say in final argument is privileged under the law of defamation. The rule makes sense. It would not do to try to argue a case and worry whether your remarks would subject you to liability. On the other hand, the privilege is apparently not absolute. What you say in argument must be at least relevant to the case at hand for it to be privileged. *Annot.,* 61 A.L.R. 1300 (1958).

Probably the most common objection made during final argument is that opposing counsel has misstated the evidence. If you think about the position that objection puts the judge in, you will understand why the ruling is almost always the same throughout the country. The chances are that the judge has been listening to argument with only one ear. He is concentrating on the charge he must give to the jury in just a few minutes. He may not have heard what you think is objectionable—and if he did, he may not remember the exact testimony. Result?

"The jury will be the judge of the testimony."

This does not mean you should not object when your opponent misquotes a witness. Even if the ruling is equivocal, it will call the jury's attention to the misstatement.

But there may be a better way. Understanding that juries are mistrustful of lawyers anyway, you may decide to give your opponent all the rope he wants when he misstates the testimony. When it is your turn you can say, "When the plaintiff's lawyer said that, the law permitted me to object right then. But I did not, because I wanted to see just what it was that Mr. McCormick thought you had to believe to find in his favor."

The rule against misstating evidence is not a requirement that the court agree with everything you say. Poor logic is not normally a matter for the court's concern, *Alabama Power Co. v. Goodwin,* 210 Ala. 657, 99 So. 158 (1923). And mere exaggeration is not necessarily improper, *Nashville Ry. & Light Co. v. Owen,* 11 Tenn. App. 19 (1929).

Misstatements of the law are just as objectionable as misstatements of the evidence. Understandably, experienced trial lawyers do try to avoid making either kind. It is damaging if the jury thinks it cannot trust what you say.

Some trial lawyers try to guard against these objections in advance. They defer to the authority of the judge and remind the jury that his instructions will be given when the arguments are finished. When talking about the evidence, they tell the jury to follow their own recollection if it is different from what they say.

A law teacher might tell you that this is logically the same rule as misstating the evidence. After all, both involve making an argument on the basis of some fact that is not in evidence. But if there is a philosophical unity between the rules, there still is a practical difference.

An example will make the point clear. It is one thing for an attorney to remember incorrectly what a witness said. It is quite another to say, ''I am truly sorry that Mr. Demetrio was not here to testify as we had hoped. If he had taken the stand, he could have told you exactly what he saw the defendant do when he left the Gem Cocktail Lounge on April 27, and you would understand just how intoxicated the defendant was. . . .''

When a lawyer argues off the record, it is usually obvious, and it is wrong for two reasons. First, the lawyer is actually serving as an unsworn witness, usually to hearsay. Second, it is ethically improper because a lawyer should not be a witness for his client. The consequence is that while objections to misstating the evidence are seldom sustained, objections to arguing off the record are often upheld. The reason is functional—evidence off the record is easier for a judge to spot.

The prohibition against arguing off the record does not mean that a lawyer is limited to what is in evidence and nothing else. It is permissible to argue common sense, general knowledge, and understanding. Like the difference between legislative and adjudicative facts in judicial notice, there is a distinction between facts that illustrate a principle of common understanding and facts that go to make up the proof in a particular case.

That distinction is the justification for lawyers using analogies, parables, or anecdotes in final argument. They are not testifying to what happened in this case, they are urging that common sense be used in assessing the evidence. Not surprisingly, Texas has made its approval explicit. ''It is well settled law in Texas that the facts of a case may in argument be related to history, fiction, personal experience, anecdotes, Bible stories or jokes.'' *Sheffield v. Lewis*, 287 S.W.2d 531, 539 (Tex. Civ. App. 1956).

But there it stops, and when lawyers argue that similar cases decided by different juries should serve as a guide in this case, it is improper. *Salgo v. Leland Stanford Jr. University Bd. of Trustees*, 154 Cal. App. 560, 317 P.2d 170 (1957).

484

Lawyers sometimes like to compliment each other during argument, fighting for the position of David by describing the opposition as Goliath. It should be no surprise that others have complained about this on appeal—and that within bounds, complimenting the opposition is not improper. *Commercial Standard Ins. Co. v. Noack,* 45 S.W.2d 798 (Tex. Civ. App. 1932).

Lawyers are not always complimentary in the heat of battle, and the cases recognize that, too. Again, considerable latitude is the rule before criticism of opposing counsel becomes improper. One case is instructive, *Missouri K. T. R. Co. v. Ridgway,* 191 F.2d 363 (8th Cir. 1951).

Counsel made a vituperative attack on his opposition, and argued at length that he had engaged in a studied effort to conceal facts from the jury. If the proof had supported that, it would have been appropriate. But since the lawyer was simply commenting on his opponent's conduct, it was held improper.

What about arguing the other side's failure to produce evidence, call a witness, or personally testify in the case? It is often litigated, but the principles are plain enough. An admission is anything said or done inconsistent with the position a party takes at trial. Failing to call a witness who would normally be helpful can give rise to an inference that his testimony would not be favorable.

The proper question, then, is simple. Under the facts of this case would it be fair to conclude that the failure to produce this particular evidence is an admission? If the answer is yes, then it is proper argument. This means that it is normally permissible to comment on the failure of the opposing party to testify in a civil case. *Flowers v. Green,* 420 Pa. 481, 218 A.2d 219 (1966). That same argument becomes improper in a criminal case, where it is an unconstitutional comment on the defendant's exercise of his freedom from self-incrimination. *Griffin v. California,* 380 U.S. 609 (1965).

It is wrong to state your personal belief in the justice of your client's cause in final argument. *State v. Miller,* 271 N.C. 646, 157 S.E.2d 335 (1967); MODEL CODE OF PROFESSIONAL RESPONSIBILITY, EC 7-24 (1977).

In one sense it is a specialized application of the rule against arguing off the record. It is worth separate consideration because it is often violated, easily complied with, and important.

The prohibition against stating your personal belief in the justice of your cause is an ethical rule that many thoughtful lawyers

485

who would never consider doing anything improper regularly violate without knowing it. One reason is that in some parts of the country the phrase "I believe" is a customary way to avoid being too opinionated; it is an American understatement. It is understandable that it sneaks into final arguments. The second reason is that when you tell a jury what verdict you expect, it is easy to make the same mistake.

You do not need to stop using understatement or to avoid telling the jury what you expect from them. People like to do what is expected of them, and saying what you want will help. Telling the jury the verdict you expect does not require violating the rule.

The cure is easier than that. Just avoid using the phrase "I believe" in final argument.

Even though juries are a humanizing influence on the law that we keep in part because they are not entirely rational, we make a great effort to keep them as logical as we can. Nearly the entire law of evidence is a monument to the notion that juries can only be expected to give reasonable verdicts when the information they get is restricted. The law of argument makes a similar effort by limiting the sorts of argument. The rule against appeals to passion or prejudice is an open recognition of the power of persuasion.

The approach of the law is an understanding one. First, lawyers are expected to be zealous on behalf of their clients. There is a fair amount of latitude allowed in the heat of oratory. Second, trial judges (who can sense the mood of the courtroom far better than can an appellate court reading a record) are given considerable discretion.

Still, it is possible to go too far. For example, the existence of dependents may be irrelevant in an injury case, but it may still be permissible to have them present in the courtroom during trial. *Delaney v. New York Cent. R. Co.*, 68 F. Supp. 70, 72 (S.D.N.Y. 1946). But in a wrongful death case in which the children are parties—and they are in the courtroom as a matter of right—it was held improper to speak directly to them about their dead father during the course of final argument in *Brabeck v. Chicago & N.W.R. Co.*, 264 Minn. 160, 117 N.W.2d 921 (1962).

Reading poetry is permitted. "[C]ourts should not smother the genius of some rising orator, nor lay an embargo upon the ancient art of oratory by undue limitations." *Colorado & S. Ry. Co. v. Chiles*, 50 Colo. 191, 114 P.661 (1911). What if your emotions get the best of you and your eyes mist up a bit? At one time in our history, there was no question: "Tears have always been considered legitimate arguments before a jury . . . we know of no rule or jurisdiction in the court below to check them. It would appear to be one of the natural rights of counsel which no court or constitution could take away. . . . Indeed, if counsel has them at his command, it may seriously be questioned whether it is not his professional duty to shed them whenever proper occasion arises." *Furguson v. Moore*, 98 Tenn. 342, 39 S.W. 341, 343 (1897).

Harsh words are sometimes justified, *Texas & P. Ry. Co. v. Smith*, 115 S.W.2d 1238 (Tex. Civ. App. 1938). But it can be improper for a prosecutor to appeal to the self-interest of jurors in social, class, and business matters or as taxpayers. *State v. Majors*, 182 Kan. 644, 323 P.2d 917 (1958).

Appellate courts are not happy with arguments that play on personal emotions or individual feelings. It is wrong to single out a particular juror and appeal to him or her during argument, *Peters v. Hoisington* 72 S.D. 542, 37 N.W.2d 410 (1949); or just to address individual jurors by name, *In re Maier's Estate*, 236 Iowa 960, 20 N.W.2d 425 (1945). It was even too much in a false imprisonment case to say that the plaintiff's dead wife was watching the proceedings, with her "face pressed against the window pane of heaven," waiting to hear the verdict. *Fort Worth Hotel Co. v. Waggoman*, 126 S.W.2d 578, 586 (Tex. Civ. App. 1939).

The "per diem" argument is a favorite with plaintiff's personal injury lawyers. It involves making a modest-appearing suggestion for what one day's pain and suffering (for example) should be worth—then multiplying it by the remainder of the plaintiff's expected life to reach an astronomical sum. It has been the subject of serious controversy, with some courts forbidding it, while others approve. *Annot.*, 3 A.L.R. 4th 940 (1981).

The Ohio rule is a good compromise. The per diem argument can only be introduced by the plaintiff during the initial final argument, and cannot be saved for rebuttal when the defendant does not have a chance to answer it. *Grossnickle v. Germantown*, 3 Ohio St. 2d 96, 32 Ohio Ops 2d 65, 209 N.E.2d 442 (1965).

Perhaps the easiest rule to break is the one that forbids asking the jury to put themselves in the shoes of either party. *Annot.*, 70 A.L.R.2d 935. It is almost always improper to make the argument, even though it may not always amount to prejudicial error under the circumstances of the particular case.

That it is forbidden to ask jurors to put themselves in the position of a party is an interesting study all itself. The rule seems to fly in the face of elemental justice. What idea is more basic to the notion of fairness than "treat this party the way you would want to be treated"?

The answer—right or wrong—is that courts feel that asking the jury to put themselves in the shoes of one of the litigants is actually an appeal to passion or prejudice, especially for damages in personal injury cases. *Smith v. Merzolf*, 59 Ill. App. 3d 635, 375 N.E.2d 995 (1978). It is thought that arguments such as "would any of you sell your right arm for $500,000?" is too powerful an appeal to the emotions, since a juror might think no amount of money is enough payment for losing his own arm, but could be more impartial with someone else's limb.

No one is surprised that it is wrong to argue that insurance shows a defendant was careless or that a personal injury award should be reduced because it is not subject to income tax unless you are in a minority jurisdiction that admits this evidence. Like the remarriage of the widow in a wrongful death case, these are matters that are not likely to be in evidence, and litigants may fight to get rulings in advance of trial, so that questions about them will not even be asked.

It is easy to understand rules that keep information from the jury. But some of the more difficult evidence rules neither fully admit nor exclude evidence. They do something in between. One of the first hurdles for the evidence student is limited admissibility—evidence that is admitted to prove one fact in issue, but cannot even be considered for some other disputed point.

The insurance, for example, that was not admitted to prove the defendant's negligence, may be admissible on the issue of bias, if an insurance investigator takes the witness stand to testify about the prior statement he took of the plaintiff's witness. Rule 411 of the Federal Rules of Evidence says, "This rule does not require the exclusion of evidence of insurance against liability when offered for another purpose, such as proof of agency, ownership, or control, or bias or prejudice of a witness."

What happens when this evidence is admitted for a "limited purpose"? The jury hears it, the judge gives a limiting instruction, and the lawyer may only talk about it in final argument as it relates to its admissible purpose.

In other words, the law of evidence admitted the testimony, but limited the purpose for which it could be used.

You might wonder whether a rule of evidence is actually something else when its main effect is to regulate instructions and the conduct of final argument. Your suspicion is correct. Except for those rare cases when limiting the admissibility of evidence results in a directed verdict, the rules of limited admissibility are simply rules of final argument.

So what?

Just this: Unlike the implication in the course of evidence you took in law school, the game is not over once a clever lawyer manages to convince a trial judge that this bit of evidence is relevant for *something*.

Never mind, for the time, whether the jury can "compartmentalize their minds" in thinking about the proof and apply it only to the proper purpose. The question at hand is what can the lawyer *say* about the evidence in final argument.

The answer is, it is limited. And lest you be tempted to doubt it, understand that some of the most important "evidence" cases are actually "final argument" cases. *Shepard v. United States*, 290 U.S. 96 (1933), is a good example. In *Shepard*, the defendant was charged with poisoning his wife. Before she died, Mrs. Shepard told her nurse, "Dr. Shepard has poisoned me."

If the statement had qualified as a dying declaration, that would have been an end to it. The statement would have come into evidence for any purpose. But it did not qualify as a dying declaration. On appeal the prosecution tried to justify the evidence as proving Mrs. Shepard's "state of mind."

In Justice Cardozo's famous opinion, the Supreme Court said that declarations of state of mind could not look "backwards to the past." Thus the doctrine of *Mutual Life Ins. Co. v. Hillmon*, 145 U.S. 285 (1892), was limited to statements that look to the future. In other words, after the *Shepard* case, declarations of a person's state of mind were admissible to prove that he later did what he said he was going to do—but could not prove he had done what he *remembered*.

It is an important case in the law of hearsay, but just what does it have to do with final argument?

One of Dr. Shepard's defenses was that his wife committed suicide. Her statement, "Dr. Shepard has poisoned me," is inconsistent with the intention to take her own life—and was admissible for that purpose. If the evidence was admissible, how was the Supreme Court able to reverse Dr. Shepard's conviction?

The prosecution's final argument used Mrs. Shepard's statement the wrong way. "It did not use the declarations by Mrs.

489

Shepard to prove her present thoughts and feelings, or even her thoughts and feelings in times past. It used the declarations as proof of an act committed by someone else, as evidence that she was dying of poison given by her husband.''

The practical lesson of *Shepard v. United States* applies to every case of limited admissibility:

- The prior conviction used to impeach the defendant when he takes the stand to testify cannot be used to prove he committed the act.
- The subsequent repair used to prove ownership or control cannot be used to prove negligence.
- The bad driving record admissible to prove negligent entrustment of the truck cannot be used to show the driver was actually at fault.

If you think these distinctions are hard for jurors to make, you are right. It is also difficult for the lawyer to stick to the limitations when arguing the evidence. Even with thought and care it is easy to step over the line—yet another reason why the rules of waiver and the doctrine of harmless error are necessary to make it all work.

CHAPTER 45

Solving Problems with Final Argument

The name makes a difference.

Take final argument, for example. Call it summation, and it will mean something else. The distinction may seem subtle at first, but it will be real.

Why? Final argument conjures up the picture of a lawyer engaged in intellectual combat. If the function of law is to provide a framework for advocacy, then this event—argument—is central to our system of justice. The lawyer's discussion may be gentle or hard-hitting, absorbing or dry, logical or emotional—but it will be argument.

Summation evokes something else. It is still the lawyer talking to the jury, but he is not persuading. He is summing up. He is going over the evidence so the fact-finder will remember what was said during the trial.

There you have the distinction, but what difference does it make? The answer lies in the purpose the lawyer has in talking to the judge and jury. In the half hour or so that he has at the end of trial, what should be accomplished?

It is not an idle question. Opening statement and final argument are special times. They are the only two opportunities lawyers have to speak directly to the jury. If they are to make a difference, they must rest on a clear understanding of what the lawyer wants to do. Fine, you say, but what does this have to do with the difference between summation and final argument?

Just this: Summation—summing up the evidence—is what must be done when the facts are long and complex, there are many witnesses, or the course of the trial was somehow interrupted. It is a task to undertake when the jury needs help keeping things straight. It is a job most needed when the case has not been well tried. Summing up means going over the evidence. It is not so much argument as it is a preliminary to argument.

Unfortunately, some lawyers use summation in place of argument. That is often a mistake. It is usually a waste of time going over testimony that is already understood or hammering home facts that were accepted long ago. Why spend time convincing people to accept what they already believe? It is annoying at best, and can even make a friendly jury hostile if carried to excess. It is our tendency for plodding redundancy that makes jurors complain that lawyers go over the same things again and again.

But argument is different. Argument does not suggest a mere summary. Argument brings to mind persuasion addressed to the thorniest problems a case can present. Most cases need no summary of facts at the end, but most of them could profit from good argument. The disputes that actually get to trial are usually not clear one way or the other. They go to trial for the very reason that each side thinks it has something of merit to present.

The point is simple. Nearly every case has some serious problem that needs attention in final argument. Usually that problem is not solved by a summary of the evidence, but by a line of argument that is designed to meet the particular difficulty.

If the problem is serious enough, it can command the entire argument. It should not surprise you that the best final arguments are often those that do not follow a standard pattern. An example comes from Philip H. Corboy's brilliant argument on damages for the bumped airline passengers in *Kluczynski v. Delta Air Lines*, reported by James Touhy in *Effective Final Argument for the Plaintiff*, 8 LITIGATION, No. 3, at 41 (Spring 1982). Instead of a model of conventionality, it was a masterpiece of persuasion that explained why the airline ought to pay something substantial to two people who had only been inconvenienced.

And that is the justification for this chapter. Not to discuss the issues that come up in *every* case, but to deal with the kind of special difficulty that can arise in *any* case.

Let us start with the burden of proof. It is a subject that can excite only lawyers, and even for us, enthusiasm may be hard to muster. In civil actions most of us are content to let the judge do most of the explaining, just taking a minute or so to anticipate the court's instructions with a demonstration of the scales of justice, the slightest tilt representing a preponderance of the evidence.

That is fine. It can be an effective standard argument, but it attacks no special problem. That is because for the most part the burden of proof does not make much difference in the outcome of the case.

But sometimes it does.

Sometimes a case hangs on the jury's understanding of the burden of proof. Then simply juggling the scales of justice with outstretched arms will not be enough. Recognizing the problem, some lawyers instinctively respond the wrong way when the case is a close one—they pour on even more zeal, insist that the case is truly simple and can be decided only one way.

To be sure, it helps to be positive. It is wrong to think that the jury will accept something you will not. You cannot sell what you will not buy. But being over-positive is not good persuasion. Overstatement in final argument is usually a needless withdrawal from your personal credibility account. It takes away without giving you anything in return. If the case is truly close—and everyone knows it—it is an opportunity for genuine candor. It is more effective than any gimmick, and can make a difference:

I know how seriously you view this case—and that is right. It is also right to want every bit of possible evidence. And surely you must want more. It is only natural. Deciding a case is important business, and you want to take everything into account.

And certainty—actually *knowing*—would make your job much more comfortable. No one blames you if you want more information.

Only there isn't any. Mr. Kiefer and I have been living with this case for years. We have done our best to supply you with every bit of relevant, admissible evidence the law allows.

There are unanswered questions, and you undoubtedly would like more information—more knowledge—more facts—and yet it is not available. But on the other hand, you must decide this case. That's why it is here—for you to decide. Only how do you go about it when there is information you would like to have, but cannot get?

Fortunately, the law provides some help. It gives you a viewpoint, a way of looking at things when there is not

493

enough proof. In a case like this, that viewpoint becomes essential.

If you have been following what this argument has done so far, you probably pictured yourself saying something like it to the jury, and then picked up in your mind where it would go from there. But for whom—the plaintiff or defendant? That is the beauty of this approach. It serves as a good introduction to the burden of proof no matter which side of the line you are on. Let us continue.

First, for the defendant: "Here is what the law does. It gives the party who is trying to change the way things stand the obligation of proving that the something ought to be done. That is only common sense. Courts—judges and juries—people—do not make judgments on suppositions. That is the role of the burden of proof. It tells you who must prove his case, who has the obligation of convincing you.

And as Judge McMonagle will instruct you before you deliberate, it is the plaintiff who must prove his case. With that understanding, what might otherwise be difficult becomes easier because of the viewpoint the law gives you—the assistance it gives in resolving a situation where you might otherwise be uncertain what to do.

There is more, to be sure. Besides the common-sense approach to what is a burden and why it is there, words like *obligation, convincing, duty, proving, burden,* and (at the right time) *preponderance of the evidence,* all play a part. They make it easier to understand that a plaintiff can fail to prove his case. If they contribute to the feeling that the obligation to prove the case is a heavy one, that will help the effort.

But what about the plaintiff? The introduction was supposed to be adaptable to the party with the burden of proof. Remember that the first part of the argument said that the law would help the jury out of the difficult position in the middle. Just a little modification (take out that phrase, "when there isn't enough proof," for example) and you will be ready to go on behalf of the plaintiff:

Fortunately, the law provides some help. It understands that we can rarely be positive about anything. Certainty is not required. If it were, we could never accomplish anything. We cannot recreate the past—and it might not help if we could. So the law does not put that kind of impossible burden on someone who seeks justice.

494

It takes a very practical approach instead. It says, 'You have heard the evidence. If you lean one way or the other, then that is the way you should decide the case. Only if you are caught completely on dead center, will you resolve the case in favor of the defendant.

There is a reason for this approach. It is a recognition that the case must be decided, and we must get on with the business of the world. It says we must use common sense in deciding the case. And the words for that common-sense approach are a *preponderance of the evidence.* It is a term that his honor, Judge McMonagle, will tell you about in his instructions before you retire to deliberate.

And on you go, ready now to show the scales of justice and explain how the slightest tilt is enough.

You noticed how both the plaintiff and the defendant referred to the trial judge and his instructions. There are good reasons for doing that. First, many lawyers feel that if they incorporate words from the judge's charge, there will be an identification between the charge and the argument. In other words, they think that when the jury hears the judge say "preponderance of the evidence," it will bring back the setting in which it first appeared.

Second, the judge symbolizes justice, and parties like to align themselves with that idea. Third, most jurors think that the judge is the smartest lawyer in the courtroom. Whether true or not, it is an impression that should not be corrected unless there is an excellent reason for it.

But there are more serious problems than deference to judges and arguing the burden of proof. If we were to conduct a poll of trial lawyers to find out what were the most difficult problems in persuasion, we would get a wide variety of answers. But there would be some common ground. If you looked at the answers long enough, you would probably conclude that prejudice heads the list.

It is not hard to see why. Prejudice is a human failing that seems to lurk everywhere. There are racial, ethnic, religious, and social prejudices, to be sure. But they do not stop there. There are prejudices that influence our attitudes toward occupations, employers, and even recreation. They may be harder to deal with than the sort we are more accustomed to thinking about.

A few examples might help. Imagine yourself in trial in what is called a company town. There is a single industry, a giant employer who influences or controls everyone's life. Pit an employee against the company, and you will suddenly pay more attention to who identifies themselves with labor and who with management when you select the jury. The dynamics change when it is the local company against a competitor or supplier. They change again when times are hard and folks are getting laid off—especially if the attack comes from outside.

We are used to thinking about these issues during jury selection, and rightly so. But once the jury is impanelled we are not free to turn to other things. When it is time for final argument, there is the difficult decision whether to talk about what may be the most important aspect in the entire case—the underlying prejudice.

Sometimes lawyers are reluctant to approach prejudice directly. Mentioning something out loud can give it a certain dignity it did not have before. The result is that some trial lawyers approach prejudice obliquely—talking instead about the power of the jury and the importance of doing justice. Most arguments like these were designed to lift juries out of their parochial concerns and make them think about the problems of others on a higher level than they were accustomed to doing. It is interesting that these exhortations are often copied by other lawyers who apply them to any case, whether it calls for it or not.

There are times when prejudice must be confronted head-on. Take the case of a plaintiff who was injured in a motorcycle crash. There are many people who think of motorcyclists as outlaws on the road, who invite injury by simply driving down the street. Some motorcyclists flout safety rules—like helmet laws—that are made for their own protection. Then there are motorcycle gangs in some communities that are a serious threat to ordinary citizens.

Small wonder that representing a motorcyclist is difficult. Is this prejudice something that should be dealt with on final argument? Certainly. Jury selection has only served to eliminate those who *admit* to their feelings about motorcycles. That means the careful lawyer for the plaintiff will be aware of the underlying prejudice against motorcycles and motorcyclists throughout the entire trial. On final argument it can come out into the open again:

There is something that we must talk about simply and directly before you consider your verdict in this case. You will remember from jury selection two days ago that none of you owns or rides a motorcycle. And yet all of you are bound to have feelings about them. There are lots of people who

496

would never dream of getting on a motorcycle because they feel they are just too dangerous—that when you ride a motorcycle, you are taking your life into your own hands—and that whatever happens to you, you have it coming.

That is an understandable feeling—just as it is for parents who, knowing that motorcycles can be dangerous, might refuse to let their child buy or ride a motorcycle.

But that is not what we are here to decide. This case is not about whether it is a good idea for you or me or anyone to ride a motorcycle. It is about something more basic. It is about whether a young man who was doing what he had a right to do—and doing it in the proper way—carefully and lawfully—will be denied the justice that he is entitled to because of the *personal* feelings—perfectly understandable feelings—that many of us have about motorcycles.

That is the special problem *you* have in this case. You are going to have to separate your personal feelings about motorcycles from what you know is right and what you know is wrong in *this case.* And when you go into the jury deliberation room, you are going to have to leave your personal feelings aside—leave them at the door—and do what you know is right—and fair—and just.

It does not stop there, even though we will. There are other ways to approach the problem, of course. The point is that directly or indirectly, you must deal with the prejudice in the case because it was there before you were.

Turn now to another kind of problem—the sort that threatens to destroy the entire case. It is the client caught in a lie.

If you are alert and doing your job, you have already done what you can to keep this from happening. But there are some people who cannot resist trying to make things seem better than they are. The irony is that sometimes a congenital liar spoils a perfectly honest and justified case by exaggeration.

Consider this situation, based on a recent case: A surgeon lost the thumb and the first two fingers of his primary hand, and brought an action in negligence for their loss. In deposition and at trial, he could not help trying to improve his case. He painted a picture of marital bliss that was destroyed by the loss of his profession. He told how he had graduated third in his class and had started a brilliant career. He testified to his high earnings, which were now gone.

The defendants were suspicious and checked the doctor's

background more thoroughly than his own lawyer had. What they found was devastating. The doctor had a serious alcohol problem and his wife had filed for divorce before the injury ever occurred. He had not graduated third in his class, but *thirty-third*. And his income tax returns showed he was only reporting half the income he claimed when he gave his deposition.

It was not a situation that called for a standard final argument. Here is what the plaintiff's lawyer said instead:

Ladies and gentlemen, there is something I must talk about before we get started.

You should be very angry. The plaintiff—the man I represent—the one who has come to you and asked for justice—has done some things he should not have done and said things he should not have said.

And if you are not angry—if you are not outraged—then something is very wrong, because you should be. It would surely be understandable if your anger, your outrage, caused you to say to this man, 'Stop. Say no more to us. Leave this place. You are not entitled to justice. How can we give you justice if we cannot trust what you say?' And if that is what you said, if that is what you did, then most people would understand.

And yet you know that would not be the right thing to do. It would be understandable—but not the *right* thing, not the *just* thing to tell him to leave.

Why? Because you know that he was wronged. You know his professional life has been taken from him, and you know it was not his fault. And you know that not only from him, but from all the evidence in the case. You even know it from what the defendant has told you from the witness stand.

So what should you do? As the conscience of the community, what action should you take? It is not an easy question to answer, but there is one suggestion that I would like to make right now.

The plaintiff has asked for money damages for what has happened to his hand. And when you look at the two fingers that are all that remains of his right hand, you may decide he has been punished enough. But then you may say, 'Wait a minute. What about his income? How much was he really making? Was he cheating on his income tax, or was he exaggerating his income to us?'

That is a question that, fortunately for you, you do not have to answer. It belongs to another court, another jury, and another lawyer. So what can you do if you are to rise above retaliation and be just, instead? There are times when a misstatement contains its own punishment. One of the things you can consider—when you calculate the plaintiff's lost income—is to *base your award on his income tax returns rather than what he has told you here in court.*

Drastic action? Certainly. Did it work? In the special issue verdict that followed, damages were assessed at more than $2 million.

If you think about attacking the serious problems in a case on final argument, you will see that it is usually a better use of your time than merely reviewing the evidence. On the other hand, you may be skeptical. You may wonder whether it makes any difference.

By the time a case reaches final argument, many of the jurors have already made up their minds. If that is true, why bother to give final argument much time and effort? Why not give more attention to jury selection and opening statements?

While thoughtful trial lawyers are aware of the limitations of final argument, no one wants to abolish it. It is too valuable. Good argument is what separates the masters from the apprentices.

What, then, should you expect from final argument? For the most part, it is true that there are no great conversions at the end of trial. As Jack Liber, of Cleveland, says, you cannot persuade jurors to do what they do not want to do. The goal of argument is to help the jury want to do the right thing, to feel comfortable in making the proper judgment.

That is probably the best way to look at final argument—and yet sometimes more is accomplished. But how can you know? It is rare that we get the chance to test the effect of what we say. That is an opportunity John Burgess of San Francisco had at the convention of the American Bar Association in 1979. He was defense counsel in President Tate's Showcase program, "Cameras in the Courtroom."

He was representing the hypothetical "Bonnie Lynch," who was charged with knowingly harboring and concealing a fugitive from a federal warrant and then helping him cross a state line, knowing it was his purpose to commit a felony.

It was a case that had been used by the State Junior Bar of Texas as the problem for the National Mock Trial Competition, and the facts were simple. Bonnie Lynch had put up a man in her apartment over the weekend. His name was Frank Adams. He was the fugitive from justice whom Bonnie Lynch had driven to the bus station—across the state line—in Texarkana.

There was only one question: Did Bonnie Lynch *know* about Frank Adams, or was the entire business an innocent coincidence?

It was a question that Burgess got to argue twice during the convention—before two different juries composed of legal secretaries from Dallas law firms.

The principal evidence against Bonnie Lynch came from her old acquaintance, Jesse Nolan. Nolan was involved in the transaction, too. He is the one who talked Bonnie Lynch into putting up Frank Adams for the weekend. But instead of being prosecuted, Jesse Nolan received a grant of immunity in return for his testimony. And on the witness stand, he *insisted* that he told Bonnie Lynch "all about" Frank Adams.

Each day the lawyer acting as United States Attorney tried the case the same way, and each day Burgess defended it the same way—with one exception. At the end of the first trial, the jury found Bonnie Lynch guilty by a vote of seven to five. It was an effective defense, but Burgess was not happy, and he decided to do something special in attacking the testimony of the immunity witness, Jesse Nolan.

As you might expect, each time he explained how the grant of immunity gave Nolan a motive to lie. But the second day, Burgess decided to "reenact" the telephone call. Here is what he did:

Ladies and gentlemen, there is only one way that Bonnie Lynch can be guilty: This 'immunity witness,' Jesse Nolan, must be telling the truth.

You remember his testimony. He told you that he called Bonnie Lynch on the telephone to see if she would be willing to put up Frank Adams for the weekend. He admitted that she was reluctant to do so at first because she lives alone with her little girl, Gretchen. But Adams says that he talked Bonnie into it and insists that he told Bonnie Lynch all about Frank Adams in that conversation.

Now, his honor, Judge Higginbotham, is going to instruct you at the end of the case. He will tell you the law you must follow. One thing he is *not* going to do is tell you to leave your common sense at the door when you go in that deliberation room.

If Jesse Nolan is telling you the truth, how *must* that telephone conversation have gone? [Then, armed with two imaginary telephones—one in each hand, and changing his voice to suit the character, Burgess relived the telephone conversation.]

'Hello?'

'Hello, Bonnie?'

'Yes. Who is this, please?'

'This is Jesse—Jesse Nolan.'

'Oh, hi, Jess. How are you?'

'I'm fine. Say, Bonnie, I wonder if you might do me a favor.'

'I will if I can. What is it, Jesse?'

'I have this friend here from out of town, and I have to find a place for him to stay. I wonder if you might put him up for the weekend?'

'Gee, Jesse, I don't know. There is just me and Gretchen living here—I am not sure.'

'Oh, he wouldn't be any trouble. He's a real nice guy.'

'I'm really not sure, Jesse. Who is this person, anyway?'

'His name is Frank Adams, and he is an old friend of mine.'

'Oh, Jesse, I don't think so . . .'

'Bonnie, don't worry. He is a real good guy. He is a bag man for the mob in Nashville. There is a federal fugitive warrant out for his arrest, and he is on his way to Dallas to bribe a local official.'

'Well, if that's the case, send him right over.'

Everyone on the jury—everyone in the courtroom—burst out laughing, and after an extensive rebuttal by the prosecution, it took the jury five minutes to return a verdict of 'not guilty.' The vote was unanimous. Instead of just urging that the immunity witness was not telling the truth, Burgess did something far more effective—he demonstrated it, so that the jury reached the right conclusion on its own.

CHAPTER 46

Analogies in Final Argument

Think back to your first semester in law school. Remember the time when you raised your hand in response to a question the class was struggling with? You saw a clear solution to their difficulty. By a stroke of sensible insight you were going to untie the Gordian Knot.

The trouble was, your answer did not come out quite as you intended. Something happened between the thought and the statement. It suffered in translation.

Even if it was beautifully articulated, the instructor picked up the idea and held it aloft for critical examination, and you started to feel uneasy. After a few probing questions you backed down just a bit. Then others joined in the attack on what you had said. When your original suggestion was reduced to an absurdity, the process was complete.

How did you feel?

Terrible.

You were embarrassed. Humiliated.

You felt as if you had been personally attacked.

Why?

You had not been in any physical danger.

Despite the ''Paper Chase,'' probably nothing was even said about *you*—just your idea.

Then why did you react so strongly?

Because people are protective about their own ideas. They hold them dearly. When you attack a person's idea, for most people it is as if you attacked them.

502

It is a fascinating human characteristic.

Teachers who are aware of the phenomenon (either by study or intuition) can take advantage of it to heighten student awareness and participation. If they go too far, they learn that students can have their intellect blocked by emotions just as surely as if they were in physical danger.

Do you doubt it?

Try seriously insulting a friend's idea and see the effect on a previously restrained, intelligent discussion.

And there it is: intellectual pride. It is a trait that most people have. It is real, it is powerful. It is one of the keys to effective advocacy.

Why?

If the fact finder—judge or jury—reaches a conclusion on its own, it will hold that conclusion more firmly than if it had merely been told what conclusion to reach.

Lloyd Paul Stryker put it superbly in the *Art of Advocacy* 125 (1954):

> No point is ever better made than when not directly made at all but is so presented that the jury itself makes it. Men pride themselves on their own discoveries, and so a point which the jury are allowed to think their own ingenuity has discovered can put the advocate in a position where the jury begin to regard him as not only their spokesman but their colleague.

The problem, then, is to discover how to guide the jury so that it reaches the conclusion you want and thinks it has figured things out for itself.

Enter the analogy.

It is perhaps the most powerful form of argument we know. Craig Spangenberg said in *Basic Values and the Techniques of Persuasion*, LITIGATION No. 4 at 13, 16 (Summer, 1977): "the greatest weapon in the arsenal of persuasion is the analogy, the story, the simple comparison to a familiar subject. Nothing can move the jurors more convincingly than an apt comparison to something they know from their own experience is true."

Analogies are effective, and it is worth knowing why.

The answer is simple. Analogies work for two related reasons. First, good stories command the attention of the audience. They want to find out what happened.

Second, analogies challenge an audience to test their appropriateness to the point made. When someone tells a story to prove a point, it is almost impossible to resist testing it to see if it fits the situation.

What is the net effect? You are right. The audience, in testing the aptness of a comparison, reasons the problem through and reaches the conclusion on its own. That is just what Lloyd Paul Stryker told us to get the jury to do.

Analogies—whether simple allusions or detailed stories—are a distinguishing mark of outstanding final arguments. They lead juries to draw their own conclusions, which they believe more fervently than if they had merely been told what conclusion to reach.

This does not mean you should not tell the jury or the judge what you want. You should. People are pleased to have their ideas reinforced. But you should try to work out your argument so that the fact finder gets to the conclusion before you do.

Because comparisons are so powerful, it is tempting to work them into jury selection, opening statements, and even the examination of witnesses. And within reasonable limits, analogies can fit in almost any part of the trial, particularly if they are short.

But the real place for analogies and comparisons—even protracted stories—is in final argument.

Whether the analogy should be a short comparison or a real story depends to some extent on how important the point is to the case and how much persuasion is required for people to accept the idea.

One of the serious difficulties language presents is that minor points often take longer to explain than important matters. Consider, for example, how annoyingly difficult it is to explain a strange sound in your new car to the automobile service manager, and how much easier it is to tell him that the engine fell out. This is a particularly irksome trait of language, because the ordinary understanding is that the longer it takes to say something, the more important it is.

Analogies can help solve this communication problem. When you choose stories to argue for you, it is much easier to tailor them to suit the relative importance of the issue.

Take stories about circumstantial evidence. First, suppose that circumstantial evidence is a minor point, but one that must be dealt with. Here is how you might approach it.

Well, you have heard the defense attack our evidence and

say it is 'just circumstantial.' [pause] 'Just circumstantial.' [pause] You know, the people upstate have a saying about circumstantial evidence. They say that if you go into the woods and find a turtle on a tree stump, you know he didn't get there by himself.

There are, on the other hand, more involved circumstantial evidence stories for use when it is a bigger part of the case. Craig Spangenberg's ''Robinson Crusoe'' is one:

> This reminds me of my father reading *Robinson Crusoe* to me when I was a little boy. Remember when Robinson Crusoe was on the island for such a long time all alone? One morning he went down to the beach and there was a footprint in the sand. Knowing that someone else was on the island, he was so overcome with emotion, he fainted.
>
> And why did he faint? Did he see a man? He woke to find Friday standing beside him, who was to be his friend on the island, but he didn't see Friday. Did he see a foot? No. He saw a footprint. That is, he saw marks in the sand, the kind of marks that are made by a human foot. He saw circumstantial evidence. But it was true, it was valid, it was compelling, as it would be to all of you. We live with it all of our lives. So let's look at the facts of this case—for those tracks that prove the truth. Spangenberg, *supra*, at 16.

It is a good story about circumstantial evidence, and it deserves a little extra comment. Not only does this analogy explain its basic point, it serves another function as well. It tells you that the lawyer who is telling the story had a father who loved him and read to him. At the very start there is a subliminal picture of a boy sitting beside his father, listening raptly as his father reads *Robinson Crusoe*.

So what, you ask.

So, remembering that scene fondly is a stroke of genius. It signals to the jury that this is a man who loves and reveres his father or his memory. It demonstrates the sort of basic values that make us accept that lawyer as a decent, credible person. It follows—in the trial's emotional undercurrent, which is often as important as the evidence itself—that we are more likely to accept what this lawyer says as true.

This is something that jurors will tend to do no matter how they feel about their actual fathers. Somewhere in the heart of every person is a father who read to the child, no matter what the real father may have done.

Usually it is the plaintiff or the prosecutor—the one with the burden of proof—who seeks to validate circumstantial evidence. Sometimes, however, the defense counsel in a criminal case needs to talk about circumstantial evidence.

When the Honorable R. Eugene Pincham of the Circuit Court of Cook County was defending criminal cases in Chicago, he sometimes used a story about his boyhood on the farm. The story is designed to show that seemingly little points from the prosecution's case add up to a major flaw.

Since it is impossible for mere print to recreate the beauty and power of an urbane and eloquent black lawyer's speech—thoroughly sophisticated, yet mellowed by the lingering touches of the rural south—you will have to imagine it for yourself:

> I grew up on a farm in Alabama. As you know, things were really different there than they are here. You couldn't just go to the store when you wanted something. You couldn't just walk a block or two when you needed a pound of sugar.
>
> Sugar is important on a farm. Besides using it for cooking and at the table, my mother would put up preserves and sometimes cure meat with it. Because it was so important, we didn't buy sugar by the two-pound paper bag. We bought it by the barrel. And my mother kept it in the kitchen.
>
> Momma had *one rule:* 'Stay out of my sugar!'
>
> My brother and I used to like to make what we called 'milk shakes.' We would take a glass of milk, a few drops of vanilla flavoring and a spoonful of sugar, stir it up and drink it. It's good. Try it sometime. Sometimes Momma would let us make one on the weekend.
>
> We didn't like to wait for the weekend. Sometimes we would fix one when we came home from school—and that was against the rule: 'Stay out of my sugar!'
>
> I would be careful. I would see which way the handle was pointing on the lid, so when I put it back, it would be pointing the same way. When I took the spoonful of sugar, I would smooth it out like it was before. Then after I made my 'milk shake,' I would even wash the glass. I didn't want to leave any traces.
>
> When Momma came in the house, she would say, 'Gene, you've been in my sugar!'

506

'No, Momma, I haven't been in the sugar.'

'Yes, you have, and now you get two whippings—one for going in the sugar, and the other for lying about it.'

How did she know? I grew up thinking mothers had clairvoyant powers. They knew what happened even when they weren't there.

After I got married and my wife and I had children of our own, I asked her, 'Alzata—do you have clairvoyant powers?'

'What are you talking about, Gene? I don't have any more clairvoyant powers than you do.'

Not long ago, I took my own children back to the farm, to visit their grandparents. I asked my Momma how she always knew when I was in the sugar. She answered as she sat, rocking a grandchild by the fire:

'You always wasted a few granules on the floor.'

[a short pause]

Now you heard Officer Walsh testify he didn't see anything in the trunk of that car, and Officer Smith swears he saw a gun. Do you know what that is?

'Granules on the floor!'

And when the Cook County Police—one of the largest police forces in the country—backed up by the F.B.I. crime laboratories—can't tell you where that bullet came from—do you know what that is?

'Granules on the floor!'

Like "Robinson Crusoe," this story is worth a few remarks.

The reverence for the family relationship—the image of three generations seated around the fire—is compelling. It says that this lawyer is trustworthy. Interestingly, the credibility gained is not at all harmed by the narrator being the culprit. Remember, he got two whippings. The one in seeming favor who lies about his misdeed—like the policeman, is doubly wrong.

Beyond that, the story is just plain interesting. We want to find out how his mother knew he was in the sugar, and when we hear the explanation, it makes perfect sense. It fits our own experience. We did not have to grow up on a farm—everyone has stepped on sugar.

Finally, the whole story is an introduction to a powerful rhetorical device—"Granules on the floor."

It is interesting that many of the stories about circumstantial evidence are designed to show its validity. Are there no antidotes?

That challenge led Cyril McIlhargie, a public defender in Cleveland, Ohio, to use this analogy in a recent case:

When I was going to law school, like a number of other students, I had to work in the summer to pay for my tuition. But even with loans, that wasn't really enough to keep me going during the school year, so I got a part-time job when I wasn't in class.

I got a job as a security officer with the Natural History Museum, over on the east side of town, not far from the law school. And one of the things I had to watch out for was junior high and high school students who would come to the museum in large groups. There often were kids who would try to pick up some change from the fountain in the middle of the foyer near the courtyard.

Because the coins tossed in the fountain were contributions to the museum, whenever I could, I tried to stop the kids from dipping in and committing petty larceny.

One day after classes at the law school, I arrived at the museum about 2:00 in the afternoon. There was a large group of junior high students—oh, maybe twenty-five or thirty—and just one teacher, taking a tour of the museum's displays.

One group of boys broke away from the rest, and casually sauntered over to the fountain. They formed a protective little group—about five or six of them—so that the one nearest the fountain was almost hidden from view.

But just then, I saw one head duck down, an arm reach out, and heard a splash of water. I was certain I had seen the culprit.

It was circumstantial evidence, but it was compelling. I saw the head duck down behind the others who were gathered around the fountain, I saw the arm, I heard the splash, and when I went over to the fountain, the water was still disturbed.

So I grabbed the boy whose head ducked down, and said, 'All right, open your hands.'

As it happened, just as I was doing that, Mr. Snow—the man who runs the planetarium—was coming down the stairs, overlooking the fountain. He had seen everything, and he called out.

'Cyril. You've got the wrong one. It's that one over there, with the striped shirt.'

> Sure enough, when I looked at the boy in the striped shirt, I saw the wet sleeve, and told him to hand over the money. He opened his hand and dropped more than a dollar in change into mine.
>
> You know, *I* was lucky. I almost grabbed the wrong one. And the evidence against the one whose head ducked down seemed so clear. . . .
>
> It's the same way in this case. The only trouble is, the prosecutor doesn't have a Mr. Snow who can tell him what really happened.

Not every analogy deals with circumstantial evidence— although there are still some good ones left on that subject. More-over, not every analogy is used to prove a point. Sometimes, for example, an analogy is used by a witness, and becomes a key phrase in final argument to bring back testimony.

Suppose a hypothetical situation. You represent a man who has, it is claimed, posttraumatic epilepsy. You call a leading neu-rologist to the witness stand. Because some people find it difficult to accept that the brain can be seriously injured without a skull fracture, your witness compares the head to a watch during his testimony:

> In some ways the head is like a watch. You can drop a watch on the floor, and the crystal will break, the case will be all scratched up, and still the watch runs perfectly. Other times, you can drop a watch, and it looks as if nothing has happened. Not a scratch on the outside. Yet no matter how many times you take it back to the jeweler, it never keeps good time again. It always runs either fast or slow—always just a little off—never the same as it was.

Later on, the doctor talks about the strength of the brain:

> Your brain is really very delicate. It has a consistency about like jello, or maybe a chocolate mousse. And just as a chocolate mousse might tear if you hit the bowl hard enough, the brain can actually tear—and bleed—and form a scar if you hit the skull hard enough.

Now then, what happens when you talk about the watch? You do not have to dwell on the doctor's testimony at length. When you mention "watch" in final argument, all the doctor's images come pouring back.

In other words, besides being an effective argument, an analogy can be an efficient reference.

Stories are fine for problems like circumstantial evidence or bringing back testimony. But where they are most valuable—where they really sing—is in persuading juries to agree with ideas they might otherwise be reluctant to accept.

Take the problem of the witness whose testimony is false in part. The general rule on the subject is that the judge may instruct the jury that if they find a witness was deliberately false in part of his testimony, they may disregard the rest. We even have a Latin maxim to describe it—*Falsus in uno, falsus in omnibus.*

The trouble is, the jury may well look at the problem from the other way around: the lawyer proved that part of the testimony was wrong. It stands to reason that the rest is true.

The net effect is that the rule, the Latin maxim, the instruction and the ensuing argument may not be convincing. It is not very persuasive to say, "The witness was wrong about the color of the plaintiff's car, and that means you cannot trust anything else he says."

Instead of doing that, John Burgess of Montpelier, Vermont, approaches it this way:

> You folks have a real problem, as a jury, with the testimony of Mrs. Norman. You will remember her. She was the very pleasant appearing woman who just simply turned out to be wrong in some of her testimony. Well, I know you do not have any difficulty with disposing of her mistakes and misstatements. The problem is what should you do with the rest of her testimony. Accept it, reject it, or what?
>
> You know, since my mother was called away (Vermont talk for 'passed away') we usually take my father out for Sunday dinner. And there is a restaurant here in town that we like to go to.
>
> It is interesting how people will always order their favorites. Dad's favorite is beef stew—has been for as long as I can remember. Mother fixed it for him when I was a boy. No matter what is on the menu, if they have beef stew, when the waitress asks for his order, he says, 'I guess I'll try your beef stew.'
>
> The other weekend we took Dad out to a new place not far out of town—they call it an 'inn'—that advertised home cooking. When Dad saw beef stew on the menu, his mind was made up.

When they brought out his plate of stew, it looked terrific. But the very first bite he took, the meat was spoiled—rancid.

Now what did he do? Did he pick all through that plate, looking for a good piece of meat? Or was he entitled to call the waitress over and ask her please to take it back because it was rancid?

What are you entitled to do with the testimony of Mrs. Norman?

By now it is easy to recognize how the family roles help us feel that the lawyer telling this is the kind of person worthy of belief. But the symbols go a little deeper than that.

It was not the old, familiar restaurant that produced the bad plate of stew. It was the new, pretentious, good-looking on the outside, but ultimately unreliable place that did it. The 'inn,' and the stew—like Mrs. Norman and her testimony—just turned out to be bad. The jury—like the father—is to be forgiven for having been taken in at first, but are now fully justified in rejecting the whole business.

Another thorny problem for the advocate is a client's pre-existing injury. Obviously, if it is concealed and the defense exposes it, the entire case looks fraudulent. So plaintiffs' lawyers are usually careful to bring out all the pre-existing injuries. But then, how do you convince the jury that a minor injury that hurt the weakened plaintiff is attributable to this defendant, and not to the earlier injury? One of the best analogies for this is Craig Spangenberg's:

> We have come to damages and a difficult field of decision. I wish it could be a simpler case, oh, like a farmer driving his pickup truck along the highway, when someone crashes through a stop sign and hits him and turns him over. He is not injured, just the truck is. Windshield out, dented fenders. And if you, as a jury, were asked what's fair compensation, I do not think you would have much problem. You would give him the kind of truck that he had. He is not entitled to a new truck, because he did not have one. But he should not have to drive a wrecked truck with mashed fenders and no windshield, because he did not have that either. So a fair result, a fair compensation, would be the cost of putting the fender back in the condition that it was in and replacing the windshield. You would have no problem with it, and I am sure my learned brother on the defense would accept that.

Well, suppose the farmer was a poultry farmer, and he was taking eggs to market. And he had a hundred dozen grade A eggs in the back of his pickup truck. After it is turned over, there are a hundred dozen grade A fresh eggs all over the highway, with the broken yolks and whites running over the pavement. What is fair compensation? Those were his eggs. They were marketable. His property has been taken away. His income has been taken away. What is fair compensation? Ninety cents a dozen retail? No. He was not going to sell them retail. He was going to sell them wholesale, and the wholesale market prices reported in the newspaper were forty-six cents a dozen. So he is entitled to forty-six cents times a hundred dozen. Forty-six dollars. Now in that situation, wouldn't you think a defense lawyer was completely out of his mind, if he said, 'Don't give him forty-six dollars for those eggs! Why, if they had been golf balls, not a one would have been broken.'

I don't mean my client was an egg, but he was like an egg. He was fragile. But he was still useful and marketable. He could sell what strength he had in the marketplace of labor. He was certainly not a golf ball and he didn't bounce. But fair compensation is to restore the loss that has actually been inflicted upon the actual man. And when you break an actual egg, fair compensation is paying the value.

One of the most difficult problems for criminal defense lawyers is arguing that an "immunity witness"—the kind that used to have been said "turned state's evidence"—should not be believed.

It is a serious problem because the government often successfully argues that "immunity witnesses" have no motive to tell anything other than the truth.

Disloyalty is not a very effective attack. Many jurors reason that criminals are not entitled to a lot of loyalty, anyway. Besides, disloyalty is really a confession without any realistic avoidance.

Selfishness is not much better.

If the "immunity witness" first denied involvement and then admitted guilt—for which there is now no punishment because of the immunity—the situation is a little better. Good cross-examination and final argument combined support the theory that the witness lied before to stay out of jail, and he is doing it again.

But not every "immunity witness" is on record denying involvement before the immunity grant. Many remain silent until the immunity order is issued. Besides, what is really wanted is an argument that the immunity witness has demonstrated his *greater guilt* than the defendant that the government has erroneously put in the dock.

Here is Gene Pincham again, with a story he told in a Chicago trial and shared with the National Institute for Trial Advocacy in Boulder, Colorado, in the summer of 1978:

> I have one rule [it seems that whenever Gene Pincham has a rule, it is 'one rule'] around my house:
>
> 'Stay out of my wallet!'
>
> If you need money, come ask me for it. If it is worthwhile and I have the money, I'll give it to you, but 'Stay out of my wallet!'
>
> There is one exception. That's my wife, Alzata. After thirty years of marriage to me, she has the right to go in my wallet. But for the children: 'Stay out of my wallet.'
>
> The other night when I went to bed, I put my wallet on my dresser like I always do. And when I got up the next morning, I checked my wallet to make sure I had enough money to park the car and have lunch.
>
> When I checked my wallet, I only had one or two dollars, and I knew I had a twenty in there the night before. So I asked my wife, 'Alzata, did you take that twenty dollar bill I had in my wallet?'
>
> 'No, honey, I haven't been in your wallet.'
>
> 'All right,' I said, 'call the family together.'
>
> 'Get everybody downstairs, because somebody took a twenty dollar bill out of my wallet, and I *know* there has been no burglary in the house.'
>
> Well, Sandy was off for the weekend, and had not returned, so that left the two boys, Scooter and Jim.
>
> Scooter—he's eighteen—he's the slick one. Jim—he's twelve—he's the naive one. They came downstairs, and I said,
>
> 'All right, one of you two's been in my wallet, and I want to know who.'
>
> Scooter, he said, 'I haven't been in your wallet, Daddy.'
>
> And Jim, he said, 'I haven't been in your wallet, Daddy.'
>
> I was mad. 'Now one of you is lying, and I'm going to find out who. I am going to get to the bottom of this.'

513

'Tell you what I'm going to do. I am going to give me out some *immunity*.'

Then Jim, he's the naive one, he says, 'Immunity? What's immunity?'

And Scooter, the slick one, says, 'Immunity is where you can't be punished for what you did, but you got to talk about it.'

So Jim says, 'I don't need any of that, 'cause I didn't take any money.'

And Scooter says, 'You going to give out immunity?'

I said, 'That's right.'

Scooter said, 'Sign the order. I took the money from your wallet.'

'O.K.,' I said, 'What did you do with the money?'

Scooter said, 'I gave some of it to Jim!'

'Jim,' I said, 'You are convicted. No more bowling for a month. No movie on Saturday night. No more television. You are going to your room and you are going to stay there. You are guilty.'

That night I heard something no parent ever likes to hear. I heard my boy in his room, crying.

Alzata asked me, 'Gene, why did you do that to Jim?'

I told her, 'Because he's guilty. I gave Scooter immunity. He's got no reason to lie.'

Alzata looked at me and said, 'That's no reason not to believe *Jim*. He's your flesh and blood, too.'

There it ends, a magnificent argument, worthy of some additional thought.

Notice that the family role is a little different this time. Jim, the young, innocent, naive boy is in the position of the defendant. What is the jury by implication to do? Think of the defendant in this case as a child—their symbolic child—entitled to the benefit of the doubt.

The immunity witness is "slick." The point makes sense, since that is the one that will ask for immunity—not someone who is innocent. Innocent people, Jim tells us, do not need immunity.

The "trial" Jim is given would offend the most rudimentary sense of fairness. Jim is first permitted to talk, but is given no chance at all once the immunity witness speaks.

The prosecutor in the family "trial" is human. He is, after all, the defense lawyer in the real case. It tells us that the prosecutor is

514

not to be disliked for wrongfully bringing an innocent person to trial, but to be forgiven for being misled. It is much easier to believe that the government is innocently mistaken than to accept the idea that it has been deliberately unfair.

Finally, Alzata, the wife and mother, is the voice of reason, and her thoughts are accepted by the authoritative father.

Good stories not only provide solutions to problems of persuasion; they sometimes help advocates around roadblocks created by the law.

For example, take the "golden rule" followed in many states. *See, e.g., Chicago, R.I. and P. R. Co. v. American Airlines, Inc.*, 408 P.2d 789 (Okla. 1965); and *Stanley v. Ellegood*, 382 S.W.2d 572 (Ky. 1964). It got its name from its function. The rule forbids asking the jurors to put themselves in the shoes of one of the parties to the action. It is called the "golden rule" because you are *not* permitted to ask the jury to do unto the parties the way they would want things done unto themselves.

That means it would be absolutely improper in a final argument for the plaintiff to say,

> Now we are asking that you award $250,000 for Bill Markle's right arm. I know that sounds like a lot of money, but think about it for a while. Just suppose that it would be possible to remove your right arm without any pain at all. Which one of you would be willing to go into a doctor's office tomorrow morning and sell your right arm for $250,000?

On the other hand, consider what can be accomplished with a short analogy:

> Now we are asking that you award $250,000 for Bill Markle's right arm. You decide that is fair compensation for what the defendant did to Bill. And then later you wonder—was it too much money?
>
> Well, suppose Bill Markle goes home with that money, and the very next day his friend, Joe, comes over and says, 'Come on, Bill. It's Saturday, and the fish are biting in the lake. Grab your tackle and let's go fishing.'
>
> Bill says, 'Gosh, Joe, I wish I could. But you know, ever since this terrible auto crash I was in I can't go fishing, because I lost my good right casting arm. But I tell you what—the jury said the man who made me lose my arm owed me $250,000. I just got that money yesterday, and I still have it

all. So I will give you every penny of that $250,000 if you will sell me your right arm.'

What do you think Joe would do? Would there be any chance he would even consider selling his arm—even if he could—for *any* amount of money?

Just because this argument is in the form of an analogy does not mean that every jurisdiction would permit it. Apparently some courts feel even this argument comes too close to violating the "golden rule." On the other hand, there are other jurisdictions permitting this sort of story but never allowing the direct request that the jury put themselves in the shoes of one of the parties.

Whether an argument is proper raises a question that may occur to you about analogies. Why should they be permitted? Do they not necessarily argue "outside the record?" Stories, analogies, comparisons are permitted on the theory that matters of common knowledge and understanding may be argued without specific proof. It is a rule of convenience that helps keep trials from getting even longer than they already are.

It should be obvious by now that stories and analogies come in all different shapes and sizes. They also are adaptable to a wide variety of styles. Not everyone would feel comfortable starting out final argument for a defendant in a criminal case saying, "This case is like the Mountaineer's Pancakes. He said, 'No matter how thin I makes em, they allus have two sides.' " But if that does not seem to fit your self-image of a controlled businesslike lawyer in a three-piece suit, you can still take a quarter from your pocket and hold it up in front of the jury, saying, "This coin—a United States quarter—has two very different sides. This case is the same way, and so far you have only heard the plaintiff's side. Let's take a look at Mr. Mercer's side."

The opposing party made some subtle but important changes in his story, and you want to discuss them. You might talk about the chameleons they used to sell outside the circus when you were a child—and how they changed color when they got scared. If that does not suit you, try the comparison to the squid—that clouds everything with ink and swims backwards out of danger. The squid is in some ways a better choice than the chameleon anyway, because some people think chameleons are cute little things, but it is a bit more difficult to think of a squid or an octopus that way.

Where do these stories come from, anyway? The good ones

516

have common roots: they illustrate ideas that the jury can quickly verify by their own background or understanding.

Usually, good stories involve you, your family or your client and his or her family. Think how much power would be missing from Gene Pincham's story about "Scooter and the Wallet" if it were about mythical people or nameless individuals: "Once I heard about this man who found that $20 was missing from his wallet one morning. . . ."

That raises an interesting question: How true do these stories have to be? Do they really have to have happened just the way you want to tell the story?

All the stories you tell should be true in the larger sense. By that, they will be more effective if they are based on something that really happened. The details that come through, your tone of voice, add to the interest and believability if your story is based on a real event. But "truth in the larger sense" means it could have happened that way—and indeed perhaps should have happened that way—not that every detail actually occurred.

Because you are arguing common sense, your obligation is to be faithful to common sense and human nature—not history.

This suggests that you should not be afraid to steal some other lawyer's story or analogy. That, of course, is true. But do not call the process theft. It is scholarship. You may take some comfort that society does not expect you to footnote your final arguments and give credit for where you get your lines of reasoning, apt comparisons or even full-fledged stories.

It also means you should not be afraid to repeat what you find is successful. Benjamin Franklin said that itinerate preachers have the advantage of "many rehearsals." Think of it this way: each jury is a new congregation. If you have a great story that has worked before, do not hesitate to use it again.

If you gain sufficient success, you may notice that some of your opponents will anticipate your arguments, and that can be a disadvantage. On the other hand, you may prefer to respond as Gene Pincham did when a Chicago prosecutor interrupted his final argument and said,

"Oh, your honor, we're not going to hear about the sugar barrel *again*!"

Gene replied, "Yes you're going to hear it again, and you're going to keep on hearing it until I lose a case."

Pincham's client was acquitted.

You may not be accustomed to telling stories in your argument, and thus might be tempted to start out a story with something such as,

"It all reminds me of a story, ladies and gentlemen. . . ."

Do not bother with that sort of substitute for "once upon a time." When you have come to the point in the argument when you need the story, just start telling it.

But, you protest, you are not a *raconteur.* Good stories are the mark of superb argument. You may feel this is not the sort of thing ordinary lawyers can do well.

Nonsense.

In the summer of 1979, I taught a class in Trial Advocacy at the University of Tulsa. The students were bright, eager, enthusiastic—just like trial advocacy students in many schools across the country.

As a new experiment, I required each student to use an analogy in final argument. They were reluctant to believe they could do it, but threw themselves into the task.

The results were magnificent. Here are two of them.

The first, told by Peter K. Sampson, was tailored to fit a will contest where the beneficiaries tried to take quick advantage of a situation they suddenly found themselves in. An old man was staying with his relatives for a short time, and they suddenly discovered he had accumulated some money. These relatives— Bosley and Mildred—quickly produced a will form for the old man to fill out—and the will left nearly the entire estate to them. Here is Mr. Sampson's analogy:

> Funny things happen when people try to take advantage of a situation. A few years ago I had some friends, a young couple, who bought an old, old Victorian house. It needed a lot of repair. One thing that was particularly troublesome was what to do with the floors.
>
> When the house was new, the floors must have been beautiful. But that was sixty to seventy years ago, and they looked as if nothing had been done for them since the house was built.
>
> These people didn't know what to do: have the floors sanded and refinished, lay new hardwood flooring on top, or what. So for a while, at least, they did nothing, and the floor in the living room was absolutely filthy—fifty years of ground in dirt and grime.
>
> Well, one morning they read one of those carpet ads in the

newspaper—'One day only, special purchase—regular $7.95 carpet now just $3.95—installation included.' They decided that's what they should do, install new carpeting over the floor.

They went down and ordered this carpet (picking a mousey, blue grey that frankly, I didn't care for—but I didn't say anything, because it looked a lot better than the old floor).

In fact they were in such a hurry to get that carpeting down, they didn't even clean the old floors, and you *know* the 'factory installation' workers didn't clean those floors either.

So they took advantage of the situation and acted quickly.

About four or five weeks after they put the carpeting in, they started having trouble. The carpet was getting dirty, and they were having a hard time keeping it clean. The dirt, you see, was not coming down on top from people's feet—it was working its way up from underneath the carpet.

Now, if they had put a carpet pad down, or bought a better carpet, or even cleaned the floors, I suppose this wouldn't have happened. But they didn't do any of those things.

After the dirt started appearing, they vacuumed and vacuumed and the dirt kept coming through. They shampooed and a short time later, the dirt showed through. Then they rented one of those combination rinsing and vacuuming things. That seemed to work. The carpet looked good for about two weeks—and then the dirt came back.

Why?

Because the dirt was there, under the carpet, and nothing they did could make it go away. They had tried to cover it up, but it just didn't work.

Well, now let's take a look at this will. Bosley and Mildred acted quickly. They took advantage of the situation. Let's look at what's underneath this will, working its way through—no matter what they do.

This analogy is an interesting one. The obvious point is that coverups do not work—the truth will out. But there is more. You will notice that there is not a complete parallel between the exercise of undue influence on the one hand and having carpet laid over a dirty floor on the other hand.

Or is that so?

Instead of attaching great moral fault to Bosley and Mildred for what they did, this analogy compares undue influence to mistaken, impulsive behavior. It is culpable conduct of a sort, but perhaps makes it a bit easier to find them guilty of undue influence than it otherwise might have been.

Finally, there is the story told by George H. Penn.

It was devised for the difficult task of convincing the jury that it is indeed possible to find a defendant guilty beyond a reasonable doubt on primarily circumstantial evidence.

> I grew up in south Louisiana in a little town that is actually on the Gulf of Mexico. There was a bayou near town, and of course, even when we were very young, we would go fishing in the bayou.

> You knew you were growing up when your dad would take you out fishing in the Gulf. It was one of those signs that you were more than just a kid.

> I remember the first time my dad took me out in the Gulf. I was eleven, and a friend and I went out with our fathers to go mackerel fishing.

> Now a mackerel is a big fish. And you use live bait. I remember riding in the boat over to the place where we bought the bait—some sort of small, trout-like fish. When we were leaving there, I saw something in the water that gave me a chill.

> I saw a black fin cutting through the water, near our boat.

> Well, because I was so excited about going fishing out in the Gulf with my father, I forgot about the fin pretty quickly.

> When we got out where the mackerel were supposed to be biting, my dad showed me how to tie the fish on the hook without killing it, and how to cast with two hands, because with a big pole like that with a live fish on the end, it isn't like fishing in the bayou.

> I wasn't very good at it, but I must have gotten it far enough, because on the second or third cast, I got a strike. The line sang out of the reel, and it took me a while before I started bringing line back in. I would crank in five or ten yards, and then the fish would fight out four or five yards. My progress was pretty slow, but after a while I could tell that the fish was getting tired.

> Just then, I saw that black fin cutting through the water.

There was a sudden thrashing, a boiling in the water—and my line went dead.

Now, I didn't see what happened. It took place under water, and I was up in the boat. But when I reeled in the bloody head of a mackerel, *I knew beyond any reasonable doubt what had happened.*

There are fine books about final argument. You can study J. A. Stein, *Closing Argument, the Art and the Law* (1969), a good book, indeed. Lloyd Paul Stryker, *The Art of Advocacy* (1954), has a section on final argument on pages 110 to 132. *The Art of Summation,* M. Block, ed. (1963) is an excellent collection of examples and comments. L. J. Smith, *The Art of Advocacy: Summation* (1978), has a number of good analogies worth your attention.

You can pour over these books, and it will be time well spent. It is no sin to be a scholar and adopt someone else's story. On the other hand, you can take a significant step forward, and like those students in the summer course, develop your own.

CHAPTER 47

The Final Five

No matter what else happens in argument, I would never give up the final five—those last five minutes of rebuttal.

Bill Colson, Miami

I suffer through the most harrowing five minutes of every case. It is scary when you are down to the last five minutes and you have to grab the jury back.

Jo Ann Harris, New York City

If Bill Colson and Jo Ann Harris have given you the idea that rebuttal in final argument is both difficult and important, you are on the right track. And in view of how important and difficult it is, it is surprising how little attention rebuttal is given by writers, speakers, and trial advocacy training programs. Pick up the typical book on trial advocacy; see how thoroughly it discusses rebuttal. Scan the continuing legal education brochures that describe the lecture series on trial advocacy; try to find rebuttal. Go to an intensive workshop on trial advocacy for one, two, or three weeks; see how much time they spend on rebuttal.

It reflects what lawyers actually do with rebuttal. Some have developed it into nearly an art form all its own. But most lawyers just use it for a few minutes of repetitious urging, going over what they have already said several times before. They use it as a reprise of the sermon they have already preached.

Thousands of lawyers know the advantages of primacy and recency. The chances are, if they have heard of one, they have heard of the other. They understand primacy—how the opportunity to go first is an advantage because it improves the chances that an argument will be accepted or that a fact will be believed. They carefully fashion persuasive opening statements and direct examinations to take advantage of primacy.

And they understand recency, too. They know that the last word continues to ring in the minds of the jury, and is most easily recalled. But they do not prepare redirect examinations or rebuttal arguments to take advantage of recency. Instead, they rely on the whimsical (and lazy) gods of momentary inspiration to supply magic words that will turn everything around.

It is misplaced faith. As John Burgess of San Francisco, California, says, "There are no geniuses in the courtroom. There are only drudges in the office." If you want a brilliant rebuttal, you should prepare it before trial.

While a handful of states do it differently, the purpose of rebuttal is to give the party with the burden of proof the chance to respond to the opponent's argument. The prosecution in criminal cases and typically (but not always) the plaintiff in civil cases has the principal burden of proof. They have the right to give the first closing argument. That right to speak first goes with the obligation to prove your case. And the other side—typically the defendant—has the right to respond. Rebuttal is intended to be the opportunity to answer the defendant's response.

Response is important. In most states, the plaintiff is not permitted to bring up new arguments in rebuttal unless they fairly respond to the points made by the defense. Rebuttal is not supposed to be an opportunity to sandbag the opponent.

But not everywhere. In North Carolina, for example, plaintiffs and the prosecution often waive their first argument, letting the defendant go first. Then they give their entire argument last. Whatever rebuttal the plaintiff has is mixed in with his argument in chief. As Judge Charles L. Becton from the North Carolina Court of Appeals says, "the whole argument is rebuttal."

North Carolina's treatment of rebuttal is a matter of custom that is deeply ingrained. Their response to a special rule demonstrates this. Under Rule 10, North Carolina General Rules of Practice of the Superior and District Courts, "In all cases, civil and criminal, if no evidence is introduced by the defendant, the right to open and close the argument to the jury shall belong to him." That means if the defendant produces no evidence, then the defendant gets to argue both first and last. How do North Carolina lawyers take advantage of this unusual opportunity? Does the side that ordinarily only gets to talk once both open and close when it gets the chance? According to Donald Beskind of Durham, North Carolina, they waive their right to go first and make their rebuttal their entire argument.

Oddities like that aside, rebuttal means the right to answer. In Ohio, for example it is specifically improper for a plaintiff to give a "per diem" argument on pain and suffering for the first time on rebuttal. *Grosnickle v. Germantown*, 3 Ohio St.2d 96, 32 Ohio Ops2d 65, 209 N.E.2d 442 (1965). It is permissible to take an amount for one day's pain and suffering and then multiply it by the remainder of the plaintiff's expected life. But it must be done during the initial final argument, so the defense will have an opportunity to answer it.

But even if you could save your best argument for last, it is not necessarily a good idea. People—judges and jurors—identify with their ideas. And once their ideas are formed, it is tough to shake them. If you deliberately let a juror form the wrong idea— confident that you are going to knock it down in rebuttal, you are playing with the fire of ego. The danger is that the juror will stick to his idea—because it is his—and resent what he feels is your personal attack on him.

As Craig Spangenberg said, "If I have convinced the jurors in my opening argument that I am right, the defendant may shake them a little, and a short rebuttal should bring them back. But if I make a weak opening and leave the jury with unresolved questions, I allow the defendant to make up their minds in his favor with a powerful argument. Then I will not change their minds on closing, no matter what I say." Spangenberg, *Basic Values and the Techniques of Persuasion*, 3 LITIGATION, No. 4, at 16 (Summer, 1977).

Limited scope also means limited time, and rebuttal is often held to five or ten minutes. It is also a good idea to reserve time for rebuttal before beginning your initial final argument. In some courts failure to reserve rebuttal is interpreted as a waiver.

All right, if rebuttal is so important that you make sure you never waive it, what do you do with it?

Barbara Caulfield of San Francisco, California, divides it into two parts. She prepares the second half first. That is a the closing remarks in the entire case, the things she will say last. And those last words draw on the theme of the case, but do not just repeat the words she used in her argument in chief. The second half is there, ready to use, no matter whether the defendant says anything that needs answering.

524

Then Caulfield prepares the first half of her rebuttal. She says that "this part of the rebuttal has to have a refrain—an idea that you repeat again and again that ties together your attack on your opponent's case. For example, suppose you prosecute a case, and the entire defense is to pick at little police procedures that took place in the investigation of the case. The defense's final argument is to catalog the one hundred little things they say were done wrong in the case. Here is how you could do the first part of the rebuttal in that case:

> The defense says the state was wrong in not calling in the FBI so they could investigate the case, too. That is not a defense of Milo Higgins. That is a false accusation that the State of Alaska cannot investigate a criminal case.
>
> The defense says that the police should have taken more photographs at the scene of the crime. That is not a defense of Milo Higgins. That is a charge against the Anchorage Police that has nothing to do with this case.
>
> The defense says . . . and then every point is answered with the theme: That is not a defense of Milo Higgins.

With this system, the framework for the first half of rebuttal is prepared before the trial, and then all you have to do to finish up is to take notes during the defense closing and list the points you want to include in your response. And there are a number of themes that can demonstrate the defense's smoke screen in civil or criminal cases:

> This case is not about traffic lights; it's about a defective car. This case is not about weather; it's about a defective car.
>
> Morgan Electric Company broke its word. It violated its contract. Is there any reason for that? Their lawyer told you that they had just installed a new computer system. That is no justification for breaking their word. That just explains why they might have been a little slow, not why they refused to make the switches they promised. Their lawyer told you they had more business than they ever had before. That is no justification for breaking their word. . . .

When Judge Jim R. Carrigan of the United States District Court in Denver, Colorado, was trying cases, he approached rebuttal as an important part of the emotional development of the case:

> It is essential to be fair—and to be seen by the jury as being fair—throughout the trial. I always tried to be the 'Fairest

Prince' in the courtroom. In rebuttal I would talk about fairness and justice—and get in my last shot on damages.

I tried to inspire the jury to do the right thing, to give a verdict they could be proud of when they went home that night and when they looked back on that day years later. I told them that it was my last chance to talk to them, and that it would be in their hands. Then it would be their last chance to give the plaintiff a full cup of justice. If they only gave the plaintiff a half a cup of justice, it would be a half a cup of injustice, and it would not be the kind of verdict that they would be proud of.

Tom Demetrio of Chicago, Illinois, has a distinctive approach.

I almost never object during an entire trial. Unless it is outrageous, I let the defense do whatever they want. I have nothing to hide. I do not get angry, and I do not attack the defense throughout my case in chief.

And I find that the defense almost always says or does something outrageous during final argument. Then, if they react to that in my rebuttal, the jury will be impressed. They will see that I really must have a good reason for getting indignant, because I have been so calm during the rest of the trial.

Let me give you an example. In one case I represented a young man who had serious injury to his nervous system. In addition to his being a quadraplegic, he had nerve damage that impaired the movement of his face. During final argument, the defense lawyer ridiculed our request for damages. 'If you give Demetrio's client that kind of money, he will laugh all the way to the bank.' In rebuttal, I got mad. I told them what a cruel joke the defense lawyer was trying to make, when he knew that because of what the defendant had done, the plaintiff had no control over the muscles in his face—that in addition to being a quadraplegic, he would never smile again, much less laugh his way to the bank.

Once—in another case—I apologized for getting indignant in my rebuttal. I told the jury I was sorry for how I had reacted to what the defendant had said. In talking to the jury after they gave their verdict, one thoughtful, elderly woman said to me, 'Young man, you did not need to apologize—he deserved it.' If the jury is ever going to see me angry during the trial, it is in rebuttal, when they know the defendant deserves it.

Craig Spangenberg agrees:

After the defense has argued, and you rise to rebut, you can show a little more emotion. This is what we call fondly the 'rousements.' Here you can use scorn, ridicule, and vehemence, but it is important to show that the object of your anger or ridicule is the argument or the ideas of opposing counsel or the testimony of the defendant. Do not look in a juror's eyes and roar at him over something the defense lawyer said. It will only make the jury uncomfortable, particularly if you are so excited that streams of saliva spread over the jury. Spangenberg, *Basic Values and the Techniques of Persuasion*, LITIGATION, Vol. 3, No. 4 at 16 (Summer, 1977).

Jo Ann Harris sees rebuttal as the final conclusion to what was carefully set up at the beginning of final argument:

I was taught that in your opening summation you should pose a lot of questions for the other side. All these questions are absolutely designed to trap your opponent into opening up issues that you want opened up on your rebuttal.

If you do this right, either of two things can happen. First, the defense can rise to the bait and discuss your issues. Since they are *your* issues, framed your way, that sets you up to show how they should be answered when you rebut. Second, if the defense ignores your questions, you can show how he was afraid of them, and then you answer the questions you posed—your way. Either way, you have gained control again, and either way, you answer those questions your way.

No matter what your overall approach to rebuttal, there are a number of arguments that have become classics:

They Picked the Witnesses

Proving a criminal case often involves putting some pretty doubtful characters on the stand. The defense typically complains about the people who testify for the government. On rebuttal, the prosecution responds:

I can't believe it. Here is Mr. Johnson, the defense lawyer, complaining about the witnesses we called to the stand. As if it is our fault we asked them to testify. WE DIDN'T PICK

527

THOSE WITNESSES. THE DEFENDANT DID. They are his friends. If we could choose our witnesses, we would pick respectable people, community leaders. We called those people to the stand—the ones the defendant is complaining about—because they were there, and they know what the defendant did.

The Indelible Pencil

Everything about this trial has some way for correcting mistakes. If I or Mr. Williams make a mistake in one of the questions we ask or arguments we make, the judge is here to correct it. If the judge were to make a mistake on the law, there is a higher court that could correct it. Every pencil in this courtroom has an eraser on it—except one. That is the pencil you write your verdict with. What you decide in this case cannot be changed if you later discover you made a mistake. You are writing with an indelible pencil, and you have to write very carefully.

(You can see it is closely related to the next argument.)

One Day in Court

This is Mike Arnold's one day in court. Tomorrow, after this case is over, you will all be back at your regular work. Judge McMonagle will have another case, Mr. Porter will be working another case, and I will be back in my office. Now suppose you were to give Mike Arnold not the $700,000 dollars he needs. Instead suppose you see if he can get by with only $400,000. When that money is gone and Mike Arnold still can't work, he comes back to court and says, Judge McMonagle, the jury didn't award enough, and I don't know what to do. The judge will have to tell him that he has had his one chance for justice, and that he cannot come back a second time.

Immunity Protects the Truth

After the defense attacks the government witness who was given immunity from prosecution in return for his testimony:

The defense lawyer, Mr. Blanchard, wants you to think that somehow Jesse Nolan's immunity makes his testimony suspect. And the opposite is true. The only way Jesse Nolan can get in trouble would be by lying on the witness stand. He only has immunity for his truthful testimony. That immunity agreement is your guarantee that he is telling the truth.

Now take a step back from all this. Suppose that you never have a chance to rebut. Is there anything you can do about all of this?

Yes.

Anticipate Rebuttual

Meet the arguments in advance. Do not just respond to your opponent's first argument, look forward to his rebuttal. If you do it right, you can even get the jury to start thinking of themselves on your side:

> This is the last time I will be able to talk to you about this case, and there is so much more that I would like to say. The plaintiff's lawyer, Mr. Rawlings, is going to get to talk to you one more time. The rules of court let him get the last word, and I do not get a chance to answer what he says. So there is something important that I want you to do. You know that there will be things he will say that I would answer if I could. And you know what all the evidence is in this case. So please listen carefully to everything he says, and whenever he makes an argument, make the response I would make if I could. And if you do that, I know that you will be fair.

Parallel Table

The chapters in this book were originally published in the following issues of LITIGATION.

Parallel Table

The chapters in this book were originally published in the following issues of LITIGATION.